Natural Theories of Mind

NATURAL THEORIES OF MIND

Evolution, Development and Simulation of Everyday Mindreading

Edited by
Andrew Whiten

BASIL BLACKWELL

Copyright © Basil Blackwell 1991

First published 1991

Basil Blackwell Ltd
108 Cowley Road, Oxford, OX4 1JF, UK

Basil Blackwell, Inc.
3 Cambridge Center
Cambridge, Massachusetts 02142, USA

British Library Cataloguing in Publication Data

A CIP catalogue record for this book is available from the British Library.

Library of Congress Cataloging in Publication Data
Natural theories of mind : evolution, development, and simulation
  of everyday mindreading / edited by Andrew Whiten.
      p.   cm.
  Includes bibliographical references and index.
  ISBN 0-631-17194-0
  1. Philosophy of mind in children.   2. Attribution (Social
psychology)—Computer simulation.   3. Comparative psychology.
I. Whiten, Andrew.
BF723.P48N37   1991
155—dc20   90-37172
                                                                CIP

Typeset in 10 on 12 pt Imprint
by Photo·graphics, Honiton, Devon
Printed in Great Britain by T.J. Press Ltd, Padstow, Cornwall

Preface

This is not a book about telepathy! It is about the kind of everyday mindreading which we take for granted, which we use throughout our daily lives, explaining and predicting others' behaviour by reference to their inner mental states: their desires, beliefs, expectations and a host of other psychological concepts.

> *Jack is more afraid of Jill*
> *If Jack thinks*
> *that Jill thinks*
> *that Jack is afraid of Jill*

> *R. D. Laing* Knots *(1970)*

As adults Jack and Jill may take this everyday mindreading for granted – they do it automatically. While formal and scientific 'theories of mind' are the work of philosophers and psychologists, Jack and Jill seem to act as if they have a 'natural theory of mind'.

But from whence does this ability come? As new evidence mounts that for some disturbed children the capacity to mindread is deficient, or as we strive to construct intelligent computers and robots which interact more comfortably with us, we realize that much remains to be understood about just how such an extraordinary phenomenon as mindreading can come about.

This is the basis of the present volume. The core subject of this book is the *emergence* of mindreading from building blocks which are not-yet-mindreading, up through the earliest stages of elaboration. For the first time, studies from three broad frontiers of research are brought together, and interdisciplinary cross-talk is initiated between them. The three disciplines are those of the book's subtitle.

Development. Research on the early development of what has come to be called the child's 'theory of mind' has blossomed in the past decade or so.

A flurry of research papers and books has appeared recently, other major works are in press, and several papers by their authors in this volume offer an overview of the fascinating picture which is emerging. None of those books, however, offers the interdisciplinary attack presented here.

'Theory of mind' has been incorporated into the title of this book because it is the expression which has gained common usage. More recently, however, the question of whether such an expression is misleading has become a serious one, as the reader will discover later. 'Mindreading' is another term adopted by some writers as more theoretically neutral (and also less of a mouthful, particularly when a verb is needed!).

Evolution. Both 'theory of mind' and 'mindreading' are in fact expressions spawned not from developmental psychology, but from different perspectives on animal psychology and the evolution of behaviour (indeed there is a third: that some animals, like people, are aptly labelled as 'natural psychologists'; the title of this book also borrows from that idea). By contrast with studies of child development, empirical work bearing on the evolution of mindreading is still sparse, but nevertheless at an exciting stage where the potential for cross-fertilization with the other approaches begs to be explored.

Simulation. In the UK, a major Joint Initiative of the research councils in cognitive science and human–computer interaction has expressed 'an urgent requirement to develop computational techniques for representing the user's knowledge, goals and intentions'. The prospect here is of a two-way street in which a computational approach offers precision to modelling natural mindreading, whilst empirical research in developmental and comparative, evolutionary psychology defines what needs to be simulated and perhaps even hints at how the required complexity can be built up.

The book is not divided up into sections simply corresponding to these three areas. Instead, the reader is guided back and forth amongst them, following a rationale which is spelled out step by step in the Contents. Chapters could have been grouped in yet other ways, for there are multiple links between them, many of which have been made explicit through cross-references established during circulation of manuscripts amongst contributors. For example, the question of a mindreading deficit in autistic children is pursued in chapters by Leslie, Baron-Cohen and Harris, which occur at different points in the structure as it stands. Other major issues, such as transitions marking the emergence of different mindreading competencies, and the relationship between mindreading and behavioural analysis, recur repeatedly through many chapters, as outlined in the opening chapter.

Acknowledgements

A generous grant from the Russell Trust, supplemented by the University of St Andrews, made it possible to initiate this project with a symposium held in St Andrews in 1989: 'The Emergence of Mindreading: Evolution, Development and Simulation of Second-order Representations'. Papers were contributed by authors of all but one of the present chapters. In this connection special thanks are due to Dr David Russell, Mrs Cecilia Croal and Mr David Erdal.

I am grateful to all the contributors for the comments on my, and on each other's, manuscripts. I particularly thank Jonathan Bennett and George Butterworth for acting as formal discussants in that part of the symposium which contributed to the British Psychological Society Annual Conference in St Andrews.

Contents

In pursuit of the origins of mindreading, each of the next two groups of papers focuses on specific aspects of behaviour which have received particular attention in recent research. In the first group, 'violations' of normal behaviour, including teasing, joking and deception, are studied as providing special diagnostic power in analysing the emergence of mindreading. The papers by Reddy and Leekam, concerning infants and older children respectively, provide a counterpoint illustrating the pre-conceptual/conceptual distinction which earlier papers alluded to – although Reddy takes issue with this simple distinction.

The second group of more focused studies, which follows, picks up a suggestion made in earlier papers that the first steps towards mindreading occur in the ways in which visual attention and allied phenomena in others are handled.

Baron-Cohen's paper brings us nearly full-circle, to an attempt to understand the earliest precursors of the capacities detailed in the first chapters of the book. The concluding chapters, in very different ways, probe further the very nature of mindreading and the processes which may underlie its emergence. In turn, they address questions of ontogenetic and phylogenetic parallels; of the roles of theories and models in young children's mindreading; of whether mindreading, rather than behaviourism is the primitive state; and whether mindreading must ultimately be understood in conjunction with other ways of attributing meaning to social actions. It remains the task of the final chapter to highlight significant bridges built between the efforts of the multidisciplinary authorship.

Contributors

Janet W. Astington,
Centre for Applied Cognitive Science, The Ontario Institute for Studies in Education, 252 Bloor Street West, Toronto.

Simon Baron-Cohen,
Department of Psychology and Psychiatry, Institute of Psychiatry, De Crespigny Park, Denmark Hill, London.

Jonathan Bennett,
Department of Philosophy, Syracuse University, Syracuse, New York.

George Butterworth,
Department of Psychology, University of Stirling, Stirling.

Richard W. Byrne,
Psychological Laboratory, University of St Andrews, St Andrews.

Michael Carrithers,
Department of Anthropology, 43 Old Elvet, Durham.

Dorothy L. Cheney,
Department of Anthropology, University of Pennsylvania, Philadelphia.

Verena Dasser,
Department of Psychology, University of Pennsylvania, Philadelphia.

Judy Dunn,
Department of Human Development and Family Studies, College of Health and Human Development, The Pennsylvania State University, University Park.

Juan C. Gómez,
Facultad de Psicologia, Universidad Autonoma de Madrid, Madrid.

ALISON GOPNIK,
Department of Psychology, Tolman Hall, University of California at Berkeley, Berkeley.

PAUL L. HARRIS,
Department of Experimental Psychology, University of Oxford, Oxford.

SUSAN R. LEEKAM,
Department of Experimental Psychology, Sussex University, Brighton.

ALAN M. LESLIE,
MRC Cognitive Development Group, 17 Gordon Street, London.

STACY C. MARSELLA,
Department of Computer Science, Busch Campus, Rutgers University, New Brunswick.

JOSEF PERNER,
Department of Experimental Psychology, Sussex University, Brighton.

DAVID PREMACK,
Department of Psychology, University of Pennsylvania, Philadelphia.

VASUDEVI REDDY,
Department of Psychology, Southampton University, Southampton.

ROBERT SEYFARTH,
Department of Psychology, University of Pennsylvania, Philadelphia.

CHARLES F. SCHMIDT,
Department of Psychology and Department of Computer Science, Busch Campus, Rutgers University, New Brunswick.

THOMAS R. SHULTZ,
Department of Psychology, McGill University, Montreal.

HENRY M. WELLMAN,
Center for Growth and Development, University of Michigan, Ann Arbor.

ANDREW WHITEN,
Psychological Laboratory, University of St Andrews, St Andrews.

1

Fundamental Issues in the Multidisciplinary Study of Mindreading

ANDREW WHITEN AND JOSEF PERNER

In this introductory chapter we aim to lead the reader into the principal issues at stake in the rest of the book. We will start by expanding the hints given in the preface into a brief overview of why the topic of mindreading has simultaneously risen to such importance in the disciplines integrated here, and the ways in which the different approaches can be expected to stimulate each other.

It is equally important that we then offer an introduction to the terminologies and underlying concepts generated by such a diversity of perspectives on the central topic of mindreading. A more challenging intellectual prospect, whether for student psychologist or interested lay-reader, is difficult to imagine: after all, the whole of academic psychology is essentially an attempt to read the mind, so the questions we must grapple with, like 'what is mind?' and 'how can we read minds when we see only behaviour?' could hardly be more fundamental.

Why a Multidisciplinary Study of Mindreading?

We postpone until later in the chapter a careful definition and dissection of 'mindreading': the gist of the concept which the reader will have already assimilated (see figure 1.1) should be quite sufficient to have stimulated curiosity in what this volume is trying to achieve. We can start to explain this with a potted history of each of the three major contributing disciplines.

Josef Perner was supported by an Alexander von Humboldt Fellowship at the Max Planck Institute for Psychological Research, Munich.

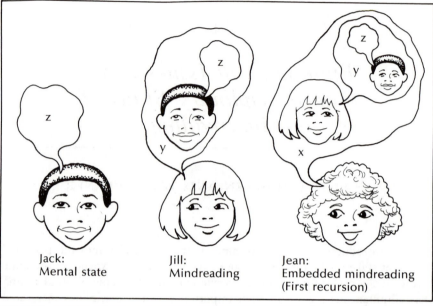

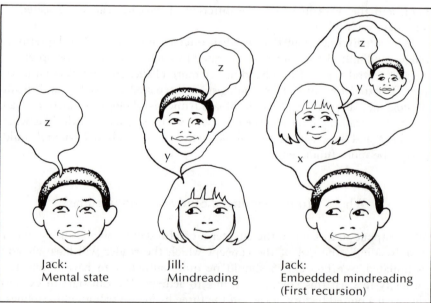

Figure 1.1 *Mindreading and embedded mindreading. In 1a with three persons, Jill, in the centre, attributes to Jack a mental state (e.g. thinks x): on the right is a more complex scenario in which Jean attributes to Jill that mindreading of Jack: Jill's mindreading (y) is thus embedded in Jean's (x). In 1b, the situations are the same except that in the final scene, Jack attributes to Jill a reading of his own mental state. Further embeddings are, in principle, possible (see text).*

Evolution and Ecology: Machiavellian Primates

The primates are the order of mammals to which the human species belongs, along with other apes (like the gorilla and chimpanzee), monkeys and a variety of living representatives of the pro-simians ('before monkeys'), such as bushbabies and lemurs. Problems presented to primates in the laboratories of experimental psychologists have shown the order to contain particularly intelligent species (Parker and Gibson, 1979; Passingham, 1982), yet, since laboratory problems are not part of the natural environment, it has always been a puzzle as to what such superior intelligence had evolved to *do* in the animals' everyday lives. Why has it arisen? Independently, Jolly (1966) and Humphrey (1976) suggested a novel answer: that higher primate intelligence was an adaptation for handling the problems of *social* life, and a body of empirical research has now been amassed which offers support for this functional hypothesis (Byrne and Whiten, 1988). A thumb-nail sketch of the social tactician depicted by this work reveals a primate who has a sophisticated knowledge of the individual characteristics and propensities of others in the group and the network of social relationships existing between them; a flexible capacity to form cooperative alliances with some, so outman-oeuvring others in competitition for resources; and a considerable repertoire of tactics for social manipulation, ranging from deception to reciprocal helping (Whiten and Byrne, 1989). Primates are thus portrayed as little 'Machiavellians', several of their strategies being just those advocated by the pioneering power theorist's advice to sixteenth-century princes and politicians (de Waal, 1982; Whiten and Byrne, 1988c; Machiavelli, 1532). Humphrey (1980, 1983) went on to suggest that such a Machiavellian primate would be better able to win the crucial social games if it could get one step ahead of its adversary through mindreading, or as he put it, acting as a 'natural psychologist'. A growing number of primate researchers have now applied themselves to the question of how such an intriguing possibility can be empirically studied, and the frontiers of this research are described later in the book (chapters 9, 12, 13, 17, 18; see also Whiten and Byrne, 1988c, pp. 60–2).

Pre-dating this functional analysis of the evolution of mindreading, the very first attempts to investigate mindreading in primates arose within experimental, comparative psychology, driven, apparently, by an interest in basic philosophical and psychological concerns about the uniqueness or otherwise of the human mind (Menzel and Johnston, 1976). Premack and Woodruff (1978) first tried to test whether chimpanzees have a 'theory of mind'. Peer commentary on that paper showed that opinion was divided on whether affirmative evidence had been collected, and in chapter 17 below further work dealing with points raised by the critics is described, along with extension of the research to human children.

We are thus dealing with a subject with only a very recent history of investigation, but the basic idea is not so new. To the special delight of one of us, having been chided for neglecting Lloyd Morgan's famous Canon of Parsimony when analysing anecdotal data (peer commentary on Whiten and Byrne, 1988a), it turns out to be Morgan himself who made perhaps the first reference to mindreading in primates (and, as Burghardt, 1988 notes, Lloyd Morgan himself advocated critical use of anecdotes and used them extensively); following a summary of some of Köhler's pioneering studies of chimpanzees, he continued: 'If I may add a comment of my own, I am led to impute to them some measure of imputation to others of first-hand experience similar to that which is theirs as current enjoyment in their own awareness in perceiving and behaving. And this, in their case, seems to be distinctively, if only incipiently, reflective' (Lloyd Morgan, 1930, p. 89).

Children's Developing Understanding of Others

Premack and Woodruff's pioneering work showed that mindreading could be subjected to experimental investigation which did not have to rely heavily on language. Whether directly inspired by those methods or not, the several lines of child research converging on the central issues have now done so under the banner of 'theory of mind'. The expression seems to have been first adopted by Bretherton and Beeghly (1982) and has recently come to represent one of the most active areas in developmental psychology, generating several books and conferences which now dwarf the still-embryonic effort within animal research (e.g. Astington, Harris and Olson, 1988; Harris, 1989a; Dunn, 1988; Perner, forthcoming a; Wellman, 1990; Moore and Frye, forthcoming; and the greater part of this volume).

The roots of this current effort are themselves diverse, even within developmental psychology. In Piaget's theory, which has held such a central place in child psychology, a core notion was that of early childhood egocentrism, in which the child operates without an understanding of the ways in which others' views and thoughts may be different to her own (Piaget and Inhelder, 1948). In the 1970s a barrage of experiments challenged and amended this view (Flavell, Botkin, Fry, Wright and Jarvis, 1968; Flavell, 1978; Donaldson, 1978), and the 1980s have seen the mushrooming of several relatively autonomous programmes of work examining the child's psychological understanding in more detail. Work has ranged over children's developing ability to compute other's perceptions, discriminate appearance and pretence from reality, take account of others' beliefs, emotions and intentions, and acquire the language with which to talk about such things. In the past few years, these research groups have discovered that they share interests aptly captured under the umbrella term 'theory of mind', seminal events being the two conferences which generated the Astington et al. (1988) volume.

This is a time of considerable ferment. On the one hand, attempts are being made to provide overarching frameworks which start to synthesize this growing body of work (Leslie, 1987a; Astington, 1989b; Wellman, 1990, Perner, forthcoming a). On the other hand, there are deep debates. How apt is the slogan 'theory of mind' when it comes to the true nature of what is emerging in early childhood – does the child really need a *theory* to mindread? (Harris and Gross, 1988; Johnson, 1988; chapters 15 and 19 below)? Further, while some debate whether the child attributes mental states by age 2½ or 4 years (Perner, 1988b; Wimmer, Hogrefe and Sodian, 1988; Wellman and Bartsch, 1988; Chandler, Fritz and Halla, 1989; Sodian, Harris, Taylor and Perner, 1989; here see chapters 2–4), others talk of 'intersubjectivity' in infant–parent interactions in the first year of life, defining intersubjectivity as 'the mutual adjustments of conscious voluntary agents (subjects) to one another's mental states' (Trevarthen, 1977; and here see Reddy's development of this position, chapter 10).

Computational Psychology and Artificial Intelligence

The relevance of work in this area ranges from the well-established to that which has the ring of science fiction. To start at the latter end, the ultimate triumph of artificial intelligence would be the construction of a robot with whom we could interact naturally; and since the way we do that amongst ourselves rests on assumptions about the mind of the other, mindreading must also be built into the robot. Closer to current reality, the steps towards this futuristic vision include a vast industry of work on making the human–computer interface operate more smoothly, with the software better attuned to the mind of the person using it (Goodson and Schmidt, 1988). An obvious example is expert systems, which need to interlock with the mentality of the person whose expertise they extend, although typically only a small part of that mentality is considered (Sleeman, 1983; Johnson, 1985).

A comprehensive integration of this enormous area of research with the two outlined above is beyond the scope of this book. However, there are particular lines of attack which seem particularly germane to our central concerns, such as work on the recognition of plans and intentional actions (Schmidt, Sridharan and Goodson, 1978; Thibadeau, 1986; Shultz, 1988).

Two chapters here (6 and 8) focus particularly on developments in these areas.

The Rationale for an Interdisciplinary Approach

These three areas of research complement each other in a number of ways and other disciplines also have an important contribution to make, notably philosophy (Bennett, 1976 and chapter 7; Dennett, 1978) and anthropology (Heelas, 1981; Carrithers, chapter 20 below). Fruitful interactions between these different areas include the following:

Methodologies We have already noted the way in which chimpanzee experiments have stimulated investigations with children; but now the converse also seems to have happened (Premack, 1988a; chapter 17). Such interplay can be expected to proliferate. While child researchers may wish to avoid dependence on language (so that proven effects are those concerning theory of mind, rather than just a different grasp of relevant aspects of language), animal behaviour researchers are intrinsically constrained to design non-linguistic tests anyway.

It has also been suggested that the complexity of social situations may ultimately confound experimentation as the only scientific approach: 'it is important to avoid the naive mistake of assuming that an experimental test of a hypothesis is necessarily more rigorous than an observational one. . . . An experiment can often be less rigorous than a well constructed analysis of observational data precisely because it disrupts the natural flow of interactions' (Dunbar, 1988). With the lessons of a century of anthropomorphism and behaviourism behind us, sharing proposals for the pursuit of rigour in exploiting spontaneous behavioural evidence of mindreading should be rewarding for students of children and animals alike (Whiten and Byrne, 1988a; Dunn, 1988; chapters 4, 9 and 10 below).

The emergence of mindreading At the heart of this book is a shared interest in how mindreading abilities are built up from simpler precursors. In child research, of course, this question is applied to *ontogenetic* change as infants grow into older children: in comparative research, by contrast, we are interested not only in this ontogenetic change, but in the *evolution* of such abilities. To be alert to the possibility of parallels in the progressive steps taken in the ontogenetic and evolutionary domains does not require us to subscribe to the doctrine that ontogeny recapitulates phylogeny (Gould, 1978; Parker and Gibson, 1979): there may instead simply be logical reasons why step B precedes step C. To date, only a little groundwork has been done on this issue, represented by shared concerns in the animal and child camps with such topics as deception, and the ability of individuals to represent what others can see, want, are attending to, believe, or know. The sequential order of acquisition is tackled in many chapters in this book, and the question of ontogenetic–evolutionary parallels in chapters 18 and 21. Premack and Woodruff (1978) argued that 'the ape could only be a mentalist . . . he is not intelligent enough to be a behaviorist', thus questioning the common assumption that behaviourism is a primitive state out of which mentalism arises. The possibility that in some important sense the reverse could be true is of equal significance for both developmental and evolutionary studies (Premack and Dasser, chapter 17 below).

As in much of developmental psychology, it is easier (although not easy!) to chart the capacities in place at various ages, than to explain *how* the child gets from one stage to the next. Interestingly, Shultz argues that one of the benefits of the computational approach lies in going beyond rigorous specification of the nature of developmental stages to models of what is involved in transitions *between* stages (see chapter 6).

The functional context In addition to these shared issues, *differences* between children and primates in the functional context of various levels of mindreading and its precursors should be instructive. Whereas young humans will tend to be buffered from the worst environmental challenges by their caretakers, adult primates with similarly primitive mindreading capacities are typically at the sharp end of the forces of natural selection. Given that in addition they are unconstrained by the more general aspects of immature sensorimotor and mental competence which complicate the picture in infancy, we may expect to see rather directly what functional benefits accrue from any mindreading abilities. In exactly which contexts will mindreading (as opposed to a behaviourist analysis) help a primate to outcompete its companions in the ultimate currency of evolution – reproductive success?

However, this perspective is not irrelevant even to the cossetted human infant. Bateson (1984) has highlighted a dichotomy of functional explanations for behaviours characteristic of early development: their function may be either to build competent adult behaviour for later stages of life; or they may have a direct utility at the particular stage in life where they occur. Although we tend to think of each step in the construction of theory of mind (like most cognitive development) as being just a stage in the building of adult competence, we should not overlook the possibility that an ability exists in the form it does because it allows the infant to exploit the ecological circumstances it is currently facing. For example, what, if any, mindreading capacities are necessary to benefit from the elaborate social support (the

'scaffolding') provided by parents in the service of infants' developing communicative and technological competences (Trevarthen, 1977, Trevarthen
and Logotheti, 1989a; Bruner, 1975, 1983; Whiten and Milner, 1984;
chapters 10, 15, and 16 below)?

Terminology and conceptual frameworks   We have already noted
the proliferation of synonyms for the core topic of mindreading. In a
similar way, different terms and concepts litter the literature of the various
disciplines and, to make matters worse, many of the terms and concepts
have everyday counterparts whose usage is not quite the same. It is our
hope that the thinking forced on us by attempting to integrate all these will
be beneficial to all those who share our interest and starting this task is what
occupies the remainder of this chapter.

What Is Mind?

Many of the issues become apparent in any attempt to answer the 'simple'
question of what the mind is. However, in our basic paradigm we have two
individuals, one the mindreader (MR) the other a target individual (TI),
whose mind is to be read. It is worth noting at this point that psychologists
in their scientific theory may need to characterize the mental processes of
TI (and MR) in a quite different way from the mental processes MR
attributes to TI on the basis of common-sense (or folk) psychology. We
shall develop the implications of this more later, but it should be borne in
mind from the start.

One quick and ready answer to the question, 'What is the mind of TI
that MR might read' is that the mind consists of mental states for which
we have expressions in our language, like *knowing, thinking, feeling, wanting*
and so on. Such mental states have been classified into *sensations* and
attitudes (e.g. McGinn, 1982). Attitudes can be further differentiated as to
whether they are attitudes towards an object or a proposition (*propositional
attitudes*, see table 1.1). However, such lists do not provide a very comprehensive answer to our basic question. Where, if at all, should we fit 'seeing
x' or 'looking at y' or 'seeking z' into this scheme? Are these mental or
behavioural or what? And by what rules would we decide? In the following
we shall discuss four different ways of defining 'the mental' which have their
roots in philosophy of mind (e.g. Churchland, 1984; Fodor, 1985; McGinn,
1982; Olson, 1988), but which have played an important part in recent
empirical investigations.

Table 1.1   Classification of mental states with examples

| | Attitudes | |
Sensations	Toward objects	Toward propositions
I feel pain.	He is happy with it.	He is happy about getting
He is happy.	He is afraid of the dog.	it.
He is anxious.	She thinks of him.	He is afraid of the dog
She is thinking.	She knows him.	biting him.
	Maxi wants chocolate.	She thinks he is dancing.
		She knows he is dancing.
		Maxi wants to put the
		candy away.

1   Inner Experience

A common-sense definition of the mental has its philosophical roots in Descartes' writing: 'the soul acquires all its information by reflexion which it makes either on itself (in the case of intellectual matters) or (in the case of corporeal matters) on the various dispositions of the brain to which it is joined which may result from the action of the senses or from other causes' (Kenny, 1970, p. 66). Thus mental states are those to which we have direct access in our inner conscious awareness. We know what knowledge or pain is because we have experienced it. This view of the mind does justice to how we intuitively feel what mind is, but for purposes of mindreading, it faces a fundamental difficulty: the *problem of other minds*. If states of mind are defined essentially by what we see in ourselves, how can we know that other people have such states too?

One answer to this conundrum is role-taking (or perspective-taking). To arrive at what another individual sees or believes, one puts oneself mentally in his position ('putting oneself in another person's shoes') and estimates what one would see or believe oneself in that situation. Most of the developmental research on the Piagetian concept of egocentrism (treating one's own mental state as absolute: see p. 97) has focused on improved role or perspective-taking skills as the route whereby the child emerges out of egocentrism (e.g. Feffer, 1959; Flavell et al., 1968; Chandler, 1977). In the evolutionary domain, Humphrey (1982; 1986) has offered an explanation for the very existence (evolution) of consciousness with his proposal that it allows us to reflect upon the psychological causes of our own behaviour.

Consciousness thereby provides a more powerful predictive model of *others'* behaviour (once we 'put ourselves in their shoes') than we could construct merely by observing their overt behaviour.

But can awareness of inner experience ever be the full story – or even the basic touchstone – of how we understand the minds of others? It requires the tacit asssumption that the other person does have similar mental states in similar conditions. But such differences between individuals as those of age and sex, political or religious belief, for example, are likely to make the assumption flawed. Furthermore, that the other be mentally like me is not always enough for role-taking to work: a systematic linkage to external observable events is also required (for example, only if there is a systematic relationship between where I *stand* and what I *see* can I work out what I would see if I stood where the other person stands). This linkage requirement is taken account of in Paul Harris' refinement of Humphrey's notion of mental modelling or simulation of others' minds (see chapter 19 below). We turn now to the other principal ways in which the problem has been tackled to date.

2 *Folk Psychology and Theory of Mind*

In everyday talk, we employ what has been called a *folk psychology* to explain the actions of others and the language of this everyday psychology relies heavily on mental terms like those given in table 1.1. Philosophers and psychologists who have pored over what is happening in folk psychology have argued that particularly central are the concepts of *belief* and *desire*, operating in a rational being: thus, Mary *wanted* an icecream and she *believed* there were some in the cupboard; and this perfectly explains her rational action of searching there. Thus folk psychology is often dubbed *belief-desire psychology*. The next two chapters in particular are concerned with children's earliest understanding of this system.

How does the system work? Dennett (1978, 1983) has argued that folk psychology need not be regarded as referring directly to the processes which truly cause and organize our behaviour (these processes are, of course, legitimate subjects of scientific psychological enquiry); rather, the utility of folk psychology is that, by *attributing* mental states to others, we achieve a powerful ability to predict their behaviour (a point relevant to the survival value of mind-probing Machiavellianism discussed above).

Far from being confined exclusively to inner experiences, mental terms thus take their place in a system very much concerned with actions. The process of mental state attribution can be seen as tied to actions at both 'ends'. Firstly, attributions are made on the basis of observations of behaviour in equally observable particular social contexts: indeed, Wittgenstein (1953) offered the revolutionary argument that the child must come to understand the meaning of mental terms not as referring to essentially private mental states, but rather by their relationship to phenomena publicly observable to the language-using community – else how could the meaning of the terms be mutually agreed? Secondly, the utility of the mental attribution is ultimately testable through its predictive power. The sophisticated folk psychology any one individual uses today can thus be envisaged as the result of repeated application, testing and reformulation – of the basic framework over generations of mindreaders – and of its particulars as refined by the individual through his or her lifetime.

Folk psychology can thus be seen as a sort of theory, in so far as it is an elaborate system of theoretical constructs, generating testable predictions on which it stands or falls. And so yet another expression has come into use to capture this: *(folk) theory of mind.*

However, although our folk theory of mind is formulated in language, it is not obvious that it must be tied to language users: in fact, an important implication of the 'theory' view of mind is that it becomes meaningful to talk of mental states in animals or even computers, and thus of mindreading occurring between them. Bennett (1976, p. 110) put it succinctly:

> there can also be languageless beliefs about beliefs. We human observers can get plenty of evidence as to what animal B believed on various occasions, and can establish and test theories which support predictions about what he will believe on some further occasion; and all our data for this consist in behaviour of B's which is perceptible by animal A as well. So A can have all the epistemic intake that would be needed for beliefs about B's beliefs.

The logic of such possibilities is pursued in later chapters on animals, computers and prelinguistic human infants. Thus, for example, Schmidt and Marsella (chapter 8) address the question of how a computer can infer another system's intentions and plans. In other studies we see the importance of Bennett's statement not only for the mindreader but for the scientist, who as observer should in principle also have access to the public 'epistemic intake' available to A and B, and be able to utilize particular patterns of behaviour to furnish evidence of mindreading; Gomez (chapter 13), for example, uses visual interplay between chimpanzee and human as evidence for mental state attribution; and Reddy (chapter 10) uses infants' teasing behaviour as a basis for this inference.

Although so far we have presented the various expressions discussed in this section as synonymous, the question of animal mindreading suggests that it should be possible to have a *theory of mind*, which is not what we mean by *folk psychology*. The latter is the result of public linguistic 'negotiation' which over countless generations has led to the system we currently use (the question of universals versus culturally different folk psychologies is another, if fascinating, issue: Heelas, 1981). Whatever animals possess by way of a theory of mind will by contrast be the result of an interaction only between innate factors and individual experience.

The situation for human children is radically different in so far as it is reasonable to see the ontogeny of a theory of mind as the acquisition of a ready-made folk psychology. Nevertheless, such acquisition cannot *always* have been possible! Perhaps the words we use to denote mental states have been grafted on to categories which already existed in our prelinguistic ancestors, and maybe exist in the prelinguistic humans and animals we are now studying: alternatively, perhaps we are handicapped by the straightjacket of the folk terms available when we study these forms of life, whose mindreading may be structured differently (in the next chapter, for example, we are asked to envisage very young children as possessing something like only a 'half' of belief–desire psychology).

3   Aboutness or Intentionality

In everyday explanations of behaviour, we refer not only to mental states, but also to the causal role of physical events and the behaviour of others. So far we have only specified the part of this folk psychology which constitutes a theory of mind rather vaguely, as that involving *theoretical constructs*. A more precise distinction between the mental and the physical has been attempted by succeeding generations of philosophers, and the central one withstanding the test of time is that of intentionality or 'aboutness' (Brentano, 1874; Dennett, 1988).

Intentionality is a technical term and not to be confused with the everyday meaning of 'intention': it is much broader in scope, and can best be explained with respect to mental attitudes (see table 1.1). Take the example of 'thinking of him'. This is not just a mental state of thinking, but the thinking is *about* a person (it *aims* at the person; latin *intendere* = aiming at). And this aboutness exhibits a curious logical feature, called *logical* or *referential opacity*.

Logical opacity   Consider the two statements 'Mary kicked her donkey' and 'Mary knows her donkey is in the stable'. Since the donkey is a *hoofed, herbivorous mammal*, it simply follows logically that in the case of the first, behavioural proposition, Mary kicked a hoofed, herbivorous mammal. But the second, mental proposition, is resistant or *opaque* to the logic which is so automatic in the behavioural case: Mary may know there is a donkey in the stable, without knowing that there is a hoofed, herbivorous mammal there. The aboutness of intentional terms is in this way *selective*, Mary knowing her donkey only in the aspect of it being her donkey, and not in other aspects, even though they be logically connected.

This is more than an abstruse philosophical discovery, because it offers a framework for examining certain psychological phenomena which are candidate borderline cases, or precursors, of the mental. For example, Leslie (1987a) has argued that early pretence, in requiring some understanding of opacity, is a sign that children have acquired an important prerequisite for understanding the mind. For this reason Whiten and Byrne compare pretence in primates with that observed in children (chapter 18) and much discussion about the social impairment of autism centres on this question (Leslie, chapter 4; Baron-Cohen, chapter 16). 'Seeing' is another important topic to examine in this context, because interpretation of seeing and related phenomena (e.g. looking, attending to, noticing) might be taken to be a first step in mindreading.

Two types of 'seeing'   Dretske (1969) distinguished between epistemic and non-epistemic uses of 'seeing'. When used with *that* – 'I saw that a burglar climbed through the window' – it is implied that I saw the intruder *as a burglar*. This is not the case in the non-epistemic, and non-logically opaque 'I saw the burglar climb through the window'; indeed I might add 'but I didn't know at the time that he was a burglar'. This distinction offers food for thought with respect to such chapters as 12 to 16; if birds, monkeys, apes or human infants take into account 'seeing' by others, is this the epistemic or non-epistemic variety?

Representation   Epistemic seeing requires the interpretation or understanding of a visual percept and the result is conventionally referred to in cognitive psychology as a *representation* of what was seen. Such a representation can be incomplete (it represents only certain aspects: the perceived individual is a man) but not others (the individual is a burglar) or it can even be downright wrong as in the case of misperception. But do all mental states have to be conceived of as representations? Take our description of what somebody wants: 'he wants to take his dog to the park'. 'Wants' is logically opaque here (try making substititions yourself), but does it entail a mental representation of self and dog in the park? Wellman (chapter 2) and Astington and Gopnik (chapter 3) question whether desires and intentions are understood as representations by young children, and Harris (chapter 19) even raises the question of whether false beliefs need to be understood as mental representations.

Metarepresentation A representation of representation is a second-order representation or metarepresentation (e.g. chapters 5, 18). Perner (1988a) has advocated that only a child or animal who comes to understand a mental state *as* a representational state be said to be engaging in meta-representation (the individual *mentally represents* **that** another individual (or itself) *mentally represents* something else). If Dretske's distinction is accepted, it follows that an individual capable of representing only non-epistemic seeing is not yet engaging in metarepresentation.

4 Recursion or Nesting

Mental states, as propositional attitudes, have another peculiar property which stems from their dual nature of being propositional attitudes (relating an individual to a proposition) and being themselves propositions. For instance, the proposition 'Jean thinks children are egocentric' expresses Jean's attitude (of thinking) to the proposition 'children are egocentric', but is itself a higher order proposition about Jean. As a proposition, it can be nested within a further propositional attitude: 'Paul believes that Jean thinks that children are egocentric'. This nesting or recursion (see figure 1.1) can be repeated *ad infinitum* in principle, although in practice we can mentally cope with only a few nestings (Dennett, 1983).

It so happens that different terminologies have arisen to count these nestings, a potential source of confusion to which the reader must be alerted (see table 1.2). The principal difference can be explained as follows, by reference to Premack's subject, the chimpanzee Sarah:

(1) 'Sarah *knows* that the bananas are in the red box' expresses a **first-order** mental state. In contrast,
(2) 'Sarah *knows* the trainer *wants* to eat the bananas' expresses a **second-order** mental state and we have mindreading.
(3) 'She *knows* he *thinks* that she *wants* to eat the bananas' expresses a **third-order** mental state (and so on).

Note that in all these cases, the same folk psychology vocabulary is used to talk about both the mindreader (MR) and the target (TI) whose mind is read. However, the scientist is not a folk psychologist, and in investigating mindreading may well wish to avoid folk psychology terms in describing MR (whilst acknowledging that such terms may be appropriate to describe what MR attributes to TI). For instance, Whiten and Byrne (1988a) and Perner and Wimmer (1985) preferred to describe (in the tradition of cognitive psychology) MR as *mentally representing* TI's mental states, the latter referred to (in the tradition of folk psychology) as *knowing, thinking, wanting* and so on. In the example with Sarah above this would mean:

Sarah (mentally) *represents* that the trainer *thinks* that she *wants* . . .

Once this first level of how the scientist describes the mindreader's mental state is separated from how the mindreader describes the mental states of the TI, a new way of counting levels of recursion suggests itself: only recursions of the folk pyschological attributions are counted. Perner and Wimmer (1985) have followed this route. In our third example with Sarah above they would, therefore, speak of Sarah as *attributing* a **second-order** mental state to the trainer (he *thinks* she *wants* . . .) where Dennett (1983) would speak of Sarah's **third-order** mental state. To further complicate the picture, Whiten and Byrne (1988a) nevertheless contrived to maintain a system of counting parallel to that of Dennett (1983), referring to such a case as the third example above as **third-order representation** (Sarah represents the trainer's representation of her representation).

A danger in this latter formulation is that it could imply that Sarah conceives of her trainer's mental states (in cognitive fashion) *as representations* (i.e., that he represents her as representing what she desires). Such an assumption, however, would pre-empt the current controversy in the developmental camp about whether children conceive of *wanting* as a representational activity (Astington and Gopnik, chapter 3; Wellman, chapter 2) or even of belief as representational (Harris, chapter 19).

However, once we are beyond such niceties of how to describe this first 'step' in mindreading, there seems no great disagreement amongst researchers about the nature of recursions (even if different numbers are, trivially, attached to them). Important combinations of recursive mental states find their way into our conceptual system; for example, Leekam (chapter 11) shows how children progressively learn to differentiate lies from mistakes (differing in speaker's first-order knowledge) and then lies from jokes (differing in speaker's second-order intention about the listener's belief).

To summarize, we have set out the major types of criterion for mentality, to help the reader ask about the evidence discussed in subsequent chapters for the attribution of mentality, whether by child, chimpanzee or computer. Does it involve understanding of *inner experience*? Or understanding of *sophisticated aspects of behaviour* (the spirit in which Krebs and Dawkins (1984) first introduced the expression 'mindreading' into ethology)? Does it require a *theory of mind* that goes beyond the description of behaviour? Does it handle *logical opacity*? Is it a sign of a *representational theory of mind*? It is our hope that answers to these questions will sharpen our understanding of the emergence of mindreading in all its manifestations.

Table 1.2 Different approaches to describing mindreading and embedded mindreading (see also figure 1.1).[a]

	Orders of representation or intentionality			
	No intentional state	Intentional state	Mindreading	Embedded mindreading[b]
Premack and Woodruff 1978 Premack 1988	[Some non-apes?]	'Behaviourist' 'We take it for granted that the ape is an intentional system'	'Mentalist' 'Does the ape *think* that other apes are *intentional systems?*' (must be equivalent to Dennett below?).	
Dennett 1983	'0-order intentional system', e.g. X is aroused by Y.	'1st-order intentional system', e.g. X *believes* Y will attack her.	'2nd-order intentional system', e.g. X *wants* Y to *believe that . . .* '	'3rd-order intentional system', e.g. X *wants* Y to *believe* that X *knows* where food is or X *wants* Y to *believe* that Z *intends* him harm.

Leslie 1987		'2nd-order representations' or 'meta-representations', examples as for Dennett.	
Whiten and Byrne, 1988a, 1988b	'First order representations', 'coding simply for physical states of the world.'	'2nd-order representations coding for mental representations in other individuals', e.g. X represents Y's actual or potential focus of attention.	'in a 3rd order representational system, the agent would represent the target's representation of the representations of someone else, which could be the agent', e.g. X knows that Y can take into account X's focus of attention.
Perner et al., 1985		'1st-order belief attribution', e.g. X attributes to Y a belief that . . .	'2nd-order belief attribution', e.g. X attributes to Y a belief that Z wants . . .

[a] For completeness, the extension of systems of counting to non-mindreading states is included.
[b] The final column shows only a first embedding or recursion. Higher orders of embedding are possible (see text).

2

From Desires to Beliefs: Acquisition of a Theory of Mind

HENRY M. WELLMAN

The topic of this volume concerns the emergence of an understanding of mind. The term 'mind', as I am using it, is an everyday one rather than a scientific one, it is a term within an everyday theory. This everyday theory construes overt human behaviour as the consequence of covert mental states, such as the actor's beliefs, hopes, ideas, and desires (see also chapter 1). When do children adopt this everyday mentalistic construal of human behaviour?

This question has a complicated and fascinating answer. To be brief, however, I am going to answer simply: at three years. To elaborate on this simplistic answer I discuss three points. First, I will sketch what I believe constitutes our everyday theory of mind. This analysis revolves around characterizing everyday mentalism as a belief–desire psychology. Secondly, I review some recent findings showing that children as young as three years understand and utilize belief–desire psychology and hence evidence a first theory of mind. Other chapters in this volume and elsewhere (e.g. Astington, Harris and Olson, 1988) review related research; I will concentrate on the research of my collaborators and myself. Thirdly, I suggest that children younger than three, say two-year olds, fail to understand belief–desire psychology. They utilize instead, a simple desire psychology.

Sketch of a Theory of Mind

There are two intuitive aspects of our understanding of the mental states of self and other. Crudely put, I will call these the hypothetical and causal

Support for this research was provided by grant HD–22149 from NICHD.

aspects of mind. The essence of the hypothetical aspect is our understanding of the difference between thoughts or ideas on the one hand and objects or overt behaviours on the other. For example, a thought about a dog is not the same sort of thing as a dog. Indeed, a thought about a dog is not the same sort of thing as even a shadow of a dog, or a photograph of a dog. Mental entities are internal, subjective, non-real and hypothetical, whereas physical entities are real, external, substantial and objective. The phrase *theory of mind*, as a label for our everyday theory, emphasizes our ordinary understanding of this hypothetical nature of mind. My collaborators and I have researched young children's understanding of the hypothetical, non-real nature of mental entities, and find that even three-year-olds appropriately distinguish mental entities from physical entities (cf., Wellman and Estes, 1986; Estes, Wellman and Woolley, 1989).

According to our everyday theory of mind, our thoughts – our beliefs, plans, ideas and so on – not only are mentalistic but are also causal. A useful and typical short-hand here is to divide our causal mental states into two generic sorts: beliefs and desires (e.g., Davidson, 1980). The causal aspect of mind, then, depicts overt human actions as the joint product of the actor's beliefs and desires. The phrase *belief–desire psychology*, as a label for our everyday theory, highlights this causal aspect of mind. The hypothetical and causal aspects of mind are intimately interrelated. Theory of mind and belief–desire psychology are different descriptive labels for the same topic, the same basic set of understandings. In this chapter, however, I approach the topic from the perspective of the causal aspect of mind.

At the centre of our everyday belief–desire psychology is a basic triad: beliefs, desires, and actions.

(1) Why did Bill go to the swimming pool? He *wanted* to swim and *thought* the pool was open.
(2) Why did Jill watch television? She *wanted* some entertainment and *thought* that a programme she liked was on.

The fundamental, obvious idea is that people engage in actions because they *believe* those actions will satisfy certain *desires*. Of course the theory is more complicated than this in a variety of important ways. It includes reasoning such as:

(3) Why did John go to the candy machine? He was *hungry* and *wanted* a candy bar, and *thought* he'd *seen* the kind he liked in that machine.

Hence, belief–desire psychology incorporates not only beliefs, desires and actions but a network of related constructs such as physiological states (e.g., 'he was hungry') and perceptions (e.g., 'he'd seen that kind'). Figure 2.1 captures the organization of these related constructs. Briefly and simplistically, physiological states and basic emotions ground one's desires. Beliefs, on the other hand, are often derived from perceptual experiences. Furthermore, one's actions lead to outcomes in the world, and these outcomes lead to reactions. As depicted in figure 2.1, at least two basic sorts of reactions are encompassed by the theory: reactions dependent on desires and reactions dependent on beliefs. That is, the outcome of an action can satisfy or fail to satisfy the actor's desires, leading, generically, to happiness reactions. You want something and get it and you are happy, or you fail to get it and you are sad or angry. Also, the outcome of an action can match or fail to match an actor's beliefs, generically termed surprise reactions. You think something will happen and it does not so you are surprised or puzzled.

In this system the key mental states – beliefs and desires – cause actions. Such states are private and not directly observable in others, albeit experienced directly in oneself. However, others' mental states (and at times our own) can be inferred from, among other things, perceptual experiences (e.g., what he sees), from physiological history (e.g., how long it's been since he's eaten) and from emotional expressions and reactions (e.g., when he's happy or when he's surprised).

This brief sketch does not provide a full or proper account of adult belief–desire reasoning. It leaves unelaborated several concepts, such as intention (see chapters 3 and 4) and traits (see Wellman, 1990, chapter 4). But even this crude sketch is sufficient to begin to ask, when do children engage in reasoning of this sort? As is clear from the many connections and links depicted in figure 2.1, if children engage in this sort of reasoning they should know several things. But, most centrally there seem to be two basic sorts of reasoning to assess, that require a direct understanding of the belief, desire, action triad. First, in the forward direction, if children know an actor's beliefs and desires they should be able to predict his behaviour. Secondly, in the backward direction, if children are given an action to explain, they should explain it by appeal to beliefs and desires.

Three-Year-Olds' Belief–Desire Psychology

Predictions

Can three-year-olds appropriately predict behaviour, given information as to an actor's beliefs and desires? In our studies of this sort (Wellman and Bartsch, 1988), we start by telling children about a character who desires

22

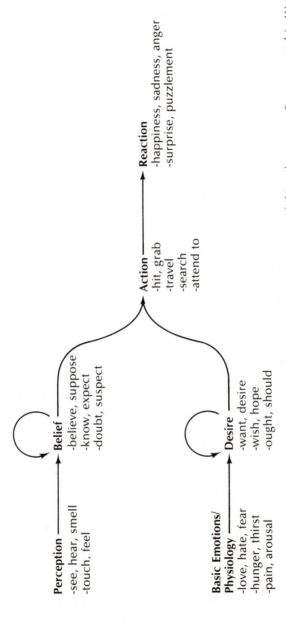

Figure 2.1 Simplified scheme for depicting belief–desire reasoning. A version of this scheme was first presented in Wellman and Bartsch (1988).

something – for example, 'Sam wants to find his puppy'. But, 'the puppy is lost, and it might be hiding in the garage *or* under the porch'. Then the child is told about the character's belief, 'Sam thinks his puppy is under the porch', and asked where Sam will look, in the garage or under the porch? This task requires the child to use information about the character's desire coupled with his belief to predict his action. For reasons that will become clear as we go along, the most critical and difficult thing to demonstrate is that young children understand belief. That is, do young children understand that actors not only will be directed towards things that they want, but that their actions will also be constrained by their beliefs? This sort of task, a *Standard Belief* task, attempts to test whether children understand that the actor's beliefs must be taken into account, in addition to the actor's desire, in order to predict action. Since the puppy might be in either location, knowing only Sam's desire leads to the prediction that he could look in either place. But, adding in Sam's belief unambiguously narrows the prediction to a single location.

Unfortunately children could respond appropriately on Standard Belief tasks without really understanding beliefs, that is, by using some less interesting alternative strategy. To control for alternative strategies we have devised a number of variations on this task. For example, in *Not-Belief* tasks children were told 'Sam thinks his puppy is *not* in the garage', so that they could not be correct simply by citing the last location mentioned in the story. Instead, the correct prediction is the unmentioned location.

Suppose by chance that our belief statements about Sam consistently coincide with the subject's own belief – the child thinks puppies will really hide under porches, not in garages. In this case, the subject might be correct not by understanding beliefs, but simply by reporting what she herself would do – 'The puppy is lost, I'd look under the porch'. In *Not-Own Belief* tasks children were first asked about their own beliefs, for example, 'Where do *you* think the puppy is?' After the child stated her belief she was told that the character in fact has the opposite belief.

A troubling possibility is that children might use what we have called *reality assessment strategies* to reason about these problems. Suppose that the young child has no conception of belief and hence does not understand belief statements such as 'Sam thinks his dog is in the garage'. Instead, children misinterpret these statements as specifying the real state of affairs. For example, on Standard Belief tasks, the statement 'Sam thinks his dog is in the garage' is understood as a statement about reality. Then the child would reason, 'Sam wants his dog, it's really in the garage, so Sam will look there'. In *Discrepant Belief* tasks we described to children a situation where there really were targets in two locations. Use of a reality assessment strategy should lead to predicting the character would search in either location or both (since targets are in both). An understanding of belief should lead to the single correct prediction.

We have conducted tests of children's belief–desire reasoning in ten different conditions such as these, controlling various alternative interpretations (e.g. Wellman and Bartsch, 1988; Wellman, 1990, chapter 3). The four conditions described above exemplify our reasoning. The top portion of figure 2.2 captures the nature of these four different conditions with respect to some competing hypotheses. On the left, if children understand this basic sort of belief–desire causation then they should be uniformly correct across all versions of the task. In the middle there is a depiction of children's responses if they simply predict what they themselves would do. In this case children could be coincidentally correct on the Standard and Not-Belief tasks if their belief consistently coincides with the belief stated for the actor. However, they would be incorrect on Not-Own Belief tasks, and they should respond at chance on Discrepant Belief tasks since on those tasks their own belief is that target objects are in both locations. The right-hand graph depicts what would happen if children make predictions based on reality assessment – predicting the character will look where there really are targets. In this case they could be correct on most tasks but only at chance on Discrepant Belief tasks.

The bottom portion of figure 2.2 shows the data from 20 to 40 three-year-olds in a condition. They are consistently correct across all versions of the task. Even on Discrepant Belief tasks three-year-olds are 82 per cent correct (significantly greater than a chance value of 50 per cent) where they have to predict the other's action on the basis of the other's belief which is discrepant from their own belief and indeed from reality.

Now it is true, as many studies have shown, that on *false* belief prediction tasks three-year-olds perform poorly (see for example Perner et al., 1987). We devised what we think of as the simplest false belief tasks possible, termed Explicit False Belief tasks. In such tasks the child is told of reality and told that the character has a false belief. For example, 'Sam's puppy is in the garage; Sam thinks his puppy is under the porch'. When given tasks of this sort, three-year-olds were only correct 16 per cent of the time. However, I believe that this result shows a peculiar difficulty that young children have with understanding *false* beliefs, it does not indicate a lack of understanding of beliefs altogether. That is, young children understand belief in spite of misunderstanding false beliefs. Children's success in our other tasks demonstrates an understanding of belief, I think, as do their explanations of actions.

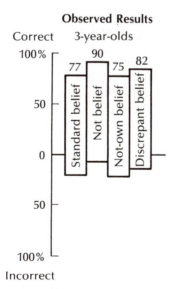

Predicted Results

Observed Results

Figure 2.2 *Predicted and observed responses to belief–desire prediction tasks.*

Explanations

Our basic explanation task is this (Bartsch and Wellman, 1989): We tell children of a simple act, for example, 'Jane is looking for her kitten under the piano', and then ask children to explain the act: 'Why do you think she is doing that?' As a look at figure 2.1 suggests, belief–desire psychologists should construct such explanations by appeal, proximally, to the characters' beliefs and desires, and by appeal more generally to beliefs, desires, perceptions, physiology, and basic emotions. Appeal to beliefs and desires narrowly I will call belief–desire explanations; appeal to any of the constructs in the larger scheme – belief, or perception, or emotion, etc. – I will call psychological explanations.

We presented three-year-olds, four-year-olds, and adults with the three different sorts of explanation items shown in box 2.1: Neutral items, Anomalous Desire items (designed to pull more for desire explanations), and Anomalous Belief items (designed to pull more for belief explanations). After each item was presented we asked 'Why do you think the actor is doing that?' And then if children did not spontaneously mention beliefs or desires we mildly prompted them by asking simply, 'What does she want?' or 'What does she think?'

Were the explanations generated of the sort predicted by the theory sketch? That is, were they psychological explanations, generally, and belief–desire explanations specifically? What else could they have been? They could have been behaviouristic explanations, invoking for example a history of conditioning – e.g., 'She's found it there again and again in the past'. Or, they could have been physicalistic explanations – e.g., 'The wind

Box 2.1

Neutral items:	Here's Jane. Jane is looking for her kitten under the piano. Why do you think Jane is doing that?
Anomalous Desire items:	Here's Jane. Jane hates frogs. But Jane is looking for the frog under the piano. Why do you think Jane is doing that?
Anomalous Belief items:	Here's Jane. Jane is looking for her kitten. The kitten is hiding under the chair. But Jane is looking under the piano. Why do you think Jane is doing that?

blew her over there'. Neither children nor adults ever offered behaviouristic or physicalistic sorts of explanations. Both children and adults did, however, make simple referrals to the external situation as in, 'the kitten was lost'. They did so about 30 per cent of the time. But, more often than that children and adults provided psychological explanations, that is, they explicitly referred to the actor's perceptions, beliefs, desires and basic emotions as explanations for his act. As figure 2.3 shows, three-year-olds used psychological explanations 65 per cent of the time in their unprompted explanations; this is not different from the percentage for four-year-olds and adults. Moreover, of three-year-olds' unprompted psychological explanations, 60 per cent referred specifically to beliefs or desires. For comparison the percentages for four-year-olds and for adults were 69 per cent and 67 per cent respectively.

So in response to 'Why did she do that?', three- and four-year-olds and adults give the same general sorts of explanations: psychological explanations broadly, and belief–desire explanations specifically. However, this analysis

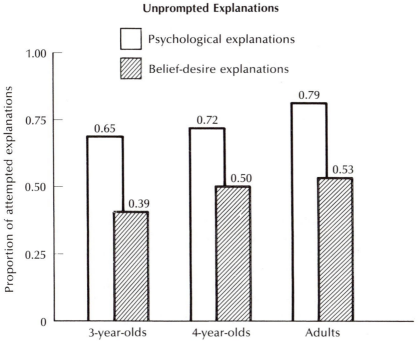

Figure 2.3 *Types of unprompted explanations of actions offered by children and adults.*

considers belief and desire explanations jointly; what about belief explanations alone? As it happens, on most items children and adults initially
prefer desire explanations. In our data, at all ages, desire explanations
outweighed belief explanations about two to one. It was because of this
general preference for desire explanations that our methods included Anomalous Belief tasks.

Subjects received three Anomalous Belief stories like the one shown in
box 2.1. Sixty per cent of the children gave an *unprompted* belief explanation
to at least one of these three stories. For example, when told 'Jane's kitty
is under the chair, but Jane is looking for it under the piano, why is she
doing that?', children answered 'She thinks it's under the piano' or 'She
doesn't know where it is'. Further, let's suppose that the child did not first
give a belief explanation but instead, a desire one such as, 'She wants to
find her kitty'. Then he or she was mildly prompted with 'What does Jane
think?' When that happened 74 per cent of three-year-olds, 91 per cent of
four-year-olds and 100 per cent of adults gave relevant, appropriate belief
explanations.

These data on children's explanations of action show, I think, that most
children by the age of three years construe human actions as the product
of mental states of belief and desire, and can reason about a person's beliefs
as well as desires. Let me reiterate the importance of the construct of belief
in this reasoning and hence in our everyday theory of mind. Desires motivate
behaviours, but beliefs frame them. Persons' actions can thwart their own
desires because beliefs are also at work. Remember Jane who wants her
kitty which is under the chair, but who looks for it under the piano. Why?
Because she *thinks* it's under the piano.

Two-Year-Olds' Simple Desire Psychology

If even three-year-olds possess a belief–desire psychology, maybe infants
do. Fodor for example has suggested that we are born with such a construal
of human behaviour (Fodor, 1987). However, I propose that three years is
just about the earliest age at which children understand belief and thus can
participate in belief–desire reasoning.

Let me begin by briefly comparing three broad classes of psychological
theory: *behaviourism*, *internal state theory* and *cognitive theory*. Behaviourism, as I mean it, attempts to explain action solely on the basis of functional
relations between observable states, specifically stimuli and responses.
Behaviourism eschews attributions about the 'insides' of the organism. In
contrast, internal state psychologies, such as classic drive theory, endow

organisms with internal states. Drive theory, for example, attributes to organisms internal drives such as hunger, whose waxing and waning propel behaviour. Cognitive theories are, in the broadest sense, internal state theories too. But they constitute a specific refinement of internal state theory, since they invoke certain very distinctive internal *representational* states that function to provide an internal mental world for the organism, such as in everyday terms, a person's beliefs.

What characterizes young children's thinking about people; do they conceive of people in behaviouristic, internal state, or cognitive terms? As reviewed thus far, by three years children are not behaviourists and are not merely internal state psychologists: they are cognitivists. Specifically, theirs is a mentalistic naive psychology, incorporating a rudimentary conception of belief. In contrast, I propose that most two-year-olds are internal state psychologists, although of a peculiar kind. Specifically, theirs is a simple desire psychology which includes no conception of belief.

Let me first elaborate on how a simple desire psychology might be possible – a psychology of action that considers only desires, and importantly considers desires only in a nonrepresentational sense. Figure 2.4 is an attempt graphically to capture this simple conception of desire and to contrast it with a conception of belief. Beliefs are representational; to attribute to someone the thought 'that is an apple' involves construing the other as representing an apple in their mind. Simple desires in the sense I am trying to carve them out here, however, require no attribution to the other of a representation. In this simple understanding, to say that 'he wants an apple' attributes to the other an internal state, for example a state of longing, but an internal state for an *external object*. Simple desires embody no notion of representing an apple in your head, simply *wanting* one. In short, I think it is possible to imagine a simple desire psychology – one resting essentially on a conception of internal states directed towards obtainment of objects in the world – and in this way quite different from a belief–desire psychology which rests centrally if not wholly on a conception of internal cognitive states representing truths about the world.

What sort of reasoning about actions might be encompassed by a simple desire psychology? Essentially, simple desires can cause actors (1) to engage in goal-directed actions, including persisting in certain actions if the goal is blocked, and (2) to have certain emotional reactions (getting what you desire yields happiness, not getting it produces frustration, unhappiness, etc.). Such a desire psychology thus provides some simple but cogent accounts and predictions of various acts. Thus, if a simple desire psychologist knows that 'Sam wants an apple', he can predict that Sam will look for an apple. And if he knows 'Sam wants a specific apple' and that 'the apple is in the kitchen', he can predict that Sam will look in the kitchen. He can predict

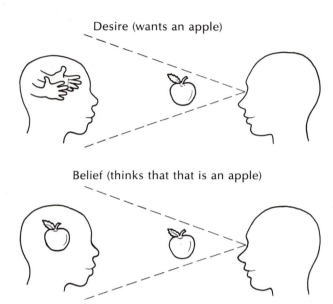

Figure 2.4   *Simple desires (top) and ordinary beliefs (bottom). Taken from Wellman and Woolley (1990).*

that 'Sam will look in the kitchen' under the general maxim that people act to fulfil their desires. A desire psychologist can also predict that if Sam finds the apple he will be happy, under the general maxim that getting what you want makes you happy.

A Study of Two-Year-Olds' Understanding of Desire Psychology

Can two-year-olds reason via a simple desire psychology? Jacqui Woolley and I (Wellman and Woolley, 1990) conducted a preliminary study to find out. As shown in the left-hand portion of figure 2.5, in our study children made judgements about the actions and emotional reactions of story characters in each of three types of situations. In the Finds-Wanted situation a doll character wants something that may be in one of two locations, the character searches in one location and gets the object. The Finds-Nothing situation was identical to Finds-Wanted except that upon searching in the first location nothing was there. The Finds-Substitute situation was identicial to Finds-Wanted except that upon searching in the first location the character found an attractive object, but not the one said to be wanted.

In making *action* judgements (at the top of figure 2.5) children had to predict the character's subsequent action, that is whether he or she would go on to search in the second location or would stop searching. An understanding of the implications of characters' desires should lead to a prediction

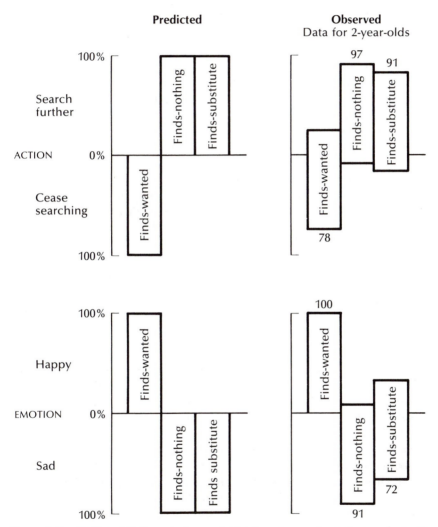

Figure 2.5   *Predicted (left) and observed (right) responses for action and emotion judgements from a study of two-year-olds' understanding of simple desires. Taken from Wellman and Woolley (1990).*

of continued search in the Finds-Nothing and Finds-Substitute situations but to cessation of search in the case of Finds-Wanted. In making *emotion* judgements (at the bottom of figure 2.5) children had to state the character's emotional reaction, whether he or she was happy or sad. An understanding of the role of desires in mediating emotional reactions should yield a prediction of happiness in the Finds-Wanted situation but sadness in the Finds-Nothing and in the Finds-Substitute situations.

So the left-hand portion of figure 2.5 shows the conditions in this study and the predicted patterns of results if children understand the role of desires in predicting actions and emotional reactions. The right-hand portion of that figure presents the data from 16 two-year-olds. As can be seen, two-year-olds appropriately predict continued searching for Finds-Nothing and Finds-Substitute story characters but not for Finds-Wanted. They appropriately predict happiness for Finds-Wanted but sadness for Finds-Nothing and Finds-Substitute stories.

I propose that very young children are simple desire psychologists rather than belief–desire psychologists. Certainly the ease with which young children solved these simple desire judgement tasks is suggestive. In contrast we and others have found that two-year-olds almost universally fail belief-reasoning tasks. It only remains, therefore, to show that the same two-year-olds succeed at desire-reasoning tasks on the one hand but also fail comparable belief–desire reasoning tasks on the other. We (Wellman and Woolley, 1990) have demonstrated this in an experimental study with tasks like those described in figure 2.5. Rather than describe that study, however, I present some similar data from young children's everyday speech.

Natural Language Evidence

If it is true that a simple desire psychology precedes a belief–desire psychology, then there should be a young age when children talk about desires cogently but never talk sensibly, or never at all, about beliefs.

In the study I preview here Karen Bartsch and I are examining children's first use of desire terms – such as *want* and *wish* – and belief terms – such as *think* and *know* – in their everyday speech, studied longitudinally from approximately two to five years. To do this we used the longitudinal English corpora of utterances from ten children in the CHILDES database (MacWhinney and Snow, 1985). This datbase includes, for example, the utterances of Adam, Eve and Sarah from Roger Brown's research programme, and similar data from seven other children. Almost 400,000 child utterances are included in the transcripts we searched. We searched these transcripts for children's use of the desire terms, *want, wish, hope, afraid, care* (about); and for the belief terms, *think, know, expect, wonder, believe, understand*. Other studies (Bretherton and Beeghly, 1982; Shatz, Wellman and Silber, 1983) have shown that these are the earliest appearing terms of the sort we sought. Approximately three per cent of children's utterances included one or the other of these terms, so the sample of utterances of interest to us includes more than 10,000 child utterances.

The question we wish to address is not when children begin to use these terms but when children begin to use them for psychological reference. By psychological reference we mean use of the terms explicitly to talk of their own or others' internal, subjective states as distinct from external, objective aspects of behaviour and events. More specifically, when do children start to use these terms to talk about desire and to talk about belief? Of course, it is possible to use the terms in other fashions, to use them conversationally, as we will call it (see also Shatz et al., 1983), without really referring to beliefs and desires. Children can and do say things like 'know what?' using *know*, but without really referring to knowing. Or 'I want the toy', simply to request a toy, meaning no more than 'give me that toy', and not really referring to desire. But it is also possible to identify instances where the terms are used to genuinely refer to beliefs and desires amidst children's conversational uses.

In this study we carefully coded children's utterances into three large categories: (1) instances of genuine psychological reference, (2) conversational uses, and (3) uninterpretable uses. Instances of psychological reference were further coded as to whether they referred to belief and/or desire, and then as to their specific sense, for example, think, know, want, wish. To make a long story short, I will focus only on children's use of the term *want* as a term for desire, and *think* and *know* as terms for belief. This is a reasonable simplification because *want* was the term earliest used to refer to desires, and *think* and *know* were the terms earliest used to refer to beliefs. Further, in this sample of very young children's speech, 97 per cent of all expressions of desire used the term *want*, and 94 per cent of all expressions of belief used *think* or *know*.

Box 2.2 shows some sample utterances that were coded as genuine expressions of desire and of belief. In most instances, such as those shown here, identifying genuine reference to belief and desire was not too difficult given the precise coding procedures we used and given examination of each child's extended discourse. Inter-coder reliabilities were very near 90 per cent.

What are the findings? Figure 2.6 shows the occurrence of genuine psychological uses of *want, think* and *know* summed across all children. Note that genuine reference to a character's desire via the term *want* begins quite early and is well established even before the second birthday. Reference

Box 2.2

Sample Utterances Expressing Desire

Dad:	What happened to your foot?
Child:	It hurt.
Dad:	Broken? Or cut?
Child:	*You want to see?*
Dad:	No, I'll see it later.
Child:	I want to show you.
Child:	Pants on. Jacket. Shopping
Mother:	We'll stay home and play.
Child:	*I want to shop . . . shopping.*
Child:	Santa Claus. Santa Claus is in town . . . street.
Mother:	It's not time yet.
Child:	*Wanna go see him.*
Child:	*Fraser (someone else) wants more coffee.*
Mother:	I'll put coffee on the fire, thank you.
Father:	What is it you're looking for?
Child:	*Want find top.* No top.
Child:	Here (offers object). That OK? *You want that?*

Sample Utterances Expressing Belief

Child:	*Which one you think could fit?* This one.
Mother:	I think that one's a little large. Oh. I guess it does fit.
Child:	You were wrong
Child:	Some people don't like hawks. *They think they have . . . they are slimy.*
Mother:	What do you think?
Child:	I think they are good animals
Mother:	Where is that thing?
Child:	*I think it disappeared. You think it disappeared?*
Mother:	Yeah, I think it disappeared.
Child:	*I didn't know you had this.* Where did you get it?
Child:	Can I put my head in the mail box . . . *So the mailman can know where I are.*

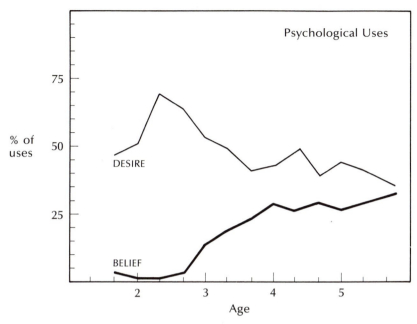

Figure 2.6   *Natural language occurrences of verbs of desire* (want) *and belief* (think and know) *used for psychological reference, as a percentage of all uses of these verbs.*

to belief via the terms *think* and *know* begins much later, just before the third birthday. More impressively, each individual child's data substantiate this general pattern. In every case (1) reference to desire precedes reference to belief, (2) reference to desire is already evident by two years, but (3) reference to belief is evident at just about three years.

In addition to these general codings, we were observant for more exacting and precise uses. For example, sometimes when children mention a belief or a desire they explicitly note that there is a difference between their own desire, say, and someone else's (or their own belief and someone else's). For example, 'Do you want me to look both ways? I don't wanna look both ways?' Or, as shown in box 2.2, 'They think they are slimy. I think they are good animals.' Such explicit self–other distinctions are rare in percentage terms but given our large data set were modestly frequent in absolute terms.

Figure 2.7 presents these data. Again, children refer to desires long before they refer to beliefs. That is, two-year-olds can clearly distinguish their own internal states from others' – they do so for desires. But only at about three years, again, do they explicitly distinguish their own beliefs from those of

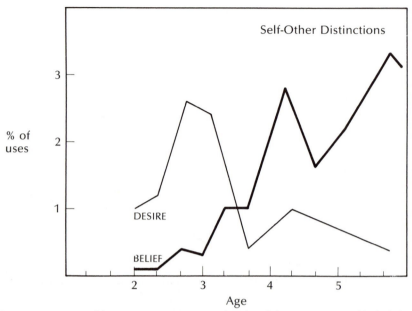

Figure 2.7 *Natural language occurrences of verbs of desire (*want*) and belief (*think and know*) used to distinguish the mental states of self and other, as a percentage of all uses of these verbs.*

others. This corroborates, with more exacting data, the general picture: Namely, evidence of a rich understanding of simple desires *before* a genuine understanding of belief that emerges at about three years.

Conclusions

My discussion thus far requires some qualifications and conclusions. First, I am not saying that three-year-olds' belief–desire psychology and concomitant theory of mind is identical to our everyday adult one. It is not. Still, it is recognizably familiar, it is a mentalistic belief–desire psychology. At least one further major transition is required after three years (see Wellman, 1990 chapter 9). I will not discuss that transition here because I have concentrated instead on the prior transition to a theory of mind in the first place. About that transition I have a simple story to tell, namely that acquisition of a theory of mind takes place in normal humans at just about three years of age. It is apparent in three-year-olds' mentalism; it is preceded by and built upon an earlier simple desire psychology. However, when I say that an understanding of belief and hence a belief–desire psychology and hence a concomitant theory of mind are acquired at age three I do not wish to be taken too literally. I do not believe that the conceptual developments I am charting are tied to chronological age at all, in any very precise way, I simply use these ages as convenient markers for talking about a sequence of early developments, namely the transition from an understanding of simple desires to an understanding of beliefs.

How does this transition take place? I do not know, but I can advance a plausible story of how it might work. In this analysis belief–desire psychology represents a theory change sponsored by and derived from simple desire psychology. Simple desire psychology provides the young child with significant explanatory resources, allowing the child to predict and understand a variety of actions and emotional reactions as stemming from the actor's internal desire states. However, a revision of desire psychology would be necessitated by predictive and explanatory failures of that reasoning scheme, failures which engender a construct of belief. For example, two characters with equal desires often engage in different actions. They do so because they have different beliefs. Same desires leading to different actions is a commonplace occurrence. It is easily accounted for in belief–desire psychology but is a theoretical anomaly for desire psychology. Similarly, actors often do things that *thwart* their own desires. Recall Jane searching for her kitty. That she should look for it under the piano when it is under the chair, is an anomaly for simple desire psychology, albeit easily accounted for by Jane's beliefs. Note, that thinking about actors in internal-state terms at all, that is with respect to their internal desires, makes it possible for the child to confront such theoretical anomalies in the first place. A behaviourist, for example, would not find these examples perplexing, he or she could easily account for them via histories of conditioning. It is desire psychology that generates *these* anomalies. Such anomalies once generated require addition of a very different sort of internal state construct to one's theoretical arsenal, specifically a conception of cognitive states of representation.

As this hypothetical scenario reveals, I believe that children's understanding of belief–desire psychology functions as a scientific theory functions in several important regards. Hence, I endorse the description of it as a theory of mind. One quality of scientific theories worth emphasizing is that they organize coherently a mass of potentially overwhelming, anomalous, even chaotic observations, experiences, data. Scientific theories do not appear out of thin air, because we have no facts, no observations, no first-hand data on which to rely. They appear just because we have so much data and observation to understand. Theories organize an otherwise immeasurable amount of data.

I wish to be clear about this characterization of theories because some people object to the phrase 'theory of mind' to describe three-year-olds' understanding (see chapter 1). Their objection seems to be that children's knowledge of beliefs and desire cannot be *theoretical* because children do not postulate beliefs and desires from the armchair, out of nothing, 'theoretically' as it were. Instead, so this objection goes, children *experience* their own beliefs, desires, emotions, perceptions (see Johnson, 1988; Harris, and also Butterworth, this volume). These are not theoretical entities for children, it is claimed, but first-hand experiences extended to make sense of others. I agree that children's database in this realm is large and immediate. Even infants accrue an extensive history of first-hand experience of their own cognition, motivations and internal states; they, further, amass innumerable experiences of interaction with and observation of others who, of course, display and express emotions, cognitions, and desires (see Wellman, 1990, chapter 8). However, the wealth of this experience does not mean that children's understanding is not theory-like. On the contrary, because there is so much experience and information available to children in so many punctate and co-mingled episodes and events, they must develop a coherent conceptual framework for organizing and distilling these experiences. This is the function of scientific theories, this is also the function of belief–desire psychology; this is the sort of theoretical understanding that children have achieved, substantially, by age three. Belief–desire psychology is a theory in this sense; it is an everyday theory forged from innumerable data, rather than constructed in absence of data.

Finally, how might my description of development of a theory of mind in humans shed light on the topics addressed by others in this volume? If I am right then the primitive condition for humans is neither behaviourism nor a theory of mind; it is instead a nonmentalistic but nonbehaviouristic, internal state theory. This might well prove true more generally. We may find that apes, for example, and autistic persons as another example, understand conspecifics as internal state organisms rather than cognitive ones. If so, we need to know this. We need to achieve a positive characterization of such subjects' understanding of others rather than simply asking if it is identical to our own and rather than simply showing that it is not a behaviourism. There is an important middle ground between these two extremes. For two-year-olds it is an impressive achievement to understand others in simple desire terms even if that does not constitute an understanding of mind. It would be a notable achievement for many other organisms as well.

3

Developing Understanding of Desire and Intention

Janet W. Astington and Alison Gopnik

There is some evidence that two- and three-year-olds and autistic children understand others' desires and intentions (Baron-Cohen, chapter 16; Premack and Dasser, chapter 17; Wellman, chapter 2), while other evidence points to the serious limitations in such children's understanding of others' beliefs. For example, three-year-olds and autistic children cannot make predictions based on false beliefs (Leslie, chapter 5; Perner, Leekam and Wimmer, 1987), and three-year-olds cannot recognize change in their own beliefs (Gopnik and Astington, 1988), understand the distinction between appearance and reality (Flavell, 1986), nor identify the sources of their beliefs (Gopnik and Graf, 1988). Children normally succeed on all these tasks by five years of age. A number of authors have suggested, in slightly different ways, that three-year-olds and autistic children fail because they do not appreciate the representational nature of beliefs and their causal relationship to the world (Flavell, 1988; Forguson and Gopnik, 1988; Gopnik, 1990; Leslie, 1988a; Perner, 1988a).

Beliefs, desires, and intentions are all intentional mental states (Whiten and Perner, chapter 1) and so we might expect that children would come to understand them at the same point in time. These states all involve relationships to representations of reality, not to reality itself. However, this relation is different for beliefs and for desires and intentions. The difference is in terms of the direction of fit and the direction of causation between the representation and reality (Searle, 1983). For beliefs, the mind has to fit the world, that is, beliefs are true if the representation matches reality. If the representation does not match reality the belief is changed, and thus events in the world cause our beliefs. On the other hand, for desires and intentions, the direction of fit is from the world to the mind, for example,

The research reported in this chapter was supported by NSERC, Canada.

desires are fulfilled if the world comes to match the representation, and it is our desires which cause changes in the world. Thus, beliefs, desires and intentions are alike in involving representational relations to reality, but they differ in the nature of that relation. Children might come to understand them at the same time, as they come to understand representational relations, or one type of state might be understood before the other, because of the difference in the character of the representational relations. Moreover, our adult conception of desire and intention is complex and different aspects might be understood at different times.

Understanding Desires

There are several components to the adult understanding of desire that might be more or less difficult for the child. First, children need to know that desire is a mental state, and not simply to identify desires with actions. They also need to understand the causal link between desire and action, and to know that different actions may stem from different desires. Wellman's work (chapter 2) suggests that even two-year-olds have this much of an understanding of desire. Moreover, this understanding of desire precedes the equivalent understanding that different actions may stem from different beliefs. Secondly, children need to know the relationship between desires and their satisfaction conditions. The satisfaction conditions for desires are outcomes, rather than actions. The work of Yuill (1984) and Hadwin and Perner (1989) suggests that three-year-olds can easily judge that other people are more satisfied when their desires are fulfilled than when they are not fulfilled. In this chapter we will show that children can also understand the distinction between satisfaction conditions and desires when they consider their own desires. Again this understanding of desires seems to precede an equivalent understanding of the relation between beliefs and their satisfaction conditions. Thirdly, children need to understand the representational character of desire, the fact that desires are intentional states and involve attitudes towards representations of things and not the things themselves. We will present two experiments that suggest children develop this kind of understanding of desire later than the first two kinds of understanding, although again there is some evidence that such understanding precedes an equivalent representational understanding of belief.

Distinguishing Desires and Outcomes

Previously we have shown that three-year-olds are not able to remember and report their earlier beliefs after they have discovered that the belief conflicts with reality (Gopnik and Astington, 1988). In a recent study (Astington, Gopnik and O'Neill, 1989) we investigated whether such children can remember and report their own desires, when the desire conflicts with the outcome of their action.

In the context of a game, children expressed a desire which was then fulfilled or unfulfilled, and they were asked to recall their original desire. We showed the child two toys, that looked very different but that could not be distinguished by feel alone. We hid the toys in a bag from which the child had to select one just by feeling them. At the beginning of the game we asked, 'Which one do you want to pick?', the child named one, and both toys were hidden in the bag. She was allowed to pick one from the bag, which had been made in such a way that we could control which toy the child picked out, although the children could not detect this. Then the experimenter took out the other toy and asked the child 'Did you get the one you wanted to pick?' Each child was given two trials so that the expressed desire was once fulfilled and once not, with the order of trials counterbalanced across children. Children's understanding of change in their beliefs was also assessed. The child was shown a closed crayon box and asked what she thought was inside it. Then she was shown that it actually contained birthday cake candles. After the candles were concealed in the box again, she was asked what she had thought was in the box when she first saw it.

Twenty-four three-year-olds and 24 four-year-olds were tested. When their desire was fulfilled, all the children said 'Yes', they got the toy they wanted to pick. Most children also remembered their unfulfilled desire. On this trial 0.79 of three-year-olds and 0.88 of four-year-olds said 'No', they didn't get the toy they wanted; both of these results are significantly above chance. On the other hand, only 0.54 of three-year-olds and 0.63 of four-year-olds said they originally thought there were crayons in the box, even though they had all said so at the beginning; these results are no different from chance.

The results of this study suggest that young children, who are unable to remember and report their earlier false beliefs, can remember their unfulfilled desires. This is relevant to Hadwin's and Perner's finding that children who could not predict the reaction to a false belief could predict reactions to unfulfilled desires. Thus it seems that three-year-old children have a better understanding of the relation between desires and their satisfaction conditions than of the relation between beliefs and their satisfaction conditions. Moreover, in the present task, while the children's actions did not conflict with their desires, they were compatible with either desire state; their behaviour in feeling in the bag could have been predicted by a desire for either of the two toys. Thus their ability to recall their previous desire also supports Wellman's claim that children do not confuse actions and desires.

Representational Nature of Desire

An important question is whether these tasks tap the child's understanding of the representational nature of desire. In these tasks, the satisfaction relation between desires and outcomes does not have to be conceptualized as a representational one, even though it is seen as a causal one. That is, in these tasks desires don't have to be seen to represent outcomes in the way that beliefs have to been seen to represent realities in the false belief and belief change tasks. Thus we might expect that a representational deficit, of the sort attributed to three-year-olds and to autistic children, might not affect performance on these sorts of desire task. Indeed, Perner (1988a) and Forguson and Gopnik (1988) argue that children with such a deficit ought to be able to understand desires. However, given the intentional nature of desire we might expect that a serious inability to understand representation should have some consequences for children's understanding of desires, that is, some aspects of desires should cause difficulty for the child. What might these be?

First of all, in many cases inferring people's desire depends on an ability to infer their beliefs (Bennett, chapter 7). If a person has false beliefs, for example, they are also likely to have inappropriate (and eventually unfulfilled) desires. In another task, developed from Campbell's (1988) suggestions, we have investigated whether children find it easier to answer questions about others' desires than about others' beliefs, in the special case where inferring another's desire depends on understanding his or her false belief (Astington and Lee, 1989). Children were shown some very small and some normal-sized Smartie (chocolate) boxes and asked which box they wanted to have. Most but not all children chose a larger box. The child was then shown that the small boxes were full and the larger ones contained only one candy. After the boxes were closed up again, the child was asked which box she had wanted when she first saw them, and which box another child, who hadn't seen inside the boxes, would want when he first saw them. Of 14 three-year-olds who originally chose a larger box, only 0.36 said when they first saw them they had wanted a larger box, and only 0.21

said that the other child would want a larger box when he first saw them.

On the basis of these results we might claim that understanding desire is sometimes as difficult as understanding belief. This experiment seems to capture the fact that beliefs and desires are both implicated in action, and that desires depend on beliefs (Bennett, chapter 7). Thus the child's lack of a representational model of belief affects her understanding of desires. However, these consequences are indirect ones. They do not stem from the representational character of desire itself, but from the dependence of desire on belief. The representational nature of desire is reflected in the fact that desirability itself is a psychological and indeed a representational fact rather than an objective fact about the world. As a consequence of this, desires may differ among different people or in the same person at different times quite independently of beliefs about the world. For example, if my tastes differ from yours we may agree in all particulars about some state of affairs and still disagree about whether that state of affairs is desirable and therefore whether we desire it. Similarly, our objective beliefs about something may not have changed since childhood but our estimate of its desirability may have changed substantially. The facts of 'desirability diversity' and 'desirability change', stem from the intrinsically representational character of desire, just as the diversity and change of beliefs stem from their intrinsically representational nature (Forguson and Gopnik, 1988). If children fail to understand this aspect of desire they should also fail to understand that people's notions of desirability, and hence their desires, may differ or change just as their beliefs may differ or change.

Wellman and Woolley (forthcoming) show that two-year-olds can predict people's actions when told about their desires, even if their desires are not the children's own immediate desires. This may suggest that children can appreciate the diversity of desires. However, understanding that desires may be different for different people isn't the same as understanding that what is desirable may be different for different people. Wellman and Woolley's task (Experiment 2, ibid.) differed from the classic false-belief task, which asssesses the understanding of the diversity of beliefs, because both alternatives that were presented were equally desirable to the children (similarly, the belief tasks in this experiment involved alternatives that were equally likely to be true). Children were asked to make a choice of which activity they would engage in, and then to predict the actions of another child, who wanted the alternative; however, the alternative choice was equally desirable. In the same way, in the toys-in-the-bag study described above, the two objects were on the face of it equally desirable and the child was invited to choose one rather than the other.

What would happen if we altered these tasks so that there was a difference in the desirability of the two objects, at least from the point of view of the child? In a recent study (Gopnik and Seager, 1988) we measured children's ability to infer the conflicting desires of another person using a version of a social role-taking task. Children were shown two books, a children's book and an adult book, and were asked which book they would choose, another child would choose, and one of the experimenters (a tall, bearded adult) would choose. A majority of three-year-olds said that the adult would choose the child's book, whereas four-and five-year-olds were far less likely to make this error. Children's performance on this task was very similar to their performance on a false-belief task; the proportion of correct responses to the adult desire question and the false-belief question, respectively, were 0.43 and 0.45 for three-year-olds, 0.64 and 0.72 for four-year-olds, and 0.89 and 0.89 for five-year-olds. This result suggests that, at least in this particular task, three-year-olds may indeed assume that other people's desires will be like their own desires just as they assume that the beliefs of others will be like their own beliefs. Or to put it a better way, they assume that desirability is an objective feature of the world and is not a function of representations, just as they seem to assume that 'believability' is an objective feature of the world.

However, perhaps they assume that believability is a more objective feature than desirability is. Flavell, Flavell, Green and Moses (1989) recently tested children's understanding of differences in what they called value beliefs, such as the belief that a biscuit is yummy or yucky. Unlike the Gopnik and Seager study, Flavell et al. found that understanding the diversity of value beliefs was significantly easier than understanding the diversity of fact beliefs, the sort of belief typically used in false-belief tasks. Nevertheless, the three-year-olds still had some difficulty; when the child's estimate of the desirability of an object differed from an adult's only 0.59 to 0.69 of the children passed these tasks. This is far from ceiling and is substantially worse than the performance of the two-year-olds on Wellman's and Woolley's tasks.

Do we find a similar understanding of desirability by three-year-olds in the realm of representational change? We have already shown that young children are capable of remembering their unfulfilled desires. But in these cases their representation of desirability is unchanged. The toy is still desirable even if it is not actually obtained. Could these children appreciate the fact that desirability itself is subject to change? One way to change your notion of desirability is to satiate your desires. As Mae West (we think) once said, the best way to get rid of a temptation is to give in to it. Do children recognize that their desires, or to be more exact their representation of desirability, may change as a result of satiation?

In a recent study (Gopnik and Slaughter, forthcoming) we have constructed a task similar to the Gopnik and Seager task to measure this.

Children were presented with two books and asked which one they wanted to read. When they picked one book the experimenter read it to them and then presented them with the original pair of books. Children were again asked 'Which one do you want to read?' All the children changed their desire and picked the alternative book on this trial. Children were then asked 'When I first showed you the books, before we read, which one did you want to read then?' Children also received the representational change-belief task. Eighteen three-year-olds and 18 four-year-olds were tested; 0.67 of the three-year-olds and 0.83 of the four-year-olds correctly reported which book they had wanted originally, whereas 0.39 of the three-year-olds and 0.78 of the four-year-olds passed the belief task. These results are very similar to those of Flavell et al. and suggest that three-year-olds are better at understanding the representational nature of desire than of belief, just as Wellman's and Woolley's results show that the earliest understanding of desire precedes the earliest understanding of belief. Nevertheless, three-year-olds appear to have more difficulty understanding differences in desirability than they have in understanding the relation between desires and actions or outcomes, and this understanding improves between three and four years.

Understanding Intention

In one sense intention is like desire. Like desires, intentions have a world-to-mind direction of fit; that is, they are neither true nor false but are fulfilled or unfulfilled by outcomes in the world. And like desires, intentions have a mind-to-world direction of causation, that is, they bring about changes in the world. Intentions differ from desires, however, because their outcomes are not just things that happen, but they are actions of an agent whose intention it is to produce the outcome; indeed, Shultz (chapter 6) suggests that young children's concept of intention develops out of their concept of agency. Thus, intentions differ from desires in their role in the causal chain between the mind and the world. Intentions are actually mediators between desires and actions. So when I desire something I form an intention to obtain it, which causes me to act in a way that will fulfil the desire. The conditions of satisfaction of the intention must be achieved as a result of the intention and the actions it causes, and not in any other way. If I want someone to be dead, my desire will be satisfied no matter how he dies. If I intend to kill someone, my intention will not be carried out unless I act on that intention and murder him; my intention will not be carried out if I accidentally run over him, or if he dies of a heart attack. That is to say, the propositional content of an intention is not *it happens*, nor even *I do it*, but *I do it in order to carry out this intention*. It is this feature of intention that Searle (1983) calls *causal self-referentiality* and it is this that distinguishes intention from desire.

It is true that three-year-olds understand something about intention. They can distinguish between intentional and unintentional action, for example, as Shultz has shown in a number of studies (e.g. Shultz, 1980). Shultz got children to perform actions where they were sometimes tricked into making mistakes, and showed that 3-year-olds could distinguish between intentional and unintentional action both for themselves and for another child that they observed. However, this distinction can be made by matching goals and outcomes and we have argued that this is the strategy young children use (Astington, forthcoming a). If the goal and the situation in the world match, three-year-olds can judge that an action was performed intentionally or that the outcome will bring pleasure; on the other hand, if the goal and the situation in the world don't match, three-year-olds judge that the behaviour was unintentional or that the outcome won't bring pleasure. These judgements of match and mismatch between goal and outcome can be made in the same way for both desire and intention; they do not require a sophisticated understanding of intentional causation. It may be that such young children's concept of intention is not distinguished from their concept of desire. Both are conceptualized as mental representations of goals; but intentions are not seen as the causal link between the desire and the goal, as the means to the end.

Recently we have shown that three-year-olds are less likely than five-year-olds to see intentions as means to ends, and to focus on the future directedness of intention (Astington, forthcoming a). In that study children were shown pairs of pictures, where one picture of the pair showed a child doing something, and the other showed another child who appeared to be getting ready to do the same thing; for example, there was a picture of a boy sliding down a playground slide and a picture of another boy climbing up the steps of the slide. For each pair of pictures children were asked one question either about the action (e.g., 'Which boy's sliding down?') or about the preparation for the action (e.g., 'Which boy's going to slide down?'). This latter question used different terms to express the intention: *going to* (or *gonna*), *thinks (s)he will*, *wants to* and *would like to*. Children were asked about eight different pairs of pictures. All the children correctly chose pictures of the child who was acting in answer to questions about actions, but three-year-olds also chose this picture in answer to questions about intentions, whereas 5-year-olds usually chose the other picture. Our argument is not that it is incorrect to choose the picture of the child acting in answer to the intention question, but that the five-year-olds were more likely to interpret these questions as referring to future, not to present, actions. They distinguished between the means and the end, between the intention and the goal. Moreover, it is not that three-year-olds always choose pictures of the action, whatever question they are asked. If three-year-olds are asked 'Which boy's not sliding down?' they correctly point to the boy who is climbing up the steps, but if they are asked 'Which boy's gonna slide down?' they point to the boy who is sliding down.

What the three-year-old lacks, we would claim, is an understanding of the causal nature of intention. An intention is a mental representation caused by a desire for a goal which itself causes action to bring about that goal. It is not clear that three-year-olds, who can distinguish between intentional and unintentional action, have such a sophisticated concept of intention. Our suggestion is that at four or five years of age children begin to differentiate intention from desire. We act to achieve our goals, or we don't act and we don't achieve our goals. However, sometimes we do perform the intended action but fail to achieve the desired goal, or sometimes we may not act and the desired goal comes about anyway, what we would call luck, or fortuitous success. Such is the case in a deviant causal chain, often described by philosophers (e.g., Searle, 1983, p. 82). These chains are described as 'deviant' because although the event represented in the propositional content of the intention occurs, the intention is not carried out. One question is: at what age would children understand a case of a deviant causal chain? That is, when could children distinguish between intending to do something, and wanting to get something? There is some evidence that five-year-olds can appreciate this distinction (Shultz and Shamash, 1981) but younger children have not been tested.

Conclusion

The data we have discussed suggest both differences and similarities in the development of the understanding of belief, desire and intention. Initially, children appear to have a mentalistic but non-representational theory of mind. According to this theory there are mental entities and there are physical ones and these two are distinct, although related. They are, however, related in a direct non-representational, non-intentional way; beliefs, for example, are formed directly by exposure to the relevant entities in the world. Similarly, three-year-olds see the relation between mental entities and actions as equally direct, and so they fail to recognize how intentions mediate between beliefs and desires and actions. Five-year-olds, on the other hand, have a representational model of mind (Forguson and Gopnik, 1988;

Perner, 1988a). They understand the process of representation. They conceptualize the process by which perception causes belief, and they see mental entities, both beliefs and desires, as representations of reality. They also understand the complexity of the process by which desires lead to intentions which cause actions. We might represent these two situations graphically as shown in figure 3.1.

When we consider the three-year-old's theory, proposed here, it is hard for us, as adults, to imagine what a non-representational account of belief would be like; we don't have the appropriate terminology. An analogy might be that the child's intial theory of belief and desire is like the Gibsonian theories of 'direct perception'. Gibsonians believe that the mind directly resonates to features of the world, it doesn't represent them. Very young children seem similarly to believe that if you are exposed to real events in the world or to desirable events in the world you will automatically formulate the appropriate beliefs and desires about them. It is possible, in fact, that the child's early model of belief is based on an early understanding of visual perception (Butterworth, chapter 15; Flavell, 1978). We may ask why three-year-olds need to posit mental entities at all if they think there is a direct relation between such entities and the world. These entities may serve a

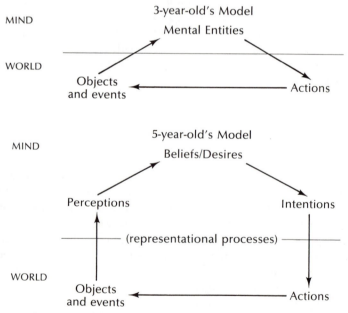

Figure 3.1 Three-year-olds' and five-year-olds' models of the relation between the mind and the world.

sort of channelling function for the young child. Because we are unable to act on all the complex events in the world, a non-mentalistic account of the relation between objects and actions would leave actions seriously underdetermined. It would be difficult to predict action, given the infinite number of possibilities.

Do three-year-olds have a concept of 'representation'? There is considerable debate about this in the literature. We have argued that three-year-olds have a mentalistic but non-representational understanding of belief. In a similar vein, Perner (1988a) proposes that three-year-olds have only the idea of an association between people and states of affairs. Wellman (chapter 2; 1990), on the other hand, argues that three-year-olds do have a representational conception of belief, although it is not an interpretivist one. Our disagreement may arise from the fact that 'representation' may be used in two ways, to refer to a process or to an entity. Beliefs, desires and intentions represent reality in the mind; this is the *process* of representation. But beliefs, desires and intentions are representations; they are mental entities, or mental *products*. We propose that initially children may understand that people have representations, mental products, without understanding that they represent or how they represent; that is, without understanding the representational process. Perhaps, in fact, we should say that young children have a concept of thoughts and wants, rather than beliefs and desires, since in the early theory these mental entities are not conceptualized as representational or intentional states at all.

What, then, of our original question: Are belief, desire and intention all first understood at the same point in development or not? We have said that non-representational aspects of both belief and desire are understood before representational ones. Cross-cutting this distinction, however, is a distinction between desires and beliefs themselves. In both cases, the non-representational 'Gibsonian' theory and the later representational one, the evidence suggests that children may understand desire problems before they understand problems of belief. Thus, the evidence from Wellman's studies suggests that the very young child's non-representational theory of desire may be formulated earlier than a similar theory of belief. That is, two-year-olds may understand the way that desires constrain actions before they understand the way that beliefs do (Wellman, chapter 2). Comparably, Hadwin's and Perner's data and the toys-in-the-bag study presented here suggest that children can differentiate between desires and their satisfaction conditions before they can differentiate between beliefs and their satisfaction conditions. However, the evidence of the other studies we have presented suggests that understanding other aspects of desire and intention only develops later. In particular, a representational model of desire in which desirability is subject to change and diversity is not developed until after children develop a non-representational understanding of desire, and until after they understand the satisfaction conditions of desires. However, there is some evidence that a representational understanding of desire precedes the equivalent understanding of the representational character of belief. Similarly, while young children understand how desire leads directly to actions and outcomes and can distinguish intentional and unintentional actions on that basis, an understanding of intention as a mediating factor between desire and action may develop only between four and five years.

A further important point from the studies we have presented is that we have shown that childen have equal difficulty, or equal ease, in understanding their own past mental states and in understanding the mental states of others. This is important in deciding between theoretical accounts of the development of the concept of mind. Both 'introspectionist' (Johnson, 1988) and 'simulation' accounts (Harris, chapter 19), that see children coming to understand the mind by constructing analogies between their own states and those of others, should predict that understanding your own mind would precede understanding the minds of others. So too should 'processing deficit' accounts (Leslie, 1988a; Wimmer, Hogrefe and Sodian, 1988) that see the child's difficulties with belief as a result of inferential problems. Knowing about your own mental states should require neither simulation, nor analogy, nor inference. However, 'theory formation' accounts (Forguson and Gopnik, 1988; Perner, 1988a; Wellman, chapter 2), that see children constructing an account of their own states and others' states simultaneously, predict that understanding your own mind and the minds of others is equally difficult (see Astington and Gopnik, 1988; Wimmer and Hartl, 1989, for further discussion of this point).

A final point relates our results to the interests of other developmentalists and primatologists represented in this volume. It has frequently been observed that primates understand the motivational states of their conspecifics, even if they don't understand their states of knowledge (e.g. Jolly, 1988). In addition, Baron-Cohen (chapter 16) has shown that autistic children understand protoimperatives, that denote desires, but not protodeclaratives, that denote beliefs. There is thus converging evidence that understanding desire is easier than understanding belief. This would make sense if our and other animals' primary motivation is to understand differences in action, since desire is more closely tied to action than belief is.

4

Understanding Others: Evidence From Naturalistic Studies of Children

JUDY DUNN

The world in which children grow up is a *social* world. From early infancy, children have diverse and complex relationships with the other members of that world, on whom they depend for love, attention, comfort and amusement, as well as for the satisfaction of their bodily needs. Understanding that those others have feelings, intentions and minds like their own, only different, is a crucial feature of becoming human, central to children's social relationships and thus to the capacities that develop through those relationships: the acquisition of language, powers of logical thought, sense of self and of emotional security. The nature of a child's understanding of why people behave the way that they do, and of what they think, feel and intend is crucial to those relationships. As children's ability to mindread changes with development, so too will the nature of their relationships change–and vice versa.

The understanding of others' intentions and psychological states is then closely tied to children's social and emotional relationships. Yet paradoxically the study of the development of children's understanding of other minds has been conducted primarily in settings divorced from children's familiar relationships, or their 'real life' social behavior. Our attempts to delineate what children understand about other people and how that changes have been conducted by studying their grasp of what puppets, toys or story-book characters might do in hypothetical situations. Imaginative experimental approaches, such as the manipulation of the false beliefs held by such characters, have illuminated the nature of both the limitations and the capabilities of young children (e.g. Wellman, chapter 2). With such exper-

The research described in this chapter was supported by the Medical Research Council and the US National Institute of Child Health and Human Development (HD–23158–03).

imental approaches the rigour and systematicity of causal inference that can
be made is clearly potentially greater than what is possible with naturalistic
observations of children in their daily lives. But there are two important
reasons why we should include naturalistic observations of children in our
attempts to describe their abilities to mindread.

First, the gap between children's understanding of what the puppet or
story-book character might know or think, and their understanding of the
minds of the real people in their own worlds could be large. We could be
misrepresenting the abilities of children by an exclusive focus on their replies
to questions that require reflection on the thoughts and feelings of puppets
in task situations, or of characters in stories. The reliance on questioning
in itself presents problems. It is evident from research in a range of different
domains that children's practical knowledge is established well before they
are able to answer reflective questions on the topic (see for instance the
work on children's conceptions of friendship contrasted with their actual
relationships with their friends (Rizzo, 1989), on their understanding of
social rules (Dunn, 1988), or on Piagetian concepts (Gelman and Baillargeon, 1983). Furthermore, it is notoriously difficult to conduct such experiments with children in the first two to three years of life. Yet the foundations
of their mindreading abilities are being laid in those years (see chapters 2,
10, 15, 16).

Secondly, it is from naturalistic observations that we are likely to gain
insight on the contexts in which these capabilities develop, and on the salient
influences that affect their development. Such insight is sorely needed
(chapter 1). Without it we are left with an account of the development of
children's and animals' mindreading abilities that is couched solely in terms
of cognitive elaboration..

To make inferences about children's mindreading abilities from naturalistic observations is however clearly hazardous (as it is, also, hazardous to
make such inferences from experiments, see below). It would of course be
foolhardy to focus on tallies of the words that children use without regard
to their functional use, or on isolated incidents of behaviour, or on pretend
play alone to draw conclusions about children's mindreading abilities. Our
strategy has been to examine a broad range of aspects of children's behaviour
and conversation, with different social partners and in different emotional
settings: their disputes and arguments, their empathetic and cooperative
behaviour, their discussion of other people, their fantasy play and jokes,
their response to the interactions between others. The evidence from these
different aspects of children's behaviour, drawn chiefly from three longitudinal studies of children at home with their mothers and siblings, has been
brought together and discussed in a recent book entitled *The Beginnings of
Social Understanding* (Dunn, 1988). This chapter will focus on the impli-

cations of that evidence, and of further data drawn from an ongoing study in the US, for two important issues relevant to the themes of this book. The first issue is the nature of very young children's understanding of psychological states in others, and the second is the issue of what contexts and processes are involved in the development of that understanding.

The Nature of Very Young Children's Understanding of Psychological States in Others

Among the aspects of children's behaviour and conversation at home in their families which reveal their growing grasp of others' psychological states, four categories stand out particularly clearly:

1 Attempts to Alter Others' Psychological States

In the first category are children's actions that relate to their attempts to alter others' psychological states. Thus in **teasing**, children attempt to annoy, disturb, upset or amuse others. As Reddy points out (chapter 10), such actions are observed very early, from the first year onwards; our Cambridge studies showed that in the course of the second year they became both far more frequent and more elaborate (Dunn, 1988). The interest of such actions lies in the understanding that they reflect of what will upset, annoy or amuse a particular person, and our observations showed that teasing the sibling and teasing the mother had developed into highly precise and differentiated strategies by 24 months. In **comforting**, children attempt to alleviate the distress of others; again such actions are observed early in the second year (Radke-Yarrow, Zahn-Waxler and Chapman, 1983), and become increasingly elaborate in the course of the next two years. **Concern** (and sometimes amusement) at others' being frightened or worried was also evident in children's behaviour during the second year, and became increasingly explicit in their talk as they became more articulate, as in the persistent questioning of his mother by the 28 month-old boy in the example from our Cambridge studies that follows. He had overheard his mother telling the observer about a dead mouse that frightens her:

Example 1   Child 28 months

C: What's that frighten you, Mum?
M: Nothing.
C: What's that frighten you?
M: Nothing.
C: What is it? . . . What's that down there, Mummy? That frighten you.
M: Nothing.
C: That not frighten you?
M: No. Didn't frighten me.

Similarly children's **helping** actions reveal their recognition of others' goals, needs and their frustration at failing to reach those goals. Such helping acts were observed early in the second year; older siblings were, for instance, often helped during their play, with unsolicited acts by the children. **Jokes** provide a further example of children's growing ability to mindread (see chapter 11). To share a joke with someone indicates some expectation that the other will be amused by what the child finds funny. In studying the jokes made during the course of the second and third year we examined those made to mothers and those to siblings, and found considerable differentiation in these. Children made jokes on certain topics to their mothers, and on different topics to their siblings. Scatalogical jokes, and jokes about disgust, for example, were directed to siblings, predominantly, while jokes about *not loving*, *naming* jokes, or *true–false* assertions were usually made to mothers (Dunn, 1988; McGhee, 1989).

It should be noted that many of such actions (but not all) are most obviously related to psychological states that either (1) can be defined in behavioural terms or (2) fail the opacity test, and are thus not 'intentional states' (Whiten and Perner, chapter 1). However Whiten's argument for including them in a consideration of mindreading seems entirely appropriate. As he put it at the Mindreading symposium, 'everyday folk psychology would at least in some circumstances class them as states of mind (and therefore fair game for mindreading)'. The children's actions that fall into the next three categories that we will consider, however, provide evidence for children's understanding of not only these classes of psychological states but also the class of 'intentional states'.

2   Verbal Discussion of Psychological States

The second category to be considered is that of explicit verbal discussion of others' psychological states. As children become more verbally articulate during the third year they begin to talk not only about the feeling states of others (as in the example above; see also Bretherton, McNew and Beeghly-Smith, 1981; Dunn, Bretherton and Munn, 1987; Ridgeway, Waters, and Kuczaj, 1985), reflected in observable behaviour, but to discuss others' 'intentional states': their *knowing, remembering, meaning to, forgetting,* and so on (Shatz, Wellman and Silber, 1983; Wellman, 1990). A clear pattern of developmental change over the third year is seen in the increase in children's active curiosity about others' internal states, and the causes of their behaviour and of these 'intentional states'. There is a steady increase, for instance, in questions about others' internal states, and in narratives that focus on such states (Dunn, 1988; and see chapter 20). Those of us who observe children of this age are often closely questioned by them about what it is that *we* know or don't know, remember or have forgotten from our previous visits. These are matters of much interest to children even before they are 36-months-old. Such discussions, in contrast to the actions in category 1 above, often are focused on situations in the past or future; that is they are not focused on the children's own immediate needs.

3   Excuses, Deceit and Evasion

The third category of evidence, in contrast, comes from situations in which the children's own interests are very directly threatened: their excuses and attempts to evade anticipated disapproval or punishment, or their attempts to gain wanted but forbidden goods. What is of interest here is not only the evidence that they anticipate the intentions of their parents or siblings, but the evidence for deceitful actions, and the children's explicit references to intentions (their own and those of others) in their attempts to negotiate their escape from anticipated or present trouble. Such excuses or justifications (described fully in Dunn, 1988) were observed during the second year and increasingly during the third, and they are particularly revealing of children's understanding of psychological states. Among the variety of strategies used we found for instance denial of future possible psychological states, reference to what other people would like, or would be upset by, and reference to transgressions made *in pretend*, as an excuse. Particularly notable is how early, in such contexts, the children used deceit, talked about intentions, or attempted to avoid trouble by reference to other peoples' psychological states. In the next example, a girl of only 21 months appears to attempt to deliberately mislead her mother in order to get her way, by indicating that she needs cleaning (she is in fact quite clean).

Example 2   Child 21 months
Child and mother in bathroom. Child points to soap with request vocalization. The mother refuses to give it to her.

M: Have a bath later, shall we?
C: Ba.
M: You put it in the bath, ready then?
C: (does so)
M: There you are. Now it's ready for you later when you have a
       bath. Come on.
C: Ba. (points to soap)
M: No, we're not taking it. I said you can get in the bath later.
C: (lies down on floor in position for nappy change and gestures
       to nappy).
M: No, I'm not taking it off.
C: Cack (word for dirty nappy).
M: No, you haven't.
C: Cack.
M: No you haven't.

And in the example that follows, a boy of 26 months refers to *lack of
intention* as an excuse for his action that hurts his mother.

Example 3   Child 26 months
Child climbs on M. to investigate the light switch.

M: You're hurting me!
C: Sorry. Sorry, Sorry. I don't mean to.

Reference to transgressions being made in pretend – used to evade anticipated disapproval during the third year – brings us to the fourth category
of evidence for children's growing understanding of other minds, that of
their ability to pretend.

4   Pretend

The significance of children's engagement in pretence for our picture of
their understanding of other minds is discussed extensively in other chapters
in this volume (see chapters 5, 18, 19). Here I want simply to note three

points that are highlighted by naturalistic observations of children's social pretend with other family members.

The first is that observations of joint pretend within the family show that children are, surprisingly early, able to share a pretend, non-literal framework with another. Most often, the early sessions of joint pretend that we observed were set up by the older sibling, but as early as 18 months, in the context of an affectionate supportive sibling relationship, children were able to participate and contribute to the shared world of make-believe. They were able not only to share the non-literal world, but to enact the part of another person or thing with the incorporation of another person into a reciprocal role (see Dunn and Dale, 1984; Miller and Garvey, 1984). The ability of two-year-olds to take on an identity other than their own, and to coordinate the actions of this pretend person with those of another pretend person, played by the sibling, is strikingly in advance of the abilities attributed to them on the basis of studies of pretend conducted outside the family setting (Fein, 1981; Rubin, Fein and Vandenberg, 1983).

The second point is that in the course of such pretend play there is often discussion of the inner state of the pretend character. Usually the psychological states discussed are feeling states, rather than mental states (indeed pretend is a key context for the early reference to feeling states (Dale, 1983; Brown, 1989)), however during the third year children were observed to play at their pretend characters remembering, forgetting as well as being angry, fearful, sad and excited; they understood that the pretend characters enacted by their siblings also forgot, remembered, were sad, and so on. The adeptness with which they played with such inner states demonstrates both their understanding of such states *in another person*, and their interest in such states.

The third point which the observations highlight is the close connection between such capacities for pretend, and the teasing – both friendly and hostile – that forms such a distinctive theme in young children's relationships (see also Reddy, chapter 10). Such evidence can only be obtained through naturalistic observations; it cannot be 'set up' or tested for. With older children especially, fantasy play is particularly sensitive to the intrusion of others, as Gottman and Parker showed in their study of the relationship between friends (Gottman & Parker, 1986). It is also highly sensitive to the particular emotional relationship between the two partners. Two separate studies have found that the establishment of shared pretend between siblings was closely related to the quality of affection in their relationship assessed on other criteria (Dale, 1983; Dunn and Dale, 1984). It is far more frequent in sibling pairs who are affectionate and friendly with one another. What this indicates is that while very young children may well enjoy and engage in pretend play in a test situation in which they are provided with suitable materials, their participation in elaborate shared pretend with enactment of roles and psychological states may well only be seen in situations of intimacy and affection between familiar play partners.

Developmental Processes

Observations of children in their familiar worlds provide us, then, with a notably rich set of evidence on the nature of their understanding of others' psychological states. But such observations do much more. With observational data we can begin to ask questions about the context of development for these capacities, and about the forces that influence their growth. Two developmental lessons stand out from considering these questions in the light of the observational data (Dunn, 1988). The first is that our attention is drawn to the significance of the emotional context in which children first begin to demonstrate 'mindreading'. The settings in which children's understanding of others' psychological states is first and most frequently evident are rarely emotionally neutral. Rather, they are either settings in which the child's self-interest is threatened and the child is intensely involved, situations in which the child is absorbedly involved in joint pretend with an affectionate partner, or situations in which the child is intensely amused in a social exchange, or (much more rarely) intensely concerned about another's state. Of these settings, it is the first in which children's understanding of others' psychological states is much the most frequently observed during the second and third year. Thus for example, causal discussion of others' psychological states is found to be much more common in the context of children's attempts to manipulate others in their own interest (Dunn and Brown, 1988, 1989). The prominence of such settings as the context for the demonstration of very young children's grasp of the psychological states of others led to an argument that situations of conflict and threatened self-interest are encounters in which children's growing understanding of the social world is not only revealed but fostered. A similar argument has been made by Dennie Wolf in her consideration of the development of children's understanding of agency during the second year (Wolf, 1982). *At least at the earliest stages*, understanding psychological states is most evident in such settings. There is a striking parallel for this conclusion in the evidence that cognitive evolution in primates (both nonhuman and human) has been driven by the adaptive importance of powers of social manipulation, including mindreading (e.g. chapter 1; Humphrey, 1976; Byrne and Whiten, 1988; Whiten and Byrne, 1989).

To stress the potential of such affectively loaded interactions for learning is not to argue that understanding others is fostered solely in contexts of heightened emotion. It is clear that by four-years-old children's passages of intellectual search into the social world often take place in conversations with their mothers when the children are calm and reflective (Tizard and Hughes, 1984). The point is rather that it is not only in such reflective and calm settings that children will learn, but that there may be special potential in the emotionally urgent situations that occur within the daily dramas of family interaction. These are the situations that psychologists have – inevitably – rarely studied; their accounts of cognitive development reflect the contexts in which they have chosen to study children. Links between social and emotional development and cognitive change are usually viewed in terms of the cognitive changes that underlie emotional development – however it is important to note first, that the emotional context of an experience profoundly affects the way it is remembered and that it bears on current functioning (Arsenio and Ford, 1985; Bower, 1981; Maccoby and Martin, 1983), and secondly, the strength of the arguments put forward, for instance by Butterworth (chapter 15) that socioemotional capacities are not so much derivative of reflection but may contribute to that reflection.

The second developmental issue that the observational evidence brings to the fore is the significance of family discourse in the development of children's understanding of others' psychological states. Children grow up in a world in which the behaviour, beliefs, knowledge, wants and feelings (though, interestingly, less commonly the thoughts) of others are frequently discussed, and from surprisingly early they are participants in this discourse. So, well before psychologists might grant them a 'theory' of mind, they not only have access to the perceptual information concerning peoples' intentions and desires to which Butterworth (chapter 15) so aptly draws our attention, but are exposed to continual discussion of why people behave the way they do, what they are feeling and why, what they remember, forget, and what their intentions are. This – obviously – is a point at which the developmental account of mindreading in children diverges sharply from that of higher primates. The connection between discourse and understanding is not merely a matter of speculation. In the case of the development of children's understanding of feeling states we have evidence that differences in children's exposure to and participation in discourse about feeling states is systematically related to their later ability to understand others' feelings (Dunn & Brown, 1989).

Conclusion

In conclusion, naturalistic observations of children in their family world provide ample evidence for children's growing ability to mindread during the second and third years. How does this evidence add to, or differ from, what is learnt through other research strategies such as experimental approaches? Two lessons stand out.

First, the observational data indicate how early actions in relation to others' psychological states appear – the evidence from the documentation of teasing, joking and social manipulation (Dunn, 1988). Naturalistic observations are the *only* source of this information: contrived situations cannot be designed to demonstrate the child's skills as a teaser, joker or as a deceitful evader. The discrepancies between the capabilities that young children display during real-life family dramas, and their abilities (or lack of them) when making judgements about hypothetical or story-book characters – at least in much of the 'classical' research – should be noted. Piaget wrote for instance that there was 'some reason to doubt whether a child of 6–7 could really distinguish an involuntary error from an intentional lie. . . . the distinction is, at the best, in the process of formation' (1965, p. 145). The discrepancies indicate that children's abilities may be seriously misrepresented if their practical knowledge and actions within the real world are not taken into consideration. Observations of early social pretend play provide powerful evidence, again, for early-developing understanding; such pretend play is extremely vulnerable to the presence or interference of outsiders – not only experimenters but mothers! (Gottman and Parker, 1986).

Secondly, naturalistic observations enable us to examine the context in which children begin to express understanding of others' psychological states. They provide evidence for the significance of the emotional context of children's interactions, for threatened self-interest as a forum for revealing and possibly fostering children's capabilities, for the significance of mind-reading abilities for children's relationships – that is, for the functional importance of this understanding. Such evidence makes it impossible to disregard the *mutual* significance of social and cognitive change.

Finally, the obvious limitations of observational data should be considered: First, the problems of making inferences about children's understanding from naturalistic observations of their behaviour, and second, the difficulty of ensuring that behaviour that properly represents their abilities has been sampled. Both are real – and substantial – problems. Clearly, the best experimental studies increase the chances of the researcher exposing children's capabilities, and of delineating precisely what their limitations might be. But the degree of difficulty of interpreting children's behaviour in what is inevitably a rather curious situation for the child in most experiments remains notably high. This point is brought home to us in a current study in which we are employing both naturalistic observations and 'false-belief' tasks for children who are just three-years-old. In some cases the same child who during the observations demonstrated relatively mature understanding of what another family member knows, performed poorly in the task setting – a performance perhaps attributable to puzzlement about what the questioner wanted as a response, perhaps to fear of performing inadequately. The point to be emphasized is not that such discrepancies will necessarily often be found, but rather that the difficulties of interpreting children's apparent incapabilities in such test situations are commensurate with those of interpreting their behaviour in naturalistic observations. The great power of naturalistic observation is that we can see what the *child* herself is interested in or curious about, and can examine her abilities in situations that are of emotional significance, interest or importance to her. What stands out from such observations is the great interest that children show in other peoples' behaviour; their practical knowledge of and curiosity about other minds, that is flourishing during the third year of life, forms one central strand in this concern with the social world.

5

The Theory of Mind Impairment in Autism: Evidence for a Modular Mechanism of Development?

ALAN M. LESLIE

Here is the general idea I have been pursuing: The normal (human) development of a theory of mind – one that includes understanding propositional attitudes – specifically requires the functioning of certain specialized innate mechanisms of central thought. I say 'specifically' because doubtless other cognitive powers play a role, particularly in performance on 'tasks', and probably there are some specialized mechanisms of perception too (see Premack and Dasser, chapter 17; and Leslie and Happé, 1989 for suggestions on this). I stress 'understanding propositional attitudes' (e.g. believing that p, desiring that p, pretending that p) because that seems to be to be one of the key notions in our common sense theory of mind (see chapter 1). The problem is to understand the nature of such a fundamental concept and, more deeply, how it can be developed uniformly and robustly in young children given exposure to an arbitrary social environment. Along with Fodor (1987), I have been arguing for a rich and specific innate endowment.

The task is to develop specific proposals about the nature of those innate mechanisms and their systems of representation that make concepts of contentful mental states available and allow the elaboration of a theory of mind (ToM). The focus of my efforts has been on the early emerging capacity for pretence and 'metarepresentation' (Leslie, 1987a, 1987b, 1988a, 1988b; Leslie and Happé, 1989; Leslie and Frith, 1990).

What is particularly important about the emergence of pretending between 18 months and two years is that the child becomes able not only to pretend productively herself but is simultaneously able to understand pretence-in-others. This is shown by the ability to share and jointly construct imaginary situations with others (Leslie, 1987a, in preparation).

The early understanding of pretence-in-others is, in an interesting sense, an elementary form of understanding another's mental state. What is so impressive is that the content of the other's pretend mental state, which the two-year-old is able to infer, is *opaque* (as philosophers call it) or *decoupled* (as I have called it). The two-year-old is able to draw inferences based on such contents while respecting its opacity. This is essential if the child is to understand the other's behaviour in the course of shared pretence. It also marks a fundamental distinction between our common sense understanding of physical mechanisms and our understanding of intentional behaviour. The *actual* behaviour of a physical mechanism is understood only in relation to *actual* states of affairs. It is not just wrong but utterly silly to blame actual bumps in the night on ghosts, if you don't think ghosts are real. But good explanations of intentional behaviour often escape this necessary connection to actual states of affairs: mother is putting that *empty* cup to her lips because she is pretending it contains tea.[1] Intentional behaviour is often understood in relation to counterfactual situations (for example, the empty cup 'containing tea'). Indeed this possibility is what is essential and special to a theory of mind and part of what makes it useful. Of course, the two-year-old does not have any idea of the particular mechanism whereby a mental state causes behaviour, but then neither do I.[2]

Understanding pretence, then, is probably the earliest (or one of the earliest) forms of understanding an opaque mental state. My hypothesis is that this ability reflects, in a developmentally rather raw form, the workings of an in-built theory of mind module. Or to put it another way, it reflects part of the initial state of the child's ToM. I want to suggest that this initial state module produces, or is involved in producing, later developments in the child's theory of mental states. Beyond this common base in metarepresentational machinery, I believe that the elaboration in development of each particular mental state concept (e.g. pretend, desire, believe) will have to be looked at case by case. These three concepts differ from one another in important ways and it is far from obvious that the course of their development in the child should be identical in all respects. But in any case, my claim is that the logical-expressive power required for expressing such concepts is available no later than around two years, by courtesy of the metarepresentational module.[3]

So much for the general idea. I now want to talk about the hypothesis that the syndrome of childhood autism, in its specific aspects, results from biological damage to and subsequent cognitive dysfunction of the ToM module. I am going to briefly review a body of recent experimental results on autistic theory of mind. I think they go along with the general idea above. The results point to a specific cognitive deficit, possibly unique to autism, certainly independent of general mental retardation. They do not fit with the classical view of autism as an affective or general social disorder (see the Leslie and Frith–Hobson debate (Hobson, 1990; Leslie and Frith,

1990). Instead, the results are consistent with a specific metarepresentational dysfunction which delays and disrupts developments.

Childhood Autism[4]

Space prevents a comprehensive introduction to the many problems of understanding autism; in any case, I could not do as good a job as Frith (1989) which the reader is urged to consult.

Autism is a developmental disorder with a variety of biological causes. While 75 per cent of autistic children are mentally retarded, 25 per cent have borderline to average IQs. This top 25 per cent still show the social and communicative impairments that are characteristic of autism. There are three broad possibilities for explaining autism (see Figure 5.1): (1) There is a basic affective disorder which somehow produces the other impairments

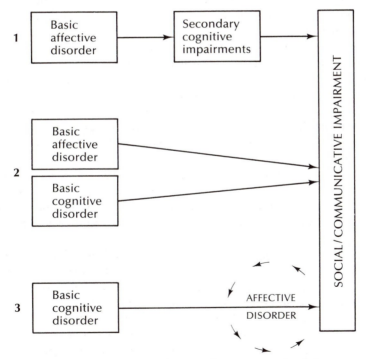

Figure 5.1 *Alternative explanations for social impairment in autism.*

in cognition and in surface behaviour. (2) There are two independent basic disorders in autism, one affective, the other cognitive, which jointly produce the surface impairments. (3) There is a basic cognitive deficit in high-ability autism which produces the secondary consequences, including affective disorder and impairment in social and communicative behaviour. It is this last possibility I want to argue for.

Experimental Studies

Baron-Cohen, Leslie and Frith (1986) tested autistic children's ability to understand different types of event using a picture–sequencing task. An important feature of this study was the use of control groups of normal preschoolers and Down's syndrome children with substantially lower mental ages (MA) than the autistic children. The relative advantages enjoyed by the autistic group allows us to evaluate conservatively any relative disadvantages in their performance.

Three types of event were studied. In the first, the pictures depicted simple physical causal sequences. Some sequences showed only physical objects while others showed a person and object, like that illustrated in Figure 5.2a. We had these two subtypes because we wanted to see if the involvement of a person made the event harder for the autistic children.

The second type of event we called 'social behavioural' because we thought they would be understood as behavioural and social routines. Again we had two subtypes: a single person performing an action like getting dressed; and two people interacting, like that illustrated in figure 5.2b. Again we wanted to see if human interaction was especially hard for autistic children to understand.

Finally, we had a type of event we called 'intentional' because it seemed to us that such events are best and most naturally understood only with reference to the protagonist's mental state – in the case of the story illustrated in figure 5.2c, the girl's expectation or belief that her teddy would be behind her.

Notice that any or all the stories *could* be understood in mental-state terms. But we assumed that the most natural and spontaneous normal understanding would be appropriate to the three different types of description: mechanical, social-behavioural, and mental-state.

The results were quite striking. For all the groups there were no differences between the subtypes *object alone* versus *person and object*, and none between *single person acting* and *two people interacting*. Figure 5.3 shows the scores for correct sequencing collapsed across story subtypes. The autistic children did best on the mechanical stories where they displayed

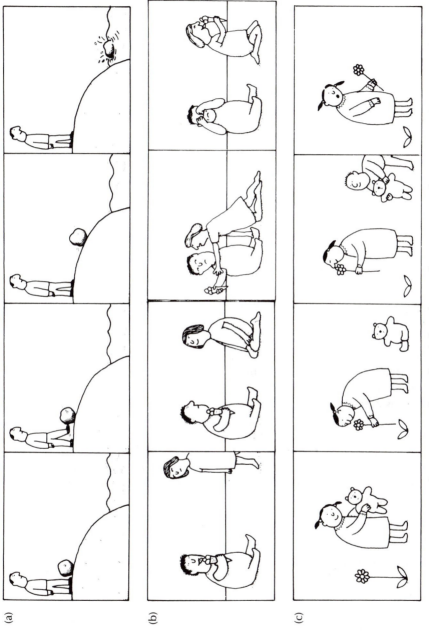

Figure 5.2 Picture sequences depicting: (a) physical causality, (b) social interaction and (c) intentionality. See text for rationale.

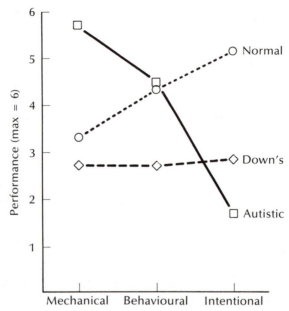

Figure 5.3   *Scores for correct sequencing of story subtypes for normal, Down's and autistic children.*

their MA advantage. They did less well on the social-behavioural stories but still well above chance (represented by a score of around two). Autistic performance on this condition matched that of the normal four-year-olds but was dramatically worse on the intentional condition where their perform-ance at chance level was signficantly worse than that of the Down's children. Protocols taken from the children at time of sequencing were analysed according to type of language used – causal, descriptive or mental-state language – producing results which paralleled the sequencing results. In particular, they showed a marked poverty of mental-state language in our autistic children relative to the controls.

These results suggest that the autistic child has difficulty in understanding certain social situations but not others. Because all the stories had emotional content and expression (except the object-only mechanical subtype), the results contradict the idea that autistic children have a general inability to deal with the social world on affective grounds. Instead, they seem to have a special difficulty with those situations in which it is necessary to take into account what someone else knows or expects.

This conclusion is supported by the results of Baron-Cohen, Leslie and Frith (1985). In this study we used very nearly all the same children as in the above experiment. This time we used dolls to present a social scenario to the children. Sally has a marble which she hides in a basket. She then goes away for a walk. While Sally is gone, Anne transfers the marble from the basket to a box. Sally then returns and wants her marble. The child is asked certain control questions to ensure he or she has understood the displacements of the object over time and that there are no memory problems, otherwise the scenario is re-enacted. Then the child is asked, "Where will Sally look for her marble?"

The results showed that 85 per cent of the normal four-year-old children correctly predicted where Sally would look on the basis of where Sally should (wrongly) *believe* her marble to be, as did 86 per cent of the Down's syndrome children. By contrast, only 20 per cent of the autistic children predicted Sally's behaviour on the basis of where the marble really was. These results provided more support for the idea that high-ability autistic children were specifically impaired in their ability to understand certain mental states, such as belief, and to predict the behaviour of others on this basis.

In a further study (Leslie and Frith, 1988), we wanted to replicate the prediction-from-false-belief study with additional controls and also to extend it to look at autistic understanding of true belief. True belief (where another person knows the 'truth' but not the whole truth) appears to be somewhat easier for normal children to understand and to base behavioural predictions upon. Among the controls we added were: all the autistic sample had verbal MAs in excess of four years five months (mean = seven years two months); the scenarios were presented by means of real people acting out rather than dolls; and we made sure in a number of ways that the autistic children could understand when the actors could and could not see something. Finally, we used a group of specific language impaired (SLI) children matched for verbal MA to help control for possible effects in these tasks of autistic language delay.

When we presented this new sample with the above described prediction from false belief task, 100 per cent of the SLI control children passed compared to 28 per cent of the high-ability autistics. This confirmed with additional controls our earlier results.

We also set the autistics a new task in which one actor watches while the experimenter hides a counter. We ensure that the autistic child notes that the actor has seen this. The actor now leaves the room. The experimenter then produces an identical counter and asks the child to hide it somewhere different (prominent hiding places are provided). The child is then asked a series of questions including a question about where the still-absent actor will look for a counter on her return. This scenario thus closely parallels the false-belief situauion except that instead of there being one object which changes place there are two objects, only one of which the actor knows about. The results showed that slightly (but not significantly) more autistic children passed this task than passed false belief. But despite a mental age in excess of seven years, 56 per cent of the group still failed. For instance, they pointed to where they themselves had hidden an object while the experimenter was absent and said that she knew it was there. The autistic child's difficulties, then, apply to understanding both false and true belief.

In a subsequent study (Perner, Frith, Leslie and Leekam, forthcoming), we extended the results on false belief by employing Perner, Leekam and Wimmer's (1987) 'Smarties' task. The child is shown a box or tube of a well-known European confectionary (US equivalent = M&Ms) and is asked what he or she thinks is 'in here'. In both studies children invariably said 'Smarties'. The box or tube was then opened and the child shown that its contents consisted simply of a pencil. The pencil was replaced in the box and the child was questioned to check whether they remembered what they had said when first shown the box and that they now knew what it really contained. In effect, the child had just undergone a false belief situation. The child was then told that X (a friend) was going to come in and that X would be shown the box all sealed up 'just as I showed you' and would be asked what was in the box. Then the child was asked to predict what X would reply. From Perner et al. (1987) we know that most four-year-olds correctly predict their friend's false belief. Now in the Perner et al. (forthcoming) study we found that 92 per cent of the SLI children (mean verbal MA = six years nine months) also correctly predicted their friend's false belief, while only 17 per cent of the autistic children (mean verbal MA = eight years three months) could likewise make a correct prediction of belief.

Perner et al. (1989) also looked at autistic understanding of true belief using a different paradigm from Leslie and Frith (1988) but with very similar results (67 per cent failed to show they could infer someone else's belief even when that belief would be true). This study also found that autistic children were no better at understanding the conditions under which they themselves did or did not know something than at understanding this for another person.

Let us take stock of the results from the four studies. First, autistic children as a group are severely impaired on tasks which tap their ToM even relative to their *own* level of general intellectual functioning or MA. This is true both in the sense that their performance is very poor even though they have a MA several years greater than that at which the normal child performs near ceiling, and in the sense that none of these studies has found a reliable association between passing and failing on any of the tasks and MA, verbal or non-verbal, and in the sense that other clinical groups with as great or greater mental retardation (e.g. our Down's syndrome group) perform comparatively well at these tasks.

Secondly, some tasks appear to be slightly easier for some autistic children (true versus false belief) and *some* autistic children do reliably pass even false-belief tasks. For example, Baron-Cohen et al. (1985) found four autistic children who passed the Sally/Anne prediction task; of these, two children also passed on the Baron-Cohen et al (1986) picture-sequencing task and produced mental-state language in their protocols as well. Where we have been able to look at it, passing or failing has been reliable on retest (for instance, see Leslie and Frith, 1988).

What of these approximately 17 per cent to 28 per cent of high-ability autistic children who pass 'theory of mind' tasks? In a recent study by Baron-Cohen (1989a), a special group of ten autistic young adults was assembled by screening for those who could pass the Sally/Anne task. A group of ten MA-matched Down's syndrome adolescents acted as controls. These subjects were given a higher-order false-belief task, modelled on Perner and Wimmer (1985). In this, two protagonists simultaneously acquire the same false belief but then each has his or her belief corrected independently so that neither knows about the other's correction. The child is then asked to predict one of the protagonists behaviour on the basis of the one's false belief about the other's false belief. Naturally, this kind of task is harder for the normal child but is passed by most children between seven and nine years old. Baron-Cohen found that six of his ten Down's subjects passed the higher-order false-belief task as expected from their MA. In contrast, none of the matched autistics could do so.

Taken together, then, the results of these studies suggest that high-ability autistic children are specifically and grossly delayed in their ToM understanding, relative to their own general intellectual functioning. Work on the development of ToM in normal children (see e.g. chapters in Astington, Harris and Olson, 1988) suggests that there may be a 'watershed' around the fourth birthday. It is only around this time that the normal child reliably solves false-belief and other related tasks. Are grossly delayed autistic children, then, like normal three-year-olds in this domain? Do they simply get stuck at the three-year-old level or is there something more to their impairment?

There are four reasons which we would offer for thinking that autistic children are not simply like normal three-year-olds in this domain. First, as noted in Leslie (1987a; cf. Leslie and Frith, 1987), autistic children have been widely reported as impaired or delayed in pretend play (e.g. Ungerer and Sigman, 1981). This would set them apart from the normal three-year-old who can bring sophisticated cognitive powers to bear on pretending.

Secondly, interesting comparisons can be made by matching autistic performance on a standard false-belief task to that of normal three-year-olds and then comparing the two groups' performance on other ToM tasks. For example, figure 5.4 compares autistic performance on Leslie and Frith's (1988) tasks with that of normal three-year-olds on analogous true-and false-belief tasks reported by Wellman and Bartsch (1988). The two groups perform similarly on false belief but appear to differ substantially on true belief. The procedural differences between these two studies have prompted us to undertake an experiment drawing the two procedures within a single design. Until these results are at hand we must, of course, draw only limited conclusions from the comparison made in figure 5.4.

A third piece of evidence comes from a recent study by Harris and Muncer (1988) in which their high-ability autistic sample was impaired in their understanding not only of false belief but also in their understanding of desires, particularly *unfulfilled* desires where what someone desires does not match up to reality. Again studies of normal children suggest this is within the grasp of the three-year-old (e.g. Wellman and Bartsch, 1988).

Finally, Baron-Cohen (forthcoming a) has found that autistic children (with mean verbal MA of six-and-a-half years and mean CA of twelve) fail on tests of the mental–physical distinction (for example, a banana can be eaten but the thought of a banana cannot) while most Down's syndrome

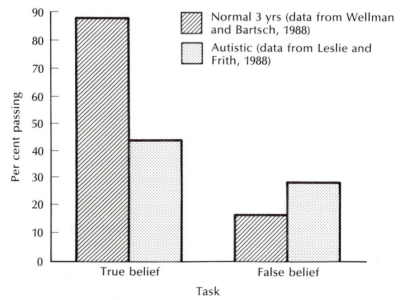

Figure 5.4 *Comparison of autistic and normal three-year-olds' performances on analogous true- and false-belief tasks.*

children pass (mean verbal MA of four-and-a-half years and CA thirteen). Wellman and Estes (1986) found that this distinction was well within the grasp of normal three-year-olds.

The pattern we see emerging from the seven existing studies is one of gross delay, plus, in a large proportion of autistic children, some further impairment in ToM.[5] This pattern provides a compelling argument for a *cognitive* deficit. What sort of cognitive deficit could produce this pattern? I see no choice, if this question is ever to be answered, but to develop a neuropsychological account of autism. In this spirit, I and my colleagues, Uta Frith and Simon Baron-Cohen, have been advancing the 'metarepresentational conjecture'.

I have used the term 'metarepresentation'[6] in a specific sense: to mean (e.g., in the case of understanding pretence-in-others) an internal representation of an epistemic relationship (PRETEND) between a person, a real situation and an imaginary situation (represented opaquely). For example, **Mother** PRETEND **the empty cup 'it contains tea'.** (Solitary pretence is the special case where person = **I**.) Metarepresentations are associated with specialized mechanisms which are expressed early in normal development – the ToM module.

The metarepresentational conjecture for autism stated generally[7] is:

> Autistic children are impaired and/or delayed in their capacity to form and/or process metarepresentations. This impairs (/delays) their capacity to acquire a theory of mind.

This opens a number of empirical questions such as: Are autistic children impaired in a metarepresentational capacity only as it specifically relates to theory of mind or do they also show deficits in understanding representations other than mental ones? Do autistic children have a set of metarepresentational dysfunctions producing, for example, conceptual deficits (e.g. affecting informational relations themselves (PRETEND, MEAN, BELIEVE, DESIRE, etc.), representational deficits (e.g. affecting embeddedness or opacity) and processing deficits (affecting e.g. inferences involving metarepresentations)?

The results reviewed above showed that high-ability autistic children vary in their degree of impairment on theory of mind tasks. This raises questions about the nature of the impairment itself. Because the underlying impairment is biological, we are discussing the effects of hardware problems on cognition and more particularly on cognitive development. The neuropsychology of autism (and possibly the neuropsychology of mental deficiency as a whole) has to take into account not just the modular organization of cognition but also how this organization produces development, in particular, conceptual development. I have suggested using the term 'engine' of development to encourage us to consider modules in relation to development (see e.g. Leslie, 1986, 1988a; Leslie and Keeble, 1987).

I assume that the operating behavioural criteria in the diagnosis of autism leads one to sample a group of brain-damaged children where the pattern of damage particularly includes the theory of mind module; in the case of severely retarded autism, other severe general damage will also be present, while, in the case of high-ability autism, collateral damage will be correspondingly less important. In other forms of retardation, damage to this module may be absent or minor. I assume also that the consequences of damage to this module could in individual cases range from complete functional absence to partial or inhibited functioning. It may be that some high-ability autistics who develop ToM, to some level, do so slowly, late, and by means other than via the ToM module, e.g. by using conscious general purpose problem-solving over a large body of accumulated experience.

But whatever the role of cognitive science in understanding autism, we can also look to autism (and to mental retardation syndromes in general) and ask how it may help us with cognitive science. For example, perhaps the study of autism can help with the very difficult problem of understanding how particular modules function as engines of development and how an impaired engine leads to impaired development.

The Precocity of Pretence

It is not obvious (at least from a *pre*theoretical point of view) why the capacity for pretence should emerge so early in development. Is it just an aberrant manifestation of a still primitive and relatively unorganized system? Piaget (1962) seems inclined to some such view. On the contrary, I would argue that pretence is linked to three major cognitive capacities: ToM (Leslie, 1987a), counterfactual reasoning (Leslie, 1988b), and intentional communication (Leslie and Happé, 1989). These powers are so important that we may suppose that the specific brain mechanisms subserving pretence have been selected *for* in human evolution.

Is the two-year-old's ToM module limited to pretence or does it have a more complex structure? I already mentioned at the beginning that study of infant perceptual processes might be fruitful in unearthing, say, a modular system for perceiving the goal directedness of animate actions.[8] If so, it may play a role in the development of the early concept of desire as an 'internal drive' as discussed by Wellman (in chapter 2).

In fact, the theory of mind module may have a complex internal (and modular) architecture as, for example, the visual (Marr, 1982) and language faculties appears to have (Fodor, 1983; Chomsky, 1986). I would like to suggest, in this vein, some speculative connections between pretence systems and other components of the theory of mind module that may develop even earlier than pretence. In Leslie (1987a), I referred to work by several students of infancy (e.g. Bates, Benigni, Bretherton, Camaioni and Volterra, 1979; Bretherton, McNew and Beeghly-Smith, 1981; Bruner, 1976) which, in one way or another, drew upon work in philosophy and the pragmatics of language to raise the question of whether the communicative abilities of infants (around the first birthday) implied that they had some sort of grasp of the mental or epistemic states of their audience. I pointed out that substantiating this remained an attractive but still-elusive goal. I believe that the metarepresentational theory of pretence may make it possible to assault this problem from a previously untried direction.

My approach to the child's understanding of pretence-in-others has, in effect, been to treat it as a form of ostensive communication where the child makes an inference from the other's perceived behaviour to a metarepresentation of the other's intended message in acting the way they do. This metarepresentation expresses a relationship, PRETEND, between that person as agent (e.g. **mother**), an *actual* situation (e.g. **the empty cup**), and an *imaginary* (typically counterfactual) situation (e.g. **'it contains water'**). The reasons for adopting this sort of analysis seem to me to add up to something quite compelling (see Leslie, 1987a, 1988a, 1988b). Yet it seems unlikely that PRETEND should exist all by itself and not be part of some *system* of initial concepts (see also Whiten and Byrne, chapter 18).

I believe that similar sorts of arguments to those I mounted for pretence could be mounted for infant understanding of gestures as intentional communications. Such argument can be patterned after the insights contained in Sperber and Wilson (1986). Thus, I gesture towards a vase of flowers with upturned palm. There is little or no interest in the primary description of this stimulus as an end in itself: a hand oriented with such and such geometry for such and such a time. if that was all, there would be little reason to attend to the gesture. What *is* interesting about a gesture is what someone *means* by making it. It is important to understand that this kind of meaningful event has special properties. Contrast: smoke rising from a forest means fire. But the forest does not mean 'fire' by the smoke!

Intentional communication and shared pretence acts have interesting properties in common. A communicative gesture must obviously be noticed if it is to communicate; but just being noticed is not enough. It must be made apparent to the audience that it is intended to be noticed. Let us suppose that communicative acts *display* an intention to communicate in the sense of engaging a direct perception in the audience. This presupposes perceptible properties of action that allow a perception of intention or goal-directedness. I do not suppose that this display is some further act in parallel to the gesture but rather is carried in the manner of the act itself. Falling down stairs is attention grabbing but it is not communicative; nor is it more communicative if the faller simply intends to fall (perhaps he wants to injure himself); but it is communicative if the faller intends *to make a display of* falling down the stairs. So I am suggesting that deliberately making an attention grabbing display of an act itself signals the intention to communicate.

There are inherent limits to what can be directly perceived. Although the intention to communicate may be perceived along with other general aspects of goal orientation, the specific intended message has to be inferred and inferred metarepresentationally. This is the psychological counterpart to the special category of meaningful events comprised of intentional communication acts referred to above. Essentially, the same act can be used to communicate radically different messages; after all, the message is determined, not by the act, but by the particular intention that lies behind the act.

We can now begin to make sense, for the first time, of a commonly noted property of shared pretence acts: their form is 'exaggerated'. Pretence can turn any act into a communicative gesture. For example, take the act of drinking from a cup. To communicate that I am pretending the cup contains water, I lift the cup ostentatiously in front of my mouth and smack my lips. The act is not carried through to its normal goal (from which it is, of course, decoupled), and at the same time, the form of the act is exaggerated to turn the action into a display. The interest of the audience is not in this truncated and grotesquely performed mechanical event, but in what the pretender means by it. *What the symbol means.*

Finally, I would like to hypothesize that the hardwired perception of an intention to communicate could be operational in quite young infants. Such a perceptual module should be connected to the central, and perhaps slightly later developing, ToM module; such perceptions may then trigger its metarepresentational processes.

Understanding counterfactual pretence communications between one-and-a-half and two years could provide us with a bridgehead for exploring the more limited communicative abilities of infants younger than this. Pretence may be part of a developing system which includes other relations such as MEAN and its reciprocal UNDERSTAND, and which will include more differentiated notions like DESIRE and BELIEVE. It would not be too surprising if the demands of a system for ostensive communication have played an important role in the evolution of the capacity to acquire a ToM nor too surprising if this is reflected in the initial state of our ToM module. The peculiar communicative problems of autism add weight to this conjecture (Leslie and Happé, 1989; see also Baron-Cohen, chapter 16).

NOTES

1 Of course, it's the pretending *relation* which is actual here, and its content which describes something non-actual. ToM explanations are still good causal explanations. The point is that *pretend* is one of those special relations that allows non-actual situations to enter into good causal explanations of actual behaviour. There are no such relations in (folk) theory of mechanics.

2 I have been persuaded that I should abandon the idea (in Leslie 1987a and particularly 1988a) that three-to four-year olds have to acquire a general causal view of mental states. Henry Wellman (Wellman and Bartsch, 1988; Bartsch and Wellman forthcoming) and Debbie Zaitchik (in press, pers. com.) provided the evidence and arguments that helped me see the light. Susan Carey (pers. com.) softened me up for this by reminding me of a few lessons I should already have learnt.

3 The question of the relation between information-processing machinery and the development of concepts is one of the most difficult and general problems of cognitive psychology. Needless to say, it bedevils the interesting questions in ToM. Nevertheless, we can now rule out one major class of explanations for the child's relatively late success on false belief tasks, viz. that he lacks a basic logical capacity to represent contradictory descriptions of a single situation as was originally proposed by Wimmer and Perner (1983).

4 This section is drawn from Leslie and Frith (1990).

5 Tager-Flüsberg (1989) has extended the findings of Baron-Cohen et al. (1986) on autistic poverty of mental-state language to show that this poverty does not include reference to simple emotional states.

6 In the collection of papers in Astington, Harris and Olson (1988) one will notice at least two different ways of using this term. On this terminological point, it can be slightly confusing that 'metarepresentation' can mean something like 'a kind of proprietary (internal) representation in ToM mechanisms' and something like 'a particular concept of representation which someone grasps'. This ambiguity is inevitable but it helps to bear the distinction in mind, especially when a lot of the questions one is interested in have to do with the relation between metarepresentation in the former and metarepresentation in the latter sense (see also chapter 1).

7 A more specific example of the metarepresentational conjecture was given in Leslie (1987a). This was allied to the 'quotation' approach to opacity taken there. The quotation metaphor has limited usefulness, however, in capturing the way inference works with metarepresentation. Quotation marks in my meaning are perhaps better interpreted as marking levels within metarepresentations under

which inferences are closed (see Leslie, 1988b; Leslie and Frith, 1990).

8 Tantalizingly, I obtained results from six-month-old infants' perception of a hand picking up an object in an anomalous way that make me suspect they were perceiving goal directedness in a dynamic hand–object interaction (Leslie, 1982, 1984). This is a very difficult question to approach with young infants but the role-reversal technique (Golinkoff & Kerr, 1978; Leslie and Keeble, 1987; Dasser, Ulbeck and Premack, 1989) may produce progress. It may be that the rich phenomena described by Reddy (chapter 10) may bear on this question.

6

From Agency to Intention: A Rule-Based, Computational Approach

Thomas R. Shultz

Introduction

It is my belief that research on early theories of mind (ETM) can now benefit from computational modelling. ETM has recently been one of the most active areas in developmental psychology. It has been based on verbal theorizing and has generated a considerable amount of interesting and reliable developmental data. Most of these data concern the timing or sequencing of particular abilites or beliefs. Understanding false beliefs (Perner, Leekam and Wimmer, 1987), grasping the distinction between seeing and knowing (Chandler and Helm, 1984), adopting the visual perspective of another person (Flavell, Everett, Croft and Flavell, 1981), and distinguishing between appearance and reality (Flavell, 1986) may be cited as well-known examples of important developmental ETM changes that occur between about three and five years of age. This diagnostic work sets the stage for future efforts to explain the reasoning mechanisms underlying these abilities and their development. How is this sort of reasoning done, and what sort of transition mechanisms might account for its development?

As in most areas of cognitive development, the search for rigorously formulated reasoning mechanisms and transition mechanisms is likely to be slow and difficult. At least some of the blame for the difficulties can be traced to an absence of mechanistic approaches. Rather a lot is known about what concepts follow what other concepts in development, but very little is known about how the child actually reasons with these concepts and how these reasoning mechanisms might construct more advanced concepts. It is very unlikely that merely analysing the content of the concepts at adjacent

Portions of the research for this paper were supported by grants from the National Sciences and Engineering Research Council of Canada and from IBM Canada.

stages will shed sufficient light on how the child moves from one stage to the next. It is essential to know, in addition, about the mechanisms the child employs to manipulate these concepts in reasoning. Only then will we be in position to understand the mechanisms of transition.

There is some room for optimism in this recommended approach. Both reasoning mechanisms and transition mechanisms are likely to be far more general than ETM in their application. Thus, the search can benefit from related work on reasoning done in cognitive psychology, cognitive science, artificial intelligence and other aspects of cognitive development, and simultaneously contribute to these other domains of enquiry.

My first effort to model ETM phenomena concerned a program called JIA (Judging the Intentionality of Action) that simulated the processes involved in determining whether an action or outcome is intended (Shultz, 1988). In subsequent work, I explored whether a variety of embedded intentional phenomena, such as false belief and strategic deception could also be modelled in a rule-based approach (Shultz, forthcoming). Intentional states more generally have the properties of *aboutness, referential opacity* and *embeddedness* (Whiten and Perner, chapter 1; Dennett, 1987). Although such properties pose a number of computational complexities, there are a variety of symbolic computational techniques for dealing with them. We have been using the OPS5 production system (Forgy, 1981), which can represent embedded propositions with so-called *linked data structures*. Basically, some slots of a data object can contain links or pointers to other data structures. Reasoning that takes account of these links exhibits the requisite properties for reasoning about embedded intentional states.

In this paper, I explore a rule-based computational approach to a particular problem in ETM, the concept of agency. I begin with a brief review of some of the psychological evidence on agency, then proceed to describe the current model of agency, and finally turn to a discussion of related issues such as transition mechanisms, concepts related to agency and continuity in development.

Psychological Evidence on Agency and Intention

The concept of agency explains that a being moves or behaves on its own, without the influence of external causation. Agency is undoubtedly one of the most primitive and fundamental aspects of ETM. The concept of intention elaborates on agency by postulating an internal mental state that guides or controls behaviour. We have proposed that the child's notion of intention develops out of an earlier grasp of the concept of agency (Poulin-Dubois and Shultz, 1988).

A variety of evidence from studies of language, play, attention, communication, manipulation, emotional reaction and habituation phenomena suggests that the concept of agency precedes that of intention. There is, first of all, the pervasive use of the agentive case in children just starting to use language (Bloom, Lightbown and Hood, 1975; Bowerman, 1976). The agentive case expresses the notion of an animate being initiating some action (e.g. *Nancy run*). Moreover, syntactically, young children are known to consistently place agents before the verb (Bloom et al., 1975; Bowerman, 1976).

Agency also appears to be salient in the perception of non-linguistic stimuli. Attribution of agency to human-like dolls has been observed in children as young as 20 months (Fenson, 1984). By 18 months, infants typically attend to the agent in an observed agent–action–recipient sequence both during and after the action (Robertson and Suci, 1980). At 17 months, infants begin to turn towards other people to request help with re-creating an interesting event (Sexton, 1983) and begin to restrict their communicative overtures to people (Bates, Camaioni and Volterra, 1975). Ten-month-olds who were taught to activate a manipulandum to create animate and inanimate events more often used it to create inanimate than animate events (Carlson, 1980). Fourteen-month-olds habituated less rapidly to autonomous movement by inanimate objects than to movement by a person, whereas eight-month-olds looked longer when the agent was a person (Poulin-Dubois and Shultz, forthcoming).

In contrast to this relatively early appreciation of agency, hard evidence on the concept of intention in preverbal infants is difficult to find (but see Reddy chapter 10). It has been argued that purported evidence based on turn-taking and communication can be interpreted in other, less sophisticated ways (Golinkoff, 1983; Poulin-Dubois and Shultz, 1988; Scoville, 1984). Firm evidence of the understanding of intention, in terms of the ability to distinguish intentional acts and outcomes from accidents, mistakes and passive movements does not appear before about three years of age (Shultz, 1980; Shultz, Well and Sarda, 1980).

Modelling the Concept of Agency

One of the central things infants will need is to distinguish agents from non-agents (or *patients*). In a rule-based account, this will be accomplished by classification or *synchronic* rules. There are two principal types of rules in our program, both related to the program's sense of time (Holland, Holyoak, Nisbett and Thagard, 1986). *Synchronic* rules are essentially atemporal. Their function is to categorize objects or events. In contrast, *diachronic* rules specify how the environment changes over time. They deal with predictions and actions.

Synchronic Rules

What sort of rules would enable the child to distinguish objects that are agents from objects that are patients? A first hint comes from the literature on the concept of animism. This literature goes back as far as Piaget (1929) who claimed that young children have a tendency to attribute the characteristics of living things to some inanimate objects. What sort of objects receive such an attribution? Many researchers on the concept of animism agree that autonomous movement is critical for an attribution of animacy by young children. Rule *agent-move* (box 6.1: for notational details see Appendix, p. 93) reflects this belief. It specifies that if an object moves and its movement has no external cause, then it is an agent. As noted above, the psychological research suggests that infants possess such a rule near the end of their first year.

Another, synchronic production rule would be needed to enable the classification of an object as a patient, or non-agent. Rule *patient-move* (box 6.2) specifies that if an object moves, its movement has an external cause, and it is not already known that this object is a patient, then it is a patient. Again the psychological evidence, reviewed above, suggests that such a rule is present by the end of the first year (see chapter 13 for the development of similar rules by gorillas).

It is noteworthy that both of these synchronic rules for classifying objects as agent or patient embody an embedded structure. In each case, the object's

Box 6.1   Rule agent-move

```
(p agent-move

  (s ^id <id1> ^agent <object> ^action move ^object nil ^embed-in <id2>)
  (s ^id <id2> ^agent <id1> ^action is ^object uncaused ^embed-in nil)
  – (s ^agent <object> ^action is ^object agent ^embed-in nil)
  →
  (make s ^agent <object> ^action is ^object agent ^embed-in nil))
```

Box 6.2   Rule patient-move

```
(p patient-move
  (s ^id <id1> ^ agent <object> ^ action move ^object nil ^ embed-in <id2>)
  (s ^id <id2> ^ agent <cause> ^ action cause ^object <id1> ^ embed-in nil)
  – (s ^agent <object> ^ action is ^object patient ^embed-in nil)
  →
  (make s ^agent <object> ^ action is ^object patient ^embed-in nil))
```

movement is embedded in a statement about the cause (or lack of cause) of that movement. The reason this is noteworthy is that it might be thought that embedded representations would occur only in the service of more advanced intentional concepts (see chapter 1). The present modelling suggests that embedded representations must occur much earlier, even when dealing with the relatively primitive notion of agency.

Both of these synchronic productions will require other productions to enable decisions about how object movements are caused. In the present paper, this type of causal reasoning is treated as an unanalysed problem, but some progress has been reported elsewhere on mechanisms of causal reasoning (Anderson, 1987; Lewis, 1988; Pazzani, 1987; Shultz, 1987; Shultz and Kestenbaum, 1985).

Diachronic Rules

The above synchronic rules for classifying objects as agents or patients appear to be used in the service of other, diachronic rules that specify how to act towards objects and what to expect from objects.

How to cause object movement   Carlson's (1980) evidence suggests that infants know how agents and patients are set into motion. In other words, infants know how to cause these two different types of motion. Rule *move-patient* (box 6.3) specifies how to get a patient object to move. It says that if a person wants an object to move, and that object is known to be a patient, then the person should cause the object to move directly. Obviously, further production rules will be required to explicate how people can cause objects to move directly.

With respect to getting agents to move, there have been reports that nine to 12-month-olds confine their communicative overtures to people (Bates et

Box 6.3   Rule move-patient

(p move-patient
  (s ˆid <id1> ˆ agent <person> ˆ action want ˆobject <id2> ˆ embed-in nil)
  (s ˆid <id2> ˆ agent <object> ˆ action move ˆobject nil ˆembed-in <id1>)
  (s ˆagent <object> ˆ action is ˆobject patient ˆembed-in nil)
  →
  (make s ˆagent <person> ˆ action cause ˆobject <id2> ˆ embed-in nil))

---

al., 1975; Carlson, 1980; Sexton, 1983). This can be interpreted as suggesting that the infants realize that people are agents. They seem to recognize that communication works on agents, but not on patients. Rule *move-agent* (box 6.4) provides a formal description of how to get an agent to move. It says that, if a person wants an object to move, and that object is an agent, then the person should communicate to the object to move itself. Rule *move-agent*, like the other proposed production rules, also has an embedded

Box 6.4   Rule move-agent

(p move-agent
  (s ˆid <id1> ˆ agent <person> ˆ action want ˆobject <id2> ˆembed-in nil)
  (s ˆid <id2> ˆ agent <object> ˆ action move ˆobject nil ˆembed-in <id1>)
  (s ˆagent <object> ˆ action is ˆobject agent ˆembed-in nil)
  →
  (bind <id3> (genatom))
  (bind <id4> (genatom))
  (make s ˆid <id3> ˆ agent <person> ˆ action communicate ˆobject <id4>
  ˆembed-in nil)
  (make s ˆid <id4> ˆ agent <object> ˆ action move ˆobject nil ˆembed-in
  <id3>))

Note: This production contains an embedded structure on its right-hand side, in that the object's movement is the embedded object of the communication. Because of this right-hand side embedding, two new variables must be bound, namely the ids of the two right-hand side sentences. The purpose of the two *bind* actions is to do just that, to bind each of these id values to a unique atomic symbol. *Genatom* is the OPS5 command that supplies the unique atomic symbol.

Box 6.5 Rule attribute-agent

```
(p attribute-agent
  (s ^id <id1> ^ agent<object> ^ action move ^object nil ^embed-in nil)
  (s ^agent<object> ^ action is ^object agent ^embed-in nil)
  →
  (make s ^agent <id1> ^ action is ^object uncaused ^embed-in nil))
```

structure in the condition elements, such that the movement of the object is embedded in what the person wants. This rule also contains an embedded structure on its right-hand side, in that the object's movement is the embedded object of the communication. Again, additional productions would be required to specify the content and form of the communication.

Explaining object behaviour The fact that 14-month-olds habituated less rapidly to autonomous movement by inanimate objects than to movement by a person (Poulin-Dubois and Shultz, forthcoming) suggests that they had some basis for explaining how objects should behave. That is, they should expect that agents typically cause their own movements and patients typically have externally caused movements. Rule *attribute-agent* (box 6.5) explains the movement of agents. It specifies that if an object moves and is an agent, then expect that there is no external cause of this movement.

The companion rule for explaining patient movement is *attribute-patient* (box 6.6). It says that, if an object moves and that object is a patient, then assume that there is an external cause of this movement. Additional productions might specify surprise and further investigation if the attributions made by these productions were ever disconfirmed by contradictory evidence. Such productions would effectively describe the responses charac-

Box 6.6 Rule attribute-patient

```
(p attribute-patient
  (s ^id <id1> ^ agent<object> ^ action move ^object nil ^embed-in nil)
  (s ^agent<object> ^ action is ^object patient ^embed-in nil)
  →
  (make s ^agent <id1> ^ action is ^object caused ^embed-in nil))
```

teristic of the orienting response on which the phenomenon of dishabituation of attention is based (Sokolov, 1960).

Earlier Stages in the Concept of Agency?

The foregoing production rules provide a partial glimpse of a mechanism for more or less adaptive reasoning about the concept of agency by children near the end of the first year of life. But, in order to examine some developmental variation, let's imagine somewhat younger infants who fail to show successful discrimination between agents and patients.

These younger children may fail either because they use a different, probably less-refined, diachronic rule or because they possess an incorrect synchronic rule for classifying objects. A diachronic rule may be faulty because it lacks a condition element referring to object classification, thus making the rule too general in its application. For example, an overly general version of rule *attribute-agent* is rule *attribute-agent-faulty* (box 6.7). It specifies that, if object moves, then expect that there is no external cause of this movement.

Whether or not the infant possesses correct synchronic rules for distinguishing agents from patients, the lack of a condition element that identifies the object type in rules like *attribute-agent-faulty* will lead to over-inclusive errors.

Another possibility is that the synchronic rule on which the diachronic rules depend is either missing or faulty. It might be missing due to lack of relevant experience, or it might be faulty in the same sense that rule *attribute-agent-faulty* is faulty. That is, the synchronic rule could be too general due to the lack of a critical condition element. An example of the latter is provided by rule *agent-move-faulty* (box 6.8) which says that if an object moves and is not known to be an agent, then it is an agent. Such a rule would create problems even for diachronic rules such as *move-agent*

Box 6.7   Rule attribute-agent-faulty

```
(p attribute-agent-faulty
 (s ^id <id1> ^ agent <object> ^ action move ^object nil ^embed-in nil)
 →
 (make s ^agent <id1> ^ action is ^object uncaused ^embed-in nil))
```

Box 6.8   Rule agent-move-faulty

```
(p agent-move-faulty
  (s ^agent <object> ^ action move ^object nil ^embed-in nil)
 - (s ^agent <object> ^ action is ^object agent ^embed-in nil)
 →
  (make s ^agent <object> ^ action is ^object agent ^embed-in nil))
```

and *attribute-agent* that include a condition element referring to the object type. This sort of incorrect synchronic classification of objects will make these diachronic rules too general. That is, they will fire even when they should not.

Transition Mechanisms

Developmental psychologists have an enduring interest in accounting for developmental change. In the present context, the search for transition mechanisms can be focused on locating mechanisms that can create or modify production rules. Artificial intelligence researchers are currently experimenting with a variety of techniques for learning productions, and at least some of these techniques are good candidates for psychological transition mechanisms.

Rule Modification

Modification techniques include discrimination, generalization, composition, compilation and strength-adjustment. Discrimination involves increasing the specificity of a rule's left-hand side, typically by adding condition elements or by instantiating variables (Anderson, 1983; Langley, 1987). There is mounting evidence in developmental psychology that children's knowledge does become increasingly differentiated as they mature (Smith, Carey and Wiser, 1985). Examples of the increasing specificity of rules were provided in the previous section on early stages of the concept of agency. Thus, a discrimination mechanism is likely to figure importantly in explaining much of cognitive development.

Generalization accomplishes the opposite of discrimination in that it makes a production rule more general in its application (Anderson, 1983). Usually this is accomplished by deleting condition elements or by changing constants to variables. An algebra-learning program, for example, generalizes procedures from specific numbers to variables that can assume a range of values (Neves, 1978). There also appears to be a place for generalization of procedural knowledge in cognitive development, although it seems less useful overall than discrimination.

Composition works by collapsing a series of rules that typically fire in sequence (Anderson, 1983; Lewis, 1987). It creates a macro rule that includes the condition elements of the first rule on the left-hand side and all of the other condition and action elements on the right-hand side. Composition accelerates performance because it reduces the amount of matching of rule conditions against working memory that needs to be done. Unlike discrimination and generalization, composition can function without the benefit of corrective feedback.

Rule compilation is another technique for reducing the relatively expensive matching process. It works by replacing variables with constants, typically in frequently used rules that continually match to the same set of values (Anderson, 1983).

Strength-adjustment has to do with modifying a numerical index associated with a rule. Such indices often concern the tendency of a rule to be considered or the certainty of the rule's conclusions (Anderson, 1983; Holland et al., 1986). Generally, positive feedback increases these quantitative indices, whereas negative feedback lowers them.

Rule Creation

The creation of rules is considered to be a more difficult problem than that of modification in the sense that the learning mechanism has less relevant knowledge to work with. Creation is essential, however, because the system may function in novel domains. Creation may be more general than modification since an excellent scheme for creation may obviate the need for modification. If new rules can be continuously created from scratch, why bother modifying old ones? The principal creation techniques studied so far include induction, analogy and chunking.

Inductive techniques typically attempt to abstract the necessary and sufficient conditions for some action by analysing a number of examples or instances (Holland et al., 1986; Mitchell, Utgoff, & Banerji, 1983). There is some doubt that humans have the working memory capacity for this sort of creative process, at least with extensive data.

Analogy involves finding a similar problem where the rules are known, mapping these rules to the novel target problem, and then tweaking the rules to adjust for possible differences between the target and analogous problems (Winston, 1980). Despite some promising work on analogical mapping (Gentner, 1983), the problems of analogy retrieval and tweaking remain difficult and obscure. There is the existence proof of some humans sometimes using analogy to good advantage, but there is not yet much understanding of how they do it.

Chunking is a technique for caching the results of so-called weak problem-solving techniques such as search. A program called Soar uses rule knowledge whenever it can, and resorts to search through problem spaces when its knowledge runs out (Laird, Rosenbloom and Newell, 1987). Then it chunks the results of the search, thereby forming new rules. Soar has been successfully applied to a variety of both toy-size and realistic problems, and is beginning to be applied to problems in cognitive development.

To this list of creation techniques, I would like to add causal reasoning. Attempting to abstract across the numerous rules I had proposed for various ETM phenomena (here and in Shultz, 1988), I was left with a strong impression that these rules were all related to causal connections between events. This raises the possibility that these ETM rules could be created by a system that is able to detect causal relations between events. Once the system establishes that one set of events causes another set of events, it could create two sorts of production rules. One sort would employ the causal statements as conditions and the effect statements as actions. This new rule would enable effects to be predicted from their causes. Rules *move-agent* and *move-patient* are examples of this in the present work. The other sort of created rule would have the effect events as conditions and the causal events as actions. Such rules would enable the explanation of effects by reference to their causes. Obvious present examples would be the rules *attribute-agent* and *attribute-patient*. Somewhat less obvious examples would be rules *agent-move* and *patient-move*. These latter two synchronic rules might qualify for this sort of creation because they attribute internally caused movement or externally caused movement to a dispositional quality of the object, namely agency or non-agency, respectively.

The drawback to this creation technique, of course, is that it pushes the problem of rule creation onto another unsolved problem, that of causal reasoning. But a variety of psychological and computational techniques are converging on promising solutions to the causal reasoning problem (Anderson, 1987; Lewis, 1988; Pazzani, 1987; Shultz, 1987; Shultz and Kestenbaum, 1985). If causal reasoning is solved, and rule creation techniques can be built upon it, then causality would figure in the development of the concept of agency in a formal sense as well as in terms of conceptual content. We've already seen how the concept of agency grows out of a concern with the causation (or lack of causation) of movement. Now I am proposing as well a syntactic device for the construction of production rules that is based on causation.

Agency and Intention

Psychological evidence referred to above suggested that children develop a notion of agency by the end of the first year, but develop a notion of intention only by about three years (see chapter 3). It was also speculated that intention involves an elaboration of the concept of agency. The infant may realize that an agent acts on its own, but not yet understand how the agent's intentional states control and produce it's actions. I would further speculate that intentional predicates will figure only in analysing the behaviour of objects already classed as agents. The child will see intentional predicates as being irrelevant or inapplicable to objects that he or she has classified as patients.

Agency, Animacy and Animalness

A concept related to agency that has been much studied in developmental psychology is that of *animacy*. As early as the 1920s, Piaget (1929) was asking children which things were alive and which were not. It might be thought that children's notions of agency would be restricted to, or be synonymous with, their notion of animacy. Perhaps they believe that only animate beings can be agents. However, developmental data on the contents of children's beliefs can be cited to rule out this possibility. Contemporary research has indicated that the child's use of biological functions such as growth and reproduction to characterize animate beings begins to appear only in the elementary school years (Carey, 1985). Agency, of course, is known to appear much earlier than this. Habituation experiments with four-year-olds suggest that they can attribute agency and perhaps even intentionality to inanimate objects which move in particular patterns (Dasser, Ulbaek and Premack, 1989; chapter 17). So agency is not identical to, nor does it derive from, the concept of animacy.

Another related concept is what we might call *animalness*, the distinction between animals and non-animals. Massey and Gelman (1988) have proposed that children's concern with causation of movement constrains their concept of animal. They claim that the animal–nonanimal distinction serves as a basis for the later animate–inanimate distinction. I would add to this the claim that the concept of agency serves as basis for both of these later concepts: animalness and animacy. The child may use agency to differentiate animals from non-animals (animals often move on their own) and to differentiate animate from inanimate objects (animate objects often move on their own). This leads to the occasional classification errors that Piaget (1929) and others have observed (e.g., claiming that a floating leaf is alive), but it at least gives the child a promising start in constructing these more subtle concepts.

A methodological key to distinguishing among the child's concepts of agency, animalness, and animacy is *plants*. Plants are alive, but they are not animals or agents. Psychologists should question children about plants and their capabilities!

Behaviour or Motion?

Throughout this paper, I have been stressing that detection of agency depends on analysing the motion of objects. But motion is only one sort of behaviour that objects can engage in, albeit a particularly vivid sort of behaviour. *Emission of behaviour* would be a more general notion than is motion *per se*. Objects can, for example, emit noise. Although noise is motion, children undoubtedly do not view it as such, at least initially. So the possibility exists for production rules dealing with agency to rely on behaviour in general, not just on motion.

Continuity of Development

Another point concerns the issue of continuity of development in the emergence of the concept of agency. Is development in this area continuous and gradual or is it rather marked by discontinuities? On this issue, I tend to agree with Siegler (1986) who claimed that continuity depends mainly on how closely one looks at the phenomenon. When viewed from afar, many changes appear to be discontinuous. But when viewed close up, the same changes can be seen to be part of a continuous, gradual progression. From afar, we notice the appearance of qualitatively different concepts of agency, intention and embedded intention. But closer up, one can see that fairly small, modular changes in individual production rules can produce enormous qualitative differences in the system's overall performance. We saw, for example, that if a single synchronic rule lacks a condition testing for the presence or absence of an external cause of motion, this can affect predictions and explanations about large numbers of objects.

Relating to Psychology and Primatology

In multidisciplinary study, it is common to provide an explicit statement of how one's work is related to other disciplines. In the present case, the relevant disciplines are developmental psychology and primatology. I believe the primary implication of my work for these other approaches is a plea to consider reasoning mechanisms and transition mechanisms in addition to documenting beliefs and abilities in children and other animals. Knowing how the animal reasons with beliefs and other knowledge states is likely to provide needed constraints on the much-sought-after theories of transition.

Conclusions

A line of research in our laboratory has been concerned with developing psychologically plausible and computationally sufficient models of reasoning about intentional states. A program called JIA simulates, in a rule-based framework, the processes involved in determining whether an action or outcome of an action is intended. Subsequent work showed how embedded intentional phenomena, such as false beliefs and strategic deception, could also be modeled with rules. The use of linked data structures was seen to offer a coherent solution to the problems created by embeddedness.

Psychological work with young children suggested that the concept of intention develops out of an earlier notion of agency. Agency explains that a being moves or behaves of its own accord. Intention elaborates on this by postulating an internal mental state that guides or controls behaviour.

In the present paper, I began to offer a computational account of early knowledge of agency. The goal was to gain some insight into how such knowledge is represented, how it figures in later knowledge of intention, and how it develops. Some key performance productions were identified and tested in a working program, but a more complete model would contain additional performance productions and mechanisms for modifying or creating new productions. A collection of such productions would implement a theory whose predictions can be tested against actual data.

One of the essential things infants need in this arena is to distinguish agents from non-agents. Computationally, the required knowledge can be formulated by synchronic, classification rules. Many infant researchers agree that autonomous movement is a critical element in making this distinction. Recent evidence suggests that such synchronic rules are typically present by the end of the first year of life. These synchronic rules are used in the service of other, diachronic rules that specify how to act towards objects and what to expect from objects. This paper examined the structure and content of such rules and identified supporting psychological evidence for their existence.

Young children's failure on agency tasks is likely due to their use of either less-refined, diachronic rules or rules with an incorrect synchronic classification of objects. Such faulty rules could be based on a too limited degree of experience with agentive phenomena. The primary symptom of these faulty rules is a tendency to generate false positive errors. Such errors can often be corrected by adding relevant condition elements to the rules.

The concept of agency was seen to be an important precursor of several more advanced concepts including intention, animacy and animalness. It was argued that intentional predicates would only be applied to objects already known to be agents since intention essentially elaborates on how agents plan and produce their autonomous behaviour. It was surmised that the child might use agency to build the concepts of animalness and animacy. Animals, but not non-animals, often move on their own. So do animate, but not inanimate, objects.

Although the present work emphasized motion as an important discriminating feature of objects, it was noted that the emission of behaviour would be a more general concept to generate knowledge of agency.

Finally, it was argued that issues about the continuity of development depend on how closely one looks. When viewed from afar, many developmental changes appear to be discontinuous. But when viewed close up, the same changes are seen to be part of a continuous, gradual progression. Small, modular changes in even a single rule can produce enormous qualitative differences in a system's overall performance.

APPENDIX: NOTATION

All of our ETM production rules are written for an interpreter called OPS5 (Official Production System; Forgy, 1981). OPS5 allows the use of both primitive and compound data types. Primitive data types are either numbers or symbolic atoms. One of the most useful compound data types is the *element class*. An element class is declared as follows:

```
(literalize class
   attribute₁
   attribute₂
   . . .
   attributeₙ)
```

Literalize is an OPS5 command, *class* refers to the name of the element class, and this is followed by the names of the various attributes of this class. Both the class and attribute names are arbitrarily specified by the programmer. As instances of element classes get created, each attribute can take a value, in the form of a primitive data type (i.e., a number or symbolic atom). Readers familiar with frame data structures will recognize that OPS5 element classes are fairly simple frames, without the elaborations one often sees in full-scale frame representation languages. In frame systems, the class name is typically known as the frame name, and the attributes are typically called slots.

In our work on modelling ETM phenomena, we have found it sufficient to use a single, uniform element class that we call *s*, for sentence. Each sentence is composed of three principal syntactic components: *agent, action* and *object*. The agent and action components are required; the object component is optional. Whereas actions are constants, represented as symbolic atoms, the agents and objects of a sentence can be either constants or variables and can be further elaborated as another sentence. This elaboration provides for the possibility of nested or embedded representations, which, as explained above, are critical to the successful modelling of intentional phenomena. To help keep track of the semantics of this embedding, we have added two other attributes, *id* and *embed-in*. The id attribute provides each sentence with a unique name, which in actual data elements is rendered as the name of sentence's action followed by a unique number. The embed-in attribute indicates where this particular sentence is embedded. Its value will be either the id of the embedding sentence or *nil*, to indicate that this sentence is not embedded but rather exists at the top level. Comments in OPS5 code are preceded by the ; symbol. They are not read by the program but exist solely for the convenience of human users. Here is the commented declaration of the element class *s*.

```
(literalize s  ; sentence
   id        ; action + unique ;needed only with embedding
   agent     ; name of agent or id of embedded sentence
   action    ; name of action
   object    ; name of object or id of embedded sentence
   embed-in); nil or id of embedding sentence
```

In boxes 6.1–8 one can see that OPS5 productions consist of an OPS5 command p (for Production), a unique name, a left-hand side that consists of one or more condition elements, the symbol→, and a right-hand side that consists of a sequence of actions. Each condition element in our models consists of a sentence (as defined above). Sentences, whether in working memory or in production rules, employ the ^ symbol as a prefix to attribute names. The attribute values in each such sentence may be constants, represented as symbolic atoms, or variables, surrounded by angled brackets <>. Each such condition specifies a pattern that is to be matched against working memory. When all the condition elements of a production are simultaneously satisfied with consistent variable bindings, the production is said to be instantiated and thus becomes a candidate for firing. If an instantiated production is selected for firing, then all of the OPS5 commands on the production's right-hand side are executed in order. The principal command used in the present programs is the *make* command. *Make* takes a sentence as its argument and creates a new element in working memory having the class and attribute values of this sentence. More formally, *make* takes as arguments an element class name and a sequence of attribute–value pairs. Any variables in this sentence are bound to values consistent with those in the production's left-hand side before the new element is deposited in working memory.

7

How to Read Minds in Behaviour: A Suggestion from a Philosopher

Jonathan Bennett

1 Introduction

Underlying empirical questions about how human and non-human animals behave and why, is this: By what formula should we go from premises about behaviour to conclusions about thoughts? In discussing this I shall focus on two thoughtful states – belief and desire.

Neither of these can help to explain behaviour except when combined with the other. Behaviour shows what the animal wants only if we know what it thinks, and conversely. The guiding idea is triangular: cognitive explanations of behaviour are possible only because the animal *does* what it *thinks* will produce what it *wants*. In chapter 2 Henry Wellman reports that very young children interpret the behaviour of others through a psychology using something like the concept of desire but not the concept of belief. Wellman suggests that the child's conative concept is that of a 'simple want', where 'Sam wants the apple' relates Sam to the apple without requiring him to have any kind of mental representation of the apple. I would rather say this: Whereas a five-year-old predicts what x will do on the basis of what it thinks x wants and *what it (the child) thinks x believes about the world*, a two-year-old does it on the basis of what it thinks x wants and *what it (the child) believes about the world*. The very young child is using a belief–desire psychology, but a restricted one in which only the attributer's beliefs are attributed to the subject. This account may even be substantively equivalent to Wellman's own. Either way, there is no conflict between his work and mine.

So we need to build our account of an animal's beliefs and desires by tackling both at once. That might seem to expose our theory to the risk of vacuity, leaving too unconstrained a choice about what thoughts and wants to attribute to the animal because whatever we say under one heading can be made to fit the behaviour by an adjustment under the other. The animal uttered that piercing scream because it wanted to eat the eagle and thought that the scream would make the eagle fall dead. That is absurd, of course; but we should be able to reject it for some more disciplined reason than that – we need a principled, theoretical protection against uncontrollably free trade-offs between the attributions of beliefs and the attributions of desires.

We are somewhat protected because we can connect attributions of beliefs to facts about the animal's environment. The tie must be mediated by theory about what the animal is sensitive to, but there are ways of checking on that. We are further protected because we can safely attribute to animals desires that are fairly constant across time, except for changes linked to knowable changes in the animal's condition – it wanted food an hour ago but since then it has gorged, and so on. That constancy lets us check attributions of desires at one time against later attributions; and that constrains attributions further, helping to stop the slide into absurdity. If the constancy were not there, and an animal's basic desires changed rapidly with no external pointers to the changes, its behaviour would be unpredictable and therefore unexplainable. For evolutionary reasons, however, there are no such animals.

I shall now take for granted that we have principled ways of avoiding interpretations of animal behaviour that are absurd and obviously not worth entertaining.

That, however, leaves plenty of choices needing to be made, and plenty of disagreements about them. I want to clarify what is at stake in those disagreements and help to resolve them. When front-line workers on animal cognition disagree about what states of mind are revealed by what behaviour, they often seem not to agree about what evidence *would* settle the disputes. Everyday working and arguing standards seem to be insecure and idiosyncratic, and that is the situation in which I shall offer some ideas that may be helpful.

2   The Economy Rule

One popular methodological idea is the view that we should always explain behaviour as economically as possible: don't atrribute cognitive states to an animal whose behaviour you can explain without invoking them, and in your cognitive attributions don't go 'higher' on the scale than is needed to explain the behaviour. This 'economy rule' condemns saying that when the chimpanzee Sherman made the sign for a rake he wanted Austin to *think that he (Sherman) wanted the rake*, because the behaviour could as well be covered by supposing that Sherman merely wanted Austin to *bring the rake*. That condemnation seems right, and probably a lot of what goes wrong in psychology and cognitive ethology comes from the kind of interpretative overreaching that the economy rule forbids.

However, the rule could not do all our work for us. If we have competing cognitive explanations that do not differ in complexity, sophistication, or whatever it is that feeds into the notion of 'higher', the rule is silent. There, at least, we need more theory.

Even where the economy rule does have something to say, we should ask for its credentials. *Why* should we always accept the 'lower' or more economical of two unrefuted explanations? Is it because we should always assume things to be homogeneous or unstructured unless we have positive evidence to the contrary? But then why should we believe that?

Having accepted the economy rule for years, I now think that we have mistaken its status, and that no deep truth underlies it. I shall justify this in the next two sections.

3   The Economy Rule as Advice

If the rival explanations are not empirically equivalent – if they predict different behaviour – then we should look for or try to elicit further behaviour that fits only one of them. Suppose we are trying to decide whether, when the animal screams like that, this is because it wants others to climb trees or because it wants them to think there is a leopard nearby. Then we should simply try to find out which of these is right. These hypotheses differ in what they imply for the animal's behaviour, I shall argue, and that behaviour should be the final arbiter. The economy rule does no real work here.

Still, it might function as good advice, telling us to expect that the behavioural data will eventually favour the 'lower' rather than the 'higher' hypothesis, and perhaps advising us to adopt the former as our provisional opinion until the facts are in. This may be generally good advice, but only because on our planet most mentality happens to be fairly low-level. There could be planets where most vaguely goal-seeking behaviour really did involve cognition, and high-level cognition at that; on such planets the advice issued by the economy rule would be bad.

Because I am interested in the *foundations* of the activity of attributing cognitive states on the strength of behaviour, I exclude linguistic behaviour. Much cognition is expressed without language, and we need to understand how. Also, even where language is present, we can recognize it as language – can know that the speaker means something – only because we can, independently of language, discover things about what he thinks and wants. (so I argue in Bennett, 1976). But although I exclude language, my 'animals' include very young humans; and where they are concerned the economy rule's advice – 'Expect the "lower" hypothesis to be right' – may be bad.

Andrew Whiten has remarked that the same might be true for chimpanzees. I agree. Some observed chimpanzee behaviour certainly 'feels' like an expression of fairly high-level cognition (see for example the best cases in Whiten and Byrne, 1988a; chapter 9), and even where one can produce a 'lower', deflating explanation of the data (as in Bennett, 1988a) we may reasonably suspect that in some cases a 'higher' explanation is right. Eventually, however, suspicion should give way to firm evidence.

That, incidentally, will often require not merely hands-off observation of animals' natural behaviour (see chapters 9 and 10) but also conduct that is elicited from the animals by experimentally rigging their environments and their experience (e.g. chapters 12 and 17). Experiments involve certain theoretical risks, which are the price for great practical advantages. Hands-off work is the best *if it can be done*; but I conjecture that definitive answers to our questions will always require experiments. (For good remarks on this, see Dennett 1988 and forthcoming.)

4   Empirically Equivalent Rivals

There can be rivalry between hypotheses which, though one goes 'higher' than the other, are empirically equivalent. The 'higher' one must include something explaining why the extra psychological capacity is not used. The lower one might be:

L: The animal has the concepts of one, two, and three, and the concept of equal-numberedness, but not the number four,

and its rival:

H: The animal has the concepts one, two, three, four, and equal-numberedness, but it cannot use its concept of four except in doing number comparisons between quartets and other groups.

How could we choose between these? Well, H credits the animal with two more items than L does – namely an extra concept, and a blockage to its exercise – so it makes the animal more complex than L does. Whether we should accept H depends on whether we can justify the extra complexity.

What would justify it? Well, in developing a theory of the animal's internal cognitive dynamics – about how some changes in its beliefs lead to others – we might find that our smoothest explanation for its grasp of one, two and three implies that it also has the concept of four; and we might have evidence for its having a natural class of cognitive obstacles that would include an inability to employ *four* except in that one way. In that (admittedly fanciful) case, we should prefer H; but without something like that L should be preferred, not because it is lower but because it is less complex and greater complexity is not justified. This coincides with what the economy rule says, but it comes not from that rule but from perfectly general considerations about simplicity and complexity.

5   A First Stab at Answering My Question

Faced with rival hypotheses that have different empirical consequences, I said, we should get evidence that knocks out one of them. That is easier said than done. Even harder than devising and conducting the tests is figuring out what would count as evidence for or against an hypothesis. That was my initial question: What behaviour indicates what states of mind? So far, all I have done is to take the economy rule down from the throne, while not banishing it from court. Let us start again.

Any explanation of animal behaviour is answerable to a *class* of behavioural episodes. If we have only one episode to go on, we can interpret it only by guessing what *would* happen on other relevant occasions. I shall assume henceforth that we are always trying to explain a longish sequence of behaviours, trying to bring them all under a single explanation.

Suppose we have observed a class of behaviours of which something of this form is true: 'Whenever the animal receives a stimulus of sensory kind S, it engages in behaviour of motor kind M.' For example: Whenever its visual field presents a clear sky with a black patch near the middle of it, and occupying at least one per cent of the field, the animal utters a specific kind of noise.

Here are two rival explanations for this behaviour. (1) The animal has an innate or acquired stimulus–response disposition; it is hard- or soft-wired to make that noise upon receipt of that visual stimulus. On each occasion in the class it received such a stimulus and accordingly made the noise. (2) The animal has the safety of its group as a goal. On each occasion in the class it thought it saw a predator and called to warn others of danger.

To test (1) we should vary the circumstances while still presenting that kind of stimulus, and see whether the animal still gives that call. To the extent that it does, the hypothesis is confirmed. Of course, the call might be triggered by another kind (or other kinds) of stimulus as well. Suppose we discover that the animal does also make such a cry whenever it gets a stimulus of some third kind, then a fourth, a fifth . . . and on into dozens of different kinds of sensory intake, each leading to the same kind of behaviour. If this happens, we are under increasing pressure to find some unifying account of all this behaviour, some *one* explanation to replace the multitude of separate stimulus–response ones that we have accumulated.

(1) There might be no way of doing this. (2) Or we might find that there is after all a single sensory kind of stimulus on all the occasions – a subtle smell or a high-pitched sound – enabling us to cover all the cries by a single stimulus–response generalization, after all. (3) Or we might find that we could bring all the episodes under a single generalization but not a stimulus–response one. Even if no one *sensory kind* of stimulus is shared by all the episodes – no configuration of colour, shape, smell, etc. – they may have *something* in common that lets us generalize across them, namely the fact that each of them *provides evidence to the animal that there is a predator nearby*. If they share that, and there is no more economical way of bringing them under a single generalization, that gives us evidence that the episodes are united in that way for the animal itself. That is tantamount to saying that in each episode the animal thinks there is a predator nearby.

What entitles us to bring the proposition *There is a predator nearby* into our description of the animal (through the statement that that's what it believes) is our having a class of behavioural episodes that can be united with help from the proposition *there is a predator nearby* and cannot be united in any simpler way. Our best unitary account says that in each environment where it calls *the animal has evidence that there is a predator nearby*. (What about 'There is a predator nearby'? *That* fact could not immediately help to explain the animal's behaviour. No fact about the environment could explain its behaviour except by being somehow registered upon or represented within the animal's mind.) The fact that we can unify the occasions with help from an embedded 'that P', and in no other way, justifies us in using an embedded 'that P' in explaining the behaviour.

I don't know a long history for the 'unification' idea proposed here, though it may have one. I propounded it in Bennett, 1964 (section 2) and Bennett, 1976; it is put to good effect in Whiten and Byrne; 1988a, where acknowledgement is also made to Dawkins, 1976.

The proposal is not merely about when we may explain behaviour by attributing beliefs, but also about what beliefs we may attribute. We get at belief content through what is perceived as common to all the environments in which the behaviour occurs. I shall return to this, the central theme in my paper, shortly.

First, a small correction is needed. The basic belief–desire–behaviour story must focus on beliefs about means to ends; that is, about what movements on the animal's part will bring about what it wants. We can attribute beliefs of other sorts – e.g. that there is a predator nearby – only *through* attributing beliefs about means to ends, which alone are immediately tied both to wants and to behaviour. When, therefore, we hypothesize that the animal calls because it thinks *there is a predator nearby*, that should be based on the hypothesis that it calls because it wants its companions to be safe and thinks that *that cry is a means to their being safe* because it thinks there is a predator nearby.

6 Thoughts About Thoughts: Preliminary Tidying

What would count as behavioural evidence for us that our animal has a thought about some other animal's mind? This thought could be either a belief or a desire, and what it is about could be either a belief or a desire.

Or an animal might have a thought about another animal's perceptual state. Our subject animal might behave in a certain way because of what it thinks about what another animal might hear or smell or otherwise take in. Supposed evidence for that kind of thought is often misleading. Usually, behaviour that is supposed to manifest the thought 'This will stop x from seeing y' or 'This will stop x from smelling y' could just as well be manifesting the thought 'This will put a physical object between x and y' or 'This will put y upwind from x'. How to get good evidence for thoughts about perceptions or sensory states is an interesting question, but I shan't discuss it here. (The chapter by Cheney and Seyfarth in this volume says interesting things about it). My topic is the more ambitious attribution of beliefs or desires whose topic is other beliefs or desires.

Such an attribution might fit into our explanatory schema in various ways. Here is one: We have evidence that our animal wants to achieve goal G and thinks that doing A will bring this about; and we don't see how it could arrive at that belief except through attributing a certain mental state to some other animal. For example, don't see how it could think its cry will make its companions safe except through thinking that the predator *wants* to eat them.

It will be hard to make that stick, however. Almost certainly, we shall be able to explain the basic attribution through the animal's thinking merely that the predator *will* eat the other if it catches them. That is, a supposed belief about a want should give way to a belief about a simple behavioural disposition if the latter covers the data as well.

I shan't discuss what would entitle us to attribute a belief about a predator's desire. I choose for detailed discussion the attribution of a desire to produce a belief. My treatment of that will indicate how in outline I would deal with the other belief–desire combinations.

7   Desires to Produce Thoughts: a Dilemma

What sort of evidence could entitle us to hypothesize that our animal behaves as it does because it *wants to produce a thought* in its companions, e.g. because it wants to get them to think there is a predator nearby?

It is highly improbable, in the non-human world, that our animal should want its companions to have the belief that P just for itself, as an intrinsic good. Let us focus on the less wild possibility that our animal wants its companions to believe that P because of how that belief will affect their behaviour. For example, it calls so as to get them to think there is a predator nearby, which it wants as a means to their behaving thus and so.

To be entitled to say that, we must rule out everything like this: The animal calls so as to get its companions to crawl under a bush. If they do behave thus whenever it calls, our animal may see its call as a trigger to produce the crawling, with no thought of what is companions will think. If it sometimes calls when its companions are already under bushes, that doesn't help, for it might always call so that it companions will *be* under a bush – going there or remaining there.

Objection: 'If our animal thinks that the cry will elicit the hiding behaviour, it must have some belief about *why* it will do so; and the most likely candidate for this is a belief that the cry will cause the others to believe that there is a predator nearby.' This presupposes that a means-to-end belief must be accompanied by a belief about why that means leads to that end; which is absurd. Across the centuries most human means-to-end beliefs have been merely empirical – accepted without any grasp of why they are true, simply because they are confirmed by past experience. If we can do that, why not other animals?

If our animal is to be credited with wanting to produce not merely behaviour but a belief in its companions, the evidence must be enriched – but how? We have to suppose that our animal wants to give the others a belief as a means to their using it in their behaviour, but we don't want evidence that: our animal calls as a means to producing a belief which it wants as a means to producing behaviour

to collapse into

evidence that: our animal calls as a means to producing behaviour,

with the intended belief dropping out, not attributed because there is no work it needs to do.

8 A Way of Escape

I know only one solution to this dilemma. Suppose that in the series of episodes when our animal calls, its companions act variously, depending on their states and situations: if they are F, they run; if they are G, they search; if they are H, they freeze; if they are J, they climb; if they are K, they dig . . . and so on; and whatever each animal does is appropriate to the information that there is a predator nearby. Can we still interpret our animal's purpose in calling as merely to elicit behaviour? Here is how such an interpretation would go:

The animal's past experience has shown it that when it calls like that its companions run if they are F or search if they are G or freeze if they are H or climb if they are J or dig if they are K or . . . and on this occasion it wants them to run if they are F or search if they are G or freeze if they are H or climb if they are J or dig if they are K or . . . and so it calls.

This is now crediting our animal with a thought of implausible complexity. We can simplify the story and make it more credible by supposing that our animal unites the complex thought

run if they are F or search if they are G or freeze if they are H or climb if they are J or dig if they are K or . . .

into the unitary thought

behave appropriately to the fact that there is a predator nearby.

That brings their behaviour under a description – call it D – that has nested within it the complete proposition that *There is a predator nearby.* If D is our best way of unifying all the behaviours of the group, that is evidence that on those occasions the animals believe that there is a predator nearby. And if our simplest statement of what our subject knows about its companions and of what it wants also uses D, that is evidence that when it calls it does so because it wants them to believe there is a predator nearby.

9   A Further Difficulty Resolved

This is still not right, however. In the story as I have told it, the calling animal's success on each relevant occasion consists in this: Its companions don't get eaten. Suddenly we slump back into a simple story that is purely physicalistic once more, and not psychological. What it knows from past experience is that if it gives that cry when there is a predator nearby, its companions don't get eaten; it doesn't want them to get eaten now when there is a predator nearby; so it calls again. That is not horrendously complex, and it does not credit our animal with a thought about a thought.

So we are back at square one! But if my general strategy has been right, we can see what would in principle deal with this latest trouble and – at last – have a chance of keeping us out of trouble. What is needed is that the animals have a variety of uses for the information that a predator is nearby. There is little hope of that, so let us switch from predators. Suppose there is some other kind of object – call it a Quark – which our animals can use in different ways, depending on their condition and circumstances: they can eat it, shelter under it, use it to crack open coconuts . . . and so on. If the range of appropriate responses to the information that there is a Quark nearby is sufficiently various, and if it doesn't all come together again in some one upshot of all these different activities (like escaping the predator), then we can say that the calling animal calls so as to get the others to think there is a Quark nearby. Without such variety, I can find no justification for attributing to our animal any desire to produce a belief.

I have brought us to a point that may seem to lie beyond anything that is true of actual non-human animals. If so, then I am committed to saying that we shan't ever get good evidence that any non-human animal wants to produce a belief. Maybe we could still have evidence that animals sometimes want to produce desires, or have beliefs about beliefs or desires; though I suspect that those would be no easier than the other. I don't know how pessimistic to be about this: it is early days yet, some observations of chimpanzee behaviour (at least) are suggestive, and there is much more experimental work to be done.

10   A Final Unsolved Problem

I have described a procedure for deciding what mental content to attribute to an animal. I have offered contentions of the form: If an animal's behaviour is thus and so, such and such thoughts can be attributed to it; and secondly I have suggested that the attributions will be unjustified if the animal's behaviour does not conform to the patterns that I have described. Never mind the second bit; let us focus on the first, which says that my procedure is correct, so that adherence to it will reliably lead to true attributions of thoughts to animals.

If my procedure is in that sense correct, *why is it correct*? What is the logical status of truths of the form 'If the animal's behaviour exhibits this and that input–output pattern then it has such and such mental content'? Two broad kinds of answer, introduced by Whiten & Perner in chapter 1, should be distinguished.

(1)   When we attribute a belief or desire to an animal, we are saying something about its inner state – something that goes beyond any facts about how it behaves – and the facts about its behaviour are merely reliable pointers to those inner states.

(2)   When we attribute a belief or desire to an animal, *all* we are doing is to say something complex about its patterns of behaviour. The behaviour is not evidence of the animal's having inner states of belief and desire; rather, to behave like that *is* to have beliefs and desires.

There is much controversy between the adherents of the two positions. In earlier decades, the friends of (1) would characterize beliefs and desires as 'mental' in some way that puts them outside the physical world. This Cartesian view has fallen into deserved disfavour, but (1) still has its friends, who say that what makes it the case that an animal thinks that P or wants G is some fact about its brain-state and not about how it behaves.

This has its attractions, and just twice in this chapter I have allowed myself turns of phrase that align me with it.

In section 5, I wrote that if a class of behavioural episodes share some feature F 'and there is no more economical way of bringing them under a single generalization, that gives us evidence that the episodes are united [by F] for the animal itself'. That implies that when the animal has (whether in a belief or a desire) a thought that is applicable to a variety of situations, it really does *have something* that *enables* it to treat all those situations in one same way. This implies a kind of inner realism about mental content. If I wanted not to commit myself to that, and to remain free to give answer

(2) to the status question, I ought to have written not 'that gives us evidence that the episodes are united in that way for the animal itself' but rather 'that entitles us to avail ourselves of that unity in what we say about what the animal thinks'. For a (2) theorist, the concepts of belief and desire are conveniences, aids in the management of certain complex facts about animal behaviour, but they don't have to correspond to items in the animal which enable it to manage its complex data.

In section 8 I wrote that if in a certain case we credit an animal with a thought about behaviour but not one about thoughts, we must credit it with a thought of implausible complexity. That was in the spirit of Premack's statement, quoted in chapter 1, that 'The ape could only be a mentalist . . . he is not intelligent enough to be a behaviourist'. My remark and Premack's both imply that when we credit an animal with a simple thought about a thought rather with a complex thought about behaviour, our attribution doesn't merely apply a conceptualization that serves our theoretical purposes but credits the animal with having a simplifying *something* inside it, a something that makes its behavioural data more manageable to it.

Well, I do sometimes find it natural to write like that. But at other times I am not so sure. Suppose we discovered for sure what enabled the animal to engage in the complex behavioural pattern on the basis of which we have attributed the belief that P. Suppose, specifically, that we found that this pattern of behaviour was possible simply because the animal's brain contains thousands of different though interrelated mechanisms, each dealing with a different input-output pair, and that no *one* item in the animal was in any way responsible for the belief-manifesting pattern. If we knew all that, would we still be willing to attribute to the animal the belief that P? Sometimes I am strongly inclined to answer 'Why not?', which aligns me with answer (2) to the status question.

This issue is discussed in chapters 1 and 21 of this volume. The present chapter scrutinizes it, but has made no attempt to answer it.

8

Planning and Plan Recognition from a Computational Point of View

CHARLES F. SCHMIDT AND STACY C. MARSELLA

Introduction

Beliefs, goals and intentions are particularly interesting entities to the psychologist. They are interesting because an organism that has the capacity to use representations which capture the semantics associated with their use can reason about states of affairs that are not true of its current world, and, perhaps, not even true of any possible world which the organism will enter. By definition, planning to achieve some goal involves the use and representation of states of affairs that are not true of the current world. And, plan recognition involves attributing to some other acting agent beliefs about past, present, and possible future states of affairs as well as an intent to bring about some future state of affairs. Further, the ability to plan and recognize the possible plans of other agents does not require an ability to use language. Thus, the absence of language does not imply that the organism does not have the ability to plan or recognize the plans of other agents.

The possession of a symbol system is required in order to achieve the full semantics that are typically associated with the capacity to represent beliefs and goals. In order to explicate the sense in which this statement is true, we will focus on the possible role of such representations in the various models of planning and plan recognition that have been developed within AI. It is necessary to consider such models because the question of whether an organism possesses and uses such representations cannot be decided on strictly empirical grounds. As will become clearer as we proceed, it turns out that for any particular situation within which some pattern of behaviour is observed we can always write down a computational model that can generate that behaviour without resorting to any symbolic representation of beliefs and the like. Consequently, we will complement the empirical arguments with a more top–down argument. This argument will involve showing what must be presumed if particular observed patterns of behaviour are explained without resorting to the use of representations of beliefs and goals. Thus, the pattern of the argument will be similar to that of *reductio ad absurdum* rather than the presentation of a specific computational model that utilizes beliefs and goals to control its behaviour and to recognize the plans realized in the behaviour of another organism.

From a computational point of view, questions of the specific content of a representation are subsidiary to questions of how it is used. In particular, the concern is with whether the use of a particular representation is required to realize the computation of some function or allows a more efficient realization of the computation of some function. What function corresponds to our intuitive ideas about planning or about plan recognition? This can not be answered directly. But, we can develop various computational models of planning or plan recognition. Such models provide a basis for understanding the computational role of beliefs as well as the difficulties and advantages that accrue from reasoning with such representations.

Computationally Characterizing Planning

Artificial intelligence (AI) has focused much of its research efforts on problems which humans can usually solve successfully but for which it is known or believed that any algorithm that guarantees a correct solution to the full set of problems will for some subset of these problems be so inefficient that the algorithm's use is not practical. We will say that problems with this characteristic are intractable.

An AI approach to studying planning and plan recognition begins by specifying a functional definition, the desired input/output behaviour, of planning or plan recognition. The next step is to attempt to define, implement and study an algorithm that meets these specifications by viewing the problem as one of symbolic search. That is, the algorithm is designed to transform syntactically structured symbolic expressions until some expression is recognized that constitutes a solution to the given problem. Thus, the AI method begins with a computational system that represents and uses a symbolic system (cf. Newell and Simon, 1976). This computational approach is useful since creating some well-defined models of planning and plan recognition can at least provide a basis for describing what might be meant when we say that a person can plan or can recognize the plans of other agents.

Planning is generally defined within AI as a function that takes as input a problem and provides as output a solution to the given problem. More specifically, a problem is defined as a pair of partial situation descriptions where the first member of the pair describes the starting or initial situation and the second member describes the goal situation. A solution is typically defined as a fully or partially ordered sequence of actions such that the final action in this sequence results in a situation that implies that the partial description of the goal situation is true. A more general definition of the idea of a solution, and the one that we employ, is that a solution is a structuring of the information required to support the execution of a sequence of actions that result in a situation implied by the goal description. A partially ordered sequence of actions is a special case of this definition of a solution. This more general definition is preferable for studying planning when the planner is actually going to execute the actions.

Note that it is assumed that a method for realizing the planning function represents initial and goal situations symbolically. More informally, situations represent the planning system's beliefs about the world and its own goals. If its world is populated by other intelligent agents, then it may also have beliefs about the beliefs and goals of these other agents if these are required by the planning process.

Planning algorithms usually employ some variation of a search method known as *problem reduction*. In this method a problem is decomposed into sub-problems. A sub-problem is syntactically of the same form as a problem, that is, it consists of a situation pair describing its starting situation and goal situation. These sub-problems may themselves be further decomposed until only primitive sub-problems remain. In planning, a sub-problem is primitive if the agent can carry out an action in the starting situation of that sub-problem which yields the goal situation associated with that sub-problem. The recursive decomposition of a problem into sub-problems yields an ANDed hierarchy or tree of sub-problems. The sub-problems are ANDed in the sense that the problem dominating the ANDed node is solved only if each sub-problem dominated by that node is solved. Thus, a problem is solved if the AND tree terminates in primitive sub-problems. This search through a space of possible problem decompositions is realized using two types of rules. One type is referred to as non-terminal rules and the other as terminal rules. Non-terminal rules serve to rewrite a problem as a set of ANDed sub-problems. Terminal rules recognize primitive sub-problems.

In this method, planning is determined by (1) the problem, i.e., the starting situation and the goal situation; (2) the planner's knowledge of possible decompositions, the non-terminal rules; and (3) the actions that an actor is capable of carrying out, the terminal rules. The planner's knowledge is extensible if new non-terminal rules can be acquired. Note that the *derivation* of a course of action, i.e, the tree of sub-problems, is obtained in a top-down and goal-driven fashion. This derivation constitutes the solution to the planning function. Planning via this method is very similar to the style of reasoning involved in providing a proof for some conjecture (cf. Amarel, 1967). The conjecture in planning is that a particular goal can be achieved from a particular starting situation. The non-terminal rules can be thought of as introducing further conjectures about the intermediate situations that, if reached, will yield achievement of the goal. The terminal rules allow a conjecture to be 'proved'. Retention of the derivation tree allows a plan to be critiqued and revised in a potentially efficient fashion. Retention of the derivation can also serve to support monitoring the execution of the plan. The assumptions on which the plan was based can be checked and, if incorrect, attempts to revise the plan can be initiated or the plan abandoned. Thus, plans that fail are still in some sense rational, they were simply based on an incorrect model or set of assumptions.

Computational Difficulties in Planning

There are two major difficulties that are encountered by this method of planning. Recall that the assumptions introduced in planning are assumptions about some partial ordering of situations that can be achieved. These situations represent assumptions or beliefs about a possible history that can be realized in the world. Now, the world is usually quite a complicated place and our model of the world is at best only partially correct. Further, we often don't have certain knowledge about the world on which to base our model. So one major difficulty is simply that of modelling the world and the effects that our actions might have on the world. And, to make matters worse, it appears that for most worlds that we are interested in, a true model would itself be computationally intractable even if we possessed it. Consequently, planning is limited by the ability to reason correctly and efficiently about the effects of actions on the world. This limitation becomes even more serious when we must reason about the effects that other causal agents may have on the world in which we are planning to achieve some goal. No computational model solves this problem of tractably modelling a complex world. What problem reduction does provide is a way in which to plan and act despite its ultimate ignorance. That is, a plan is based on the assumptions about the world that the planner possesses. To the degree these assumptions constitute a good approximation to the way the world works, the planner will on average be successful. In social situations there is the additional possibility the actors can attempt to constrain their actions to accord with their assumptions about each other in order to sucessfully achieve coordination and cooperation.

In addition to the problem of modelling the effect of actions on the world, there is also the problem of dependency among sub-problems. It is usually the case that goals and sub-goals involve a conjunction of conditions and no single action can bring about this conjunctive goal or subgoals. Sub-problem dependency holds whenever the choice of *how* or *when* a sub-problem is achieved affects the ability to achieve other sub-problems. Sub-problem dependency is the norm rather than the exception. For example, if the goal is to have dinner and to see a play in New York City then seeing-a-play and having-dinner are two quite dependent sub-problems. One had best work out the seeing-a-play sub-problem first since the location and time of the performance will constrain how the having-dinner sub-problem is solved. None the less, the actions that achieve having-dinner may be executed prior to those involved in seeing-a-play.

There are three basic ways in which planning systems have attempted to cope with sub-problem dependency. One is to solve the sub-problems as if they are independent and await the 'verdict' of the terminal rules which in essence determine whether the action(s) associated with each primitive sub-problem can be carried out in the starting situation of the sub-problem. If not, the procedure backtracks and tries another. If this procedure is followed exhaustively, the search is through a space of possible decompositions and their permutations (e.g., Fikes, Hart and Nilsson, 1971). This can be a very large space to search (Chapman 1987). Another procedure defines a metalevel of knowledge which can access the current tree of derivations and recognize such dependencies and then potentially adjust the current derivation appropriately (e.g., Sacerdoti, 1977; Amarel, 1983; Stefik, 1981; Schmidt, 1985). A third way is simply to know in advance that such dependencies exist and allow this knowledge to guide the derivation of a solution (Bresina, Marsella and Schmidt, 1987). These variations on ways of dealing with sub-problem dependencies yield differing planning models that have been developed within AI.

In summary, the method of problem reduction provides a computational model of planning that: (1) ensures that each action selected is logically related to the goal; and, (2) depends on the agent's beliefs about, and model of, the world in which the plan is to be executed. Further, the employment of this method yields a tree of derivation which, if retained in some fashion, can be used by the agent to critique and modify the plan as well as intelligently monitor its execution. These features of the computational model of planning accord quite well with our informal concept of a plan.

From Planning to Plan Recognition

Given a definition of planning, recognizing (others') plans can be defined as a kind of inverse of the planning function; that is, as a function which takes as input a temporally ordered description of a sequence of actions and associated situation changes and provides as output the assumptions about the actor's beliefs, goals and plan or plans that imply the observations. Because plans can fail or be abandoned, assumptions about the actor's beliefs often must be explicitly provided. An action sequence describes what happened whereas the plan attributed to the actor describes what the actor intended to happen.

If actions are understood by attempting to recover the plan or plans that the actor was executing, then this model of planning accounts for a sense in which the observer attributes rationality to the actor. The derivation of a plan creates a logically coherent structuring of the beliefs, intents, and goal of the actor. However, a cursory glance at a statement of the basic axioms that govern the inference of plans from actions suggests quite force-fully that this might be a computationally formidable problem (cf. Schmidt, 1976). These axioms are presented in Box 8.1. The statement termed the Axiom of Personal Causation asserts that for all actions, A, if some person, P, causes the action then there is some plan, M, of which A is a part. In addition, P believes that P can do M and P has some reason for choosing to do M. Thus, each action is assumed to be constrained by the situation,

Box 8.1   Some 'mindreading' axioms

Axiom of Personal Causation:

(Act A) (P cause A) → ((Some Plan M)
                     (A part of M)
                     (P believe (P can M))
                     (P choose M))

Axiom of Shared Assumption of Rationality:

(Person Q) (Q believes
                ((Person P) (Act A) (P cause A) →

                                ((Some Plan M)
                                  (A part of M)
                                  (P believe (P can M))
                                  (P choose M))))

capacities and beliefs of the actor together with the actor's reasons for choosing to carry out the action. The reasons for the actions are typically either the actor's belief that this action is necessary for the achievement of the overall goal or the action is a final action of the plan which achieves the overall goal directly. Note that the axiom simply states that each action is part of some plan. If one action is observed followed by another, the axiom states that they are each part of some plan. It does not state that each contiguous action is part of the *same* plan. Although the construction of a plan follows an orderly and logical process, this process is not necessarily reflected in a simple way in the action sequence. Contiguous actions may be part of the same plan or differing plans which happen to be temporally interleaved during execution.

Plan recognition is further complicated by the next axiom which states that this axiom is shared over all persons. This, of course, gives rise to the familiar recursive nature of beliefs (see chapter 1) and also provides a basis for cooperation, competition and deception. This creates, from a logical point of view, an extremely complex world in which to plan and recognize plans. Note, there is nothing that guarantees that any of the actors possess correct beliefs about the physical world or about the beliefs and goals of each other. Nor can there be any guarantee that the actors share the same beliefs, correct or incorrect. In fact, in general there is no way in which to guarantee that asynchronous distributed processes can always maintain a consistent 'set of beliefs' that constitute their common knowledge (cf. Halpern and Moses, 1984; Fischer and Immerman, 1986).

The observer's uncertainty about the beliefs and motivations of the actor, the fact that the actor may have based the plan on incorrect beliefs, the fact that plans can be interleaved, and the fact that a plan can fail or be abandoned all conspire to make plan recognition a challenging task. Further, the sequence of actions that are observed is simply a temporally ordered sequence of events. It may have a temporal rhythm or temporal breaks associated with it, but it has no logical beginning and end. A plan, on the other hand, has a definite beginning, the beliefs about the starting situation that served as a basis for the plan. It also has a definite end. When the world satisfies the goal situation of the plan, it has been completed. If the plan fails or is abandoned, it ends as well but in a less satisfactory sense. The planning process was driven by the planner's goal, but goal achievement is the last observation that the observer has available and goal achievement is an inference that results from the recognition process itself, not something that is perceptually marked.

A Plan-Recognition Strategy: Hypothesize and Revise

For these reasons, a plan-recognition process that exhaustively maintains the space of plans consistent with a set of observations will generally be intractable. A more tractable computational model generates a predictive hypothesis about the actor's goal or goals and utilizes these goal hypotheses to focus the observations and their interpretations. We have referred to this type of recognition strategy as a *hypothesize and revise strategy* (Schmidt, Sridharan and Goodson, 1978). It proceeds by generating the higher levels of the plan derivation as early as possible. This hypothesis is then revised in light of the unfolding observations. There is no guarantee that such a heuristic strategy will always succeed in identifying a set of plans that cover the observations. And, there is certainly no guarantee that the hypothesis is correct. None the less, it can yield a tractable strategy which can serve the observer well especially if the goals of the actor and the actions of the actor's plan obey the norms and conventions that are used to guide the observer's process of hypothesize and revise. Further, the logical coherence of a plan serves as a quite reliable basis for *disconfirmation* of the observer's hypothesis. Thus, even if we are not sure as to exactly what someone is up to, without an explicit attempt by the actor to deceive us, we often know that we don't know. This is more than an interesting consequence. It is crucial since it can itself serve as a basis for action on the part of the observer. Again, this ability to recognize failure to understand the beliefs and intents of another is crucial for the eventual achievement of cooperation and coordination of action among several actor/observers. If the logical coherence were not assumed, then even this strong basis for disconfirmation would be unavailable.

An Alternative to Symbolic Representation of Beliefs

Now up to this point, we have simply presented a brief sketch of some of the ways that planning and plan recognition have been formulated from a computational point of view. This computational approach assumes beliefs, beliefs about beliefs, intents and goals as part of its method for planning and plan recognition. But, must we make such seemingly strong assumptions about the cognitive ability of a device in order to achieve performance that we might informally characterize as intentional and plan-like? For many, the idea that young children, much less primates, have such capacities is at least debatable if not downright absurd. We leave to others in this volume who are much more expert in these matters to debate the specific merits of the case.

However, we can briefly sketch the alternative, again from a computational point of view. That is, let us systematically consider some computational models that can be phrased in a formalism in which symbols, and therefore beliefs and goals, cannot be represented. One reason for this tack is that the arguments *against* attributing beliefs and goals to some biological organism almost never present a constructive alternative account. There is, as we hope to briefly illustrate, good reason for this. Alternative accounts, accounts which do not resort to a computational model which can represent beliefs and goals themselves suffer from some rather severe problems.

It is often argued that a psychological theory of an organism's behaviour that does *not* assume that the organism can represent beliefs and goals is *simpler*, and thus preferable, to one that does make this assumption. Consequently, the burden of proof is often placed on the theorist who claims that such representations are part of the cognitive mechanism. But what would a computational theory that does *not* assume that the organism has the ability to represent and use beliefs look like? In this final section, we turn to an examination of the kind of theory of 'planning' or 'plan recognition' that can be stated if we restrict ourselves to a computational framework in which symbols, and thus beliefs, are unavailable. Planning and plan recognition are placed in quotes because these terms are defined in terms of the computational model that carries out these processes. A computational model in which beliefs and goals cannot be represented and used explicitly will obviously result in a different characterization of the process of planning and plan recognition.

In what sense is a theory that eschews the use of symbols and thus beliefs simpler? To say that one thing is simpler than another presumes that we have some uniquely appropriate metric to use to determine the simplicity of theories or explanations. If we take the view that our theories of behaviour are computational in character, then there is a well-defined metric used to order formal models of computation. Associated with each formal model of computation is a set of functions which can be computed using that model. If the set of functions that can be computed using one model are strictly included in the set that can be computed using another model, then we say that the more inclusive model is more powerful than the first. This yields a hierarchy of formal models of computation. At the bottom of this hierarchy, the least powerful, are finite state machines (FSM) or equivalently finite state grammars (FSG). At the top of this hierarchy are Turing machines or equivalently, unrestricted grammars. In this hierarchy, it is only the finite state machine model (FSM) that provides a formal model of computation that does not employ symbols. Thus, one well-defined construal of *simpler* is to say that a computational model or theory of behaviour is simpler than another if it is computationally less powerful than another. On this interpretation, any theory that is cast as a finite state machine would be simpler than another theory that is cast in a more powerful computational formalism. Then, a decision procedure might be to only state our theory within a formal system more powerful than a FSM when the 'data' demand it.

There are difficulties with this seemingly straightforward approach. The difficulties can be more easily appreciated if the basic structure of a finite state machine is defined (cf. Hopcroft and Ullman, 1979). A deterministic finite state machine (DFSM) is a 5-tuple (Q, Σ, ∂, q_ϕ, F), where Q is a finite set of states, Σ is a finite input alphabet, q_0 in Q is the initial state, F subset of Q is the set of final states, ∂ is the transition function mapping $Q \times \Sigma$ to Q, that is, $\partial(q,a)$ specifies a state from Q for each state q and input a. The input to a DFSM is a string, s, of elements from Σ. The set of all such possible input strings is symbolized as L, subset of Σ^*. This set may be infinite. The output of a DFSM is typically defined as 1 if the device accepts the string and 0 otherwise.

Figure 8.1 provides a transition diagram of a DFSM that accepts L, where L is the set of strings of the form $a^n b^m$ where $n > 0$ and $m > 0$. In this example, $\Sigma = \{a,b\}$; the set $Q = \{q_0, q_1, q_2\}$ are represented as nodes; q_0 is the initial state and q_2 the final state. The transition function ∂ is represented as the set of directed arcs between elements of Q annotated with an element from Σ.

It will often be more natural for our purposes to associate an output with

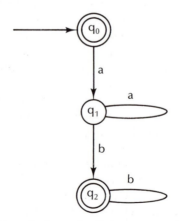

Figure 8.1   *State transition diagram of a finite state machine that accepts $a^n b^m$.*

each transition of the machine. In this case, the DFSM is defined by the 6-tuple $(Q, \Sigma, \triangle, \partial, \lambda, q_0)$. Here Q, Σ, ∂, and q_0 are defined as before. The set $\triangle$ is the output alphabet and λ is a mapping from $Q \times \Sigma$ to $\triangle$. DFSM with an associated output function are equivalent to the standard DFSM.

Figure 8.2 provides a transition diagram that exemplifies this type of DFSM. In this example $\Sigma = \{N, D, Q, C, P\}$ and $\triangle = \{a, r, c, p\}$. In the diagram, states are represented as nodes and the arcs represent state transitions. Each arc has a label of the form 'x/y' where 'x' is the input symbol associated with the transition and 'y' is the output. This machine can be thought of as accepting (a) nickels (N), dimes (D), or quarters (Q) as long as they contribute to an exact sum of 50 cents and rejecting (r) them otherwise. In the state 50 it accepts C and emits the action of providing a coke (c) or accepts P and emits the action of providing a pepsi (p). For future reference we will refer to this DFSM as the structured soda seller (SSS).

Finally, it will be useful to define a nondeterministic finite state machine (NFSM). This is again defined as a 5-tuple $(Q, \Sigma, \partial, q_0, F)$, where $Q, \Sigma,$ q_0, F have the same meaning as before, but ∂ is a mapping from $Q \times \Sigma$ to 2^Q rather than to Q. The set 2^Q is the power set of Q; that is, the set of all subsets of Q. An equivalent DFSM can be constructed for any NFSM.

It is important to keep the algebraic structure in mind to avoid reading more into this formal model than is really there. The state-transition view of this model of computation makes clear that the control of the computation is realized by the states and their connections. At any point in the computation, only the current state and current input event can affect the state transition. There is no memory for the path of state transitions that led to the current state and no memory for the previously processed input events. Similarly, future input events and future possible state transitions are unavailable to control the choice of a state transition.

It would seem to be extremely difficult to account for observations of an organism's actions or outputs in response to inputs from the environment using such an austere computational model. Surprisingly, the opposite is the case. As long as the set of <I,O> pairs is finite, we can always write down a FSM that can generate these <I,O> pairs. This can be done by adding, as needed, new elements to Σ, new states to Q, additional actions to $\triangle$, an extension of the transition function, ∂, and extension to the output mapping, λ, depending on which may be required to include any additional <I,O> pairs that may be observed. Even the most driven experimentalists among us will never observe more than a finite set of <I,O> pairs. Thus, we have a kind of paradox. What has often been taken by psychologists as the simplest and most parsimonious model, can in fact be very hard to

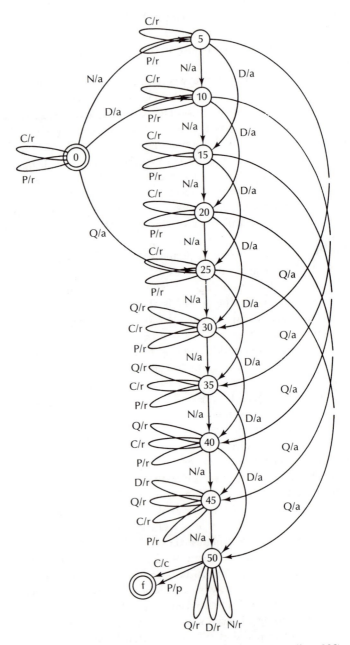

Figure 8.2 *State transition diagram of the Structured Soda Seller (SSS).*

falsify empirically. At the limit a finite state machine can have no more structure than an arbitrary finite list of rules. A theory that is simply a list is certainly simplistic. Whether it also corresponds to our intuitive notion of a simple theory is another matter.

Figure 8.3 illustrates a NFSM that is nothing more than a list of a set of <I,O> pairs. For purposes of this example we again consider a machine that sells soda, but in this case the rules for selling the soda are represented in this list form. Only some of the states required to define this machine are represented in figure 8.3, since there are a great many. We will refer to this version of our soda seller as the list soda seller (LSS). Note, that in contrast to the SSS, the structure of LSS does not at all reflect the combinatorial structure of L. There are two consequences of this difference in the structure of the machine from the computational point of view. First, L, the input language or event strings accepted by SSS is infinite and L' the input language accepted by LSS is a finitely bounded subset of L. Secondly,

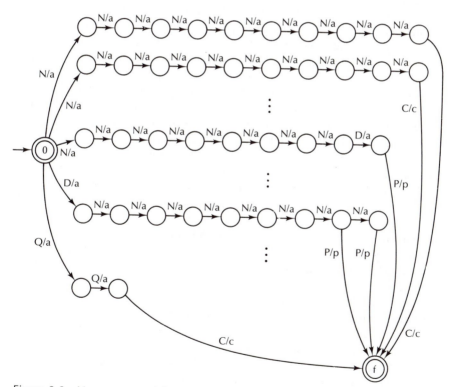

Figure 8.3 *Very, very partial state transition diagram of the List Soda Seller (LSS).*

the LSS requires many more states than SSS. However, neither SSS nor LSS appreciate their respective intelligence or ignorance regarding the combinatorial structure of L. We can see the structure or lack thereof in the respective graphical representations of these machines. But the processes realized in each of these machines 'see' only the current state, current input event, and next state.

Now the discovery or conjecture that an input language, L, possesses some combinatorial structure is of little relevance unless there is concern with the issue of creating or modifying an FSM. If a FSM comes prepackaged with the hardware or neuronal wetware, then aside from physical considerations of its size or density of connections, one is just as good as the other. But, modifying or building an FSM suggests the need for use of a computational model more powerful than a FSM. Thus, we are left with the dilemma that either our organism or device must already possess a suitably general set of FSMs to handle all of the exigencies of its everyday life or it must possess a computational model more powerful than a FSM.

To appreciate and illustrate the inflexibility of a given FSM let us return once again to our soda sellers. Now, obviously, what is crucial to this soda selling game is not the particular sequence in which the money is received and the type of soda specified. What is crucial is that the purchase price be provided and the item desired be specified. A permuted sequence of inputs such as <quarter, coke, dime, nickel, dime> is just as good as any other sequence that satisfies these requirements. Thus, using such permutations, there is a very abstract, at least for this mundane example, way in which to form an equivalence class over the particular input language. But the only way in which to capture this equivalence class in an FSM is to increase drastically the number of states. For example, one can extend the SSS to accept the input of soda selection followed by a sequence of coins summing to 50 cents by creating two additional copies of the existing machine and attaching these to the start state. One of these copies covers the selection of a pepsi and the other the selection of a coke. These copies allow the dependency between soda selected and soda dispensed to be retained over the ensuing coin sequence. To accept the permutation set created by specifying the selected beverage somewhere within the sequence of coins will again require an enormous proliferation of states.

This equivalence class is quite simple to capture within the more powerful planning formalisms discussed earlier. Planning can capture the equivalence class at a level of description quite removed from the input actions by referring to abstract situations or sub-problems; having-received-the-price and having-received-the-request. The dependency among events can be stated correctly and generally at this level of abstraction. Further, the enumeration of the permutation set of events is no longer required. What is required is only the ability to generate a correct sequence from this set in order to achieve this goal. Thus, for a problem reduction planner, generating a correct sequence would entail recursively decomposing these abstract sub-problems (having-received-the-price and having-received-the-request) into primitive sub-problems that represent the various actions, such as depositing a quarter. On the plan-recognition side, what is required is the ability to recognize if a sequence does achieve the goal. In part, the flexibility and economy is achieved because planning and plan recognition are captured as a generative process, the problem reduction search, rather than as a fixed and fully enumerated structure.

At this point, it should be obvious that these same problems beset any attempt to characterize plan recognition as a FSM. Indeed, it is difficult to even distinguish 'planning' and 'plan recognition' within a FSM model. The difference between generation and recognition can be captured by a change in the input and output alphabets of the machines. There is, however, something interesting to be said if we consider the possibility that two interacting machines/agents may have differing structure. By interacting machines we refer to a case where some of the inputs to one are the outputs of the other and conversely. Consider first the case where both machines are FSMs. To illustrate this, let us create a soda purchasing machine whose outputs are precisely the elements of the soda selling machine's input language. In this case, the soda purchaser may be a generator of output sequences where either the selection is first specified and then the money provided or vice versa. Assume that the soda seller is our now well-understood soda seller, SSS. In this case, the soda buyer will be successful whenever the money is provided prior to the selection and unsuccessful otherwise.

To take an even more extreme case, consider the degenerate soda seller (DSS) shown in figure 8.4. This machine has a single state and provides

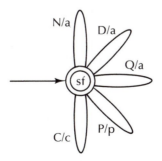

Figure 8.4   *State transition diagram of the Degenerate Soda Seller (DSS).*

the specified soda as soon as it is input. It will also accept as much money as the interacting machine cares to provide it. Note, that if the soda purchaser always provides 50 cents followed by a selection of a soda, the DSS will seem to accept exactly the same input strings as the SSS. Alternatively, the soda purchaser may actually be a planning system of the type reviewed earlier. In this case, this planning soda purchaser may provide any permutation of coins summing to 50 cents and a soda selection and DSS will consistently provide the appropriate soda. In fact, the DSS might appear to the planning soda purchaser to be more powerful than the SSS; and, DSS will now receive all of his business. The only anomaly that might suggest to the planning soda purchaser that DSS is not itself a powerful plan recognizer rather than a FSM is that DSS provides the soda as soon as requested regardless of whether the proper amount of coinage has been output by the soda purchaser. But, perhaps our planning soda purchaser simply assumes that DSS is a very trusting soul/machine!

Now we have rather thoroughly and painstakingly illustrated the limitations of finite state machines as a model of computation. However, despite their limitations they also have certain advantages. First, as the DSS has illustrated, a very simple and computationally tractable model can perform quite appropriately in a suitably benign world. Secondly, we have illustrated that as long as the input events are of finite length, it is always possible to specify a FSM that 'behaves appropriately'. Again, this can yield an extremely tractable computational solution to the generation of action. The FSM model may well be an appropriate computational formalism in which to capture the generation of actions by some organisms or by some organisms at various stages of development or by some organisms within certain types of problem domains.

As some in AI have turned to problems of real-time control that arise in robotics there has been increased interest in the ability to map from plans to a corresponding FSM. Note, the plan is not created via a FSM, but once created the plan and an associated logic of belief can serve as a basis for constructing a FSM whose behaviour is correctly correlated with the plan (Rosenschein, 1985). In general it is not possible to predict if and when a planning algorithm of the type specified earlier will arrive at a solution. If a real-time response is required, this requirement can sometimes be met by mapping a symbolically generated plan onto a suitable FSM. Consequently, it is certainly possible that we, along with other species, have the ability to, in some fashion, 'compile out' the representation of beliefs, goals, and actions by creating a structure of control akin to the simplicity of a finite state machine model.

Concluding Remarks

Where does this leave us as psychologists interested in determining the kind of computational model required to explain some observed behaviour? It certainly reaffirms what most of us knew all along; namely, the explanation of behaviour is not a simple task. However, our hope is that we can draw some more interesting conclusions from this examination of the computational approach that will inform our empirical attempts to study behaviour. These conclusions were implicit in many examples that were presented.

The first conclusion is that attempts to characterize the computational model required to explain an organism's behaviour must begin with a careful analysis of the combinatoric structure of the problems presented to, or in the case of naturalistic studies, responded to by the organism. Precisely what input events can appropriately be grouped into equivalence classes? What are the dependencies among these equivalence classes and how do these dependencies constrain the permissible action sequences?

If the combinatorial structure or structures allowed by a problem are understood, then this provides several ways in which to attempt to probe the generative power of the organism's computational model. The first is to ascertain whether or not the full combinatorics of the input language, the equivalence classes allowed, are evidenced by the organism's observed behaviour. The second is to violate systematically the combinatoric structure of the input language to determine if such violations are evidenced in the organism's behavior. Thirdly, if by hypothesis a generative model of planning or plan recognition is appropriate, then it may be possible to devise problems which differ in their difficulty of solution. And finally, if a planning or plan recognition model is appropriate, then the organism's knowledge may be at a level of abstraction that allows the transfer of appropriate portions of this knowledge to an entirely different problem.

We have probably meandered down this computational path at a rapid enough rate to catch our breath and provide a brief summation of the gist of what we have tried to communicate. First, as you undoubtedly expected, we have not come to any final answers to the various questions that have been posed. Rather we have tried to direct your attention and intuitions here to a certain quandary. It appears that any device, whether biological or artificial, that is required to engage in flexible and asynchronous modes of social interaction, especially if that social interaction includes a cooperative component, needs to be able to compute functions, create plans and recognize the plans of others, that are from a computational point of view generally intractable. None the less, we do interact with each other quite successfully.

The answer to this success is probably to be found in several places. First, just as in the case of natural language, we will probably be led to conclude that biological devices are biased by their nature in ways that make effective social interaction tractable. Second, and this is not independent of the first point, devices which can interact successfully are probably able to find and learn computationally tractable approximations of the function that seems to be logically required to interact with guaranteed success. The task of understanding our understanding of ourselves and others is certainly a challenging one, and, probably one that will all keep us all occupied as long as we wish.

9

Computation and Mindreading in Primate Tactical Deception

RICHARD W. BYRNE AND ANDREW WHITEN

Animal deception is common and pervasive, and does not usually require that the animals possess any special mental aptitudes. This is particularly obvious in cases like those of camouflage by close resemblance to an inanimate object, mimicry of the form of another species, and mimicry of behaviour or form of the opposite sex. In these instances there is a long-term commitment to the misleading resemblance, and we have therefore referred to them as 'strategic deception', to contrast with cases in which behaviour can be flexibly alternated by the animal agent between the misleading and the transparent, at will (Byrne and Whiten, 1985). This alternative, 'tactical deception', we have defined as *acts from the normal repertoire of the agent, deployed such that another individual is likely to misinterpret what the acts signify, to the advantage of the agent* (Byrne and Whiten, 1988). Even here, it is perfectly possible for the deception to be learned and carried out by an animal agent that does not attribute intentions to its victims and social tools, and who therefore has no understanding of why its behaviour is effective in attaining its goals (Byrne, forthcoming). In our initial survey of tactical deception in primates (Whiten and Byrne, 1988a), we emphasized the implications for primate psychology of obtaining *good* evidence which implied an understanding of others' intentions (and thus of deception) by the animal. We then attempted to say what would convince us to accept such an explanation, and evaluated – usually in the negative – the evidence available at the time. We now have a much greater corpus of data available against which to test the preliminary conclusions made at that time, and to do so is the purpose of this chapter.

It may be useful to distinguish three levels of evidence that observational data can furnish about an act that seems to be deception by an animal (see Byrne, forthcoming). Level Zero is simply *not* intentional behaviour: for instance, where the result of an act is a windfall gain to a rather surprised animal, or the 'result' is not really connected with the act at all – except in the mind of the observer. Level One is defined as behaviour that is convincingly intentional, in the sense of goal-directed, and this therefore includes most animal behaviour. The category is agnostic as to the animal's mental states. With a non-verbal animal to say that it 'acts as if it wants or knows something' is not empirically any different to saying that it 'wants or knows something' (see Bennett, chapter 7). Animal behaviourists may either use, or dislike, the teleological shorthand, but there is no difference that shows up in behaviour. Given an individual acting as if it wanted something, some researchers (e.g. Premack, 1988a) 'take it for granted' that their subjects really *do* have wants and beliefs and treat such behaviour as diagnostic of the mental states. Instead, we here leave aside this difficult issue and treat any purposive device (for instance, a windmill with a tail-wheel that makes it appear to want to face into the wind) as displaying Level One evidence of intentionality; some of these devices tell us they have wants and beliefs, others remain mute. To qualify as tactical deception, an action must therefore indicate at least Level One evidence *of intention to achieve a goal which can only be reached if an individual is deceived* (*not* the same thing as 'evidence of an intention to deceive').

A claim that primates were in any sense 'mindreading' would have to rest on evidence of *higher* order intentionality than these: Level Two evidence of deception. Here, *deception* itself must be intended and the agent must attribute intentions to other animals; we have to be sure that 'animal-1 wants (animal-2 to believe X)' where X is false (also see Whiten and Perner, chapter 1). When examining the 1988 corpus for evidence of this kind, we had to admit a verdict of 'not proven'; indeed in many cases an account in terms only of instrumental conditioning seemed perfectly plausible (Whiten and Byrne, 1988a), implying Level One evidence. This should not surprise us. Primates are famed for their rapidity of learning (see Passingham, 1982), and recent work on social learning (Visalberghi and Fragaszy, forthcoming) has shown how rapid trial-and-error learning can easily mimic the greater understanding needed for true imitation and cultural transmission. In collecting together data from many primatologists, each of whom has had many years experience, our trawl was intended to net even rare behaviour patterns: the scope for instrumental conditioning was thus wide. To see whether any species of primate attribute intentions to others, we need more than simply evidence of tactical deception: we need evidence that an animal intended to deceive or understood that it had been deceived.

In analysing the evidence for animal ability to attribute intentions, in what was known at that time about primate tactical deception (Whiten and Byrne, 1988a), we found that chimpanzees, but not other primates (see also Cheney and Seyfarth, chapter 12), convinced us of their capability (Byrne and Whiten, 1988). We discussed three possible markers or *diagnostics* of mindreading in deception: inadvertent 'giveaways' of an intention to deceive (suggested by Reynolds, 1988, but even now without any clear case among non-human primates and therefore not discussed further), righteous indignation (suggested by Humphrey, 1988), and counterdeception. In evaluating the much larger '1990 corpus' (Byrne and Whiten, forthcoming, from which all unreferenced quotations are drawn), we will begin with these markers, then move to examine whether there are other ways of diagnosing mindreading from behaviour observed without experimental control.

Righteous Indignation

Plooij's observation (Byrne and Whiten, 1988) is still the only record. In it, he describes tricking an over-attentive young chimpanzee by acting as if he had seen a distant object of interest. When she found nothing, she 'walked over to me, hit me over the head with her hand and ignored me for the rest of the day'. Convincing as this record seems, while it remains the only example we cannot rule out the possibility of an improbable series of coincidences.

Countering Deception

If deception can be acquired by instrumental conditioning, then so should acts that reduce the losses suffered from being deceived (see Dawkins and Krebs, 1978, for a discussion of arms-races of deception). Among the many examples we now have of counterdeception in primates, some go on to suggest an understanding that deception has been practised (rather than merely that a resource has been lost). For instance, T. Nishida describes Chausiku, a mother chimpanzee, rejecting by covering her nipples her son Katabi's attempts to suckle, and an apparent attempt by him to gain her comfort: 'Katabi came towards me, and began to screech/scream loudly, reaching his hand towards me (as if pointing). Then, he went round me repeatedly screech/screaming loudly, while still reaching a hand to me. Chausiku and her male consort at once glanced at me, with hair erect. I retreated a little bit away from Katabi.' Nishida was sure that the adults believed (falsely) that he had threatened or teased the infant, and the infant was, as a result, then allowed to suckle. Six months later, Katabi did just the same, but this time with a conspecific instead of a human as 'fall guy'

– an older adolescent male, Masisa. Masisa showed immediate nervousness, displayed submissively at the adult male present, and left Katabi: Nishida comments that this was 'the same reaction as I did' and that 'Masisa completely understood the dangerous situation'. It is tempting to believe that he saw the actions as attempted deception, but it is possible that he had simply learnt to react to the situational *Gestalt*. Experience of defensive and high-rank mothers could have allowed a juvenile like Masisa to acquire the rule, which we can describe using the (pattern) => (procedure) notation from artificial intelligence:

> (mother of high rank or with consort male) & (infant scream) & (infant near/reach-at self) => (retreat)

Each rule is called a 'production', and memory consists of many productions. The idea is that the current state of knowledge about a situation automatically triggers the production whose pattern matches it most closely, and its procedure is then executed. This may cause observable behaviour, or a change in knowledge state, or both. A change in knowledge state might in turn cause a new production to match, and so on.

Countering Deception with Deception

In other cases of counters to deception, a learning environment which requires no understanding of deception is much more obvious. Consider, for instance, the arms-race that resulted in one of Menzel's famous experiments (1974) where one chimpanzee, Belle, was shown hidden food but repeatedly lost it to Rock, a dominant male, when she led the group to the food (D_i and C_i are deceptive tactics and counters to them):

D1: Belle accordingly stopped uncovering the food if Rock was close. She sat on it until Rock left.

C1: Rock, however, soon learned this, and when she sat in one place for more than a few seconds, he came over, shoved her aside, searched her sitting place, and got the food.

D2: Belle next stopped going all the way (to the food).

C2: Rock, however, countered by steadily expanding the area of his search through the grass near where Belle had sat.

D3: Eventually Belle sat farther and farther away, waiting until Rock looked in the opposite direction before she moved toward the food at all.

C3: and Rock in turn seemed to look away until Belle started to move somewhere. On some occasions Rock started to wander off, only to wheel round suddenly precisely as Belle was about to uncover some food. Often Rock found even carefully hidden food that was 30 feet or more from Belle, and he oriented repeatedly at Belle and adjusted his place of search appropriately if she showed any signs of moving or orienting in a given direction. If Rock got very close to the food, Belle invariably gave the game away by a 'nervous' increase in movement.

D4: However, on a few trials she actually started off a trial by leading the group in the opposite direction from the food, and then, while Rock was engaged in his search, she doubled back rapidly and got some food. In other trials when we hid an extra piece of food about 10 foot away from the large pile, Belle led Rock to the single piece, and while he took it she raced for the pile.

C4: When Rock started to ignore the single piece of food to keep his watch on Belle, Belle had temper 'tantrums'.

Rock's tactics C1, C2 and C4 could all be accounted for in learning theory terms, but when he begins to feign disinterest, then suddenly wheels round to catch sight of Belle's action, the evidence becomes compelling that Rock understands Belle's (deceptive) intention. If this is once accepted, then of course it becomes parsimonious to account for all D_i and C_i as derived from mindreading.

Is it that countering deception with deception is always compelling Level Two evidence of deception? Surely not, since if tactics which are deceptive can be freely linked to problem situations by the 'short-cut' of instrumental conditioning without understanding of other animals' mental states, then why should not some of these problems have arisen themselves from tactical deception? But as well as functioning to deceive, Rock's looking away and suddenly wheeling round is an *unusual* chimpanzee behaviour: the appropriate use of a rare or novel behaviour to thwart deception is the combination that convinces us of higher intentionality. This is equally true in a record concerning another chimpanzee; when another individual withheld information from him about a food source, he left but 'as soon as he was out of sight, he hid behind a tree and peered at the individual' (Plooij, discussed in Byrne and Whiten, 1988, and Whiten and Byrne, chapter 18). This tactic unmasked the other's attempt at deception effectively, but we suggest that the *novelty* of an adult chimpanzee hiding and peeping out is important in implying that the animal understood the other's attempt to deceive. In both cases, what we find *convincingly* Level Two could, if we took an intentional stance (Dennett, 1983; see also Whiten and Byrne, 1988b, p. 220), be glossed as fourth-order: 'Rock *believes* that Belle will *think* that he no longer *wants* to discover what she *knows* about hidden food' and 'the chimp who hid *believes* that the other will *think* he does not *guess* that he really *knows* about hidden bananas'. Once we are convinced of Level Two evidence, of course, we no longer need to refer to a 'stance'. An intentional system becomes the only parsimonious way of describing the animal.

Telling Tales

Another way of dealing with deception if one *can* understand that it is being practised, is by telling tales to a superior. This has two aspects to it, the use of a third-party as a social tool (which need not in itself imply mindreading, e.g. Byrne and Whiten, 1987), and the mechanism of use – conveying that a *forbidden* act is being practised, which appears to rely on understanding the ideas of secrecy and permission. Low-ranking monkeys and apes often mate or feed out of sight of dominant animals who would prevent these acts if they saw them (Whiten and Byrne, 1988a), and 'telling tales' about this has been reported. For instance, Colmenares describes in baboons how 'a third individual witnessing [this type of behaviour] starts screaming and looking back towards a dominant individual to attract its attention. The dominant individual comes onto the scene and interferes with the activity', and de Waal (1982) describes the chimpanzee 'Dandy, witnessing a secret contact involving an oestrus female, Spin, with whom he had a very close friendship. Loudly barking, Dandy ran to the alpha male, who was far away, unaware of the contact, and led him to the scene where the two others were in the middle of mating.' Whether the first record implies knowledge of another's likely reaction depends crucially on whether the agent was indeed looking back at the dominant *to attract its attention*, or for some other reason; the problem is that interference with copulation is known in primates to sometimes involve screaming, which could by coincidence attract further unwelcome attention without any intention to tell tales. Interference does not, of course, normally involve leading third-parties to the scene, so the chimpanzee record implies understanding of the third-party's likely reaction, somewhat as:

(subordinate mating) & (line-of-sight to dominant) & (dominant alert)
=> (dominant attack subordinate)

Spelling out the necessary representation as a production rule makes it easier to see that this too could be learnt without insight into the mind of the dominant, given knowledge of other animals' ranks (Seyfarth and Cheney, 1988) and appropriate experience, and such experience does not seem unlikely in captive chimpanzees.

Suppression of Another's Behaviour

A situation with a most urgent requirement for secrecy is the 'border patrols' of Gombe chimpanzees, since being in a patrol that is intercepted and outnumbered may result in death (Goodall, 1986). Youngsters sometimes are noisy none the less: 'On two separate occasions the adolescent Goblin vocalized during patrols. Once, he was hit; the second time, embraced. During another period of noiseless travel an infant got loud hiccoughs; her mother became extremely agitated, repeatedly embracing the child until eventually the sounds ceased. A human observer who is too noisy on such occasions may be threatened.' In a circumstance of mortal danger, trial and error learning is not likely, but the need for silence could perhaps be passed on by social tradition without any understanding of why, just as we must presume for these animals' use of natural antibiotics (Wrangham and Nishida, 1983). At the very least, the record shows an ability to combine two rules, represented here as productions (1 & 2 or 2'):

1 (border patrol) => (need silence)
2 (own infant noisy) & (need silence) => (comfort infant)
2' (adult noisy) & (need silence) => (threaten)

A carefully documented observation by Bauers on stumptail macaques (*Macaca arctoides*) goes beyond this. When a low-rank male Joey mated, he did so in a way not typical of the species: when no other adults were in view, without resistance from the female, silently and quickly after little preliminary indication of sexual interest, the two participants separating immediately afterward. On one occasion during such a mating, the female Honey 'suddenly turned and stared into his face, grasped his upper arm, (still looking into his face), then covered his mouth with her hand briefly. The latter behaviour was most striking, as it was my strong impression that she had been afraid he would begin vocalizing, and thus reveal their situation.' It is difficult to analyse this without allowing the simultaneous holding of three simple rules:

1 (mate low rankers) => (need silence)
2 (certain intention movements) => (adult vocalize)
3 (adult vocalize) & (need silence) => (cover mouth)

Not only does this imply the rudiments of a problem-solving system which in larger versions is adequate as a theory of complex human problem solving (Newell and Simon, 1972) but rule 3 raises interesting questions of how it could be acquired. The key question here is whether the action was used directly to ensure silence by mouth closure, or indirectly to communicate intention (implying that 'A wants T to know that A wants silence'); no resolution is obvious. Notice that none of these production rules involves the mental states of other animals; although it may be argued that understanding others' mentality is the obvious way to gain such rules, at least the behaviour which signals them is in principle fully observable. This is not so in the next category we address.

Modification of Own Outward Appearance

By contrast, consider the case where the thing to be observed is one's own facial expression. De Waal's (1982) observation of self-correction by a chimpanzee experiencing an agonistic challenge is illustrative: 'a male, who was sitting with his back to his challenger, showed a grin upon hearing hooting sounds. He quickly used his fingers to push his lips back over his teeth again. The manipulation occurred three times before the grin ceased to appear. After that, the male turned around to bluff back at his rival.' That an experienced male chimpanzee should know the tactical usefulness of:

(rival shows grin) => (attack)

presents little explanatory difficulty, but to apply it *reflexively* shows an understanding of a facial expression as an object that can be seen by others. The necessary objectification of body parts is also what Mitchell (1989) indentifies as required for mirror self-recognition, which chimpanzees can learn (Gallup, 1970). Once again, an obvious way – not necessarily the only way – of achieving this is by realizing what another would think of oneself showing this facial expression. Alternatively, the action may have been based on a combination of computation and a sort of visual perspective-taking: learning how one's own expressions, with their distinctive muscle tensions and feedback both direct and indirect by haptic exploration, affect others. Given this crucial step, then use of the following sort of rules might suffice:

1 (self feel X) => (self show grin)
2 (individual A shows grin) & (audience sees A) => (audience attributes fear to A)
3 (individual A shows fear) => (rival will attack A)

When experiencing the distinctive feelings X, (1) allows 'I show grin' to be added to the current knowledge state; this, taken with (2), causes 'audience attributes fear to me' to be added; this then, taken with (3), allows 'rival will attack me' to be computed. Hence, the grin must be changed.

While this remains an isolated record we must be cautious in its interpretation. One cannot help wondering if this chimpanzee, living in a moated enclosure, had watched his face in the water! The closest record we have available, in terms of requiring calculation of how an individual would look to another without itself being able to see, is a record of a captive pygmy chimpanzee hiding from a caretaker with great success 'by lying flat on his stomach and pulling the blankets over him, so that only a pile of blankets appeared to be on the bed' (Savage-Rumbaugh and McDonald, 1988). Without the aspect of self-correction, this is much weaker evidence for an animal computing a visual perspective which could not by its nature be seen by itself.

Visual perspective-taking of a simpler sort, calculating what objects it is possible to see from another's point of view, has been seen in chimpanzees and baboons (Whiten and Byrne, 1988a). A new record from N. Menard is a clear illustration. She describes how partly habituated Barbary macaque monkeys, when they suddenly find themselves too close to an observer 'initially had a barely perceptible reaction of surprise, then continued to walk in an apparently unconcerned manner in the original direction. They would then pass behind a tree but did not re-appear on the other side.' They in fact walked precisely down the narrow cone of vision shielded from the human by the treetrunk, and the frequent use of the behaviour showed it was not coincidence but a tactic. The ability to represent rather accurately what another is able (geometrically) to see is in everyday terms identical to representing what another does mentally represent (see chapter 1); however, there is evidence from child psychology that the distinction is a crucial one (see Baron-Cohen, chapter 16; Butterworth, chapter 13; Gómez, chapter 15).

Acquisition of Distinctively Abnormal Tactical Version of Act

Many of the dilemmas in this area would be resolved if we knew that a behaviour had *not* had its probability of occurrence increased by conditioning. A possible hallmark of an alternative, calculated origin is a revealingly wrong performance. For instance, while giving an alarm call when no danger is present is a known form of tactical deception (Whiten and Byrne, 1988a), Savage-Rumbaugh and McDonald (1988) describe the captive pygmy chimpanzee, Kanzi, making calls that 'do not have the loud, clear sharp sound that they have when he is really alarmed. Instead, they sound forced or strained. Moreover, he does not show piloerection as he normally does when he is alarmed. However, he is able to make his facial visage appear quite concerned.' This kind of deceit has been practiced towards the animal by human caretakers, so imitation cannot be ruled out (though Whiten and Byrne, chapter 18, argue that imitation itself requires second-order representation). It would seem odd if certain parts of a display but not others were conditioned by the same rewards; nevertheless, 'overacting' or otherwise variant forms of behaviour are of course familiar to pet owners in circumstances where the pet has transgressed, and can often lead to detection of the transgression. For instance, R. Pfeiffer describes a pet baboon looking 'so *conspicuously innocent* that I became suspicious'. The errors suggest incomplete representation of the circumstances triggering a desired result (i.e. the 'pattern' of a production rule), and while we are unsure of how this would mesh with a conditioning account, it presents no difficulty for an AI-based description.

Lack of Reinforcement History

Implausibility of reinforcement has already been argued for acts whose performance would have lethal consequences on a border patrol in chimpanzees; firmer rejection of conditioning would in principle be possible with knowledge of an animal's entire history, and this is approached when scientists home-rear in order to study development. Thus, while a wild baboon's use of gaze for tactical distraction of others need not imply mindreading (Byrne and Whiten, 1987), the same act performed by the Hayes' chimpanzee Viki does, in so far as Hayes guarantees the lack of any past incidents that could have conditioned it: 'Suddenly she sat up straight and stared at something behind me. Her eyes moved up and down as if sizing up a person' (Hayes, 1951). There was, of course, no one there, but Viki was able to escape from a distasteful situation. Hayes laconically notes that Viki had seen no Westerns from which to learn the 'look behind you!' trick, but with a species known to be capable of imitation and reared in the rich environment of a human child, uncertainty must remain over a single record.

New Acts

With a behaviour that is not *in* the repertoire of an individual, conditioning to a stimulus can be ruled out, and we would be forced to accept computation of a novel solution as an explanation. The difficulty here lies in being sure of complete knowledge of the repertoire. Consider two candidate examples. P. Hart describes a captive lowland gorilla that began to approach a rival, then 'changed the nature of his approach, putting his feet down carefully, with his whole body adopting a tense demeanour. He gave every appearance of creeping up on [the rival]. His gait became more springy and he lifted his limbs in an exaggerated fashion. When he got within striking distance he gave [the rival] a hefty shove in the back and then ran indoors.' Also in a captive lowland gorilla, an oestrous female ignored by a male, S. Chevalier-Skolnikoff reports 'she presented to him, turned round, sat down and stared at him and clapped her hands about eight times, and presented again. He got up and walked towards her, whereupon she laughed and ran off.' Gorilla laughter is homologous with and resembles human laughter, and the motivation would seem to have been teasing (see Reddy, chapter 10). Neither tip-toeing nor clapping are seen in wild gorillas, but the boredom of captivity is well known to cause many species to show aberrant behaviour. We cannot rule out the possibility that these animals had thus learnt the acts' effects on other individuals' behaviour without needing to calculate the acts' effect on their minds, and then later used them tactically.

Anticipating Novel Reactions of Others

A logically similar argument can be made for the reverse case, the use of a normal behaviour pattern to cause another animal to behave in a way which is novel, but predictable from an understanding of mentality. C. Boesch studies a population of chimpanzees who use stones as hammers and anvils to crack open nuts, and the stones are in short supply. At the time of the observation, males were much better habituated to the presence of a human observer than females. He describes finding

'an adult female cracking Panda nuts with a heavy granite stone, the only one available in the vicinity. Two males, including the large and dominant Pistache, were looking at her behaviour. Some minutes after my arrival, Pistache slowly left the nut-cracking site, controlling the female with backward glances. After he moved some meters, the female, which was looking towards me uncomfortably, followed Pistache, leaving the hammer on the anvil. I didn't move. 30 seconds later, Pistache came back in a straight line to the anvil and immediately cracked nuts with the stonehammer. He cracked for 20 minutes, undisturbed by my presence.'

Boesch notes that the male was 'psychologist enough to take into account the way the female would react to my presence, once alone, although this way of thinking is not his'. He considers the record a possible candidate for third-order intentionality, i.e. that 'Pistache (agent) represents the adult female's (target's) use of the agent's presence to diminish her (target's) own shyness', but notes that opportunities to see the difference in tolerance of humans were numerous.

A similar example was described by Strum, where a female baboon, evidently in order to distract a male from food which she was then able to seize, 'chased after his favourite female, attacking seemingly without provocation' (Whiten and Byrne, 1988a). The choice of the male's *favourite* female, which he could be expected to protect, argues for an interpretation in which the male's likely reaction is calculated in advance.

Does such calculation imply Level Two understanding? Monkeys like baboons are known to 'redirect' aggression specifically against relatives of those that have attacked them (see Seyfarth and Cheney, 1988, who use this fact to argue for an abstract knowledge of kin-relations in these animals). Thus the choice (for attack) of a friend of the male which, though not actually attacking her may be presumed to have earned a negative assessment by the female, is consistent. Consistent, that is, with some rule like:

(animal X annoys) & (X dominant to self) => (attack X's allies)

This could then be reinforced as an effective *tactic* in just those cases where the 'annoyance' concerns a failure to share food, given the windfall food gain (see Byrne, forthcoming):

(distraction of X required) & (friend of X near) = (attack friend)

The same 'debunking' exercise can be carried out in the chimpanzee case: if Pistache in fact merely gave up waiting, with no understanding that the female would then be forced to relinquish her hammer site, he might have noticed that she had and returned immediately to take possession – without understanding her mental processes. Even if the departure was tactical, this could be based on just knowing that females avoid humans when alone, rather than knowing about females' likes and dislikes. As so often, a 'short-circuit' explanation exists which causes apparent evidence of attributing intentionality to collapse.

This exercise, of working out ever more complex ways of avoiding having to believe that animals can attribute intentions to others, despite data of a kind which, in humans, is routinely taken as good evidence, may or may not be a good way of proceeding. But what *is* clear is that, in the case of the current category of evidence, our decision to claim intentional, Level Two, deception or not entirely determines the verdict on a logically quite separate issue: whether the animals are performing interestingly complex mental computations. This is not true of some other categories considered above, and we therefore suggest it will be fruitful first to concentrate on these clear cases, to generate a better understanding of computation in primate social problem solving – only returning to the others once we have better evidence of the actors' likely level of intentionality. In the meantime, let us not *lose* the great bulk of data that is intrinsically ambiguous between a behaviourist and a mindreading explanation, just because its ambiguity frustrates us. Future generations of scientists, who may well have been able to decide to their satisfaction that certain primates and not others have a theory of mind, are accordingly liable to regard these data very differently and will not thank us for 'filtering them out' of the literature.

Absence of Common 'Simple' Tactic of Deception

We noted that in the 1986 corpus of data, there was a strange absence of triadic forms of tactical deception in great apes, especially considering the chimpanzee's reputation as a social manipulator (Whiten and Byrne, 1988a). This lack continues, and contrasts with the strong evidence for triadic manipulation in *Cercopithecine* monkeys.

A simple metric is to take a count of (categories × species × observer): that is, the number of different categories of deception recorded for a species by each independent observer, summed over every species of a larger taxon. When this is done for the current corpus, excluding records that may be coincidences, chance windfalls or a result of any form of redirection, it shows dyadic forms of deception to be equally recorded in monkeys and great apes (*Cercopithecines* 31, *Pongids* 34) whereas triadic deception is almost confined to monkeys (*Cercopithecines* 13, *Pongids* 1); this difference is statistically reliable (1-tailed chi-square = 7.16, significant at P = 0.01, 1df). The single exception, the case described by Nishida (above), failed in its evident goal, as the target was *not* deceived.

It seems then, a serious possibility that apes may be too 'intelligent' to be deceived by such ploys. If so, this could be for two reasons, either because they learn more rapidly than monkeys and so soon acquire counters to some forms of deception, or because they can represent others' intentions and so anticipate their behaviour – Level Two understanding.

Discussion

This chapter should have made clear the amount of hard work needed to confirm successfully that an animal can understand another's intentions. Would it not be much easier to adopt an assumption of this ability and then see whether this leads to consistent and predictive interpretations of the data? We believe not. First, if some animals are capable of attributing intentionality we *need to know* – perhaps most importantly because it would completely change our standards of ethics as applied to them. Secondly, we do not believe that this knowledge is unobtainable – in fact, we consider the case for the common chimpanzee now to be well established from tactical deception (and see Premack, 1988a, for discussions of his own claim to this effect from experimental data).

In examining the available data, and filtering out each case that can be explained with recourse only to conventional learning theories, we have repeatedly felt the risk of throwing out computationally interesting babies with the murky bathwater of animal mentality. This risk arises for two reasons. Some categories of evidence cannot in principle convince us of mindreading, yet imply complex problem solving. Our approaches to explaining primates' suppression of other individuals' behaviour illustrates this most clearly, but the point applies also to 'telling tales' and other behaviours. Secondly, the decision as to whether a behaviour has a complex or simple mechanism of operation sometimes depends on whether we decide mindreading was involved. Thus, on a mindreading interpretation, the Boesch record is complex, but otherwise it is not.

To deal with these difficulties, we propose a dissociation of the degree of complexity of primates' mental computations and the nature – mental state or otherwise – of objects in those computations. This would involve semi-independent approaches to intentionality and problem-solving in tactical deception. For the former, it is evident that the currently most useful diagnostic applicable to spontaneous behaviour is the occurrence of novel deceptive solutions to the problem of being deceived, although several other categories of data could in principle be employed, and we believe that the approach of filtering out any evidence which can be explained without allowing animals to attribute intentions must continue to be used. For the latter, the whole range of well-observed, multiply-corroborated records of tactical deception is of interest, and results should then be validated in appropriately designed experiments. Whether the species is known to be capable of attributing intentionality may of course be taken into account (and we suspect that observers with long experience of chimpanzees find it difficult to avoid doing this already); this would have the advantage of revealing the true complexity of computations performed by 'intentional' species – with the concomitant risk of allowing species bias (see Menzel, 1988).

Finally, we recommend the use of the production-system notation, derived from artificial intelligence, to make explicit just what mental program or plan (Miller, Galanter and Pribram, 1960) is being hypothesized to underlie a behaviour. In this chapter, we have used it to help clarify our thoughts, and we hope it aids communication of them.

10

Playing with Others' Expectations: Teasing and Mucking About in the First Year

VASUDEVI REDDY

Developmental psychologists have been accused of not knowing what is 'obvious to almost everybody' else – that 'childhood is an extremely emotional period both for children and adults' (Dunn, 1984). This neglect seems especially true of the literature on children's play. While there are, for example, vast tomes on symbolic play and its links with language and cognition, there is comparatively little written on playfulness as a phenomenon in itself, and extremely little on infant playfulness revealed in what is variously called teasing, joking and 'mucking about', which forms such an important part of the experience of interacting with babies in any extended and secure relationship. Like humour, playfulness is a difficult 'behaviour' fully to define or explain. One of the problems with previous attempts was the treatment of an interpersonal phenomenon as an individual behaviour e.g. Lieberman (1977) attempts to look for the links between combinatorial play and playfulness, and to trace the survival of playfulness into adulthood as a personality trait related to creativity. The present approach views playfulness as a cause of developmental advances, and playful behaviour as an important source of data.

Most psychological research on teasing has looked at the very negative effects which teasing can have – e.g. on children with oddities or handicaps when they are teased by their schoolmates. And, indeed, such teasing also happens with chimpanzees (Köhler, 1927, pp. 83–5). The more positive forms of teasing have occasionally been mentioned in the psychological literature (e.g. Trevarthen, 1980; Dunn and Munn, 1986a, 1986b and Stern,

I am greatly indebted to Alan Costall, University of Southampton, and Colwyn Trevarthen, University of Edinburgh, for their encouragement and criticisms.

1985) but have never been systematically, or even directly, studied. I believe it is an important mode of interacting for three reasons, of which I shall in this paper be discussing the latter two:

1 for its effects on relationships
2 for what it shows about the understanding of others' minds (see chapters 4 and 11), and
3 for its links with deception and pretence (see chapters 5, 9 and 18).

Teasing sometimes involves deception and pretence, but sometimes occurs without either. Its chief criterial feature seems to be that it is behaviour directed to achieve affective effects on other 'organisms' and not for obtaining other 'benefits' – such as food, toys, status, mates, etc. Teasing, like deception, is not so much a particular pattern of behaviour – it is an element in a relationship. Altmann (1988) gives a potentially operational description of teasing, namely that it involves the rapid alternation of metasignals, which create and then remove doubt. Similarly Trevarthen (1987a, p. 49) sees a mingling of behaviours in teasing – of affectionate or affiliative and aggressive or defensive behaviours 'as the interactants attempt to predict one another's moves, and jump ahead or forestall each other'. This approach to teasing would include animal teasing as well as human, and is reminiscent of Mitchell's (1986) sensitive descriptions of play between dogs and humans.

To look for the origins of teasing this paper goes further back in infancy than most in this book (see also chapter 16). This age in human infants – between nine and 12 months – is known for the beginnings of clearly intentional communication, for joint object–person interaction or secondary intersubjectivity as it is sometimes called, but is obviously well before 'pretending' as it is usually studied occurs (i.e. pretending about object existence, properties, etc.) and also well before the child is believed to develop an explicit 'theory of mind' – i.e., have causal or theoretical knowledge of others.

Infants' Engagement with Others' Intentions and Expectations

So what is this 'mucking about' and teasing that infants do in the first year? And what can it tell us about mindreading? The set of categories and examples in box 10.1 should give a flavour of the kinds of interactions and games involved. They are phrased in explicitly 'intentional' language, although their intentionality and the knowledge of intentional states they involve are indeed part of the debate under question. They cover a range

1   Performance of varied actions as invitation to appreciation/game/interaction:
Stephanie (7 months) developed a very shrill shriek which her parents saw her as using primarily in situations when she was getting no attention; for example in a supermarket her mother would hear the shriek and turn around in a hurry with some alarm, to find Stephanie sitting in her trolley grinning at her.

2   Performance of specific actions which amuse others:
Shamini (11 months) noticing great-grandmother snoring with open mouth, makes a face with jaws open wide but mouth pulled down to a small 'o' as an imitation of what was an extreme facial gesture. This causes enormous though slightly embarrassed hilarity in rest of family. Shamini responds directly to the laughing others, looking at their faces, laughing, and repeats her 'face' with great amusement several times.

3   Repeating semi-annoying actions within established game:
Rebecca (8½ months) A game which had been developing for two weeks; Rebecca 'accidentally' discovers the impact on others of going over to the television in her walker when somebody is watching it. It has now turned into a game in which as soon as the television is turned on Rebecca, if in her walker, shoots over to it and stands in front of it, giggling and waiting. Mother (M) or others usually say 'no' verbally and try to get her to come away, but Rebecca continues to giggle until M eventually makes a game of 'coming to get you' and grabs her away. Rebecca continues to giggle. This is in interesting contrast with a different game also played at the same age – Rebecca was dropping things and getting someone to pick them up from about 7½ or 8 months – but no smiling accompanies the dropping or the waiting.

4   Opposing other's actions/intentions with amusement:
Rebecca (11 months) Mother playing recorder, not specifically *to* Rebecca, who takes it away from her. M allows her, not thinking about reasons for Rebecca's action. Rebecca laughs, then gives it back to M. M takes it, laughing, and then resumes playing the tune. Rebecca reaches out and takes it again, laughing. M allows her. Rebecca then gives it back with a 'wicked grin'. M laughs 'because it was so obvious that she was teasing'. This was just a single episode which did not turn into a game.

5   Opposing other's directives/expectations with amusement:
Rose (9½ months) has been reliably complying with prohibitions for over a month, including prohibitions for extremely 'tempting' actions such as pulling sibling's hair; starts to move towards the fireplace where the fireirons were a regular attraction, Mother says from across the room, 'No, Rosy'. Rose looks back at M, pausing in her crawl, with a 'cheeky smile' crawls forward, M repeats prohibition, Rose looks back smiling at M, then crawls forward

again, then looks back again with a smile. Sequence repeated a few more times.

6 Creating a false expectation and disrupting it:
Shamini (9 months) within a chatting session following some showing-off with eye-crinkling etc., and following a few pleasant give and take exchanges, offers object to F saying 'ta' and waving her fingers with it as an additional call, looking at F's face intently; F stretches hand out to take it, as F's hand comes closer, Shamini with eyes intently on F's face begins to smile, then withdraws object with smile broadening and turns away, then looks back, F laughs, and says in a voice acknowledging being teased 'You, gimme, gimme, gimme' stretching his hand closer to her face; Shamini makes briefly as if to run, but is caught by the high chair she is in, then turns around again, by which time F has withdrawn his hand. She repeats offer saying 'ta, ta' with her face this time less intent and with a slight smile, F holds out hand again, Shamini repeats withdrawal with smile broadening as F's hand approaches and as she turns rapidly away.

7 Non-serious use of affect signals, 'pretending to cry':
Carla (8 months, 8 days) Father reports that Carla pretends to cry when she wants the breast. Mother: 'I'm still feeding you see and I've been trying to cut it out, and if she wants it and I'm not going to give her a feed then she sits there shouting, as in crying, but there's no tears, I mean she carries on and on and on.' M reports incident the night before: trying to get Carla back to sleep in middle of night, after several attempts of going in picking her up and putting her down again, M got fed up with it and watched her from the door, without being visible herself. Carla would 'shout, sort of as in crying but no tears, for about thirty seconds and she'd stop and listen to see if she could hear me coming or moving, and because she couldn't hear anything move, she'd start again, this went on for about five minutes. I was watching from the doorway, she just lay there and she'd shout and then she'd stop and listen and when she realized that I wasn't there she'd carry on screaming but no tears, not one single tear, and she carried on and on and on and on and on'.

8 'Sly' performance of desired actions:
Philip (8 months) Mother: '. . . he likes the curtains – to try and close them, he doesn't like to be told off for that; he usually waits to go for the curtain when I'm in the kitchen, when I'm around here he doesn't tend to go that much because he knows he's not really allowed to do it, because if I just go into the kitchen and get something, he thinks I'm not looking and makes a beeline for the curtain. Makes a dash for it, you can see him looking over his shoulder to see if I'm watching him, and if I tell him from the kitchen "no" – he stops and looks at you and grins for a while and if I sort of say no really loudly – not loudly it's actually more deep – he lets go and gives a start and whimpers a bit. As soon as I've turned my back he makes another move for it – tends not to do it if I'm actually watching'.

of phenomena all of which can be said to involve the infant's engagement with the intentions and expectations of the adult. The interpersonal significance of these infant initiations is that not only are infants for the first time interested specifically in fulfilling others' intentions (e.g. giving, complying), but also for the first time in being playful with these intentions and expectations and *not* fulfilling them. Not all 'mucking about' *contradicts* others' intentions and expectations (e.g. 'showing-off', making funny faces, moving funnily); it always, however, *assumes* them.

Of this list in the box, 1 and 2 are varieties of *showing off*; 3 is a game with origins in *accidental initial obstruction*; 4, 5 and 6 are perceived as *teasing* games initiated by the infant; 7 and 8 are perceived as *tricking* actions which occur for meeting the infant's interests/desires. Categories 6, 7 and 8 appear to involve deception of some sort, 7 and 8 being roughly similar to the categories of Creating an Image and Concealment (Whiten and Byrne, 1988a), though of much simpler form than their examples of animal deception. Category 6, however, meets no direct parallel in Whiten and Byrne's examples, but is similar to Chevalier-Skolnikoff (1986)'s lone example of a 19-month-old human infant's 'humorous deception'.

I would like to concentrate on category 6 and in particular the teasing with offer and withdrawal of objects, and discuss various interpretations one might give to it. I think it is important for several reasons. It appears to be the most sophisticated of the teasing interactions in this sample of nine to 12 month olds. It is undoubtedly a positive and humorous form of teasing, a fact which is important in view of the largely playful interactions frequent with infants at that age. It would appear to involve some knowledge of others' expectations separated from the act of fulfilling them and it appears to involve the 'pretend' use of a gesture which by all accounts should not be possible in infants under about 18 months. The particular video-taped observation described in box 10.1, category 6, reveals an interesting parallel with Altmann's idea of the alternation of metasignals. The infant's facial expression is serious while offering the object, and relaxes into a smile as she begins to withdraw the object. The claim here is not that these are metasignals; none the less the alternation is suggestive.

Alternative Explanations

Of 11 infants in this study who were old enough, seven were observed or reported to have played some variation of this offer–withdrawal game which the parents described and interpreted as teasing. The following are some alternative explanations of the 'game' which need to be considered.

Could it be an inability to let go? This is an easy alternative to check. If the infant is able to offer and release an object at other times it seems a safe bet that early difficulties with letting go of objects have been overcome. Of the cases discussed here two out of the seven infants were not yet reliable 'givers' (see box 10.2). All the other infants, however, had been giving objects, both spontaneously and in response to requests, for a few weeks prior to the 'teasing' episodes.

Could it be change of mind about giving the object? This is also an easily verifiable charge. Occasions where the offer–withdrawal is a playful act are quite distinctly marked by smiles or 'cheeky' expressions, contrary to instances where the infant has changed her mind. In the latter cases, the infant's face is clearly serious. Such examples are fairly common and are hard to confuse with playfulness, 'mucking about', cheekiness and teasing.

Could it be a solitary exploration of the actions of giving and taking back? Playful offer–withdrawal upon the parent's outstretched hand with the parent only incidental to the game does happen, but is again

Box 10.2   Two infants apparently teasing before reliably giving

Stephen at 11 months was reported to 'hold . . . something out spontaneously, you reach out and he takes it back laughing'. He often held objects out to his parents, but sometimes didn't quite let go. He had never offered *and* given anything as yet. In this case the 'game' didn't follow upon a run of serious albeit enjoyable giving and taking.

Natalie at 7½ months also reportedly teased before being a reliable giver. At that time she had been responding to her mother's open palm request for objects by holding out the object in her hand, but not being able to quite let go. Then she started spontaneously offering and giving one particular doll (about 1½ inches long) to her mother for a few days. Following that she seemed to discover dropping the object. Mother: 'I thought she was giving it to me and I put my hand out and she gave it to me . . . and then I took it the first couple of times and then when I put my hand back for it she'd first look at me and then she'd just, my fingers would be just half an inch away and she'd just drop it in the gap like that, and giggle!' This game lasted for two days and then disappeared. The giving continued to develop with only occasional letting go of things, and even by about nine months depended upon her mood. In the absence of reliable serious giving, and a reliable response to requests, it is difficult to interpret this game as a manipulation of the other's expectations in the act of giving.

fairly clearly distinguishable from an interactive act through markers such as the infant's direction of gaze. As Bruner showed (1975) when the infant gives an object with gaze directed at the other's face, it usually implies a view of the other as active participant rather than as recipient of the action, which latter is implied by giving with gaze directed at the object or the palm of the other's hand. One of the remaining five infants (Rose, ten months) 'teased' with gaze directed at the other's palm rather than the other's face, although with several accompanying play signals: jerky body movements, 'funny' vocalizations and a half-smile. Interestingly, all Rose's serious 'gives' at this period were also without eye contact.

Could it be a direct imitation of a parental game? Infant imitations are frequently a complex indication of interest in the actions and motives of others even when they do not concern the self; and this is precisely a feature of the nine to twelve month period in humans (Bretherton et al., 1981; Trevarthen, 1980, 1987b). But although other kinds of teasing by parents involving the hiding of objects was very common, most parents reported not liking to tease such young babies in *that* manner, remarking that it felt cruel to get their expectations up and really disappoint them. There was no evidence to suggest that the exact forms of parental teasing were imitated in reverse by infants at this age. Examples such as roaring and being 'frightening' (or, in one case, knocking away objects just as the infant reached them) caused hilarious laughter in some infants, but did not later appear in the infant's actions in the same form or same type of game. Direct imitation therefore seems an unlikely origin for most of the cases reported here. Only one mother reported often doing a quick holding out of an object, and then withdrawing it for 'getting him to play' and that she had done that for several months now. This infant, Stephen, didn't meet the first check either (that of being able reliably to let go).

Could it be behaviour which is merely interpreted as teasing by the parents? Unless one accepts a completely preformationist stance, all social behaviour, especially that of such complexity, depends for its 'meaning' upon the situations in which it develops and in which it is able to occur and on the effects it creates. The intention to tease can only be realized through social interaction and the nature of the intention must always, at least partly, be dependent upon the context it takes shape in. This context includes participants' reactions to one's behaviour and perceived intentions. To this extent, teasing is in the perception of it (at one point in time and over time), not in abstract, context-free, pre-formed impulses. Teasing, as a communication, inevitably involves the experience of at least two people. This is different from an intention towards an inanimate object or situation which has only one psychological origin – in the subject. While the latter may be called a subjective intention, the former is *inter*subjective (Trevarthen, 1980). It does not follow, however, that the 'teasing behaviour' is devoid of meaning until some sudden point in time when meaning accompanies the physical shell of the behaviour. It is much more likely to involve gradual development and change of meanings throughout life. The answer to this argument in the abstract is ultimately a metaphysical choice[1], as is the answer to the four questions posed in the next section. Our best recourse in a psychological enquiry appears to be to use indirect evidence to interpret these episodes, and to question the assumptions upon which current interpretations are based.

Could it be a learned response?   Parental responses to what are perceived as tricks, jokes and teasing usually consist of amusement and pleasure. It is surely possible that this response acts as a *reinforcer* for the child's previous behaviour. This is undoubtedly true, but does *not* imply that any behaviour which is learned through reinforcement, is therefore devoid of meaning in any other terms than that of reinforcement. Learning excludes the possibility of neither meaning nor intentionality. Yet it is also true that these teasing games are *specific* to dyads and families. Could this strengthen the argument that the games are merely specific behavioural contingencies? Only if one were looking for a 'wired-in' behaviour or skill would one expect it to show up in fixed and similar behaviour patterns. Since teasing is unlikely to be such a pre-formed motive, it is quite likely to be specific to dyads and situations. Could these examples of teasing be *ritual* play sequences whose social significance lies merely in the repetition of behaviour which amuses others rather than in any engagement with their expectations? While there are plenty of such ritual games at this age where the indignation or surprise is regularly feigned and marked as such by signals (see example of Rebecca blocking the TV, category 3 in box 10.1), these particular examples of teasing are notable for the genuine ambiguity which they induce in the parent, and for their relative brevity. Most importantly, the teasing in the case of offer–withdrawal involves the 'inappropriate' use of a newly mastered *gesture* which is also used seriously to mean something else. In the other games the actions such as blocking TV have no prior serious meaning; they derive their meaning solely from the game.

So what do these episodes show us about the child's understanding of others' expectations?

Understanding Others

Stern (1985) points out, 'You can't tease other people unless you can correctly guess what is "in their minds" and make them suffer or laugh because of your knowing'. Can we assume that the nine-month-old infant has some understanding of what is in other people's minds?

Does the infant understand the 'meaning' of an offering-to-give gesture? The infant *responds* to an offering-to-give gesture from others correctly, i.e. with a reaching-out-to-take gesture. The infant makes *spontaneous offers* (that is not just in response to an open palm request from other) of objects to others, accompanied by eye contact and interest in other's response. The gesture is therefore understood in a number of ways.

Does the infant expect a specific response from the other to an offer? The infant *waits for a specific reaching-out-to-take action* from the other before turning away; the other's response is therefore expected, and is seen as a completion to the act of offering.

Does the infant expect an expectation in the other? If the infant offers an object, and expects the other to reach out for the object in response, then the infant also expects the other to wait to be given the object. To the extent that the infant knows that the other will wait to be given the object, the infant may be said to know that the other expects an action by the infant.

In terms of recursion this is not a very complex level of mental state understanding. The analysis here requires only that the infant understand the presence of an expectation of an *action* in another, not the understanding of the other's expectation of a *mental state* in the infant (see chapter 1 for a discussion of levels). It is likely, however, that what *is* characteristic of the nine to 12 month period in human infancy is the development of an understanding of *others' expectations-of-my-action* (or others'-intentions-for-my-action).[2]

Does the infant expect amusement in the other in response to his actions? Laughter in others tends to excite the infant and attract interest, and actions which produce such reactions tend to get built up into idiosyncratic games. Laughter and attention are, furthermore, deliberately sought in a variety of ways with the infant sometimes running through a bag of tricks. It is therefore clear that the infant expects laughter from the other. The nine-month-old infant also shows an understanding of fearful, etc.,

emotional expressions of others in connection with situations which the
infant faces (Emde et al., 1978; Klinnert et al., 1983). This suggests that
others' laughter need not simply be seen as an 'interesting spectacle', but
understood as an affect.

However, it is possible to explain these sequences in a purely behavioural
way, by making a distinction between understanding physical behavioural
contingencies and understanding the psychological meaning 'behind' behaviour. The give and take exchanges and the emerging compliance of the nine-
month-old infant can be explained physicalistically: the knowledge involved
can be seen as a knowledge simply of the physical actions involved, with no
knowledge of the psychological significance of the actions for the other.
There seems, so far, to be no 'proof' that teasing in pre-verbal infants
involves the attribution of expectancy to another person (see Bennett, chapter 7, for a discussion of criteria for proof). However, there could be a
theoretical reason for this lack of proof.

Physical and Psychological Explanation in Understanding
Others

I would like to ask the question – *is this dualism* – this complete separation
of the physical from the psychological – *really necessary*? Do we need to
assume that infants learn about others through their physical behaviour
alone and later get to the psychological meanings of these behaviours and
to their 'minds'? This picture of a behaviourist infant becoming a mentalist
adult has its roots in a very influential but now troubled cognitivist theory
(Butterworth, 1989).

The Piagetian tradition in developmental psychology which embraces this
dualism *and* another one between individual and society, has the following
argument: 'others' come to be known through their physical behaviour alone
until such a time as the infant can conceive of minds other than his
own. The infant's knowledge develops through her own actions upon other
objects, both social and non-social. *People* are physically no different from
any other objects, so their actions cannot be a direct source of knowledge
for infants any more than can the actions of a doll which the infant is not
acting upon. Thus, understanding of others as psychological beings similar
to self can come only after the self's actions on the world have allowed the
formation of cognitive structures which can yield second-order representations – that is, a mechanism for enabling the isolated infant to 'get into
other minds'. If one doesn't accept this theory of profound egocentrism in
infants which is based upon the dualism between self and other selves

(and most infancy research since the mid-1970s has been concerned with challenging and rejecting it), then one is free to reject the dualism between the physical and the psychological as well. If others are knowable directly through their own actions, and as essentially different from non-social objects, then the split between the meaningless behaviour of another and the meaning somehow behind it or added to it, disappears.[3] Instead, one could see psychological meaning as intrinsic in the understanding of actions – developing only in complexity.

Rejecting this dualism could also explain a persistent discrepancy in the literature between infant communication studies, and cognitive experimental studies (see Flavell, 1985). Communicative acts which begin at about nine months include complying with directives, giving objects, issuing directives (proto-imperatives) and commenting (proto-declaratives). These cannot be explained without assuming that the infant recognizes the other's capacity to understand a message – thus attributing to the other an internal state of *knowing and comprehending* – revealing an 'interfacible theory of mind' (Bretherton et al., 1981). Joint attentionality or the capacity to share the focus of another's attention (Murphy and Messer, 1977; Scaife and Bruner, 1975; see also Baron-Cohen, chapter 19) and social referencing or the infant's search for and use of maternal expressions as a guide in ambiguous situations (Emde et al., 1978; Klinnert et al., 1983), are seen by communication theorists to demonstrate the infant's knowledge of the other's capacity to *perceive*, *understand* and *respond* to particular actions by the infant. Infants from nine months of age discover that they have minds and that other people have minds as well (Stern, 1985), and that other people's reactions can be messages about shared surroundings.[4]

On the other hand a variety of studies from the cognitivist tradition maintains that knowing internal aspects of other minds such as their intentionality, or even their very existence as minds (Flavell, 1985) does not become possible until the middle of the second year, and that a causal–behavioural theory of mind is not possible until about three years of age at the earliest (see chapter 2).

By some the discrepancy is explained as *slippage between world knowledge and word knowledge* (Stern, 1985), or as *implicit versus explict knowledge* (i.e. knowledge versus the ability to talk about it [Bretherton et al., 1981]). Some interpret having an implicit theory of mind to be distinctly different from the ability to '*impute*' mental states to others' (Astington, 1989b). By this distinction an implicit theory of mind can only mean the *presumption* and *use* of others' mental states without the ability to *attribute* them. Some leave the interpretation of these early skills unresolved and open 'awaiting methodological discoveries' (e.g. Poulin-Dubois and Schultz, 1988). Some make the distinction between understanding something and understanding it conceptually. But exactly what is meant by a non-conceptual understanding of others without an understanding of mind itself, is very unclear and confusing.

This confusion is due to the dualism of assuming that understanding behaviour precedes understanding mental states. Having begun with no understanding of other minds – nor any channel for gaining it until very much later – *one cannot explain how intentional communication can imply an understanding of mental states, when the very* existence *of mental states is not known*. One is either forced to an explanation of intentional communication in behavioural terms, or one accepts the confusion. Rejecting the dualism avoids the confusion.

A similar contrast arises in this volume between infants who tease others from before the end of their first year, and the conceptual understanding of teasing and joking that doesn't come until after four years (Leekam, chapter 11). The existence of *some* understanding of teasing intentions is undoubtedly present in the one-, two- and three-year-olds who continue actively to engage in such interactions, although understanding lying does not emerge until later. It is likely that early understanding of others' teasing consists of distinguishing between serious and non-serious intentions. It is also likely that teasing which involves the self is understood better than that which is reported in others. What is needed here is an attempt to explore the different *ways* in which understanding of others' intentions and beliefs is possible.

The existence of playful teasing and other explorations of oppositional interactions in nine-to-12-month olds adds a further piece of evidence to support the theorists who argue for an implicit understanding of others' expectations by this age.

Pretending

Let me return to the episodes of infant and parent teasing and cheekiness that I began with, and conclude with the suggestion that such interaction both sets the ground for, and forms the interpersonal basis for, pretending itself. Can the 'teasing' seen in these examples be seen as a form of pretending? What is the difference between such pretending with gestures, and similar pretending which is reported later at around 18 months?

1   The actions themselves are much more fleeting and less 'robust'.
2   They are less frequent.

3 Other cognitive capacities evident at the time are different – i.e. at 'lower' levels.
4 They are *purely* interpersonal pretences. Pretending about object identities and properties never happens at this age, while they are the most dominant form of pretence after about 18 months or two years (as well as almost the only recognized form of pretence in the second year).

There are, however, structural similarities between the two. An act of offering-to-give which has shared meaning for both participants, and is used by each in both recipient and agent roles in serious situations is sometimes used with a different 'meaning', without the original serious meaning being lost or corrupted. Offering to give an object with playful rather than serious intentions can be seen to involve the abstraction of the serious gesture into a non-serious context. The gesture is used as a means by which either amusement or a game ensues.

Piaget's (1951, 1962) has been the dominant theory of the development of pretence for decades, with only minor modifications. The problem with his view of pretend play is that: (a) it sees pretending as being a solitary production of individual representations, rather than being primarily a replay of actions which are important because other people do them (Vygotsky, 1933; El'Konin, 1966); and (b) it sees the symbol as an individual construction. Developmental psychologists today would argue for the contrary – that symbolic knowledge is constructed through interpersonal interaction (Trevarthen, 1980, 1987a).

Leslie, in his welcome modification of the ambiguities in Piagetian theories of symbolic representation acknowledges that early pretence is not necessarily undertaken in solitude (Leslie, 1987a, p. 415). He notes (Leslie, 1988a, p. 31) that some specialized 'mannerisms' like knowing looks and smiles, melodic intonation and exaggerated gestures may in fact be critical for engaging early shared pretence, and that in this sense social context acts as a limitation on the (decoupling) mechanism. From the playful behaviour of nine- to 12-month-olds I think there is evidence for *precursors* to 'knowing looks', 'knowing smiles' and 'pretence', which are visible in 'cheeky looks' and 'teasing'. The latter display an 'as if' quality within social interactions, not evident at all within solitary play with objects. Leslie sees pretence as inherently involving the characterization and manipulation of attitudes to information. When dealing with very early forms of pretending – and possibly later as well – pretence has probably more to do with an attitude to *people* than an attitude to information.

Although parents pretend to drop, eat and smack their infants from very early on, infant appreciation of such pretence need involve nothing more than an understanding of the playful quality of the parents' intentions. The pretence itself need not be grasped as a contrast between the 'real' act and the play one. When infants begin to engage in 'trickery' and 'pretence' themselves, (and generally in dissimilar forms from earlier parental tricks or pretence), then an understanding at some level of the difference between serious and non-serious versions of the same interactions must be present. Episodes of teasing, cheekiness and mischief, originating in humorous games with other people very early in infancy reveal the first signs of pretence.

Trevarthen (1987b, Trevarthen and Logotheti, 1987) traces the beginning of the 'symbolic potential' to the nine- to 12-month period in infancy. With the new ways of relating to others, and to objects and others together, objects and actions gain symbolic potential; their existence is not merely as distal objects in one mind – they are intermental 'meanings' and therefore ready to be represented by a symbol in any form. If such an alternative to symbolism is developed, we are led to an explanation of the development of pretending which allows social interaction to be something more than merely peripheral to it as an activity. Further, it avoids the implications of 'all-or-none'-ness that surround most explanations of development which look for particular clear differences in time or in behaviour between when a skill or capacity is there and when it is not.

This kind of teasing also demonstrates an advance in the infant's understanding of other people's expectations however one understands the term. Therefore for both pretence and understanding others, interpersonal relations should be the first source of data and the source of their origins. Olson makes an interesting point about the function of cultural or folk-psychologies in building up a language of mind 'It is the acquisition of this metalanguage that, I suggest, is central to the development of a theory of mind' (Olson, 1988).

I would suggest that the issue now is the kinds of metalanguage involved. Could this metalanguage consist not only in the formal language of the culture but also in the forms of interacting and relating between parents and infants – e.g. in teasing, joking, tricking, lying, that occur pre-verbally as well – and allow the realization of different ways of having mind? Could interpersonal pretence form the basis for the development of Leslie's Informational Relation of PRETEND through a similar process? The study of such naturally occurring forms of interaction (especially in conjunction with the beliefs and interpretations of parents and their larger communities) might hold the key to these questions.

NOTES

1 Olson (1988, following Fodor) defines three philosophical stances: one denying mental states, one equating them with a folk-psychology, and one giving them a 'real' existence; Olson's solution is to accept the validity of all three stances, at different developmental points in time. I would prefer to have a constant and developing combination of all three. Indeed, I don't see how this solution can be avoided. The ground-level intentionalist position of Searle does not imply that intentions don't get built into a folk-psychology, or that the latter help to give social reality to intentions and intentionality.

2 Premack and Dasser, chapter 17, distinguish between perception of intention and perception of expectancy, saying that the former is a hard-wired perception and the latter a mental state, and therefore not present very early. It is possible to interpret the teasing sequences as involving knowledge of intentions rather than expectations: following his/her offer and the reach by the other, the infant perceives that the other intends-that-s/he-give-object; and playfully opposes this intention. However, it remains to be seen whether the difference between perceiving intention and perceiving expectation *is* such a clear one of *perception* of physical events *versus knowledge* of mental state; there is a lack of agreement in the literature on this point. For the present, I am assuming that both intentions and expectations are mental states.

3 Both behaviourism and mentalism are dualistic in this way (Coulter, 1979; Markova, 1982). Mentalism maintains the separation by insisting mind follows behaviour; and behaviourism maintains it by denying mind altogether. The behaviourist solution runs into the problem of not being able to explain our apparently mentalistic explanations, understandings and theories of other people's actions as adults. The mentalist solution runs into the problem of having to invent mechanisms which *suddenly* allow the entry of mind into a world of behaviour.

4 Intersubjectivity is an important but often vague term referring to the *experience of sharing* subjective states and *to the search for the 'sharing of* experiences about events and things' (Trevarthen and Hubley, 1978). It is dependent upon the recognition by infants of the psychological similarity between themselves and separate others. Although there is argument about the innateness of intersubjectivity, and the manner of its development, most theorists are agreed that by nine months of age infants have the ability to impute internal states to self and others and to recognize that his or her mind can be interfaced with that of a partner, i.e. have a theory of 'interfacible separate minds' (Bretherton and Bates, 1979). By postulating an innate intersubjectivity Trevarthen can avoid the trap of the question: 'when do infants come to understand others psychologically?' He argues

that the capacity to recognize similarity between oneself and other persons is present from birth as evidenced by studies of magnetic imitation (Maratos, 1973; Meltzoff and Moore, 1977, etc.) and in studies of neonatal interactive behaviour with persons (Brazelton, 1982).

11

Jokes and Lies: Children's Understanding of Intentional Falsehood

Susan R. Leekam

In this chapter I look at two verbal forms of teasing and deception; jokes and lies. My aim is to show how children's understanding of falsehood is related to their developing understanding of other people's intentions and beliefs. I focus particularly on the child's understanding of jokes and lies because the distinction between these two acts seems to rely on distinguishing higher-order intentions and beliefs (i.e. what A *wants* B to *believe*).[1]

My study of the relationship between mindreading and falsehood started with a conceptual analysis of falsehood based on intention and belief. This analysis led to a set of studies to test children's understanding of the distinction between lies and jokes. The results of these studies suggest that even quite young children of four and five years understand the difference between jokes and lies and can grasp complex, embedded mental states related to this distinction. These results are striking because they contrast with previous evidence on the abilities of five- to nine-year-olds and later in the chapter I consider why these younger children should be doing so well. In addition, I look at the connections between my results and the work of Reddy (see chapter 10) on infant teasing and Byrne and Whiten (chapter 9) on primate deception. Whilst my enterprise differs from theirs in focusing on conceptual knowledge rather than mindreading evidenced in spontaneous behaviour, I think there are some important links to be made between the approaches.

Classification of Falsehood

False statements include a range of different communicative acts, including mistakes, lies, jokes, irony, hyperbole, banter, understatement and hypocrisy. My proposal is that all these acts can be classified quite simply in terms of the mental states of speaker and listener.

Two levels of classification are proposed. These levels are based on first- and second-order mental states.[2] At the first level we can distinguish unintended falsehood (mistakes) from intended falsehood (lies, jokes, etc.). We do this according to the speaker's first-order intention and belief. So a mistaken speaker *intends* to be truthful, believing that he or she is saying something true while the lying or joking speaker *does not intend* to be truthful, knowing that he or she is saying something false.

At a higher level we can make a second-order distinction. This distinction separates intentional falsehood into two classes on the basis of the speaker's second-order mental state. In one class we have lies, hoaxes, white lies, etc. In the other class we have jokes, teasing, irony, etc. This second-order distinction is based on the *speaker's intention concerning the listener's belief*. For the deceitful speaker the sole aim is to deceive the listener, whereas for the joking speaker the ultimate goal is not to deceive but to be disbelieved. The speaker's intention to deceive is therefore defined in terms of what the speaker *wants* the listener to *think*. The deceitful speaker wants the listener to think that the statement is true while the joking speaker wants the listener to know that the statement is false.[3]

The two levels and different types of speech act are depicted in figure 11.1.

Children's Understanding

This analysis assumes that understanding the difference between different forms of falsehood depends on understanding mental states at different levels of complexity. Children's ability to distinguish mistakes from lies should therefore depend on their understanding of first-order beliefs and intentions (i.e. wants, beliefs). Children's ability to distinguish two forms of intended falsehood, (for example distinguishing white lies from irony), will depend on their understanding of second-order beliefs and intentions (i.e. what A thinks B thinks: what A wants B to think, etc.).

How closely does this proposal match the evidence from existing literature? The first suggestion, that the distinction between mistakes and lies depends on first-order beliefs has already been confirmed by Wimmer

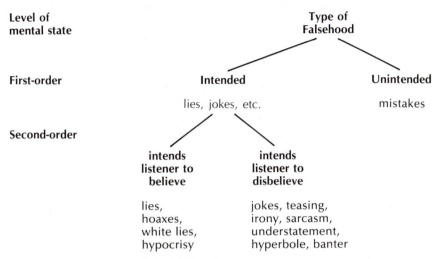

Figure 11.1   *Classification of falsehood.*

Gruber and Perner (1984, 1985). These authors found that as soon as four-year-old children were able to understand a speaker's false belief (Wimmer and Perner, 1983), they were also able to distinguish mistakes from lies.

However when it comes to the second suggestion, that intentional false-hood depends on second-order beliefs and intentions, the picture starts to become less clear. As far as children's understanding of *second-order beliefs* is concerned, studies by Perner and Wimmer (1985) and Yuill and Perner (1987) have shown that children become able to attribute second-order (false) beliefs such as 'John thinks that Mary thinks' or 'John thinks Mary can see him' between the ages of six to eight years. The literature on children's understanding of *intentional falsehood* however suggests that the ability to distinguish between different types of intentional falsehood might come much later. Observations by Piaget (1965) indicate that children might not be able to distinguish lies intended to deceive from other forms of falsehood such as jokes and exaggeration, until the age of nine or ten years. Research on irony comprehension (Demorest et al., 1983, 1984; Ackerman, 1981, 1983) indicates that it is not until about 13 years that children can easily distinguish deception from teasing types of sarcasm. More recent studies (Andrews et al., 1986; Winner, et al., 1987) show rather better performance than this but still only from eight years can children consistently distinguish sarcasm from other forms of falsehood (Winner et al., 1987, experiment 2).

From all this evidence, it looks as though children's understanding of intentional falsehood might not emerge at the same time as their ability to attribute higher order mental states after all. Another possibility though, is that these earlier studies might have simply underestimated children's ability. In the studies of intentional falsehood just described, the first-level intentions and beliefs of speaker and listener were not controlled. This made it possible for children and even adults to make errors by basing their responses on the speaker's first-order *belief* rather than the speaker's second-order *intention* about the listener's *belief*. In the following set of experiments therefore I ensured that the crucial second-order mental state was experimentally isolated. Only this aspect was manipulated while the first-order mental state of both speaker and listener was held constant.

Distinguishing Lies from Jokes

The task I gave children was to compare a *joking lie* with an *unsuccessful deception*, that is, a lie that goes wrong and is discovered. I used the same kind of story method used in earlier studies mentioned above, but presented these stories in the form of a paired comparison, a technique first used by Piaget (1965) to investigate children's moral judgements.

Here is one pair of stories children were asked to compare: A boy, on his way out of school with his mother, points to another child's beautiful painting and says, 'I did that picture'. His mother is very pleased and praises him. In the *joking lie* story, the boy immediately directs his mother to the true artist's name on the picture, to show the mother that it was a girl who painted it and not him at all. In the *deceitful lie* story the boy doesn't show his mother the girl's name. Instead the boy and his mother go home, but the next day, while waiting to collect the boy from school, the mother discovers the truth on her own. She goes up close to get a better look at the picture and discovers the name of the true artist written in the corner. So in both stories the mother found out about the artist's true identity, but in one case (deceitful lie) the boy *did not want* her to *know* the truth and thought at the end of the story that his mother still believed him. In the other case (joking lie) the boy *did want* his mother to *know* the truth and knew that his mother no longer believed him.

To summarize, the first-order mental state of the boy and the mother is kept constant across the two stories: the boy *intends* to say something false and his mother eventually *knows* it is false. Only the second-order mental state is varied: what the boy *intends* his mother to *know*. Childred aged six, seven, eight and nine listened and followed the illustrations for both stories. At the end of the second story they were asked the following questions:

Moral judgement: 'Which boy was naughtier for saying he did the picture?'
Belief question: 'In both stories, the mother believed what the boy said at first, but now she doesn't believe it any more. But one of those boys still thinks that his mother *does* believe him. Which one?'

This procedure was repeated with another almost identical story pair about a girl and her mother and a different work of art. Then, at the end, after the other two questions, a third question was asked:

Joking question: 'Which one was joking?'

The complete set of all three questions was asked on only the second pair. Table 11.1 therefore shows the percentages of correct responses for all three questions for the second pair only.

These results show perfect performance on the belief question from six years. By eight or nine years children are also giving perfectly correct answers to the moral and joking questions (50 per cent = guessing level).

The remarkably good performance by all ages on the belief question therefore shows that even six-year-olds can distinguish deceitful lies from joking lies on the basis of the mental states of the speaker and listener when these elements are properly controlled.

It is interesting that children gave correct answers to the belief question before they were able to give perfect answers to the moral and joking questions. These findings are similar to those reported by Yuill and Perner (1987) who found a lag of one to two years between children's ability to attribute second-order beliefs and their ability to make moral judgements in terms of attributing responsibility for accidents.

Why should there be a lag between understanding second-order beliefs and distinguishing lies from jokes? In follow-up work I tried to pin down the reason for this delay. One possibility is that children missed the point in my experiment when it came to the moral and joking questions. Both

Table 11.1 Experiment 1: percentage of subjects with correct answers

| Test question | Age[a] | | | |
	6	7	8	9
Belief	100	81	100	94
Moral	50	69	100	100
Joke	56	87	87	100

[a] N = 16 in each age group.

these questions concern the boy's *intention*. My second-order belief question however did not ask about intention; it asked about belief: 'Which boy *thinks* his mother believes him?' It may be fairly obvious from the joking story what each boy thinks his mother believes. The clue may come from the story illustration for the joking story, in which the boy points to the name, the mother sees it, so the boy *knows* she *knows*. However, it is less clear from the story exactly what the boy *wanted* his mother to know.

Is Second-Order Intention Important?

In the next experiment, therefore, I tried to make the boy's *intention* to show his mother clearer by changing the joking version to include the boy telling his mother that he didn't do the picture. So instead of 'the boy points to show his mother that there's a girl's name', the story went, 'The boy points to the name. He shows his mother that there's a girl's name written there and tells her that he didn't really do it.' With this improvement, even if children do not recognize one boy as 'joking' they should at least recognize him as less naughty (moral question), because it should be clear that one boy intended to own up while one boy did not.

In this second experiment children also had two story pairs but the belief question was asked only after the second story whereas the other questions were asked after both pairs. As before, therefore, I show percentage of correct responses for the second story pair in table 11.2 (guessing level = 50 per cent).

Again, these results show extremely good performance on the belief question for all age groups. The results for the moral question are also very good and the age gap between second-order belief attribution and moral judgement has considerably narrowed. While 12 six-year-olds and 15 seven-year-olds correctly answered the belief question, 11 six-year-olds and 16

Table 11.2 Experiment 2: percentage of subjects with correct answers

| Test question | Age[a] | | | |
	6	7	8	9
Belief	75	93	100	100
(think–believe)	69	100	100	100
Moral	56	69	69	100
Joke				

[a] $N = 16$ in each age group.

seven-year-olds gave correct moral judgements. This result suggests that it may be second-order intention (want other to believe) that is the crucial thing for distinguishing lies from jokes rather than second-order belief (think other believes).

When looking at the performance on the joking question however, we should note that a delay between second-order belief attribution and joking judgement still persists until age nine. One could argue that the joking story in this study is a rather weak example of a joke anyway and amounts to no more than someone 'owning up'. Perhaps behavioural cues such as smiling, laughing, etc. should be present before children can accurately judge a person's joking intention. In fact, this could not have been a problem to nine-year-olds who performed perfectly on the joking question in both experiments. Nevertheless, younger children perhaps do rely on these behavioural cues as evidence for joking and this is something I decided to investigate further. First, though, I extended the existing study to younger children of four and five years, taking a closer look at the difference between second-order intentions and second-order beliefs.

Does Second-Order Intention Precede Second-Order Belief?

Children below six years of age normally fail miserably on tests of second-order belief (Perner and Wimmer, 1985, 'John thinks that Mary thinks'). However, so far we know nothing about their ability on tests which ask about second-order intention (what the boy wants his mother to think). In the next experiment I tested children aged four, five and six. For this experiment I used exactly the same procedure as in experiment 2 but included a new test question. Half the children had the original belief question as used in experiments 1 and 2 while half had the new form of question. This was:

> *Want–Know Question*: 'At the end of both the stories the mother knows that the girl really did it (painted the picture). One of those boys *didn't want* his mother to *know* that a girl really did it. Which one?'

The results showed remarkably good performance on both questions and although four- and five-year-olds were slightly better on the want–know question, there was no significant difference between the two questions. For both types of question combined, 62 per cent of four-year-olds (10 of 16 subjects), 81 per cent of five-year-olds (13 of 16 subjects) and 69 per cent of six-year-olds (11 of 16 subjects) gave correct answers. (Once again, in order to compare results with experiments 1 and 2, performance here is for the second story pair only. Guessing level = 50 per cent.)

The most remarkable thing about these results is that children as young as four- and five-years-old were able to use second-order mental states for the basis of their discriminations. These results are particularly striking when compared with those of Perner and Wimmer (1985) who found only 37.5 per cent of five-year-olds (experiment 6) giving correct responses on their second story. (Four-year-olds were not tested.)

To examine this further, it is worth taking a look at the number of children who give *consistently* correct answers on two rather than one story trials as children tend to improve across story trials. This reduces the guessing level to 25 per cent. My experiment 3 showed consistently correct performance by 38 per cent of four-year-olds (six of 16 subjects), 69 per cent of five-year-olds (11 of 16 subjects) and 56 per cent of six year olds (nine of 16 subjects). This is still better than Perner and Wimmer's five-year-olds (25 per cent correct performance, experiment 6) although six-year-olds in Perner's experiment performed at the same level as mine (56 per cent).

Distinguishing Second-Order Intentions and Second-Order Beliefs

The previous experiment did not show any significant difference between second-order intention and second-order belief questions. However, in all three experiments described so far I manipulated *both* second-order beliefs and second-order intentions together. The deceitful boy *wants* and *thinks* that the mother believes the statement while the joking boy does *not want* and does *not think* mother believes it. From this confounding it is difficult to tell whether children's good performance was because they based their judgements on second-order intention, second-order belief or both. In this final experiment I isolated second-order intention and examined 4- and 5-year-olds' judgements again, this time with a behavioural cue; smiling, included in the joking version. In experiment 4, therefore, only second-order intention was manipulated. A summary of the mental state of each boy is shown in table 11.3.

In this new experiment, second-order belief was controlled by inserting an extra picture and adding to the story. So in both versions the boy knows his mother knows. For the joking speaker this extra passage was: '*The boy is standing right next to his mother so he can see she is looking at the girl's name on the painting.*' For the deceitful speakers the passage was: '*Just at that moment, the boy comes out of his classroom. He sees his mother is looking*

Table 11.3   Summary of speaker's second-order mental state in experiment 4

	Type of lie	
Mental state	Joking	Deceitful
Second-order belief	KNOWS mother KNOWS	KNOWS mother KNOWS
Second-order intention	WANTED mother to KNOW	DIDN'T WANT mother to KNOW

at the girl's name on the picture.' Half the subjects had a joking boy with a smile on his face and were told 'he smiles and points to the name'. Half had the no-smile version from experiments 1 and 2.

To summarize, the only difference between the joking and lying version was the boy's second-order *intention*. In addition, half the subjects saw the joking boy with a smiling expression and half saw the joking boy with a neutral expression so we can also see whether this behavioural cue has any effect on children's judgements. Sixteen four-year-olds (aged four-and-a-half to five) and 16 five-year-olds (aged five-and-a-half to six) were tested and two questions were asked.

> *Want–Know question*: 'One of these boys wanted his mother to know that a girl painted the picture and one didn't want his mother to know. Which boy wanted/didn't want his mother to know?
> *Joking/Lying*: 'One of these boys was joking and one was lying. Which was joking/lying?

The results showed no significant difference between the smile and no-smile version for either type of question. So the behavioural cue of smiling had no significant effect on children's judgements. To give the most accurate picture of children's ability, I report in table 11.4 the percentage of subjects

Table 11.4   Experiment 4: percentage of subjects with correct answers (both story pairs)

	Age[a]	
Test question	4	5
Intent (want–know)	81	87
Joke/lie	69	87

[a] $N = 16$ in each age group

in both smile and no-smile versions who gave correct answers on *two* story pairs (guessing level = 25 per cent). As table 11.4 shows, children are already performing at a very high level on both questions. With this manipulation based purely on the speaker's second-order *intention* even four-year-olds are consistently giving correct answers to both the want–know question and the joking/lying question.

Implications and Relevance

Understanding Higher-Order Mental States

My main aim in this work was to look at the role of second-order beliefs and intentions in children's understanding of falsehood. My hypothesis was that children should be able to discriminate different forms of intended falsehood at around the age six to eight, when they become able to attribute complex second-order beliefs. What I discovered was that even children of four or five years could distinguish lies from jokes and did so by attributing complex second-order mental states. This result suggests that children understand second-order mental states at a much younger age than we previously thought. The results of experiment 4 showed that over 80 per cent of four- and five-year-olds could make correct judgements of second-order intentions. Why should young children do so well on these tasks? Two suggestions for young children's competence are proposed. The first concerns the issue of recursion. The second concerns the nature of mental states.

Recursion   The main feature of higher-order mental states is that they are recursively applied (Shultz, forthcoming; Perner, 1988b). It has been proposed (Perner, 1988b) that understanding second-order beliefs may give evidence for children's understanding of the recursive nature of mental states. Originally, Perner proposed that this understanding might develop at the age of six, two years later than the understanding of first-order mental states. My findings imply that this understanding might develop earlier. Children already know something about embedded propositions when they understand a sentence such as:

'Boy knows that (girl painted picture).'

The difference for the second-order construction:

'Boy thinks or wants (mother doesn't know [girl painted picture])' therefore is that it forms a doubly embedded proposition. Perhaps, once children understand the notion of propositional embedding the idea of repeated embedding quickly follows. This does not of course explain the difference between Perner and Wimmer's results and my own but perhaps these can simply be accounted for in terms of the different methodology between the two studies.

The nature of higher-order mental states However, another possibility is that there is a critical distinction to be made between different types of higher-order mental state. That is, between second-order *intentions* (or desires) and second-order *beliefs*. This distinction has already been made by Wellman (chapter 2) and Astington and Gopnik (chapter 3) for first-order mental states. There is evidence that children understand desires and intentions before they understand false beliefs. It is possible that the same applies to second-order beliefs. If so, this would support Astington and Gopnik (chapter 3) and Perner's (forthcoming, a, c) argument that the problem for younger children lies in the representational nature of the mental states. Therefore, five-year-olds' difficulty with second-order beliefs might be due to their difficulty with recursive *representational* states, rather than with understanding recursive mental states in general.

At this stage I cannot yet conclude that understanding second-order intentions does precede understanding second-order beliefs because in experiments 1 to 3 second-order intention and belief were always varied together. In experiment 4 once second-order intention was isolated from second-order belief four- and five-year-olds did in fact show better performance than in the previous experiment where intention was varied with belief. However until a direct comparison between second-order beliefs and intentions has been made experimentally we cannot tell whether there really is a difference between the two. We would also need to go further to demonstrate that there is a difference in complexity between other different second-order mental-states. For example, would beliefs about intentions be more difficult to understand than intentions (desires) about desires?

If such a difference of 'representational complexity' between higher-order mental states was demonstrated, we might have to think again about our use of such terms as 'higher-order representations'. If not all higher-order mental states involve representations about representations, it might be useful to distinguish between 'higher-order representations' and 'higher-order intentionality'. This might be applicable particularly in the case of animal research where the question of representation is still being debated.

Nevertheless, one might argue, as Whiten and Perner do in chapter 1, that deception which is based on 'A *wants* B to (wrongly) believe' is good evidence that the child or animal understands the mind as representational.

In this case surely my term 'second-order intention' is not quite accurate. Shouldn't this count as a 'second-order *intention* about a *belief* and therefore as a 'higher-order representation'? My view is that we should be careful about what we accept as evidence for higher-order representations in deception. First, in real life, as Bennett (chapter 7), Byrne and Whiten (chapter 9) and Cheney and Seyfarth (chapter 12) argue, it is very difficult to find evidence that an animal intends to manipulate *beliefs* and not just *behaviour*. Second, even if one could show that the animal did intend to manipulate another's knowledge, this might not involve representational understanding. It is quite possible to deceive someone by saying something false to them in order to prevent them from knowing the truth. This might require understanding their knowledge state (i.e. ignorance), but it does not require understanding how the person views your false statement (i.e. that they perceive the false statement as true rather than false). So in this case what you want to influence is the *content* of another person's thought but not necessarily the way in which they represent your statement. (See Perner, forthcoming, a, c; Astington and Gopnik, chapter 3).

Another consideration in all this is that intentions about knowledge can be based not only on what you want another to know or not know, but more simply, on what you want the other to see or not see. This in turn may be based on non-epistemic mechanisms such as the line of sight. The use of sophisticated looking strategies to achieve goals is discussed by Byrne and Whiten (chapter 9) and Gómez (chapter 13).

In sum, where second-order intentions seem to be involved in deception, these do not need to be intentions about wrong *beliefs* and as such do not need to be representational.

Understanding Deception and Teasing

What does my study of the conceptual distinction between lies and jokes tell us about the child's understanding of deception and teasing? Others have shown that even infants participate in teasing exchanges (Reddy, chapter 10). We also know that primates (Byrne and Whiten, chapter 9) and even birds (Ristau, chapter 14) show deceptive behaviour at different levels of complexity. Does this evidence suggest that the distinction between lies and jokes might be grasped much younger, say even in the first year, given the right conditions and context?

The answer to this question is that we do not know. The youngest children I tested were four-year-olds and even at this age they were performing very well. So at this stage we do not know when children first start to distinguish lies and jokes or their non-verbal equivalent in teasing and deception. My guess though is that children below three or four years would not understand the distinction. Before I give grounds for my speculation however I should make clear what I mean by the terms 'deception' and 'teasing'.

Defining deception Mitchell (1986) has described deception in animals as occurring at different levels. At the lowest level are 'programmed' behaviours without purpose. This is followed by repetitive behaviours repeated for an effect such as material gain, food, safety, etc. That is, using means to achieve ends (see Ristau, chapter 14 for discussion). At the third level are means–ends strategies which are *intentional*. The animal *intends* to influence the behaviour of the other. At the fourth level is *intentional deception* which involves representation of another's beliefs. Higher levels of analysis have also been proposed (Chisholm and Feehan, 1977; Dennett, 1987). However, it is this fourth level, analysed in terms of 'A wants B to believe' which I investigated in my study and which I want to consider here.[4]

Defining teasing I would like to suggest that acts of teasing might also be analysed according to the same levels. At the lowest level teasing might be described as pure play without purpose. However, perhaps we cannot yet describe this as 'teasing'. The first acts of teasing though probably do emerge from an early notion of play and non-seriousness. The second level is perhaps where teasing as we know it might start: that is repetitive behaviours used for an effect. For example, the infant might enjoy breaking conventional sequences of behaviour which they have learned. The give–take sequence for example always starts with an offer of an object and ends with the object being taken. The infant may enjoy the effect of breaking the sequence and the reaction that follows, i.e. smiling and laughing by the other and this behaviour is repeated for the effect it has (smiling reaction, laughing). At the third level the infant might use this action *intentionally* in order to get a reaction and influence the other's behaviour. Only at the fourth level however would the infant be using the act in order to influence another's beliefs and expectations.

When do children distinguish teasing and deception? So here we have four levels of teasing and deception; programmed behaviours, means–ends behaviours, intentional means–end behaviours, and behaviour showing understanding of beliefs. Only the third and fourth levels involve mental states; *intentions* about behaviours or *intentions* about *beliefs*.

If what we are now interested in is whether children or animals are attributing mental states how can we get evidence for this? One way is to make a distinction *between* teasing and deception as I have done in my experiments. Deception can be distinguished from teasing at the third level of Mitchell's scheme: in terms of A's *intention* to influence B's *behaviour*. In the case of deception this might be, A wants B to go away or to look (turn head) in another direction in order that A might obtain some benefit such as food. In the case of teasing, A wants to influence B's behaviour in a different way. The *effect* of teasing is usually some emotional reaction or 'affective effect' by the recipient (Reddy, chapter 10); for example, surprise, amusement or annoyance. However, these affective states are manifested in behaviour; laughter, smiles, frowns. At this level of analysis therefore the teaser wants to influence the recipient's behavioural reaction. The teaser enjoys the effect of this reaction as an end in itself. Where teasing involves temporary deception, the teaser wants to influence the recipient's behaviour (e.g. get them look away) in order to obtain a second behaviour or reaction (laughter, surprise, etc.).

Deception can therefore be distinguished from teasing in terms of A's intention to influence B's behaviour. However, the two acts can also be distinguished at the fourth level of Mitchell's scheme; in terms of A's *intention* to influence B's *belief*. This is the distinction I have been focusing on in this chapter. As I pointed out in the previous section, this level may split in two. The deceiver or teaser might intend to influence the content of the other person's *knowledge* (A wants B to know/not know, see/not see) or else may intend to influence the other person's *representation* (A wants B to view statement as true/false).

Now, to return finally to my claim that children below the age of three or four would not understand the teasing–deception distinction. Here is my proposal. I would predict that once children understand desire (Wellman, chapter 2) they will also understand 'A's intent to affect B's *behaviour*'. So, by three years old children should grasp this. Once they understand intentions and beliefs as representations they should also understand 'A wants B to (wrongly) believe'. This should be around the age of four. However, as mentioned earlier, we need to be cautious in interpreting instances of deception as representation. Many cases can be reduced to 'A wants B to see/know' which concerns the *content* of the other person's mental state but not necessarily *how* the other person represents the situation (i.e. as true or false). Children seem to grasp non-representational states such as knowledge earlier than false beliefs (Hogrefe, Wimmer and Perner, 1986) and by three years old, children seem to have a clear understanding of 'seeing' and 'knowing'.

Conclusion

My analysis of children's understanding of jokes and lies suggests that children can make a distinction between these verbal forms of teasing and deception involving higher-order mental states (A wants B to know), at least by the age of four. The question of whether even younger children might make this distinction is still an open one, although I doubt that they could do so much before the age of three. However, if we move away from children's *understanding* of the distinction between teasing and deception and turn instead to the child's own acts of teasing and deception we may find the ability to take account of other's beliefs appearing earlier. Reddy (chapter 10) and Byrne and Whiten (chapter 9) give excellent examples of teasing and deception occurring in infants and animals. Many of these examples can be fitted into the lower levels of the Mitchell scheme. Some may be level three or four examples ('A wants to affect B's behaviour or beliefs'). However, as these authors point out the critical thing is establishing whether an animal or infant's deceitful or teasing behaviour really was *intended* to influence either the behaviour or beliefs of another. Even if we can be sure of that, it is another task to decide whether an infant or animal really wants to affect the other's *beliefs* or just their *behaviour*.

If there are different degrees or levels of deception and teasing is it possible that these different levels form developmental stages? Reddy (chapter 10) makes the point that development may be continuous, with intentions in behaviour from the start and the meaning of these intentions gradually constructed in interaction with others. I favour the stage hypothesis, for pragmatic reasons.

In everyday life we do not *need* to make the complex kinds of distinctions required here. We rarely, for example, need to make complex attributions of higher-order mental states or consider someone's representation of a situation even in the case of deception. This does not mean that we do not do so, especially when things go wrong. In the case of mistakes, misunderstandings and failed jokes we are often forced to replay the situation in order to understand it. We say things like: 'I thought you knew', 'Do you expect me to believe that?' My point is that we don't always *have* to use complex mental state attributions in order to be effective communicators and effective deceivers. We can get by with far less. After all, why should we bother to represent the mind if we don't need to? However, being able to understand mental states enables us to incorporate such understanding into our social interactions and allows for greater flexibility and efficiency in our dealings with others.

In sum, my conclusion is as follows. I propose that four- to five-year-olds have a sophisticated understanding of the distinction between lies and jokes and can grasp complex embedded mental states related to this distinction. However, understanding deception and teasing does not always involve the need to attribute higher-order intentions about beliefs; that is, 'A wants B to believe x'. First, children can base their understanding of deception and teasing on behaviour (A wants B to do x). Secondly, they can base their understanding on mental states that are not representational (A wants B to see, know) and finally on mental states that are representational (A wants B to believe that x is true).

ACKNOWLEGEMENTS

I should like to express my sincere thanks to Maggie DeVos for her assistance with data collection for experiment 4. I am also especially grateful to Sylvia Turner for help with the manuscript preparation and Nicola Yuill, Josef Perner, Vasu Reddy and Dick Byrne for their helpful comments and advice.

NOTES

1   The term 'higher-order intentions and beliefs' includes second, third or fourth-order mental states. In this chapter, I use the term 'intention' synonymously with the term 'desire' since in this case there is no difference between them. 'A' both *wants* and *intends* to make 'B' believe (cf. chapter 3).

2   By using the terms 'first and second-order mental states', I am adopting Perner's (1988b) terminology (see also Perner and Wimmer, 1985; and Yuill and Perner, 1987). Here understanding first-order beliefs means the child attributes a *belief* to X. Understanding second-order beliefs means the child attributes to X a *belief* about Y's *belief*. This way of counting levels differs from that used by others (Dennett, 1978, 1987; Leslie, 1988a; Whiten and Byrne, 1988a) as explained by Whiten and Perner in chapter 1.

3   As Reddy (chapter 10) points out, joking and teasing acts often involve some kind of temporary deception. In my analysis and experiments these acts are distinguished in terms of whether the speaker is being serious in their intention to deceive and wants the listener to remain deceived.

4   Mitchell's third and fourth levels are equivalent to my first- and second-order distinction, though it should be noted that Mitchell's levels concern the animal's action while mine concern *understanding* action.

12

Reading Minds or Reading Behaviour? Tests for a Theory of Mind in Monkeys

DOROTHY L. CHENEY AND ROBERT M. SEYFARTH

To attribute beliefs, knowledge, ignorance and emotions to both oneself and others is to have what Premack and Woodruff (1978) term a 'theory of mind'. A theory of mind is a theory because, unlike behaviour, mental states are not directly observable, although they can be used to make predictions about behaviour. Monkeys and apes are highly adept at recognizing the similarities and differences between their own and other individuals' social relationships. What is not known is whether they are equally adept at recognizing the similarities and differences between their own and other individuals' states of mind.

Without the ability to attribute mental states to oneself and others, there can be no pedagogy, empathy, and very little self-reflection. Since an individual who lacks a theory of mind cannot recognize ignorance or false beliefs in others, he cannot selectively alert some, but not others, to novel information. Similarly, since an individual who cannot attribute states of mind to others fails to understand that beliefs and motives can act as causal agents of behaviour, he cannot easily generalize past experiences from one context to the next or from one individual to another. Because he is unable to assess his companions' motives, his predictions about other animals' actions derive primarily from previous experiences in a particular social context (see also chapter 1).

Despite the apparent functional advantages of a theory of mind, however, it is far from clear whether non-human primates ever act to alter other individuals' beliefs, rather than simply their behaviour (see Cheney and Seyfarth, 1990, for a review). Perhaps this is not surprising, since, as many papers in this volume clearly demonstrate, before about the age of four years it is even difficult for children to recognize false beliefs or ignorance in others.

Like many other animals, monkeys and apes are acutely sensitive to the

presence and composition of their audience. To cite just two examples, subordinate males in many primate species will often only attempt to copulate
after they have manoeuvred their partner into a position out of sight of
more dominant males (e.g. de Waal, 1982, 1989; reviewed in Byrne and
Whiten, 1988). But what is the basis of this apparent deception? Does a
subordinate male copulate behind a bush because he knows that he can
influence what the dominant male sees and therefore thinks? Or does the
subordinate male go behind a bush simply because he has learned from past
experience that he can avoid attack whenever he copulates out of sight of
the dominant male? Given the nature of our observations, there is simply
no way to distinguish between these two alternatives. At the moment, we
have very little evidence that monkeys ever act to alter other individuals'
beliefs rather than their *behaviour*. We cannot rule out the possibility that
'deception' simply results from an animal's knowledge of specific behavioural
contingencies: if I do X, he will do Y (see Bennett, chapter 7).

A consideration of alarm calls reveals similarly incomplete evidence for a
theory of mind. Alarm calls in many species of birds and mammals are not
obligatory but depend on social context. Individuals often fail to give alarm
calls when there is no functional advantage to be gained by alerting others;
for example, when they are alone or in the presence of unrelated animals
(e.g. roosters: Gyger, Karakashian and Marler, 1986; ground squirrels:
Sherman, 1977; vervet monkeys: Cheney and Seyfarth, 1985). While this
'audience effect' requires that animals closely monitor the presence and
behaviour of group companions, however, it does not demand that the
signaller distinguish between ignorance and knowledge on the part of his
audience. Indeed, in all species studied to date, signallers call regardless of
whether or not their audience is already aware of danger. Vervet monkeys,
for example, will continue to give alarm calls long after everyone in the
group has seen the predator and fled to safety (Cheney and Seyfarth, 1981,
1985).

Even in the case of loud, long-distance food calls, or 'pant-hoots', given
by chimpanzees, it seems unlikely that signallers take into account their
audience's state of mind. Chimpanzee pant-hoots are capable of conveying
quite precise information about the presence and abundance of food, but
calling rate seems to be influenced primarily by the relative abundance of
the resource. There is no evidence that chimpanzees alter their calling
behaviour depending upon whether their audience is already aware of the
food or not (Wrangham, 1975; Hauser and Wrangham, 1987).

According to the philosopher Grice (1957), true communication does not
occur unless both signallers and recipients take into account each others'
states of mind. By this criterion, it is doubtful that *any* animal signal could
ever be described as truly communicative. Does this matter, though? It

could easily be argued that there is little selective advantage to be gained from determining whether or not one's audience is ignorant or knowledgeable before uttering an alarm call; as long as the call *functions* to inform others of danger, the audience's state of mind is irrelevant.

Here again, however, having a theory of mind might well be an evolutionary asset. Among ground squirrels, for example, animals who give alarm calls put themselves at greater risk than those who remain silent, because alarm calls attract the attention of predators and those who give alarms are more likely to be taken (e.g. Sherman, 1977, 1985). Under these conditions, an individual would be at an obvious advantage if he could determine whether or not an alarm call was really necessary before uttering the call.

In this paper, we describe two experiments designed to investigate the ability of monkeys to attribute mental states to others and to distinguish between their own knowledge and the knowledge of others. The first experiment examines the issue of informing, and considers whether individuals take into account their audience's state of mind when alerting them to the presence of food or danger. Do signallers recognize ignorance in their audience, and, if so, do they make any special effort to alert ignorant individuals more than knowledgeable ones? The second experiment considers the extent to which a monkey's behaviour is influenced by her audience's apparent presence, as opposed to her audience's knowledge. Do monkeys only take into account their own visual perspective when monitoring one another, or do they recognize that another individual's perspective, and hence the knowledge derived from it, can differ from their own?

Clearly, we cannot claim to resolve ambiguities about theories of mind in non-human animals with only two experiments. Instead, we offer these tests as a preliminary attempt to address an issue that to date has been considered primarily in terms of highly suggestive, but largely inconclusive, anecdotes.

Experiment 1

Introduction

In captivity, Japanese macaques (*Macaca fuscata*) and rhesus macaques (*Macaca mulatta*) give alarm calls when they see technicians approaching with nets, and they also utter a 'coo'-like food call when they are fed preferred foods like fruit (Green, 1975b, personal observation). The aim of our first experiment was to determine whether or not mothers would utter more food or alarm calls when their offspring were ignorant about the presence of food or a predator than when they were not. Mothers were isolated from the rest of the group, either in the company of their offspring or alone, and then shown either highly preferred food or a 'predator' in the form of a technician with a net. The offspring were then released, alone, into a part of the enclosure where they were in close proximity to the food or the predator.

If monkeys are sensitive to the mental states of others – that is, if they take their audience's knowledge into account when giving food or alarm calls – the mothers should have uttered more calls (or in some other way have altered their behaviour) when their offspring were ignorant than when they were already informed. On the other hand, if informants are unaffected by their audience's mental states, their behaviour should have been similar regardless of whether or not their audience had also seen the food or danger. Given the observations that free-ranging monkeys and apes apparently fail to alter their calling rates depending upon their audience's state of mind, we predicted that the mother's behaviour would not be affected by their offspring's ignorance or knowledge.

Methods

Experiments were conducted on two groups of rhesus macaques and two groups of Japanese macaques. All animals had lived in social groups since birth. One of the rhesus groups had been constituted in 1984, while animals in the three other groups had lived together for over ten years. Each group included between one to two adult males (defined as animals aged over five years), three to four multiparous females, and five to eight nulliparous females, juveniles and infants.

The groups were housed at the California Primate Research Center in outdoor enclosures constructed from two modified corncribs (henceforth called 'arenas'), each measuring 4.7 metres in diameter with a conical roof 4.3 metres high. The two arenas were connected by a 4.9 metres × 3.0 metres rectangular intercage unit. A capture chute, mounted lengthwise along the back of the intercage unit, was used to capture and temporarily separate one or more animals from the rest of the group. During the experimental period, the two arenas in each enclosure were visually separated from each other by means of a screen erected on the side of the test arena.

We began each trial by locking all but two members of a group in one of the arenas. The remaining two animals, a mother and her juvenile offspring, were locked in the chute that connected the two arenas. In the 'knowledge-able' condition the mother and offspring were seated next to each other. Each could see the other, and both could see the empty test arena. In one set of trials, both individuals then watched a human place a highly preferred food (apple slices) in a food bin in the test arena. After observing the placement of food, the offspring, but not the mother, was released into the test arena, where it had access to the food bin.

In the 'ignorant' condition mother and offspring were also locked in the chute, but the offspring was seated at a distance from the mother, visually isolated and physically separated from her by a steel partition. Now, only the mother was able to observe the apple slices being placed in the food bin. After the food had been placed in the bin, the offspring, but not the mother, was once again released into the arena.

In a second set of trials, mothers saw a 'predator' (a technician wearing a surgical mask) approach with a net as if to capture her. After ten seconds' exposure, the technician hid behind a barrier next to the test arena. In the knowledgeable condition, the mother was seated next to her offspring and both mother and offspring saw the technician. In the ignorant condition, as before, the offspring was separated from the mother behind a steel partition and only the mother could see the technician. In both conditions, the offspring was released into the test arena immediately after the technician had disappeared.

Throughout the trial, the subjects' behaviour and visual orientation were noted by voice onto a tape recorder, and later transcribed. All vocalizations given by either mother or offspring were also recorded on a separate track of the tape recorder. In the food trials, observations lasted for 15 minutes before the mother and offspring were reunited with each other and the rest of the group. In the predator trials, observations lasted only five minutes to minimize the obvious distress caused to the animals by the sight of the technician.

All mothers with offspring aged at least two years were used as subjects. In both the food and predator trials, seven mother–offspring pairs were tested in the knowledgeable condition and seven different pairs in the ignorant condition. With some exceptions, each mother appeared as a subject only once in each trial. Those mother–offspring pairs that were tested as knowledgeable subjects in the food trial appeared as ignorant subjects in the predator trial, and *vice versa*. In three cases, a sibling pair rather than a mother–offspring pair was used. In such cases, the older sibling was given the role of the 'mother informant' (for more details, see Cheney and Seyfarth, forthcoming).

Results

Food trials If informants were influenced by their audience's knowledge, mothers should have uttered more calls or in some other respect altered their behaviour when their offspring were ignorant of the food than when their offspring already knew the food was present. The mothers' behaviour, however, seemed unaffected by their offspring's knowledge. The seven mothers whose offspring were ignorant showed no difference in their behaviour or calling rate compared with the seven mothers whose offspring were knowledgeable. Some mothers and offspring did exchange vocalizations at low rates, but the mean rate of calling by mothers of ignorant offspring did not differ significantly from that of mothers of knowledgeable offspring (mean number of calls by mothers of ignorant offspring: 3, SD = 4.1; by mothers of knowledgeable offspring: 1.3, SD = 1.5; one-tailed Mann-Whitney U test, N_1 = 7, N_2 = 7, U = 22.5, NS). Mothers' calling rate was also unaffected by offspring age or sex. Similarly, ignorant offspring did not call more than knowledgeable ones (U = 21, NS).

The mothers' apparent failure to communicate information about food to their ignorant offspring had immediate consequences. The mean latency for finding and eating food was significantly shorter for knowledgeable offspring than for ignorant ones (figure 12.1; U = 13, P < 0.05, corrected for ties). The primary factor determining whether the offspring actually acquired food, therefore, was the *offspring's* knowledge rather than the mother's.

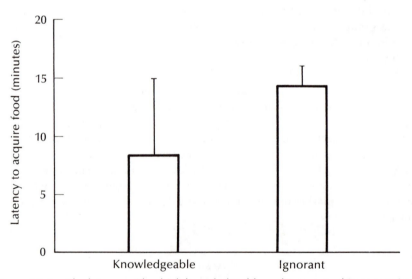

Figure 12.1   *The latency with which knowledgeable and ignorant subjects acquired food. Histograms show means and standard deviations for seven knowledgeable and seven ignorant subjects.*

Predator trials   Although all mothers showed distress at the sight of the technician and struggled to free themselves from the chute, none of them uttered alarm calls. The lack of alarm calls clearly made it more difficult for us to measure any transmission of information from informant to audience. Nevertheless, several measures suggested that mothers did not behave differently when their offspring were ignorant than when they were knowledgeable. For example, when their offspring were released into the arena, mothers of ignorant offspring did not orient themselves toward or look at their offspring more than mothers of knowledgeable offspring (U = 17.5, P > 0.1).

Despite the similarity in the mothers' behaviour under the two conditions, however, the behaviour of ignorant and knowledgeable offspring differed significantly. Upon seeing the technician, knowledgeable offspring showed distress by crouching and sitting next to their mothers at the entrance of the chute. After being released, knowledgeable offspring spent significantly more time than ignorant ones sitting within arm's reach of their mothers (figure 12.2; U = 9.5, P < 0.05). Paralleling results obtained earlier in food trials, therefore, the determining factor in the amount of anxiety shown by offspring was their *own* knowledge and not their mothers'.

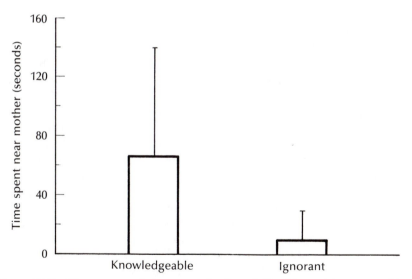

Figure 12.2   *The amount of time spent by knowledgeable and ignorant subjects within arm's reach of their mothers. Legend as in figure 12.1.*

Discussion

While the failure of mothers to give alarm calls made these experiments less informative than we had hoped, in neither the food nor the predator trials did mothers make any apparent effort to inform their offspring. Although it is possible that mothers gave their offspring some subtle behavioural cues that were not apparent to us, the juveniles' behaviour suggested that any such cues were also not apparent to them. Juveniles obtained food significantly faster when they had already seen the food themselves than when the presence of food was known only to their mothers, and they showed significantly more anxiety when they had seen the technician themselves than when the technician had only been seen by their mothers. Results support observational accounts of free-ranging monkeys and apes in suggesting that signallers do not alter their behaviour or calling rate depending upon their audience's knowledge. While the amount of food and the immediacy of danger may affect the behaviour of signallers, the audience's ignorance or knowledge appears to be relatively unimportant.

Might the mothers have failed to alert their offspring because they did not know that their offspring were ignorant? While we cannot answer this question definitively, the mothers certainly had ample *opportunity* to determine whether their offspring were ignorant. Under the ignorant condition, no other animals were in sight when the mothers were exposed to the food or the frightening technician, and their offspring were released from behind a steel barrier on the other side of the enclosure. Most important, the offspring's own behaviour was markedly different when they were ignorant than when they were knowledgeable. The question may, however, be moot. If the mothers were incapable of attributing ignorance to others, they could not, by definition, infer whether or not their offspring had seen the food or the predator.

Clearly, these negative results do not allow us to distinguish between the inability to attribute states of mind to others and the failure of this ability to alter behaviour. It could easily be that monkeys and apes *do* recognize the difference between their own knowledge and the knowledge of others, but that their behaviour is simply unaffected by this knowledge. Whenever knowledge in another species is defined operationally, through behaviour, there is a danger of concluding that an ability is absent when it is simply not manifested. Negative results *are* of interest, however, when compared with information transmission in humans. While human cultures vary in their emphasis upon active informing and pedagogy (e.g. Boyd and Richerson, 1985), in no culture are these modes of information-transmission absent. In contrast, pedagogy has yet to be documented conclusively even among chimpanzees (see Cheney and Seyfarth, 1990; Visalberghi and Fragaszy, forthcoming, for reviews). Even if non-human primates are capable of distinguishing ignorance and false beliefs in others, therefore, their apparent failure to act on this knowledge is striking.

Experiment 2

Introduction

In any analysis of social interactions it is almost impossible to distinguish between actions that result from knowledge of other individuals' states of mind and actions that result from knowledge of other individuals' behaviour. This is partly because it is difficult to present subjects with evidence of another animal's *knowledge* while simultaneously eliminating all visual or auditory evidence of the animal's physical *presence*. The problem is well illustrated by an experiment conducted by Keddy Hector, Seyfarth and Raleigh (1989) that attempted to determine if captive male vervet monkeys changed their behaviour towards infants depending upon whether the males perceived the infants' mothers to be watching them.

Among baboons, adult males frequently interact at high rates with a particular infant in an apparent effort to establish a close bond with the infant's mother (Seyfarth, 1978; Smuts, 1985; reviewed in Whitten, 1987). Since such bonds may persist into the female's oestrous period, affiliative interactions with infants may represent a reproductive strategy that allows males to offset some of the competitive disadvantage brought about by their low dominance rank. In captivity, male vervet monkeys also groom and carry infants. Keddy Hector's experiment tested whether or not the affiliative behaviour shown by vervet males towards infants might constitute a reproductive strategy to influence female mate choice.

The vervet groups were housed in cages similar to those described earlier for the 'informing' experiment, and consisted of an indoor and outdoor enclosure connected by a chute. In each trial, a male was locked in the outdoor half of the enclosure with an infant, while the rest of the group was locked inside. The mother was placed in the front of the chute, separated from the male and her infant either by a clear glass partition, a steel partition, or a one-way mirror that was transparent on one side. Neither the male nor the female could see each other in the steel door condition. In the one-way mirror condition, the female could see the male, but the male could not see the female.

All males, but particularly subordinate males, altered their behaviour towards the infants depending upon the perceived presence or absence of the mother. In the glass condition, when the mother appeared to be watching, males were more affiliative towards the infants, grooming, touching and lip-smacking at them. By contrast, in the steel and one-way mirror conditions, when the mother appeared to be absent, males were more likely to threaten the infant. The mother's behaviour under these different conditions also changed; mothers were less likely to threaten the male following the glass exposure, when both the mother and the male could see each other, than following the one-way mirror exposure, when the mother could see the male but the male could not see her.

It is impossible to conclude from these experiments that the males' behaviour was altered by their attribution of knowledge to the mothers. Males might have been friendly to infants because they wanted to influence what the infants' mothers *thought*. Alternatively, the males' behaviour might have simply been influenced by the mother's physical presence, much as alarm calls can be affected by the presence of an audience. If the males were influenced only by the presence of an audience, explanations based on states of mind are unnecessary. We cannot distinguish between these two alternatives, however, because in these tests the mother's presence and the mother's knowledge were confounded.

The experiment described below attempted to distinguish more precisely between an individual's apparent presence and her knowledge. Our aim was to investigate the extent to which monkeys recognize that there can be a difference between their own visual perspective (and the knowledge gained from what they see) and the visual perspective of others. The experiment followed the same procedure as Keddy Hector's, but with one important modification: the orientation of the one-way mirror was *reversed*, so that the animals in the arena could see the observer sitting in the chute, even though the observer could not see them.

We used as subjects the same adult female and juvenile Japanese and rhesus macaques described in experiment 1. In both of these species, offspring acquire dominance ranks similar to their mothers', and the ranks of younger animals often remain dependent on the support of their mothers and other female kin during agonistic interactions (see e.g. Kawai, 1958; Datta, 1983). Indeed, experiments conducted on Japanese macaques have shown that the juvenile offspring of dominant females can fall in rank relative to the members of normally subordinate matrilines if they are deprived of kin support (Chapais, 1988).

Our experiment measured the influence of a dominant mother's apparent presence on the agonistic interactions of her offspring and a normally subordinate older female. To do so, we locked the offspring of a high-ranking female in an empty test arena with a subordinate adult female under each of three conditions: when the mother was visible behind a clear glass barrier; when the mother was invisible behind a dark opaque barrier; and when the mother was seated behind a one-way mirror barrier. In this last case, the mother could be seen by her offspring and the subordinate female but she could not see them. The procedure represents a first step in separating an observer's apparent *presence* from her *knowledge*.

We predicted that under the glass condition, the subordinate female would behave toward the dominant offspring much as she did under normal group conditions, and would show little agonistic behaviour. In contrast, we predicted that the subordinate female would behave more agonistically when the mother was invisible behind the opaque barrier.

There were two possible outcomes to the trials using one-way mirrors. If the subordinate female was influenced more by her audience's apparent presence than by its knowledge, her behaviour under the one-way mirror condition should have been indistinguishable from her behaviour under the glass condition. On the other hand, if the subordinate female was capable of distinguishing between her own visual perspective and the mother's visual perspective, she might have realized that the mother could not see what was occurring even though she was visible. If this were true, the subordinate female's behaviour under the one-way mirror condition should have been indistinguishable from her behaviour under the opaque condition.

Given the many anecdotal observations suggesting that monkeys do not distinguish easily between their own and other individuals' states of mind (Whiten and Byrne, chapter 18; Cheney and Seyfarth, 1990), we predicted that the subordinate female's behaviour under the one-way mirror condition would be the same as her behaviour under the glass condition. Only the apparent presence of an audience would affect her behaviour; the audience's state of mind would be irrelevant.

Methods

Clearly, this experiment required that the monkeys become familiar with the properties of one-way mirrors. At least four weeks before the trials began, therefore, we placed a one-way mirror in each cage, at the entrance of the chute. Each side of the mirror was bordered with differently coloured fluorescent tape to allow the animals more easily to distinguish between the opaque and transparent sides. We emphasize that this procedure only gave the monkeys the *opportunity* to learn that each side of the mirror provided a different visual perspective. If monkeys are incapable of comprehending that their own visual perspective can differ from another individual's, they will never, by definition, understand how one-way mirrors work.

To accustom the animals to the test procedure, all groups were subjected to at least 11 separations and lock-outs prior to the trials. The dyads selected for these pre-trial lock-outs did not involve the same combination of animals that were later used in formal tests.

At the start of each trial, two technicians herded the animals into the chute and separated the subjects from the rest of the group, which was then released into the other half of the enclosure. The mother observer was then locked in the chute behind one of the three barriers and the test dyad was released into the test arena. After 30 minutes, the observer was also released into the arena, and the three animals were observed for a further 15 minutes. The animals were then reunited with the rest of the group. All comparisons of rates of behaviour before and after the observer's release are corrected for the difference in observation time. In the statistical analysis below, only significant results are presented.

The animals in the test arena could see only each other, although they remained in auditory contact with both the mother observer and other group members. The observer was visible only through the barrier that separated her from the animals in the test arena, and was therefore not visible to us. Our inability to monitor the behaviour of the observer was unfortunate, because subsequent analysis suggested that the observer's behaviour and apparent attentiveness toward the animals in the test arena affected their behaviour.

With one exception, each individual was used in only one set of trials. All possible triadic combinations of two females and one juvenile were used, to produce a sample of eight sets of animals for each of the three test conditions. Since the number of juveniles was limited, we were not always able to control precisely for offspring age or sex, and in two cases we were forced to use older offspring (aged four and five years) whose ranks were probably relatively independent of their mothers' support. Similarly, in one set of trials, the 'observer' was not a mother but a sister of the test animal.

Each set of subjects was tested under each of the three conditions. To minimize order effects, four sets of animals were tested in the glass condition first, and four were tested in the mirror condition first. The opaque condition occurred as the second trial for all eight sets of animals. All trials involving the same individuals were separated by at least three days.

Although subjects almost never exchanged affinitive interactions during the test period, they did exhibit agonistic behaviour in the form of approach–retreat interactions and threats. An approach–retreat interaction (or supplant) was defined as occurring whenever one animal approached to within two metres of another, and the other animal moved at least 0.5 metres away. A threat occurred whenever one animal bit, chased, hit, pushed or gave an open-mouth display at another.

We also measured the relative frequency with which subordinate animals approached and left their dominant companions under the three conditions, using the index derived by Hinde (Hinde and Atkinson, 1970). This index is defined as the percentage of approaches due to the subordinate minus the percentage of leavings due to the same animal (and then multiplied by 100), where approaches and leavings were defined in terms of changes in distances of two metres.

The ranks of all subjects were determined prior to the onset of the trials from data on agonistic interactions obtained during the previous two years (Owren and Dieter, personal communication). Dominance rank was defined in terms of the direction of approach–retreat interactions. We refer to the mother in the chute as the 'observer'. The two animals in the outdoor arena are referred to in terms of their relative ranks under normal group conditions. Thus the offspring of the observer is called the 'dominant' subject even though his or her rank may have been dependent upon the presence of the mother. The older lower-ranking female is called the 'subordinate' subject (for more details see Cheney and Seyfarth, forthcoming).

Results

Time spent near chute   All subjects spent some time during each trial sitting on the ground within two metres of the chute's entrance. This behaviour provides a measure of both the observer's visibility to the subjects and the subjects' interest in her under the three test conditions.

On average, both dominant and subordinate subjects spent the most time near the chute under the mirror condition, the next most under the glass condition, and the least under the opaque condition (see figure 12.3. For subordinates, glass versus opaque: glass more = 6 subjects, opaque more = 1 subject, tie = 1 subject; one-tailed sign test, P = 0.062. For dominants, glass versus opaque: glass more = 5, opaque more = 0, ties = 3; P = 0.031. Mirror versus opaque: mirror more = 6, opaque more = 1, ties = 1; P = 0.062.)

It seems probable that the greater amount of time spent by subjects near the chute under the mirror condition was due to the fact that, although the observer was visible, she was not responsive or attentive toward the subjects. Her behaviour was therefore somewhat abnormal, and attracted the subjects' attention. Given our inability to monitor the observer, however, this can only remain conjecture.

Agonistic behaviour   (1) *Pre-release.* As might be expected if the ranks of normally dominant juveniles were to some extent dependent on

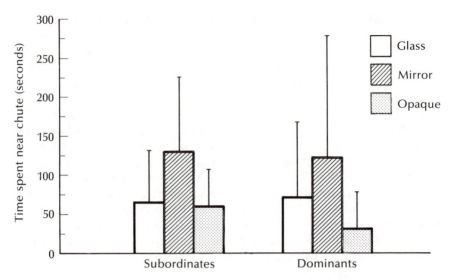

Figure 12.3   *The amount of time that subordinate and dominant subjects spent near the chute under the three test conditions. Histograms show mean and standard deviations for eight subordinate and eight dominant subjects.*

their older relatives' support, subordinate subjects on average supplanted and threatened their dominant companions least under the glass condition and most under the opaque condition, with the mirror condition being intermediate between these two extremes (see figure 12.4. Glass versus opaque: glass more = 0, opaque more = 5, ties = 3; P = 0.031.) The behaviour of dominant subjects showed the opposite pattern. Dominant animals showed most agonistic behaviour under the glass condition, less under the mirror condition, and least under the opaque condition (see figure 12.4. Glass versus opaque: glass more = 6, opaque more = 1, ties = 1; P =0.062. Glass versus mirror: glass more = 5, mirror more = 0, ties = 3; P = 0.031.)

(2)   *Comparison of agonistic behaviour before and after the observer's release*. Because subjects were sometimes distracted by activity elsewhere in the colony, it was necessary also to analyse our data using a method that controlled for variation in the subjects' behaviour from one day to the next. To this end, we compared subjects' behaviour before the observer's release with their behaviour after her release under the three conditions. If the subjects' agonistic interactions were influenced by the observer's visibility or apparent attentiveness, we would predict little difference in behaviour

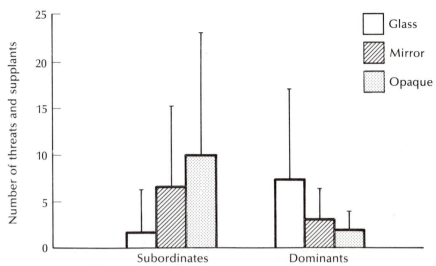

Figure 12.4   *The number of threats and supplants given by subordinate and dominant subjects to their companions under the three test conditions. Legend as in figure 12.3.*

before and after release under the glass condition and a substantial difference under the opaque condition.

As predicted, under the glass condition there was no difference in the agonistic behaviour of subordinates before and after the observer's release (figure 12.5). Under the mirror condition, there was also no significant change in the behaviour of subordinates following the observer's release. In contrast, under the opaque condition, there was a significant change in subordinates' behaviour, with six subjects showing more agonistic behaviour before the mother's release than afterwards, and two showing no change (P = 0.016).

For dominants, the mean number of supplants and threats given to subordinates before and after the observer's release was the same under both the glass and mirror conditions (figure 12.5). As predicted, under the opaque condition the mean number of supplants and threats given by dominants was higher after the observer's release than before. This difference, however, was not statistically significant.

The observers' behaviour following release also differed somewhat under the three conditions, although in no case were these differences statistically significant. Observers showed slightly less agonistic behaviour under the glass condition, when they had been able to watch the subjects' interactions and when subordinates had been least aggressive, than under either the mirror

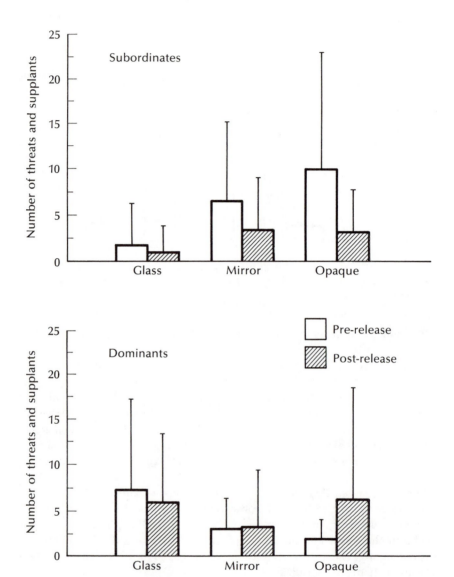

Figure 12.5   *The number of threats and supplants given by subordinate and domi-nant subjects to their companions before and after the observer's release under the three test conditions. Legend as in figure 12.3.*

mirror or opaque conditions, when they had been unable to observe the subjects.

Curiously, the dominant subjects' behaviour following the observers' release never seemed to alert the observers to what had transpired earlier. Dominant subjects never threatened or attempted to recruit the observers' aid following their reunion with the observer, even when they had been threatened or bitten prior to the observer's release.

Approach–leave index for subordinates (1) *Pre-release.* The approach–leave index provides a measure of the relative role of subordinate subjects in maintaining proximity with their dominant companions. A negative figure indicates that the subordinate subject left her companion more than she approached her; the magnitude of this figure therefore provides some indication of the extent to which subordinate females avoided dominant animals under the three test conditions.

As might be predicted if the observer's visibility had some influence on the subjects' relative ranks, a larger number of subordinate subjects had a more negative approach–leave index under the glass condition than under either the mirror or the opaque condition (see figure 12.6. Glass versus opaque: glass more negative = 6, opaque more = 1; $P = 0.035$; glass versus mirror: glass more negative = 6, mirror more = 2). In contrast, under mirror and opaque conditions the subordinates' indices were slightly positive, suggesting that the subordinates were behaving as if the observer was not present (figure 12.6).

(2) *Post-release.* As predicted, there was little difference between the behaviour of subordinates before and after the observer's release under the glass condition; in each case, subordinates had, on average, high negative scores. Under both the mirror and the opaque conditions, however, there was an overall change in subordinates' behaviour, with the index becoming more negative following the observer's release (see figure 12.6). Under neither condition, however, was this difference significant.

Discussion

The results of the trials using glass and opaque barriers support many previous studies in suggesting that the dominance ranks of juveniles are to at least some extent dependent upon kin support. Juvenile subjects were supplanted and threatened significantly more by normally subordinate females when their close kin were hidden behind an opaque barrier than when their close relatives were visible. Subordinate females also approached their dominant companions more often (or moved off from them less

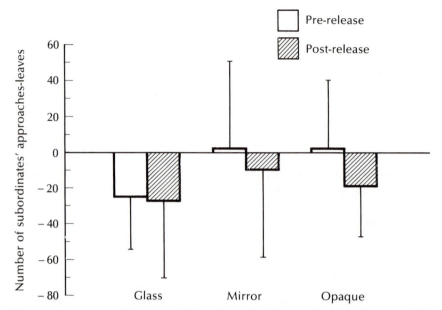

Figure 12.6 *Approach–retreat indices for subordinate subjects relative to their dominant companions before and after the observer's release under the three test conditions. Legend as in figure 12.3.*

frequently). Conversely, dominant juveniles showed more agonistic behaviour when their relatives were visible than when they were not. They also spent more time near the entrance of the chute when the observer was visible, suggesting that their rank was to some extent dependent upon her proximity. Finally, both dominant and subordinate subjects showed more changes in their behaviour following the observers' release from the opaque barrier than from the glass barrier, further suggesting that their behaviour was strongly influenced by the observers' visibility.

Some aspects of the subjects' behaviour were the same under both mirror and glass conditions, as would be predicted if we assume that monkeys do not distinguish between another animal's presence and its knowledge. For example, both subordinate and dominant subjects spent more time near the chute under the mirror and glass conditions than under the opaque condition.

According to other behavioural measures, however, subjects treated the mirror barriers as if they were opaque, and therefore behaved as if they *could* distinguish between the observer's presence and her knowledge. Dominant subjects showed more agonistic behaviour under the glass condition than under either the mirror or opaque condition, while subordinate subjects showed more agonistic behaviour under mirror and opaque conditions than under the glass condition. Similarly, subordinate subjects were more likely to avoid their dominant companions under the glass condition than under either mirror or opaque conditions.

The similarity between mirror and opaque barriers becomes less apparent when we contrast the subjects' behaviour before and after the observers' release. Only under the opaque condition, for example, was there a marked change in the agonistic behaviour of dominant and subordinate subjects following the observers' release. According to this comparison, at least, the mirror barrier was more like the glass than the opaque barrier.

In summary, therefore, some of our results argue against a 'theory of mind' in monkeys, while others support it and still others are inconclusive. Can we therefore conclude that the monkeys might have been capable of attributing ignorance to others, and of recognizing that other animals' visual perspectives can be different from their own? Not really, because we cannot rule out the more conservative and likely hypothesis that subjects were simply adept at monitoring the observer's behaviour and apparent attentiveness. Rather than recognizing a mental state – the observer's ignorance – subjects may instead have been sensitive to her actions, orientation and the direction of her gaze.

Numerous anecdotes from field observations provide similarly inconclusive evidence of a theory of mind in monkeys. When subordinate males copulate from behind bushes, or when females groom subordinate males only after they have first concealed themselves behind rocks (e.g. Kummer, 1982), it is impossible to determine whether or not the animals understand that the spatial perspective and visual field of others differ from their own. Humans as young as three years old seem capable of recognizing the distinction between their own physical orientation and the orientation of others (Donaldson, 1978; Flavell, Shipstead and Croft, 1978), suggesting that they recognize at least some distinction between their own knowledge and the knowledge of others. Whether monkeys are also capable of such judgements, however, is simply not known. Animals may simply learn that they can avoid attack if they conceal their actions from more dominant individuals.

It is, of course, by no means a trivial feat to adjust one's own behaviour according to other individuals' orientation and direction of gaze. The ability certainly demands that monkeys recognize that attentiveness can strongly affect *actions*. It remains to be determined, however, whether monkeys also recognize that attentiveness can affect *knowledge*. The experiments described here support what many observational studies have suggested: that monkeys are sensitive to the composition of their audience and that they are astute observers of each others' behaviour and apparent attentiveness. They may be less astute observers of each others' minds.

ACKNOWLEDGEMENTS

We are grateful to the staff of the California Primate Research Center, Davis, California for their assistance in these experiments. Special thanks are due to A. Hendrickx and S. Cello for administrative assistance and to J. Adams, A. Cabrera and P. Telfer for their help in conducting the trials. J. Dieter and M. Owren provided essential background data on the animals. Thanks also to B. Bornstein for suggesting that we reverse the mirror. J. Astington, V. Dasser, A. Keddy Hector and M. Owren read earlier drafts of this manuscript, and we are grateful to them for their comments. Research was supported by NIH grant 19826.

13

Visual Behaviour as a Window for Reading the Mind of Others in Primates

Juan Carlos Gómez

*When one perceives that another is looking at one, one perceives that
another intends something by one, or expects something of one. In a
word, one perceives that one is being taken account of by another . . .
We can only be sure that we are being effective in what we do if the
other is taking account of it . . . Through eye-contact P knows that he
is affecting Q in some way and that he is thereby making progress in
whatever he is attempting to do.*

A. Kendon, 1967

This paper is about the use of visual behaviour as a window for mindreading
in primates. Visual behaviour has been identified as an important component
of social interactions in humans and other animals (Argyle and Cook, 1976;
Fehr and Exline, 1987). I am going to concentrate upon one special kind
of visual behaviour that seems to be particularly relevant for mindreading:
looking at another's eyes. There are two basic ways of looking at the eyes
of another person (see figure 13.1): one is *gaze monitoring* or *deictic gaze*
(see Butterworth, chapter 15), which consists of looking at the eyes of a
person who is looking away; the other is *mutual gaze* or *eye contact,* and
it involves two persons looking at each other's eyes. Typically, both patterns
are sequentially combined into a pattern called 'gaze alternation'. In it, a
person looks alternately at an object and at another's eyes.

Research mentioned in this paper was in part supported by a grant of the CAICYT
(Nr 1342–82) awarded to Dr J. L. Linaza. Our thanks to the managers of Madrid
Zoo for giving us permission to work with the gorillas in the zoo nursery facilities.

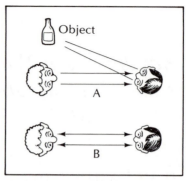

Figure 13.1   *Deictic gaze (a) and mutual gaze (b).*

Mutual gaze and its allied patterns have been extensively studied as a component of human interactions by researchers in the field of non-verbal communication (Fehr and Exline, 1987). It has been identified as an important component of interactions, although its interpretation has raised some controversy (Rutter, 1984). On the other hand, eye contact has also been identified as an important pattern in the development of early social interactions in human infants (Schaffer, 1984; Trevarthen and Hubley, 1978; Butterworth, chapter 15). It is used as an essential criterion to define intentional communication in infants interacting with adults (Bretherton and Bates, 1979; Sarria et al., 1988). It is also mentioned by ethologists as playing 'a critical role' in certain primate interactions such as reconciliation among chimpanzees (de Waal, 1989). Recent studies extend research on gaze to non-mammalian species (Ristau, chapter 14). Despite the importance implicitly attributed to this behaviour, however, it has not been explicitly interpreted in a theoretical framework. Both personal intuition and systematic observation agree that mutual gaze plays an important part in social interactions. But why is it important? In this paper I am going to propose a theoretical interpretation of the meaning of mutual gaze founded upon my own research with non-human primates. First, I will describe some of the observations on gorillas that originally suggested this interpretation.

Mutual Gaze in Infant Gorillas Interacting with Human Adults

I am going to present some data on the development of eye-contact patterns in an infant gorilla interacting with human adults in problem-solving situations (Gómez, forthcoming, a.) The subject of this longitudinal study was a hand-reared female infant gorilla (*Gorilla gorilla gorilla*) observed in a zoo nursery environment from about six months to 30 months.

A well-known problem-solving situation for anthropoid apes is when they have to move a box under an objective hanging from the ceiling in order to reach it (Köhler, 1917). In the standard experimental procedure, the ape remains alone in a room trying to solve the problem with a number of objects available to him. As we were interested in ape–human interactions, however, our experimental procedure allowed for the presence of a human adult at the scene. In figure 13.2 appears a sketch depicting the situation. The animal can solve the problem of reaching the door's latch either using the box as a support or seeking help from the human. Our aim was to compare the structure of spontaneous solutions involving humans with the structure of solutions involving objects (see Gómez, forthcoming, a).

Solutions Involving Objects

In the above example, the typical solution consists of applying force to the box in order to move it to an appropriate location under the door (figure 13.3a). This sequence of actions is accompanied by looks directed at the relevant parts of the environment (door, latch, box, ground). The function of the looks appears to be to monitor the actions in relation to the environment. The subject looks at the points with which she needs to coordinate her behaviour (e.g., the door when she is moving the box; the latch and the box when she is adjusting the position of the box in front of the door, etc.).

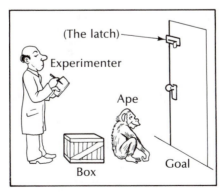

Figure 13.2   *The problem set.*

Solutions Involving Humans

We observed two different kinds of behaviour patterns used by the gorilla to involve humans in the solution of the task:

Human dragging The gorilla pushes or pulls the human towards the door and, once there, she climbs on the human to reach the latch (figure 13.3b). There seems to be no essential difference between this procedure and the previous one applied to objects. The human is apparently treated as a box. The gorilla tries to move him under the door applying to him all the force she is capable of. Once under the door, she climbs on the human and reaches the latch. As in the previous procedure, the looks of the gorilla are concentrated on the environmental parts relevant to the problem. Thus, the gorilla looks occasionally at the human, but only at the legs or the body

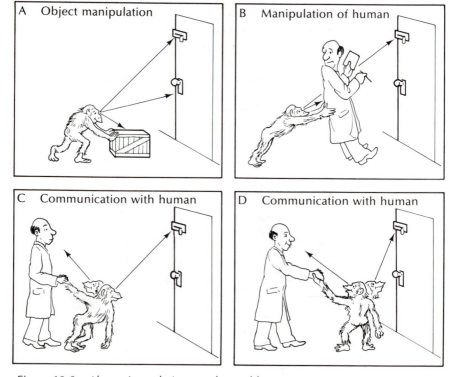

Figure 13.3 *Alternative solutions to the problem set.*

as a whole. There is no gaze directed at the human's eyes at any part of the procedure.[1]

Request to human   The gorilla takes the human by his hand and pulls him softly (applying a force well under the level she would be able to) towards the door while looking alternately at the door and his eyes (figure 13.3c). Once there, she alternates looks at the latch and the human's eyes, while taking his hand in the direction of the latch (figure 13.3d).

In the first part of this procedure (figure 13.3c), although the gorilla continues to establish physical contact with the human and directs him towards the goal, there are two essential differences with the previous behaviour. First, the action displayed by the gorilla seems not to be designed to move the human mechanically. The human is not 'dragged' by sheer force but gently 'led' by hand. And second, although the gorilla continues to look at the goal, she also looks at the human's eyes.

In the second part of the procedure (figure 13.3d), the difference with the use of objects is still clearer: In some observations there was a total absence of further action by the gorilla. She simply *looked alternately* at the latch and at the human's eyes, while waiting for the latter to act (Gómez, forthcoming, b). In most cases, however, the gorilla took the human's hand in the direction of the latch 'freezing' it midway and alternating her gaze between the latch and the eyes of the human.

Ontogenetically, the first procedure to appear was the use of boxes as supports (by the end of the first year). Shortly after that, the use of the human as a box appeared (when the animal was about one-year-old). Requests to the human appeared six months later (Gómez, forthcoming, a).

Humans as Objects and Subjects

If we compare the two problem-solving procedures involving humans, we can see that in the first one ('human dragging') only the properties of the human body as a physical object seem to be taken into account by the gorilla. In the second procedure, however, the gorilla seems to take into account something else, and her behaviour can no longer be described as:

Gorilla wants to move *human* to the door

It seems more appropriate to describe it as:

Gorilla wants *human* to move to the door

In the first description, the *human* plays the grammatical role of *object* for the action 'to move' which is carried out by the gorilla, whereas in the second it plays the role of *subject* of the action of moving. I have argued elsewhere (Gómez, forthcoming, a) that the grammatical difference apparent in these descriptions reflects the *psychological difference* underlying both kinds of behaviours. The second procedure is a *request*, a communicative behaviour addressed to another organism. The essence of communicative behaviours is that the actor's actions are adapted to the recipient as a *subject*, i.e. that they take into account and exploit the *subjective properties* of other organisms and not merely the physical ('objective') properties they share with objects. This is precisely what the gorilla does in her second procedure.

Adaptation to the human as a subject is recognized by two essential distinctive features: first, the actions displayed by the gorilla are mechanically inadequate to reach the goal (displacing the human); secondly, the visual behaviour of the gorilla includes looks at the human's eyes that would be irrelevant to the task if it were to be solved by mechanical means.

The *mechanical inadequacy* of actions is an adaptation to the fact that subjects are *agents*. In comparison with their mechanically functional counterparts (human-dragging), the communicative versions (hand-leading behaviours) are physically ineffective. They lack segments and force, or change their form, because they are not intended to carry out a movement, but merely to 'trigger' it in an autonomous agent.

But what about *mutual gaze*? The fact that a subject is an agent, i.e. that he is able to act by himself, does not explain why he is looked at in the eyes. To check whether the human is responding or not, it would be better to look at his legs, hands or whatever body part is involved in the action to be carried out. However, the human is consistently looked at the eyes. Human infants also look consistently at an adult's eyes when they begin to communicate about objects of the environment (Bretherton and Bates, 1979; Trevarthen and Hubley, 1978).

Since the gorilla seems always to look at the relevant parts of the situation when she is trying to solve a problem, the inference is that for the gorilla the eyes of the human must play a relevant part in the solution. It seems that for the gorilla it is as important to monitor the human's gaze as, for example, to monitor the position of the goal. What is the gorilla monitoring when looking at the human's eyes? My interpretation is that she is *checking if the human is attending to her actions*. When an organism is asking another to do something, it is essential to know if the addressee is perceiving the request. For a request to work, to have the attention of the addressee is as important as is physical contact between, for example, a stick and a banana for the mechanical action of dragging the latter with the former to work. Looking at the other's eyes is an excellent way to control (and to establish) this essential *attentional contact between subjects* needed in communicative interactions. Since the direction of another's gaze informs us about what he is attending to, to have eye contact with the addressee is to have its attention. Eye contact, then, is an index of attention contact – the kind of *causal link* which is essential for communication to work (cf. the opening quotation from Kendon, 1967).

Thus, whereas mechanical inadequacy is an index of an organism's adaptation to the *agentive* side of subjects (the property of acting by themselves), eye contact is an index of adaptation to their *perceptual/attentional* side (the fact that they perceive objects and events in the environment).

In the above examples, however, the ape was not simply adapting herself, on the one side, to the human as an agent, and on the other, to the human as a perceiver; her behaviour showed that she perceived both aspects of the human as *coordinated*. She used eye contact (combined with deictic gaze) at strategic moments of the interaction (for example, when first taking the human's hand or when she had already extended the human's arm towards the latch). She seemed to use eye contact to monitor if the human was *attending* to her request that he *acted*. Thus, she seemed to understand that in subjects perceiving is causally related to acting. And here is where the mind appears, since the coordination between perceptions and actions is carried out by the mind (figure 13.4).

Thus, the main achievement of the gorilla in figure 13.3 is the develop-

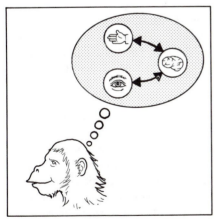 

A. Explicit representation of the mind   B. Latent understanding of the mind

Figure 13.4 *Two alternative ways of understanding the mind. A: the mind is represented as an explicit separate link between perception and action. B: The mind remains implicit in the perception of attention and action as causally related.*

ment of a form of interaction with human adults based upon an understanding of people as 'subjective' entities, whose autonomous behaviour can be influenced through a special kind of causal contact: mutual attention. This development seems to coincide with that of preverbal human infants at around 12 months, when they begin to communicate with adults about external obejcts (Bates, 1976; Trevarthen and Hubley, 1978).[2]

Sometimes it has been suggested that the beginnings of intentional communication in one-year-old infants are a manifestation of their understanding of adults as mere 'agents' (Poulin-Dubois and Shultz, 1988; Schultz, chapter 6). My interpretation suggests that they also understand them as perceivers. Intentional communication cannot be based upon the mere understanding of others as agents, i.e. as entities able to generate their own movements. To communicate there must also be an understanding of them as entities capable of perceiving the environment and behaving according to their perceptions.[3] Prelinguistic one-year-olds and gorillas show that they have at least a rudimentary understanding of the perceptual abilities of people and their relation to the behaviours they can subsequently generate. They seem to understand that an agent's behaviour may depend upon what he is attending to. Thus, they seem *somehow* to take into account the mind of the other. The core of the problem lies in this *somehow*.

Eye Contact and Mindreading

How is the mind taken into account by gorillas and pre-verbal infants communicating with adults? Why do they seek to establish eye contact and mutual gaze with others? Perhaps because the eyes are the windows through which the ape and the human infant begin to read the mind of others? I have spoken of 'attention contact' to suggest an explanation for mutual gaze. I could have spoken, however, of 'mind contact'. Mutual gaze and the information derived thereof could be interpreted as a way of sharing the contents of the minds, as a signal of mutual mental engagement. In this sense, the eyes would be windows through which we gain access to the minds of other people and display our own minds to others.

Since attention is one of the primary processes of cognition (a primary state of mind), perceiving that someone is attending to a thing must involve a reference to something that goes beyond the physical display 'looking at' into the realm of the mind. Indeed attending may be defined as 'turning the mind to something' (*Concise Oxford Dictionary*). Thus, understanding attention may involve an understanding of the mind.

Attention, however, is a cognitive process that can be directly reflected by certain behaviours: frequently, turning the mind involves turning the body, the head and especially the eyes, to something. This opens the possibility to have a good understanding of attention without having an explicit representation of the unobservable events or entities involved in this process. This understanding would be based upon the perception of the overt features of attentional activities, and it could be compared to the perceptual understanding of intention studied by Premack and Dasser (chapter 17).

Any understanding of the mind is of course based upon the perception of behaviour. The mind is always read in behaviour (Whiten and Perner, chapter 1; Bennett, chapter 7). One's representations, however, may either remain exclusively within the realm of behaviour (being first-order representations of the external, perceptible manifestations of the mind), or they may be second-order representations of the mind itself (the unobservable events or states that mediate between perception and action). My contention here is that organisms begin to understand the mind through first-order representations of behaviour (including attentional behaviour) organized in complex cognitive structures. This understanding is practical and not conceptual, and can be compared to the practical understanding of the physical world in sensorimotor intelligence (Piaget, 1936). This implies that it is not based upon the mere detection of contingencies between stimuli. It involves a focus upon the causal links that mediate contingencies and the ability to manipulate them in an intelligent way (Gómez, 1990a, b; Whiten and Byrne, 1990).

In the world of physical objects this practical understanding of causes is manifested in behaviours such as using a stick to get a goal. The realm of subjects and people, however, involves a different kind of causality based not upon the transmission of mechanical forces through physical contact,[4] but upon the transmission of information. In figure 13.3d and 13.3c the behaviour of the gorilla transmits information to the human who acts according to this information. The causal link that makes possible such transmission of information and connects the behaviour of the gorilla and the human is *mutual attention*. A practical understanding of the social world, then, must involve the ability to focus upon and exploit the external manifestations[5] of attention as causal links.

Thus, gorillas and human infants do not simply perceive the association between their own gestures and the adult's responses; they understand at least part of the causal chain connecting their behaviour with that of the adult; specifically, they understand that eye contact (mutual attention) is a *causal link* connecting their gestures with the human's actions. The gorilla understands that the human must *attend* to her gesture for it to be effective. Just as apes understand the need for contact between a stick and the object they want to move with it, they understand the need for *attentional contact* between the human and themselves when they want to communicate with the human (or the need for an absence of attentional contact when they want to avoid the reaction of the human; cf. deceptive hiding; Whiten and Byrne, 1988a).

The advantage of having a causal understanding of behaviour instead of a mere memory of contingencies is that the former allows one to focus upon the causal links when something goes wrong or when an innovation is needed. For example, a gorilla will get the human's attention before displaying her gestures, and will look for a new way of getting his attention when the situation precludes the known ones (e.g., use of pig grunt vocalizations or soft hair-pulling; see Gómez, forthcoming, b). Some deceptive behaviours of chimpanzees may also be explained in terms of a causal understanding of attention and action. For example, a chimpanzee covering his erect penis when a dominant male appears demonstrates that he understands a part of the causal chain (one that has to do with attention) which may lead to the dominant's aggressive reaction, and tries to alter it (see Whiten and Byrne, 1988a, and 1990; Gómez, 1990a).

Theories of Mind and Mentalistic Perceptions of Behaviour

A theory of mind involves a level of representation more complex than that required by the earliest manifestations of intentional communication. A theory of mind is a later stage in the development of what we could call the 'subject concept'; a stage in which the mind is explicitly represented and differentiated from behaviour. Without a theory of mind one is able to take into account only the behavioural manifestations of attention and its behavioural consequences; with a theory of mind, one is also able to understand the mental implications of attention that mediate behaviour, such as knowledge or belief (Astington and Gopnik, chapter 3; Wellman, chapter 2). Knowledge and belief are mental links in the causal chain leading from perception to action.

Gorillas and human infants seem to understand primarily the behavioural ends of this chain, but the mind is not totally absent in their understanding: it remains *implicit* in their representations of observable behaviours. This means they perceive that there is a link between the behavioural manifestations of attention and the actions of people, although they do not perceive nor represent this link (see figure 13.4). They can be said to have something like a 'latent hypothesis of the mind' rather than a theory of mind. It is only in this sense that their perception of behaviour can be said to be 'mentalistic'. At least in the case of humans, this latent hypothesis eventually becomes explicit (or can be made explicit) when the child begins to represent different aspects of mental processes and develops a proper theory of mind.

A problem that remains to be elucidated is that of the relationships between the 'theory of mind' and this early practical understanding of subjects. How does the latent hypothesis become an explicit theory? Is there a continuity between the latent and the explicit understanding of mental processes? It certainly seems natural to think that the explicit understanding of mental processes is at least partially dependent upon an adequate practical understanding of them. Baron-Cohen (chapter 16) suggests that autistic childrens failure to develop a theory of mind may be first manifested in their inability to understand and produce certain behaviours related to attention such as protodeclarative pointing. Is this failure to understand attention one of the causes that prevent autistic children from developing a theory of mind or is it another consequence of a general metarepresentational deficit (Leslie, chapter 5)? To what extent is metarepresentation involved in the understanding of attention?

Baron-Cohen (chapter 16) suggests that a proper understanding of attention may involve metarepresentation: representing others as representing something as interesting. I have suggested above, however, that it is possible to have a practical understanding of attention based upon its external manifestations. Attention, as any other cognitive process with direct behavioural counterparts, can be understood at different levels. One, that I call the practical level, is based upon the behavioural counterparts. Others may involve a reference to mental states such as 'being interested in something'. The practical understanding appears to be enough for an organism to develop proto-imperative communicative strategies, such as the requests shown by the gorilla in the above examples (figure 13.3b and 13.3c). Since these behaviours involve taking into account the attention of the addressee, they can not be attributed to a mere physical–causal understanding of people. In proto-imperatives the practical role of the recipient's attention is understood and this implies an understanding of a different kind of causality, one based upon the existence of subjects and 'subjective' properties.

Is it necessary, however, to have a representational understanding of attention in order to develop proto-declaratives? Gorillas and chimpanzees, despite their practical understanding of attention in requests, seem not to spontaneously develop full-fledged proto-declaratives (Gómez, forthcoming b; Savage-Rumbaugh et al., 1983). This would support the interpretation that proto-declaratives require something else. Furthermore, apes fail to spontaneously develop full-fledged symbolic play (see Whiten and Byrne, chapter 18). This could be interpreted as evidence of a metarepresentational deficit in apes and would support the view that proto-declaratives might require a representational understanding of attention.

Anthropoid apes and human infants develop a sophisticated practical understanding of subjects and subjective properties which does not require a theory of mind and that can not be accounted for in behaviouristic or associationistic terms. Gorillas and human infants clearly 'read' complex messages in the eyes, facial expressions, body configurations, etc., of other people, but they do not translate their readings into mental concepts. It is necessary to distinguish between 'mindreading' as the adaptation to mental phenomena through the perception or representation of the external manifestations of the mind, and 'mindreading' as the translation into mentalistic language of those manifestations. Such a translation would involve second-order representations (see Whiten and Byrne, chapter 18). Infant apes and humans do not properly have a 'theory of mind' but they are able to adapt their behaviour to some properties of the mind as manifested in the behaviour of others. Their reading of behaviour can be said to be 'mentalistic' as long as they capture some of the complex causal relations implied by the mind. Mindreading may imply a complex, 'mentalistic' perception or understanding of the behaviour of others which, however, remains different from a 'mentalistic conceptualization' of this behaviour (cf. Premack and Dasser, chapter 17).

NOTES

1   The illustration shows just *one* of several dragging procedures used by the animal. Some of them consisted of pulling in front of the human, in a position similar to that depicted in figure 13.3c. Thus, the absence of looks at the eyes is not due to the position of the gorilla behind the human.

2   This is valid for the ability to use mutual attention to organize interactions around objects of the environment. In face to face interactions without objects, such as rough-and-tumble play, the importance of attention contact seems to be understood earlier both in apes and humans (Gómez, forthcoming b; Trevarthen and Hubley, 1978).

3   Subjects also present a number of further properties, such as emotion and motivation, crucial for an adequate understanding of them (see Whiten and Perner, chapter 1), but in this paper I am going to concentrate only on the 'colder' side of subjects.

4   In the physical world there is an important causal force that operates without physical contact: it is gravity. Note, however, that organisms directly perceive it as 'weight'. This is a good example of how an unobservable entity on which a

theory may be developed may be directly perceived through its external manifestations without regard of theoretical representations.

5 The external manifestations of attention can be conceived as a set of emergent properties that can be perceived as a *Gestalt* quality of movements. Premack and Dasser (chapter 17) present an example of such a perception. Köhler (1917) was probably the first to suggest that behaviour presents a number of *Gestalt* qualities which are normally captured in everyday language with terms such as 'quiet', 'uneasy', 'looking for', etc.

14

Before Mindreading: Attention, Purposes and Deception in Birds?

CAROLYN A. RISTAU

Before an organism can attribute intentions to others, it must possess simpler abilities which are likely to be precursors to such 'mindreading'.

Some organisms may not have the ability to engage in the complicated attribution of intention, of which humans and at least some other primates seem to be capable. Possible precursors may include the following: (1) the species should itself have intentions, i.e. its behaviour should be describable in terms of purposes; and (2) it should be responsive to the attention of another. The existence of deceptive behaviour, depending on its complexity, might also reveal abilities similar to those necessary for mindreading.

Purposes

Among those attributes prior to an organism's having the capacity to attribute intentions in others, I suggest that the species in question should itself *have* intentions; its behaviours should be describable in terms of purposes. Whether the plovers' use of 'injury feigning' can be describable as purposive behaviour has been discussed in other publications (e.g. Ristau, 1983b, 1988, 1990). I make the case that it can, and is in that analogous to many other behaviours in both human and non-human species which have both innate and voluntary components. Yet while I emphasize the usefulness of applying terms such as 'purpose' to aspects of animal behaviour, I am also careful to note that there are no unassailable criteria connecting observable behaviours to specific accompanying mental states. The problem has remained unsolved for centuries by philosophers of mind and has not been solved in more recent decades by the comparatively new science of psychology. Neither, alas, am I the one to put all aright.

With these provisos in mind, I shall most briefly review my evidence suggesting that plovers exhibit purposeful behaviour. (Consult Ristau, 1983a, 1988, 1990, for more complete descriptions). Field studies were undertaken to investigate the plovers' use of 'injury feigning' or broken wing displays. Broken wing displays are so called because the bird's appearance very much resembles one with a broken wing. The full display consists in arching one or both wings and dragging them, quivering, along the ground. Sometimes the behaviour is accompanied by a raucous call. Both parents make the display, usually singly, but occasionally simultaneously. The behaviour occurs on some, but not all, approaches of an intruder towards the region of the eggs or young chicks. 'Injury feigning' is among the most intense of a repertoire of anti-predator behaviours, although occasionally some plover species behave aggressively, another very intense reaction.

Using human intruders to approach the eggs or young, the field experiments were conducted with piping (*Charadrius melodus*) and Wilson's plovers (*C. Wilsonia*) on a beach. The stance was taken that for some species, a bird engaged in 'injury feigning' or other distraction displays 'wants to lead an intruder away from its offspring' and acts as needed (within limits) to achieve that end. Data were gathered on the following questions: (1) Are the most intense displays (those resembling a broken wing) made in a direction that would usually cause an intruder who followed the displays to move further away from the offspring? (2) Does the displaying bird monitor the intruder's behaviour? (3) Does the bird flexibly modify its behaviour when the intruder changes its behaviour, for example, by following or not following the 'injury feigning' bird?

The data yield positive answers to the questions posed. (1) Depending on the stringency of the criteria used to define 'the intruder moving away from the nest/young', the bird moved in appropriate directions while displaying in 87 per cent (most stringent) to 98 per cent of the 45 cases examined in detail. (By the most stringent criterion, the bird must never in the course of displaying move in a direction which would cause an intruder following it to pass closer by the next.) (2) Monitoring of the intruder occurs and indeed quite dramatically. Photographs and videotapes indicate that, in the midst of an intense broken wing display the bird pauses to turn its head back towards the intruder. (3) Likewise, the parent plover adjusts its behaviour depending upon the intruder's actions, for example, by reapproaching an intruder who does not follow it.

I interpret these data as providing at least suggestive evidence for the purposive nature of the birds' behaviour. As noted above, I do not claim to *prove* that the plovers are exhibiting purposeful behaviour, for to do so requires a solution to the philosophical mind–body problem. However, in accord with suggestions proffered by the philosopher Jonathan Bennett (chapter 7; 1990), my criteria for attributing belief–desire states to a plover are grounded in behaviour, *and* in the plover's sensory input. The sensory input encompasses the environment, the condition of the plover's sense organs, etc. (Bennett, 1990). This quadrangle replaces the libertine belief–desire–behaviour triangle which is permissive of too many alternate belief–desire explanations. For the plover, the sensory inputs include the presence of the intruder and the bird's nest/eggs, the location of each with respect to each other and to the plover, and the behaviour of the other organisms. In short, yes, I have suggestive evidence for the existence of purposes in plovers, although such purposes are not likely to be the highly elaborated, fully conscious, pre-planned states sometimes the province of humans.

Deception

The issue of deception is raised, because at least in some instances, deception can entail an understanding of the mind state or knowledge of others, as discussed by Wellman, Shultz, Whiten, Byrne, Leekam, and Astington and Gopnik, among other contributors to this volume. In other cases, deception can be quite simple, such as the eye spots on the wings of certain species of moths. These eye spots are flashed when a predator is near, serving to deter the predator. (The 'eyes' appear to be those of a large, very close creature, such as an owl.) In these cases, it seems most likely that not the moth, but evolution, Mother Nature, is the deceiver. Gradations of deception exist between the extremes.

The possibility of avian deception arises from several studies, including laboratory experiments with domestic chickens by Marler, Karakashian and Gyger (1990), Marler, Dufty and Pickert (1986) and field observations of tropical sentinel birds by Munn (1986) and of great tits by Moller (forthcoming). The focus of the studies with chickens was the audience effect; that is, the effect of the physical presence of specific audiences on communication. The investigators noted that male domestic chickens gave more 'food calls' when a female chicken was the audience than when the males were alone. Even fewer calls than baseline were uttered when a male was the audience. When an inedible object was presented, the male called more to a strange female than to his mate. This latter has been interpreted as deceptive calling, i.e. the male utters food calls to the presumably exciting strange female to entice her approach. Another interpretation, suggested by various researchers, including W. J. Smith (1990), is that the call does not indicate the presence of food, but communicates that the signaller will interact in a positive way with an individual who approaches it. Others have suggested the message is simply 'approach'. Such interpretations do not involve deception.

Munn reports deceptive use of alarm calling by three different species of tropical sentinel birds in mixed species flocks. All three species used hawk alarm calls when no hawk was present to gain a small time advantage in aerial tumbles over flushed insect prey. The recipient bird, almost 'bug in beak', typically paused, was startled or began an escape movement when the alarm was heard, thereby losing its prey to the vocalizing sentinel species.

These intriguing results are somewhat controversial. At least some scientists are concerned that further verification be obtained that the call made is indeed a hawk alarm call rather than a threatening call to the bird with the insect. Data which would substantiate the 'hawk alarm call' interpretation could include: (1) observational data that (a) the usage of these vocalizations in contexts other than food acquisition involve the presence of a bird of prey and (b) the calls are not made in aggressive interactions between the birds; (2) experimental data that the sentinel species respond to the presence of a model hawk or tethered live hawk with the 'hawk alarm call' – at least in the presence of an audience which is typically responsive to such calls by the sentinel bird; (3) another line of evidence could be based upon the call's acoustic structure – calls might be similar to and/or part of a graded series with other alarm calls or conversely with other aggressive calls.

However, as additional support for Munn's interpretation, there are other species which also use alarm calls to gain an advantage in access to food. Sixty-three per cent of all alarm calls made by great tits in winter foraging flocks were false, in that they were emitted when no predator was present. The calls were seemingly given to drive away a dominant bird from a feeding perch. Further substantiation for this interpretation arises from the fact that subordinates gave such calls to both dominant and subordinate individuals, while dominants gave false alarms to other dominant individuals, but not to subordinates who could be supplanted with a threat display (Moller, forthcoming). The troublesome aspect of these data is that the calls were used more frequently in a presumably deceptive manner than veridically. If the calls are to maintain their communicative value, one would expect veridical use to predominate. However, some scientists (e.g. Krebs, 1977) consider animal communication to be essentially deceptive in function, so the tits' use of their alarm calls would cause no conceptual difficulty. In either case, it would be informative to have a more extensive catalogue of the tits' alarm call usage, in other seasons and in other contexts during the winter.

The question of deception arises with the plovers, particularly in their usage of the broken wing display or 'injury feigning', which was described previously. A fairly high-level interpretation of the parents' behaviour entails a second-order intentional stance, namely 'the plover wants the predator/intruder to believe that she is injured'. (Further analysis of the issue of intentionality is beyond the scope of this chapter. Instead, see discussion in Dennett, 1983; Ristau, 1983a, 1988, 1990; Whiten and Perner, chapter 1; Bennett, 1990, chapter 7). One can also pose the analogous question about the plover's understanding of her (his) own behaviour, 'the plover believes she is pretending to have a broken wing'. It is extraordinarily difficult to gather evidence about such hypotheses; most data can usually be given a more demoting interpretation concerning the predator's behaviour rather than its belief about the plover (e.g. 'the plover wants the predator to follow her', a first-order intentional statement.)

However, if one took the stance that the plover wanted the predator to believe she had a broken wing, one might predict that the plover, having once used the display with a particular intruder, 'lured' it away from the young, and then having flown away, should not immediately try the same trick again if the predator returned. But it is commonly reported that the plovers do reuse the display and that the predator continues to follow. The instances I observed were (a) with human experimenters who were following the displays of piping plovers and of Wilson's plovers, and (b) with a dog, directed by a human, interacting in one session with semipalmated plovers (*C. semipalmatus*) and in another with American golden plovers (*Pluvialis dominica*) (the latter conducted with I. Byrkjedal, University of Bergen, 1986). In the sessions with the birding dog, the dog was permitted and/or encouraged and/or commanded to approach a plover while the humans walked behind. With instruction from the experimenter, the dog's owner vocally and gesturally directed the dog, as another observer videotaped the event. Thus the plover was actually interacting not only with the dog but with two to three humans as well. This particular dog showed only minimal interest in the small semipalmated plovers and somewhat more in the larger golden plovers. The pertinent information is that plovers did make 'broken wing displays' and then flew in the presence of the intruder, were, nevertheless, sometimes observed to display again. This was by no means a complete study, so more data would be desirable, using a dog behaving as naturally as possible, with humans hidden from the bird's view.

On the one hand such episodes seem like clear evidence that the plover could not be attempting to deceive the predator/intruder. Yet, given that the 'trick' continues to work, the question must be raised as to the predator's cognitive abilities. Despite the fact that the predator has observed that the plover flys away ably, it continues to follow the 'broken wing displays'. The rapid recovery of function may not be paradoxical to the predator. With many non-humans and indeed with young children (even adults at times), the *present* situation assumes dominance in controlling behaviour (see discussion of related issues in Johnson, 1982). Knowledge from prior experience is often unable to compete with compelling, on-hand stimuli. Alternatively, the plover's display may not indicate 'injury' to the predator; it may be merely an attention getting series of movements. In that case, it is indeed unusual that a behaviour so closely resembling injury should have been the one selected for during evolution. The complete explanation could be yet more complicated in that many species may be innately predisposed to be especially attentive to stimuli, such as behaviours, which are typically associated with injury. Some of those species (and others?) may likewise learn that organisms exhibiting such behaviours are fairly easy prey. Only a select few species, and those perhaps only in some circumstances, may have the requisite cognitive powers to learn that individuals exhibiting such behaviours tend to continue exhibiting the behaviours, i.e. tend to remain injured – at least for a time. It is only to *those* select species that a 'reinjured' bird would appear paradoxical.

In short, the plovers which I have observed do not behave in ways that require an interpretation of purposefully 'deceiving' the predator/intruder. The cognitive prowess of the intruder must not be assumed to be like that of a human. The broken wing display 'works' for the plover; the intruder follows it and gets farther away from the plover's vulnerable eggs/young.

Gaze

Attentiveness to eye gaze of another is of significance as a possible precursor to mindreading for several reasons. Gaze itself figures prominently in human and other species' communication. At least for humans, mutual eye gaze (looking into each other's eyes) can be either an aggressive signal or an indication of intimacy. Who and what one looks at can reveal the structure of social hierarchies as described for non-human primates by Chance (1967) and for humans and their evolutionary predecessors by Barkow (1976). Likewise, such information about gaze can indicate the purposes or, in the least, the objects of attention of the gazer. It is this last function of gaze that I will concentrate upon in this discussion.

Sometimes two (or more) individuals will gaze towards the same object. Such joint visual gaze or 'looking where someone else is looking' is termed deictic gaze (see discussion by Butterworth, chapter 15). In deictic gaze, it is usually understood that the direction of gaze of one individual depends on that of another, rather than on the attractive qualities of the object *per se*. Butterworth and his colleagues study the developing capacity of young

human infants to be sensitive to and directed by the attention of their mothers to otherwise innocuous objects in a laboratory setting. Earlier work had shown that 'infants as young as two months would readjust their gaze contingent on a change in the focus of attention of an adult' (Scaife and Bruner, 1975). In experiments by Butterworth et al., infants of six months (the youngest studied), look to the side of the room their mother is gazing towards, but not necessarily to the correct object on that side. By 12 months, the infant is beginning to localize objects correctly; by 18 months the babies are equally accurate in localization whether or not the object is the first or second they encounter visually. But the babies' joint visual attention is restricted to objects within its own visual field; it does not search behind itself, unless (by 18 months) the field of view is devoid of objects.

An organism may react to another's gaze, not merely by looking at the same object, but by inferring what appear to be rudimentary aspects of the other's purpose. For example, gaze, posture and locomotion can, at least in chimpanzees, communicate the location of hidden food and objects (Menzel, 1974; Menzel and Halperin, 1975). That this communication involves more than merely following a conspecific is indicated by observations of differential behaviour by the 'recipient' chimpanzees dependent upon whether the hidden object is a model snake or food. If the object is a model snake, the 'leader' chimpanzee (and the 'recipient') act fearfully (e.g. fur raised) during the approach.

Furthermore, a complex scenario can emerge during repeated interactions in which the same chimpanzee is shown the location of desirable food items. During experiments at the Arnhem Zoo (de Waal, 1986), Dandy, a young adult male chimpanzee, had seen experimenters bury grapefruit beneath the sand but when released, he had casually walked over the hiding place without retrieving the treat. More than three hours later, when most other chimpanzees were napping (including the dominant males), Dandy quietly returned to the location of the grapefruit, dug it out and ate it without interference from any of the apes.

In other experiments, the 'knowledgeable' chimpanzee initially walked to the location of the hidden food. On subsequent trials, the others followed, soon outrunning the 'leader' in the correct direction. In still later episodes, the followers raced ahead even as the 'leader' began orienting in a particular direction. Soon the 'leader' began looking in the 'wrong' direction and then when the others were running off that way, the 'leader' quietly reoriented correctly, obtained the hidden food and quickly consumed it (Menzel, 1974). All these instances suggest that what is occurring is other than and indeed more than mere following of an excited conspecific, more than socially facilitated following. Rather some understanding of the purposes of the interactants seems to be involved (Byrne and Whiten, chapter 9).

In this volume, Gómez reports data from a young captive gorilla who appeared to be using her own eye gaze not in a deceptive manner, but rather to enlist the aid of a human caretaker in opening a door, a task the gorilla could not do herself. In Gómez's words, 'they understand the need for attentional contact between the human and themselves when they want to communicate with the human'. He notes that one-year-old humans begin to address gestures to adults by looking at the adults' eyes (Poulin-Dubois and Shultz, 1988). Those researchers consider such behaviour the beginnings of intentional communication in that the infants are understanding the adults as 'agents'. Gómez considers that the infants are instead understanding the adults to be 'perceivers', a more advanced kind of understanding. He notes, as particular evidence for this interpretation, that 'they look at the other's eyes at strategic moments in their actions, and that they actively seek to establish this visual contact before producing their gestures (or, conversely, to avoid the attention of others when their intervention is not wanted)'. He, as Butterworth has done for different data, also hesitates to call this ability 'mindreading'. Gómez finally opts for the description 'early practical understanding of mental phenomena'.

The reported use of gaze by a gorilla is of particular interest since mutual gaze is not an indication of intimacy in the natural communication system of gorillas, while it is with humans. Instead, for the gorilla, a direct gaze is an aggressive signal (as it can sometimes be for humans and other primates as well). It seems more plausible for a gaze which directs gestures and other communications to develop out of a signal of intimacy. (Note that some researchers do consider that the gorilla's direct gaze communicates meanings other than threat.) It would be illuminating to know if young and adult gorillas, in the wild or in captive groups having little interaction with humans, use gaze to direct communication between themselves. Likewise more comparative research with human and non-human primates about the ontogeny of gaze to direct communication would be of especial interest.

Field Studies with Plovers

Some species of plovers exhibit behaviours which I also hesitate to term 'mindreading', but which bear upon the findings discussed. My studies were conducted in the field with shore birds, specifically, piping plovers (*Charadrius melodus*), and also Wilson's plovers (*C. wilsonia*) and Semi-palmated plovers (*C. semipalmatus*). The plovers, in particular the piping plovers, are extremely well camouflaged. In order to be noticed, they must vocalize or otherwise act conspicuously. In one set of experiments with piping plovers, a human intruder approached the general area of the plover's nest or offspring and then either followed or did not follow the adult. When, in the course of these experiments, the plovers do act conspicuously, for example, by making a broken wing display, they turn towards the intruder, apparently to determine if the human is following them. Such following is one behavioural manifestation of the human's attention to their dramatic display. If the human is *not* following them, they most often alter their behaviour, usually by reapproaching the intruder. This is a behaviour which can function to regain the intruder's attention (Ristau 1988, 1990).

In another set of field experiments (the 'gaze' experiments), I asked whether a piping plover is responsive to the *attention* of an intruder to its nest in which attention is defined as the *direction of gaze* of the intruder. In other experiments, part of the data concerned the location of the plover's display as it related to the intruder's visual field. During both kinds of interactions, the bird also had available as cues the position of the intruder's head as well as the orientation of the intruder's shoulders and upper torso.

Gaze Experiments with Piping Plovers

To investigate the question experimentally, we conducted a series of simple experiments on beaches in the Hamptons on Long Island, New York, in 1984 and 1985 (details in Ristau, 1990).

In every experiment, there were two human intruders, each dressed differently so as to aid the birds' distinguishing between them. One intruder always looked towards the dunes while the other intruder always looked away from the dunes, towards the ocean. Note than on Long Island, the piping plovers' nests are located in the dunes which, on the beaches we used, were north of the ocean. Matched pairs of trials were conducted such that within each pair, the intruders walked one at a time, along the same path which was parallel to the dunes and within 15 to 25 metres south of the dunes. As they walked, the intruders actively scanned either the dunes or the ocean, turning their heads as well as their eyes from side to side as they did so. In addition, during some of the sessions, about five metres before an intruder was due south of the nest on the walk, the intruder sat down and continued scanning either the dunes or the ocean for approximately 45 seconds.

Each trial began when a parent plover was incubating eggs. The incubating bird almost always left the nest when an intruder walked by (one exception). The data consisted of the duration of time a bird remained off the nest when each type of intruder walked by. (The underlying assumption is that a bird will remain off the nest longer for a more threatening human intruder than for a less threatening one).

Adequate data were available for a total of 50 trials (25 matched pairs); 11 different birds served as subjects. Results indicated that the birds stayed off the nest longer when the intruder gazing towards the dunes walked by than when an intruder walking along the same path but looking towards the ocean walked by. There was a significant difference between the number of birds (nine) which stayed off the nest longer for the 'looking towards' gazer as compared to those (two) which stayed off longer for the 'looking away' gazer. There is also a significant difference if one examines the total number of matched pairs of trials summed across all birds; birds stayed off the nest longer for the 'looking to' condition in 21 pairs of trials, but were off the nest longer for the 'looking away' condition in only four pairs of trials. The longest duration off the nest was ten minutes, 14 seconds, which occurred during a 'looking towards the nest' trial, while the shortest duration was 0 (the bird didn't get off the nest for one 'looking away from the nest' trial) and the next shortest was 29 seconds (also for a 'looking away' trial).

Note that in all trials, the bird was initially on the nest, so that the intruder was not only looking towards the nest, but to the bird as well. In all cases but one, the bird left the nest, while the intruder continued to scan the dunes (where the nest was located). The human intruders were specifically instructed *not* to look at the birds. However, whilst walking on the beach the bird could be within the general visual field (i.e. about 180 degrees) of an intruder.

In brief, even at a fairly great distance from the nest, 15 to 25 metres, the gaze of an intruder towards the general area where the nest is located (the dunes), in contrast to a gaze in the opposite direction, causes a parent plover to behave differently. The birds act in a more intense or aroused fashion (stay off the nest longer) to walkers looking towards the nest region than away. These results strongly suggest that the plovers are sensitive to at least one measure of the intruder's attention, direction of eye gaze towards their eggs.

Data gathered during other experiments with piping plovers indicate additional behaviours of the birds dependent upon the intruder's direction of gaze and/or movement (Ristau, 1990). We observed that before beginning a broken wing display to an intruder, a parent which had been incubating eggs will walk away from the nest and then sometimes fly to a different location. We were able to examine 45 cases of broken wing displays in considerable detail. In 13 of those instances, the plover *flew* to a new location. When the plover's new location is analysed with respect to the position of the intruder and of the nest, it is found that, in all cases examined, the parent plover flew to be closer to the intruder, and in fact, in 11 of the 13 (85 per cent) of the cases, closer to the centre of the intruder's visual field. This work is relevant to Butterworth's research demonstrating that human infants will look in the same direction as their mother, refining this ability as they mature to be able to look not only in the same general direction, but at the same object, finally even, (at about 18 months) being able to follow her gaze to an object behind them, out of their initial visual field.

Unlike the babies, the plovers had cues other than orientation of the eyes and the head. In most instances, the human intruder was generally moving and looking forward, so direction of locomotion also served as a cue to the centre of the visual field. For intruders who had paused, remembered direction of movement might possibly be a cue to the plovers. Other differences between the two situations, besides the obvious one of a potentially dangerous intruder and a protective mother, are that the human intruder was not necessarily moving towards a particular item, while the mother was always looking towards one of a few conspicuous objects.

Research with other species also indicates their responsiveness to the direction of an intruder's gaze, specifically gaze directed towards themselves. For example, Burghardt has shown (1990) that hog-nosed snakes engage in 'death feigning' longer (or more precisely, take longer to recover fully from 'death feigning') in the presence of an intruder one metre away, looking directly at them, than when the intruder has its eyes averted. The snakes 'feign death' for an even shorter time when the human intruder leaves. The snake experiments differ from my work with the plovers in that the intruder is much closer to the animal in Burghardt's research (one metre for the snakes against 15 to 25 metres for the plovers); the snake experiments are done in the laboratory while the plover experiments are conducted in the field; the intruder is stationary for the snakes and moving for the plovers, and, importantly, the human intruder is staring at the snake, but scanning the general location of the plover's nest/eggs. However, since my experiments are begun when the plover is incubating its eggs, the plover is, at least initially, occasionally within the gaze of an intruder scanning the nest region.

Gallup et al. (1972) also found in laboratory experiments that chickens engage longer in tonic immobility in the presence of a human nearby, staring at them, than when the human was not looking at them. Similar results have been obtained for anoles (Hennig, 1977; general review and discussion of phenomenon by Arduino and Gould, 1984). Tonic immobility is also termed 'death feigning', though it is not so complex a behaviour sequence as that of the hog-nose snake. The simplest hypothesis being investigated in this research is whether the presence of eye spots can affect an organism's behaviour. One of the simplest instances of this phenomenon occurs when a would-be predator is startled as a moth flashes large eye spots on its wing.

The predator thereby loses a valuable time advantage in its pursuit, and the moth is more likely to escape. Most likely, this is a pre-wired, evolutionarily determined behaviour of the moth involving no voluntary action, but, in fact, no research has been done to investigate carefully the precise conditions in which a moth 'flashes'. It is very plausible that a widespread sensitivity to eye spots could be further refined and developed during the course of evolution so as to direct behaviour as appears to occur in piping plovers. Comparative research is especially important in order better to understand the limitations and differences in abilities that comprise similar, but possibly differently complex behaviours.

Several experiments with plovers would be of interest. Initially, the intruder's gaze to the nest also encompasses the incubating bird. To determine more precisely the effect on the parent bird's behaviour when an intruder gazes towards the eggs, but not towards the parent plover, one would want to conduct the gaze experiments when a parent is in the area, but is not incubating the eggs. Under natural conditions, this is a rare event, typically happening only when there is a nest exchange (one bird relieves the other of incubation duties), or when the parent is involved in a territorial encounter with another bird, or is interacting with an intruder. Very infrequently, the parent might be nearby feeding for a brief time, leaving the nest unattended. Except perhaps for the last scenario, none of these conditions is adequate for conducting the proposed experiments.

To conduct an experiment in which the intruder gazed at a displaying adult in one condition and away from it in another condition has, as yet, been impracticable. One cannot predict exactly where and when an adult will begin displaying. Thus one cannot locate a stationary observer adequately enough to gather sufficiently precise observations without the observer moving and becoming an additional 'intruder'. In other experiments, when the intruder does not have to look away from the bird and when the intruder's movements are predetermined, observations are easier to make and the intruder functions as an additional observer.

Another series of potential experiments arise from the observation that the piping plovers' eggs are better camouflaged when not being incubated than during incubation. Presumably, degree of egg camouflage and tendency to leave the eggs in the presence of an intruder co-evolved. However, might each bird also be able to assess egg conspicuousness and modify its behaviour accordingly? Pertinent evidence could be gathered by brightly and conspicuously marking the camouflaged eggs of a bird species which leaves the nest during an intruder's presence. Does the bird thereupon alter its behaviour adaptively as the parent of its now non-camouflaged eggs, for example, by remaining on the nest longer, or increasing its likelihood of attacking the intruder or of making a broken wing display rather than relying on camouflage to deter predation?

In Closing

The piping plovers do exhibit responsiveness to an intruder's attention (defined in terms of direction of the intruder's eye gaze). They remain off their nest longer when an intruder walks by, gazing towards the nest region as contrasted to their behaviour when an intruder walks by, but gazes away from the nest region. Similarly plovers are responsive to the direction in which an intruder is looking and walking as indicated by the location they choose to display in. Plovers which had flown to a new position before beginning a broken wing display always moved to be closer to the intruder and, in most cases, closer to the centre of the intruder's visual field and direction of movement. It would be useful to gather more data on this matter.

It is reasonable to interpret the plovers' use of broken wing displays or 'injury feigning' in terms of purposive behaviour which is also under hormonal and genetic control. These are likely causative factors for many behaviours, human and non-human.

It is unlikely that 'injury feigning' is deceptive in the sense of the plover consciously pretending to have a broken wing; it is a behaviour at the disposal of the plover. Using it is pragmatic in getting an intruder away from the region of nest/young. The behaviour can be construed as deceptive from Mother Nature's point of view, i.e. from an evolutionary perspective. Injured animals are selectively preyed upon by predators. It is adaptive, therefore, for a distractive behaviour to give an appearance of vulnerability, as the 'injury feigning' does. However, it is very possible that other avian behaviours are deceptive as accumulating evidence strongly suggests. More investigation of this intriguing matter is needed.

This manuscript has dealt with problems 'before mindreading'. To venture further, I see as yet no clear evidence that birds engage in 'mindreading', that is, attribute purposes to another organism, but neither do I see evidence contrary to this interpretation. It is extremely difficult to design experiments which clearly differentiate between an interpretation that an organism is trying to change another's behaviour versus change another's belief. Yet the plovers' attempts to have intruders leave the region of offspring, their increased arousal from intruders who have, in the past, closely approached the nest region in contrast to those who have not (Ristau, 1988, 1990), and their responsiveness to the intruder's direction of attention all suggest more possible awareness of another's purposes than previously thought. Contrary explanations are still possible. Experiments which would begin to clarify these issues have not been done. As Donald R. Griffin has so often admonished us (e.g. 1976, 1984), beware of scientists' 'simplicity filters' which belie the possible thinking of animals. We will begin to understand the possible cognitive abilities of animals only when we entertain those possibilities in our scientific explorations. Exciting research and thinking awaits us.

ACKNOWLEDGEMENTS

I would like to thank the following for their help in the 1982 field season: the Harry Frank Guggenheim Foundation for financial support; the Virginia Coast Reserve of The Nature Conservancy for permission to use their land; the Marine Science Consortium of Wallops Island, Virginia for living and office accommodations; David Thompson, for help in initial preparations; Laura Payne, for help in observations. For subsequent field seasons, I thank the Mashomack Preserve of the Nature Conservancy on Shelter Island, New York and its Director, Michael Laspia, for living and office accommodations and supportive services, and the Morton Wildlife Refuge and the town of Southampton, Long Island, for permission to use their land for research. I am grateful to the Whitehall Foundation for financial support of the research and the Edna Bailey Sussman Fund and Barnard College for support of research assistants. I am also indebted to Margaret McVey who was my colleague during most of the 1983 field season and to her and Elsia Hellen, William Langbauer and Terry Metwijn for help in field work and preliminary data analysis for that season. For subsequent seasons, I thank my research assistants Angela Greer, Margaret Mosteller, Karen Seidler, Samuel Hellings, Peter Sherman, Kim Pietrzak, Crista Diels, Randi Massey, Rachel Larson, Salila Shivde and Angelica Landrigans. I thank Daniel C. Dennett for philosophical insights, Stevan Harnad for helpful discussions and in particular Donald R. Griffin for his work in cognitive ethology, constructive comments on a longer manuscript from which this paper is drawn, and for his continued encouragements.

I thank Lawrence Erlbaum Associates, publisher, for permission to use and adapt parts of a longer manuscript from *Cognitive Ethology: The Minds of Other Animals*, ed. C. Ristau, 1990.

15

The Ontogeny and Phylogeny of Joint Visual Attention

George Butterworth

Introduction

The social signalling function of gaze has been widely documented by ethologists. Eyes, eye movements and eye markings serve as signals for threat, courtship, to maintain social hierarchies and to indicate the direction of attention. It is with this latter, spatial orienting function of gaze and the associated postures of the human head and hand that this paper is concerned. Joint visual attention, or deictic gaze as it is also called, may be defined simply as 'looking where someone else is looking'. Deictic gaze is thought to pave the way in human development for deictic gestures, such as manual pointing, which draw attention to a particular object by locating it for another person. For humans then, joint visual attention and pointing are thought to offer one basis in shared experience for the acquisition of language (Bruner, 1983).

In other organisms the spatial functions of gaze seem not to have been very much studied, although gaze following and gaze aversion are obviously involved in Machiavellian intelligence, where looking may be used in a misleading way (Whiten and Byrne, 1988 a, b). One of the main functions of gaze direction is primates may concern the so called 'attention structure', as studied in troops of monkeys and apes. It has been suggested by Chance (1967) that patterns of gaze reveal the social structure; that is, infants attend to their mothers, mothers to their mates and so on, through a social hierarchy to the dominant males. The argument is that gaze plays an important part in monitoring and maintaining these social hierarchies. Gaze and posture may also be used for communicative purposes, as Menzel and Halperin (1975) have documented. They noted a number of instances in which the purposive aspects of posture and locomotion may be used by adult chimpanzees to communicate information about hidden objects and sources of food.

They suggest that perceptual and cognitive structures available to chimpanzees are all that is required to explain such communication, rather than specifically symbolic or linguistic processes.

Detailed information on the communicative function of gaze is most readily obtained in controlled experiments with human infants and this paper will briefly review a series of studies carried out in our laboratories. The first series to be discussed is specifically concerned with the comprehension of gaze (see also Butterworth, 1987, for an extended discussion of the implications for childhood egocentrism). Secondly, results on the comprehension and production of manual pointing will be reviewed (for an extended discussion see Butterworth and Grover, 1988, 1989).

Comprehension of Gaze Direction

There is little doubt that adults monitor very closely the focus of the infant's attention and adjust their own gaze to maintain shared experience. Mothers vocalize at suitable moments when they can see that the baby is attending to a particular object or event and by establishing joint visual attention they create a suitable tutorial environment. Schaffer (1984) reviewed a number of studies which show that the majority of episodes of joint attention arise as a result of the mother monitoring the infant's line of gaze. Perhaps because young babies have traditionally been considered totally egocentric, it has been assumed that they must be incapable of following the gaze of an adult, since this implies taking into account another person's point of view. Furthermore, babies aged below eight or nine months are notoriously distractable and this also may have seemed to preclude shared attention with an adult.

It was therefore an important discovery when Scaife and Bruner (1975) showed that infants as young as two months would readjust their gaze contingent on a change in the focus of attention of an adult. It suggests that the capacity for joint attention is a reciprocal phenomenon; that the baby may be aware of a spatial objective of the mother's change of gaze.

General Methodology of the Studies

Butterworth and Cochran (1980) and Butterworth and Jarrett (1980) made an extensive series of studies in an attempt to establish the mechanisms serving joint visual attention. The studies were carried out under strictly controlled conditions with mother and infant seated face to face in the centre of an undistracting environment, with pairs of identical targets placed at various positions to the left and right of the room. These conditions allow relatively unambiguous conclusions to be drawn concerning how the baby is able to single out the referent of the mother's gaze since distractions and other possible artifacts are eliminated. In these experiments the mother was instructed to interact naturally with the infant and then on a signal, to turn, in silence and without pointing manually, to inspect a designated member of the set of targets. Babies between the ages of six and 18 months were studied; the interaction was videotaped and subsequently scored by two independent observers who noted the direction and accuracy of the infant's response relative to the object of the mother's line of gaze.

Three Developmental Stages

Evidence was obtained for three successive mechanisms of joint visual attention in the age range between six and 18 months. At six months, babies look to the correct side of the room, as if to see what the mother is looking at but they cannot tell *on the basis of the mother's action alone* which of the two identical targets on the same side of the room the mother is attending to, even with angular separations as large as 60 degrees between the targets. Although the babies are accurate in locating the object referred to by the mother's change of gaze when the correct target is first along their path of scanning from the mother to the target, they are at chance level when the correct target is second along the scan path. Furthermore, infants only localize the targets within their own visual field and hardly ever locate targets which the mother looks at in the region behind the baby, out of view.

If the mother looks at a target behind the baby, the infant either fixates a target in front and within the visual field or does not respond. This phenomenon is not caused by any inability of babies to turn behind them; indeed they often would turn behind them on first being seated in the laboratory or in response to some inadvertant noise. The most likely explanation is that there is a basic inability to link the mother's signal to the space outside the immediate visual field. This basic finding on failure to search 'behind' (first reported in Butterworth and Cochran, 1980) has subsequently been replicated on several occasions in our own laboratories. A similar inability to search at locations behind the infant has recently been demonstrated in a manual search task involving rotation of the infant relative to objects that were first hidden in the field of view, which suggests that inaccessibility of the space 'behind' the infant must be a general cognitive limitation (Landau and Spelke, 1988).

On the other hand, so long as all the possible locations are within the infants' field of view, they are capable of correctly locating targets presented one at a time at visual angles which introduce separations between mother and the referent of her gaze of up to 135 degrees (Butterworth and Jarrett, 1980). This experiment demonstrated that babies are perfectly capable of noting even very small changes in the mother's head orientation. Thus, failure to search behind cannot be attributed to failure to perceive the change of the adult's head orientation.

At six months, therefore, joint visual attention is restricted to targets within the infant's visual field. Accurate spatial localization of the referent among the youngest babies seems to depend not only on the adult's signal but also on the intrinsic differentiating properties of the object being attended by the mother. Grover (1988), for example, showed that adding movement to both targets elevated the probability of a response among nine-month-old babies and also raised accuracy to 100 per cent so long as the correct target was moving.

This earliest mechanism of joint visual attention we have called 'ecological', since we believe that it is the differentiated structure of the natural environment that completes for the infant the communicative function of the adult's signal. What initially attracts the mother's attention and leads her to turn, is also likely, in the natural environment, to capture the attention of the infant. The ecological mechanism enables a 'meeting of minds' in the self-same object. It is as if the change in the mother's gaze signals the direction in which to look to the infant and the object encountered completes the communicative link.

By twelve months, the infant is beginning to localize the targets correctly, whether first or second along the scan path, when the target is stationary in the visual field. The only information allowing this is the angular displacement of the mother's head and eye movements. It is interesting to note that the infant fixates intently on the mother while she is turning, then when the mother is still, the infant makes a rapid eye and head movement in the direction of the target. The mean latency of response after the end of the mother's head movement is about one second (Butterworth and Cochran, 1980, p. 268). This brief interval may be sufficient for the baby to register information about the angular orientation of the mother's head. We call this new ability the 'geometric' mechanism since it seems to involve extrapolation of an invisible line between the mother and the referent of her gaze, as plotted from the infants' position. That is, the mother's change of gaze signals both the direction and the location in which to look for the infant.

Despite this new-found geometric ability however, babies at 12 months still fail to search for targets located behind them. Again, we have carried out control studies in which the visual field is emptied completely of targets yet babies of one year do not turn behind them at the mother's signal. Instead, they turn to scan to about 40 degrees of visual angle and give up the search when they fail to encounter a target. It seems that the geometric mechanism is restricted to the infant's perceived space.

By eighteen months babies are as accurate when the correct target is first along their scan path from the mother, as when it is the second target they encounter, and this suggests that a geometric mechanism is now definitely available. Our ongoing research is attempting to establish the minimum spatial separation between targets allowing correct discrimination between the alternate referents of the mother's signal.

Furthermore, although the babies still do not search behind them when there are targets in the field of view, they will do so if the visual field is empty of targets. We found that head and eye movements to targets behind the baby would elicit turning to the correct target, so long as there was nothing in front of the 18-month-old infant, in the field of view. Thus, infants seem to be able to access the invisible portion of space at 18 months (but not at twelve months) so long as there is no competition from locations within the visual field. This leads us to postulate the development of a third 'representational' spatial mechanism for controlling joint visual attention which is based on an understanding of being contained within space.

In summary, as far as the comprehension of gaze is concerned we have evidence in the first 18 months of life that three successive mechanisms are involved in 'looking where someone else is looking'. The earliest, 'the ecological mechanism', depends on completion of joint attention by the intrinsic, attention-capturing properties of objects in the environment, as well as on the change in mother's direction of gaze. At around 12 months, we have evidence for the beginning of a new mechanism, a 'geometric' process, whereby the infant from her own position extrapolates from the orientation of the mother's head or gaze the intersection of a line with a relatively precise zone of visual space. Finally, at sometime between 12 and 18 months, there is an extension of joint reference to a 'represented' space which contains the infant and other objects outside the immediate visual field.

Relation between Comprehension of Gaze and Comprehension of Pointing

In our more recent studies we have attempted to establish how the infant's comprehension of gaze may be related to comprehension of manual pointing. Manual pointing, defined as the use of an outstretched arm and index finger to denote an object in visual space, is species-specific to humans and it is thought to be intimately linked to language acquisition. It is the specialized referential function that is of interest here since it is a particularly human type of social cognition. Could the comprehension of pointing be related to comprehension of looking?

There is a fairly sparse literature on the comprehension of manual pointing and it has been reviewed by Schaffer (1984). It is generally agreed that comprehension of manual pointing occurs towards the end of the first year, somewhat in advance of production of the gesture. Looking where others point is observed in most babies by about 12 months (Guillaume, 1962; Leung and Rheingold, 1981; Schaffer, 1984) whereas pointing for others is observed in most babies at about 14 months (Schaffer, 1984). Piaget (1952) considered comprehension of manual pointing to arise simultaneously with comprehension of other complex signs, between 10 and 12 months (e.g. p. 249). It has long been noted that comprehension of pointing is linked to cognitive development. 'When the finger points at the moon, the fool looks at the finger' is a famous aphorism which illustrates vividly the link between the development of intelligence and comprehension of pointing.

Grover (1988) has obtained extensive data on the infant's comprehension of pointing, which can be readily summarized. She replicated our earlier study and compared the accuracy of response of babies when the mother merely looked at the correct target, or looked and pointed to the target. Infants at 12 months fail to locate targets behind them, whether the mother looks or looks and points. They can correctly locate the mother's referent target within their own visual field whether the target is first or second on their scan path. Thus, the addition of pointing by the mother does not make the space outside the field of view more accessible to the infant.

The main effect of adding the manual point is significantly to increase the probability that the infant will respond. Adding manual pointing to simple change of gaze has a compelling effect on the infants' attention. When looking is accompanied by pointing, the proportion of trials to which the infant responds increases to 96 per cent (from 59 per cent of trials when the mother only looks at the target) and perhaps this is only to be expected since the extention of the arm is an attention-worthy event in itself. Babies below 12 months will as often fixate the finger of the pointing hand as they fixate the designated target; they do not comprehend the signal function of the point.

Taking the series of experiments as a whole, babies begin to comprehend manual pointing at about 12 months, the age at which the new 'geometric' mechanism first becomes available. It seems that the ability to monitor invisible displacements, in Piaget's (1952) terms, and the comprehension of looking and pointing as signs, leads these behaviours of adults to become acts of definite reference, which single out the object at a particular location in space, for the infant.

Production of Pointing

The use of an outstretched arm and index finger to denote an object in visual space seems to reflect hominid evolutionary adaptations of the index finger and thumb (Hilton, 1986). For example, the relative ratio of index finger and thumb length, as well as the position of articulation of the thumb have changed from a chimpanzee-like hand in *Australopithecus afarensis* (−4 million years) akin to that in modern man by the time of *Homo erectus* (−1.5 million years). These data on hand morphology have been interpreted in relation to the evolution of the precision grip in tool manufacture and tool use but it is easy to speculate that the same increase in the precise use of the hand might also be reflected in its species typical use in signalling; a particular contrast with the whole body orienting observed in other animals.

Theorists do not agree on the ontogenetic origins of pointing. Preyer (1896) considered pointing to be a movement originally expressing a wish to seize. Vygotsky (1962) similarly argued that pointing develops out of the mother's interpretation of the infant's failed attempts at prehension. Shinn (1900, reviewed in Schaffer, 1984) suggested that manual pointing may develop out of conjoint visual–tactual inspection of objects. The infant of eight or nine months will simultaneously touch an object with the tip of the index finger while engaged in close visual exploration. Shinn suggested that pointing may begin soon after by the application of this intersensorimotor coordination to an extended space.

A third contemporary point of view, consistent with the species typicality and universality of the pointing gesture is that it reflects a modular, coordinative structure which serves a specialized communicative function (Fogel and Thelen, 1987). Fogel and Hannan (1985) showed that index finger extensions occur reliably in face-to-face interaction in infants as young as two months. The index finger does not single out a particular object; it is not correlated with the infant's gaze direction or with arm extension. However, the 'point' is reliably preceded or succeeded by vocalization or mouth movement. By six months, the hand may spontaneously adopt the pointing posture when an object attracts the infant's attention in a social context but again, the arm is not extended to designate any object. Intentional extension of the arm and index finger, in a communicative gesture, is observed at the beginning of the second year of life. The specialized function of the index finger in relation to shared attention may be innate. The developmental changes are to be explained by successive acquisition of arm control, fine manipulative skills and cognitive integration of the communicative roles of infant and adult.

Our research on *production* of pointing has recently begun. Butterworth and Adamson-Macedo (1987) developed a technique to elicit pointing in babies using a radio-controlled car and automated doll figures. In our first study, using the car, we found that the onset of intentional manual pointing (at 13.5 months) clearly involves coordination of viewpoints, with the index finger holding the position of the interesting object to establish whether the mother is attending. We found that 90 per cent of pointing episodes occurred when the car was stationary and within 2 metres of the baby. Pointing may therefore be linked to mechanisms of focal attention specialized for object identification at fixed positions. In more recent studies, Fabia Franco has contrasted pointing with reaching in ways which suggest that these actions have different developmental origins (Franco and Butterworth, 1988). She has also come up with some interesting findings on the intrinsically social nature of the gesture; infants begin their pointing career by checking the mother's direction of gaze after she points. By 15 months, infants first check that the mother is attending to them, and only then do they point. This anticipatory checking is among the clearest evidence that a concern for communication is the motive for pointing.

Conclusion

Our results demonstrate that even very young babies may enter into a communicative network with others through comprehension of an adult's direction of gaze. On the one hand communication is not solely dependent upon the greater cognitive sophistication of the adult as has been traditionally supposed. On the other hand, there is no need to suppose that babies entertain a 'theory' that other people have minds. At six months, the signal value of the mother's head movement will indicate the general direction (left or right) in which to look. Communication occurs because the easily distractable baby will attend to the same attention compelling features of the objects in the environment as the mother. Such an agreement on the objects of shared experience might be reasonably considered a proto-communicative prerequisite for comprehension. It remains to be established whether communicative content may be conveyed at this level of development (e.g. pleasure or fear of the object being singled out) but this is likely to be the case (Campos and Stenberg, 1980). When seen in social context, the earliest 'ecological' mechanism allows communication in relation to publicly shared objects, through their common effects on the intrinsic attention mechanisms of mother and baby. This basic, inter-mental process depends on the fact that attentional mechanisms in infant and adult operate in much the same way; there is nothing 'theoretical' about the properties of mind revealed in the interaction of mother and infant.

During the first year, joint visual attention remains limited to locations within the infant's own visual space. The infant behaves as if its own field of vision is shared with the adult and this gives us an insight into the nature of infant intersubjectivity (Whiten and Perner, chapter 1). A theory of direct perception, such as that of J. J. Gibson (1966) enables us to understand that perception must originate at a particular viewpoint. This need not mean that the infant cannot perceive that others also have a perspective on a space that is common to several points of view. The phenomenon of joint visual attention is ultimately possible because perception, even in the infant, presupposes a world of objects that exist in a space held in common with other people. The infant in the first year is limited by the boundaries of the immediate visual field but this nevertheless allows inter-subjectivity. Even though cognitive development of the participants in the interaction is at very different levels, the process of immediate perception provides a basis for agreement on the objects of experience.

Superimposed on this basic mechanism, with cognitive development, comes more precise 'geometric' localization of the referent of the mother's gaze. This development seems to be one of the cognitive changes necessary for comprehension of manual pointing. A geometric mechanism lessens the ambiguity of reference, since now targets that are identical in all respects except position can be singled out by the infant. Once this geometric mechanism is available, communication does not require differential, intrinsic properties of the object being singled out, the infant will choose the correct object in relation to the angular displacement of the mother's head and arm. It seems likely that this ability arises from a cognitive developmental process of the Piagetian type which allows invisible displacements to be monitored (Piaget, 1948). This change enables the comprehension of manual pointing, itself an important, species-typical, social means for redirecting attention and for entry into language.

The production of manual pointing may also depend on acquisition of the 'geometric' mechanism. Manual pointing seems to be based on a species-specific modular coordinative structure which operates in the interpersonal context. It comprises a specialized posture of the index finger, vocalization, social referencing and attentional processes involved in object identification.

Finally, taking the problem of knowing other minds back to basics, as the infancy research does, reveals that attention mechanisms on which these abilities are based do not presuppose a 'theory of mind' in the infant. It is more parsimonious to take the data as evidence for the functioning of perceptual systems on information held in common between the participants in the interaction. In that important and original sense of 'mindreading', the minds of others are transparent to the baby and revealed in interpersonal behaviour (Coulter, 1979).

16

Precursors to a Theory of Mind: Understanding Attention in Others

SIMON BARON-COHEN

The Forked Path

A central problem in developmental psychology has been to explain how, during the course of normal development, children come to understand that they and others have such a thing as a mind, and that states of mind guide human action. Developmental psychologists addressing this problem have tended to go down one of two paths. The direct route entails testing young normal children's comprehension of different mental states, in the hope of tracing the origins of this ability (see, for example, Wellman, in press, and chapter 2). The indirect but, I would argue, equally fruitful path entails studying why some children *fail* to develop a concept of mind. I and others have been taking this 'abnormal' route by studying autistic children (Baron-Cohen, 1985; Leslie, 1987a; Frith, 1989; Hobson, 1989a). Such children reveal what may be necessary but insufficient for the development of a concept of mind. This chapter describes a journey a little way down this second path. I begin by summarizing the relevant research in autism.

The Autistic Child's Theory of Mind

In the past five years a number of experiments have suggested that autistic children are unable to attribute mental states to other people (Baron-Cohen, Leslie and Frith, 1985, 1986; Dawson and Fernald, 1987; Baron-Cohen, 1989a; Leslie and Frith, 1988; Perner, Frith, Leslie and Leekam, 1989; Harris and Muncer, 1988; Swettenham, 1990; Russell, Sharpe and Mauthner, forthcoming; Leekam and Perner, 1990; Sodian and Frith, 1990; Mitchell, 1989; Shaw, 1989). One study also suggests they may have a purely behavioural notion of the function of the brain, and may even be completely unaware of the distinction between mental and physical entities (Baron-Cohen, 1989c). Together, such experiments point to a severe deficit in autistic children's 'theory of mind', as Premack and Woodruff (1978) called the ability to attribute mental states to oneself and others. By itself this could account for the striking abnormalities these children show in their social interaction and communication (Baron-Cohen, 1988), since both social and communicative skills depend to a large extent on the ability to take into account other people's beliefs, desires, thoughts, intentions, etc. (Dennett, 1978; Grice, 1957).

How are we to account for this impairment in the development of a theory of mind in autism? And what does such an impairment tell us about the factors underlying the normal development of a theory of mind? There have been two recent attempts to explain autistic children's deficits in this area, one computational-cognitive (Leslie, 1987a, 1988a; Leslie and Frith, 1990; and see Leslie, chapter 5), and one social-affective (Hobson, 1989a, b, 1990).[1] I shall first take a closer look at these two explanations. Then I shall consider some new evidence of joint-attention deficits in autism, and explore the possibility that a critical *precursor* in the development of a theory of mind lies in the infant's understanding of attention in others.

Leslie's Metarepresentation Theory of Autism

Leslie (see chapter 5) postulates a distinction in the development of the normally functioning cognitive system, between *primary representation* and *metarepresentation*. Primary representations function as ways of storing literal information about events in the world and are, as Leslie (1987a) poetically expressed it, 'sober' (p. 414), in that they include information that the system needs for its survival in the real world, e.g. There is a tiger out there. Metarepresentations, in contrast, function to allow the system to construct descriptions of hypothetical events, such as descriptions of pretend objects, thoughts, dreams, etc. Rather than referring to the outside world, they instead refer to other representations. Hence their name.

Leslie argues that metarepresentations have the special general form **Agent-Informational Relation-**'*expression*', where an **Agent** is a person or persons, and an '**expression**' is any *decoupled* representation. (A representation is said to be decoupled, in Leslie's theory, when a primary representation is copied and the normal reference links to the outside world then suspended.) An **Informational Relation** is any Intentional state (i.e. any mental state that is *about* something), such as thinking, knowing, believing, intending, pretending, etc. So, to give an example, a primary representation might have the form *There is a tiger*, whilst a metarepresentation derived from this (i.e. a decoupled copy of it) might have the form *John believes 'there is a tiger'*.

Notice that the Informational Relation, by preceding the expression, renders the expression 'opaque', i.e. suspends its normal truth implications. That is, the sentence is still true even if there is no tiger, so long as John believes there is one. Intentional states are thus said to possess the logical property of *referential opacity*, a term derived from Quine (see chapter 1). The form of metarepresentation that Leslie proposes is, of course, identical to the analysis of intentional propositions given by Bertrand Russell, and the logical properties he outlines for metarepresentation are identical to those documented by Gottlob Frege. (For a summary of this philosophical background, see Olson, 1988.)

Metarepresentation is the mechanism Leslie sees as underlying the ability to represent mental states. In its mature form this mechanism allows for a theory of mind, and in its earliest, most primitive form, it allows for the emergence of pretend play since, according to Leslie, the logical properties of pretence and mental state attribution are similar. This has significance when Leslie applies his model to autism: he predicts that damage to the capacity for metarepresentation should in one tragic blow give rise both to an inability to employ a theory of mind and an inability to engage in pretend play. In addition, this model predicts a specific profile of both *intact* and damaged cognitive skills in autism, (intact ones being based on primary representation, damaged ones requiring metarepresentation).

Evaluation of Leslie's theory How far are these predictions supported? The evidence for autistic children's inability to employ a theory of mind has already been cited. And in line with the other main prediction from Leslie's theory, a number of studies have documented an absence or severe impoverishment in autistic children's pretend play (Riguet, Taylor, Benaroya and Klein, 1981; Ungerer and Sigman, 1981; Gould, 1986; Rutter, 1978; Wing, Gould, Yeats and Brierley, 1977; Baron-Cohen, 1987). In addition, an analysis of intact and damaged skills within autistic children's social cognition also seems to support Leslie's view. Thus, social cognitive skills which do not involve mental state attribution, such as visual self-recognition, face recognition, gender recognition, visual perspective-taking, and social schemata construction are *unimpaired* in autism (see Baron-Cohen, 1988, for a review), as are relationship recognition and the animate–inanimate distinction (Baron-Cohen, forthcoming a).

A critical test of whether autistic children have a specific deficit in representing mental representations would turn on how they perform on tests that require representation of non-mental representations. So far, the only such tests that have been tried with autistic children are a false photograph test, and a false drawing test, both derived from Zaitchik (1990). Results from these studies show that autistic children have no difficulty with such tests (Leekam and Perner, 1990; Charman and Baron-Cohen, 1990) supporting Leslie's model. The only alternative psychological theory of the deficit in autistic children's theory of mind has been proposed by Hobson, to which we now turn.

Hobson's Social-Affective Theory of Autism

Hobson's (1989a, 1990) theory assumes that, from birth, normal infants are involved in 'reciprocal personal relations with others' (Hobson, 1990, p. 116), a claim for which there is considerable evidence (see Schaffer, 1984, for a review). Hobson argues that one source of such reciprocity is the infant's ability to perceive its caregiver's expressions of emotions. He further argues that infants do not *infer* emotions from bodily action, but rather that they directly perceive them. The ability to perceive emotions, Hobson maintains, leads to the phenomenon of 'social referencing' (Campos and Stenberg, 1980), that is, the infant monitoring the caregiver's facial expression to disambiguate novel events.

Hobson goes on to argue that both the production of gestural requests and social referencing lead to the ability to construe the world from other people's positions, and to construe the world as if it were other than it really is. He holds this latter ability responsible for the ability to pretend play. For Hobson then, the autistic child's deficits in understanding other people's mental states and in generating pretend play are consequences of an inability to understand and respond to emotions in others, a deficit postulated to be present in autistic infants.

Evaluation of Hobson's theory A number of controversies, both empirical and theoretical, surround Hobson's model of normal development. First, it is not clear why normal infants' understanding of emotions would by itself enable them to attribute non-emotional, opaque mental states (such as beliefs, thoughts, intentions, etc.). Hobson (1990) is vague on this point: he says that infants' understanding of emotions 'crystallize' (p. 117), allowing them to assume alternative standpoints, but the term 'crystallize' leaves it unclear as to exactly how this operates. Secondly, by what mechanism an understanding of alternative viewpoints necessarily produces the development of a symbolic capacity (as Hobson maintains) is also left unspecified: he writes that infants 'come to grasp' (Hobson, 1990, p. 117) how symbols function, but such phrases beg many questions.

From empirical studies of autistic children there are other reasons for taking issue with Hobson's theory. Hobson's key prediction for autism is that their understanding of emotions should be markedly impaired, and their affective 'personal relatedness' (Hobson, 1989a, p. 22) should also be severely disturbed. However, the idea that there is a global affective impairment in autism is not supported by the data, since autistic children do show some signs of attachment (Sigman and Ungerer, 1984; Hertzig, Snow, and Sherman, 1989; Shapiro, Sherman, Calamari and Koch, 1987; Dissanayake and Crossley, 1989; Sigman, Mundy, Ungerer and Sherman, 1987). Secondly, autistic children can also understand simple emotions, such as happy and sad, as outcomes of situations and desires (Baron-Cohen, forthcoming d; Harris, Coles and Tan – cited in Harris, chapter 19). Thirdly, autistic children do also use some simple emotion terms in their language in an appropriate way (Tager-Flüsberg, 1989). Fourthly, although Hobson's experimental data show that autistic children have difficulty in emotional expression recognition tests (Hobson, 1986a, b), recent studies suggest such deficits may be a function of verbal mental age (Ozonoff, Pennington and Rogers, 1990; Braverman, Fein, Lucci and Waterhouse, 1989; Hobson, Ouston and Lee, 1988a, b).

Nevertheless, an affective disturbance may exist in autism. For example, a number of studies agree that autistic children have some difficulty in *expressing* emotions facially (Snow, Hertzig and Shapiro, 1987; Yirmiya, Kasari, Sigman and Mundy, 1989; Dawson, Hill, Spencer and Galpert, 1988; Kasari et al., forthcoming), although at present it is unclear if this is simply a non-verbal sign of autistic children's inability to *communicate* with others, or if it represents a purely affective disturbance.

Some Philosophical Issues

Before leaving Hobson's and Leslie's accounts, it is worth examining some of the philosophical issues underlying them. Hobson proposes that perceptual experience plays an important role in the development of knowledge of other minds. He does this on the basis of philosophical objections (by, for example, Wittgenstein) to the view that such knowledge is simply *inferred* from one's own experience: neither observation of other people's behaviour nor experience of one's own mental states could by themselves lead one to the inference that mental states underlie behaviour in others. Hobson's alternative is to assume that certain basic mental states must therefore be *directly* perceivable in behaviour and in facial configuration (cf. chapter 17).

Leslie's theory, outlined earlier, provides an alternative solution to the philosophical 'problem of other minds'. He agrees with Hobson that mental states cannot be inferred from behaviour, but disagrees with him that mental states are therefore directly observable. Instead, Leslie suggests that human beings are hard-wired (biologically pre-programmed) to develop a capacity for metarepresentation towards the end of the first year of life, a capacity which by itself allows human beings to represent that they and other systems can represent (think about) things. Such a position is similar to Fodor's (1987, pp. 132–3) nativist theory of mind hypothesis:

> Here's what I would have done if I had been faced with this problem in designing *Homo sapiens*. I would have made a knowledge of commonsense *Homo sapiens* psychology *innate*; that way nobody would have to spend time learning it . . . The empirical evidence that God did it the way I would have isn't, in fact, unimpressive . . . Suffice it that (1) Acceptance of some form of intentional explanation appears to be a cultural universal. There is, so far as I know, no human group that doesn't explain behaviour by imputing beliefs and desires to the behaviour. (And if an anthropologist claimed to have found such a group, I wouldn't believe him.) (2) At least in our culture, much of the apparatus of mentalistic explanation is apparently operative quite early.[2]

One critical philosophical difference, then, between Leslie (and Fodor) on the one hand, and Hobson on the other, is in the role they attribute to experience in the development of a normal concept of mind. Hobson sees perceptual experience as a necessary factor, whilst Leslie (and Fodor) do not. This leads Hobson (1990) to predict that *congenitally blind* children, who obviously lack perceptual experience of their caregiver's facial expressions, should also be severely impaired in the development of a normal theory of mind. In contrast, Leslie's theory suggests that the development of a metarepresentational capacity will be largely, if not completely, independent of perceptual experience. Indeed, this is why Leslie calls a theory of mind a 'module' (see Leslie, chapter 5).

From this, it follows that Leslie's theory predicts blind children should develop a theory of mind at the same mental age as other non-autistic children. (Blindness may well slow down 'mental age' development across the board, but according to Leslie's theory there is no reason to predict that their theory of mind will be *specifically* delayed.) Testing blind children on an appropriate version of the Sally-Anne marble test (Baron-Cohen et al., 1985) may be a critical next step in order to evaluate Leslie's and Hobson's theories further.[3]

This brief excursion into two major psychological theories of autism has, I hope, illustrated some of the value of exploring the 'abnormal' route as a way to understand the normal development of a theory of mind. In the next part of this chapter I move on to consider some recent evidence of *joint-attention* deficits in autism, and to examine their implications.

Joint-Attention Behaviours in Autism

From observational studies, it appears that joint-attention behaviours occur far less frequently in autistic children than in non-autistic control groups (Loveland and Landry, 1986; Landry and Loveland, 1989; Mundy, Sigman, Ungerer and Sherman, 1986; Sigman, Mundy, Ungerer and Sherman, 1986). These behaviours include 'referential looking' (as occurs when I look at what you are looking at, and attempt to get you to look at something by using the direction of my eye gaze), and gestures such as giving, showing and pointing. In normal children, referential looking is present in the majority of eight-month-olds (Scaife and Bruner, 1975), and gestures such as giving, showing and pointing emerge between nine to 12 months old (Bruner, 1983; Stern, 1985). Joint-attention deficits are likely to be the earliest *social* deficits in autism yet identified.

Do Joint-Attention Behaviours Require Metarepresentation?

Mundy and Sigman (1989) consider that the data indicating joint-attention deficits in autism refute the metarepresentation theory of autism. They argue this on the grounds that metarepresentation only emerges at 12 to 18 months (with pretend play – see Leslie, 1987a), whilst joint-attention behaviours emerge in normal development *prior* to 12 months. However, as several commentators have pointed out (Harris, 1989; Baron-Cohen, 1989b) this argument is rather tenuous, since pretend play can also be present in normal development from as early as nine months of age (Bates et al., 1979). In other words, the two abilities may not be as distant in their chronology of emergence as Mundy and Sigman suggest.

Hobson (1989b) suggests that joint-attention deficits indicate an incapacity to share or participate in other people's experiences, and suggests this incapacity stems from autistic children being unable to understand patterns of 'bodily expressiveness' (p. 199) as essentially linked with the observed person's feelings. His emphasis on joint-attention behaviours as entailing sharing experiences seems plausible. Hobson (1989b) goes on to suggest that such behaviours are likely to involve metarepresentation (p. 201) since the child is 'psychologically engaged with someone else's psychological engagement with the world and with oneself' (p. 201).

Leslie and Happé (1989) also consider joint-attention behaviours require metarepresentation. Their reasons are, however, different to Hobson's. They argue that joint-attention behaviours such as pointing and showing are examples of 'ostensive communication', and that such communication requires a theory of mind, if a Gricean analysis of 'speech acts' is accepted (Grice, 1957). And because a theory of mind requires metarepresentation, it follows that joint-attention behaviours also require this. This argument mirrors that put forward for communicative deficits in autism (Baron-Cohen, 1988).

An Experimental Investigation of Pointing

In order to tease out the role of a theory of mind in autistic children's joint-attention deficits, I carried out an experiment (Baron-Cohen, 1989b). I focused on just one of these behaviours (pointing) in more detail, testing comprehension and production of two different functional uses of pointing. The first type was called *proto-imperative pointing*, and this was defined as pointing 'in order to use another person to **obtain** an object' (ibid., p. 117). The second was called *proto-declarative pointing*, and this was defined as pointing 'in order to **comment** or **remark** on the world to another person' (ibid., p. 118).

I reasoned that proto-imperative pointing need not require taking into account the other person's mental states, in that it might merely comprise acting to cause another person to get an object or give an object – physical, not mental, interactions. Proto-declarative pointing, in contrast, is likely to involve taking into account the other person's mental states, in that it appears to comprise acting to cause another person to 'take notice of' and 'comment on' (rather than obtain) an object. Commenting, arguably, entails mental – not physical – interaction. I predicted therefore that if autistic children's joint-attention deficits were due to their inability to attribute mental states to others, then proto-imperative pointing would be unimpaired in autism, whilst protodeclarative pointing would be impaired.

Boxes 16.1 and 16.2 show the scoring categories used in this study, and tables 16.1 and 16.2 show the results. The results of this study supported the predictions: both in production and comprehension of proto-imperative pointing autistic children were unimpaired, whilst in production and comprehension of proto-declarative pointing autistic children showed severe difficulties. Such difficulties were not seen in non-autistic normal and developmentally delayed control children of equivalent mental age.[4]

If, as we assumed earlier, proto-declarative pointing requires a theory of mind, then its impairment in this study is consistent with Leslie's metarepresentation theory. What about the other assumption made earlier, that proto-imperative pointing does not require a theory of mind? It has been suggested that proto-imperative pointing can be analysed purely in terms of physical–causal understanding (Harding and Golinkoff, 1979), and

Box 16.1   Scoring comprehension of pointing

1   *Understanding proto-imperatives.* The act of labelling a pointing gesture as a protoimperative depends on the viewer interpreting it as such. We therefore recorded how the subject interpreted a pointing gesture. The experimenter said 'I am going to use my finger to say something. What am I saying?' He then faced the subject and pointed to one of four toys in turn, positioned in a semicircle close to the subject but at some distance from the experimenter. The experimenter then waited to see how the subject responded.

Scoring. Four response categories (two pass and two fail) were rated:

a   If the child picked up the object and handed it to the experimenter, this was rated as a pass, the subject interpreting the gesture as a protoimperative (request for object).
b   If the subject said 'you're saying "Give me that toy"', or some such phrase, this was rated as a pass, the subject articulating the meaning of the gesture as a protoimperative.
c   If the subject did nothing, or made some inappropriate response (e.g. touching the index finger or imitating the gesture), this was rated as a fail.
d   If the subject named or commented on the toy, this was rated as the child interpreting the gesture as a protodeclarative, in which case the experimenter repeated the gesture insistently, in order to emphasize that a different response was expected. If the child did not then produce a response described in (a) or (b) above, this was scored as a fail, although understanding protodeclarative pointing was noted.

2   *Understanding proto-declaratives.* The experimenter said 'Now I am going to use my finger to say something else. What am I saying?' He then walked over to the window, looked up to sky and pointed, and then looked across to the subject, whilst still pointing up at the sky. The experimenter then waited to see how the subject would respond. He then repeated this with three locations: through the open door, into his briefcase and into his jacket pocket. Each of these locations was selected because the experimenter could see an object which the subject could not see (e.g. a plane or bird in the sky, a person in the corridor or toy in the briefcase or pocket).

Scoring. Five response categories (three pass and two fail) were rated:

a   If the child looked in the direction of his point (often involving the child moving nearer the experimenter), this was rated as a pass, interpreting the gesture as a protodeclarative.
b   If the child said 'What is it?' or 'What are you looking at?' or named the

object, etc. (i.e. expressed interest in the gesture as a proto-declarative.)
c If the child said 'You want me to look at something you can see', or an
   equivalent phrase (e.g. 'You're saying "There's a plane in the sky"'), this
   was scored as a pass, the subject articulating the meaning of the gesture
   as a proto-declarative.
d If, however, the subject attempted to pick something up and give it to
   the experimenter, this was rated as a fail, the subject (inappropriately)
   interpreting the gesture as a proto-imperative. Understanding proto-
   imperative pointing was however noted.
e Finally,if the subject made no response, or an inappropriate response
   (such as touching the index finger, etc.), this was rated as a fail.

Box 16.2 Scoring production of pointing

Scoring. The videotapes were rated by two independent judges, using the
following criteria:

a Pointing was scored as proto-imperative if it was rated as unmistakably
   part of an attempt to obtain an object (e.g. (i) Sam points at toy held by
   Anna, and repeats the point until Anna hands the toy over; or (ii) Sam
   points to a toy held by Anna, and then abandons the gesture through
   Anna's lack of response, and finally takes the toy himself).
b Pointing was scored as proto-declarative if it was rated as unmistakably
   part of an attempt to comment on an object or event, that is, to draw
   another person's attention to the object or event, as an end in itself (e.g.
   (i) Sam points at a boy who is crying, then looks over to an adult, and
   continues pointing until the adult turns around and looks; or (ii) Sam
   points at an object or event which could not be an object of possession,
   such as an airplane out of the window, or a car across the road, and then
   looks over to Anna, and waits until she also looks at the same event).

Pointing rated as ambiguous by both judges was ignored.

as an 'instrumental' gesture (Zinober and Martlew, 1985). Since
physical–causal understanding itself only requires primary representation of
objects in a particular temporal and spatial relationship to each other (Leslie,
1988b), and indeed since physical causality is well understood in autism
(Baron-Cohen, Leslie and Frith, 1986; Curcio, 1978), intact functioning of
proto-imperative pointing in autism is also in line with predictions from the
metarepresentation theory.

Is the Gricean account that Leslie and Happé (1989) proposed sufficient
for all joint-attention behaviours? (Reminder of their account: joint-attention

Table 16.1 Average number of children (and percentages in each group) passing comprehension test of proto-imperative and proto-declarative pointing

		Proto-imp		Proto-dec		Dissociation	
Groups	n	Pass	%	Pass	%	Rate[a]	%
Autistic	20	14	70.0	2[b]	10.0	12[c]	60
Down's syndrome	14	11	78.5	12	85.7	1	7.2
Normal	27	25.25	93.5	26	96.2	0.75	2.3

[a] Dissociation rate = average number of children passing one and failing other.
[b] $P < 0.001$.
[c] $P < 0.05$.

Table 16.2 Number of children (and percentages in each group) producing proto-imperative and proto-declarative pointing[a]

		Proto-imp		Proto-dec		Dissociation	
Groups	n	Pass	%	Pass	%	Rate[b]	%
Autistic	10	4	40	0[c]	0	4	40
Mental handicap	10	8	80	7	70	1	10
Normal	10	7	70	9	90	2	20

[a] First judge only.
[b] Dissociation rate = the number of children passing one and failing the other.
[c] $P < 0.005$.

behaviours are communicative, communication requires a theory of mind, a theory of mind requires metarepresentation, therefore joint-attention behaviours require metarepresentation.) I think a Gricean account may be valid for proto-declarative pointing, and perhaps for showing, because these are, arguably, communicative, but there are some joint-attention behaviours which may not be forms of ostensive communication (e.g. referential looking and, arguably, giving). I have found it useful instead to develop a cognitive account of joint-attention behaviours, be they forms of ostensive communication or not (Baron-Cohen, 1989d). This account is sketched below.

Understanding Attention in Others

I begin with an analysis of proto-declarative pointing, although I hope to show that the level of analysis adopted is sufficiently general to be relevant for *all* forms of joint-attention behaviours. This analysis is framed in terms of the infant developing a concept of *attention*. Using this concept, what the nine- to 12-month-old infant understands by someone else's proto-declarative point is that the person is focusing his or her attention on a specific object or event. However, understanding attention cannot simply entail understanding that another person can see, since a number of experiments show that the latter is within autistic children's comprehension (Hobson, 1984; Leslie and Frith, 1988; Baron-Cohen, 1985, 1989b). An example of a test of what another person can see is illustrated in figure 16.1. The experimenter simply directs his or her eyes at one object, chosen at random, and asks the child 'What am I looking at?'.

Primary representation is sufficient for the infant to represent a person, and to represent if that person is seeing or not seeing (i.e. has his/her eyes open and unobstructed, etc.). Primary representation and the application of rules of 'geometry' and 'line-of-sight' (Lempers, Flavell and Flavell, 1977) are therefore likely to be sufficient to pass a test like that shown in figure 16.1. In contrast, understanding attention, I argue, must require understanding that vision (or audition) can be directed selectively, and that its direction depends on the person finding the object or event *of interest*. But is primary representation sufficient in order for the infant to represent a person attending, that is, to represent a person as seeing something of interest or not of interest?

The simplest computational way of achieving this that I can imagine is by the infant representing a person's representation of the object as marked by a simple **+ive or −ive valence tag**. This mechanism could be elaborated with a larger number of such valence tags (e.g. for representing an object as dangerous versus safe, etc.), but even the simple version of this mechanism suggests that metarepresentation may be required for joint-attention behaviours. On this model, then, autistic children's joint-attention deficits would be consistent with Leslie's metarepresentation theory.

Applied to pointing, this theory assumes that the autistic child develops the 'index-finger outstretched' hand configuration that is hard-wired in our species alone (see Butterworth, chapter 15), but then uses it functionally only for proto-imperatives because a physical–causal concept is all that is available to the child. Proto-declarative pointing does not develop, according to this model, because the child lacks the ability to represent that another

Figure 16.1 *Experimental test of perceptual role-taking (from Baron-Cohen, 1989b).*

person might represent an object as having a different valence (interesting versus uninteresting).

I would like to suggest that this analysis in terms of understanding attention in others applies not only to comprehension of proto-declarative pointing but also to its production, and to comprehension and production of the range of joint-attention behaviours mentioned earlier (referential looking, showing, giving, offering), all of which appear absent or severely impoverished in autism. For example, in production of all of these behaviours, normal children often look back at the other person's face and continue to point, show, give, etc., until the adult 'takes notice' of the target of the child's action. The child does not simply point, show, etc., but monitors the effect of this on the other person's direction of vision. This suggests that in producing the behaviour the child is trying to influence the other person's attention to an object (positively or negatively). Similarly, comprehension of any of these joint-attention behaviours is likely to entail understanding that another person represents an object as interesting or uninteresting, etc.

The claim that understanding attention as a mental state in others occurs during the period from seven to nine months and constitutes the origins of a theory of mind[5] is consistent with the analysis developed by Stern (1985), and corresponds to the age at which Trevarthen and Hubley (1978) have argued '*secondary* intersubjectivity' develops. Stern (1985, p. 134) has argued that Trevarthen and Hubley's claim of *primary* intersubjectivity being present at three to four months is incorrect, and instead suggests Trevarthen should replace his term 'secondary intersubjectivity' simply with 'intersubjectivity', since seven to nine months is the earliest point at which intersubjectivity or a theory of mind can be convincingly demonstrated.[6]

My formulation of proto-declarative pointing deficits in autism in terms of an inability to represent attention in others may also help to make sense of the dozens of reports in the clinical literature of autistic children taking an adult by the wrist and placing the adult's hand on a doorknob, etc., rather than using eye-gaze strategies to communicate the same intent, strategies which Gómez (chapter 13) argues rely on understanding shared attention, and which seem to be beyond many non-human primates.[7] Before placing this in the context of a broader theory of autism I am developing, I shall briefly consider the relevance of this to the child's developing theory of other mental states.

Understanding Attention and Other Mental States

Wellman (chapter 2) and Wellman and Bartsch (1988) have provided data which suggest that in the normal development of a theory of mind, under-standing of **desire** precedes understanding of **belief**. On this basis Wellman suggests that two-year-olds can be construed as *desire psychologists* only, whilst three-year-olds can be construed as *belief–desire psychologists*. In addition, Wellman and Bartsch suggest that at both ages children's under-standing of these mental states causally link with other internal states, such as emotions, and physiological drives (e.g. hunger). Wellman and Bartsch's model is shown in figure 2.1, p. 22.

As can be seen from that figure, Wellman and Bartsch posit that as part of their theory of mind young children know that perceptions can directly cause beliefs. The earlier discussion of the data from autism suggested that at a certain stage (estimated to be prior to seven months of age) children might understand perception without understanding attention. We therefore propose the following revision to Wellman and Bartsch's model: in their theory of mind, young children must first understand that perception can be directed selectively as attention, and then that attention can then cause beliefs. This refinement of Wellman and Bartsch's model is shown in figure 16.2.

Notice we postulate that understanding attention is specifically located in the development of understanding beliefs. This last claim is made on the

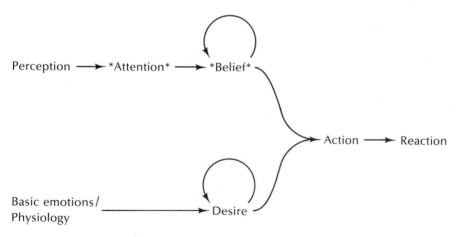

* — * internal states that are not understood in autism

Figure 16.2 *Proposed revision to Wellman and Bartsch's model (see figure 2.1 for the original model).*

basis of data from autism suggesting that autistic children are not pure behaviourists, but rather are more like desire psychologists. Thus, as cited earlier, Harris, Coles and Tan (1989) and Harris and Muncer (1988) have reported that autistic children can attribute desires to other people, given a minimum mental age, and this has been replicated by Baron-Cohen (forthcoming c). Finally, in autistic children's protocols describing picture stories of human action, of all the possible mental state terms they could have produced, only desire terms were used (Baron-Cohen, Leslie and Frith, 1986). Longitudinal language data analysed for spontaneous production of internal state terms in autism confirms this picture (Tager-Flüsberg, 1989).

Such data suggest that joint-attention deficits do not affect understanding of simple desires (or the emotions these cause), but may well affect understanding of even simple beliefs. This may be because beliefs are always opaque, whilst desires and emotions need not be: beliefs therefore require metarepresentation, whilst desires and emotions need not always (see Wellman, chapter 2). Such an analysis raises the idea that understanding attention may be critical not only as a precursor to understanding beliefs, but to all mental states that require metarepresentation. In the final section of this chapter, I will briefly consider the notion of a deficit in the autistic child's understanding of attention within the context of a broader theory of autism.

The Specific Developmental Delay Theory of Autism

Our research in autism started from the discovery that the majority of autistic children were impaired in their ability to pass tests of *first-order* belief attribution (of the form **Sally thinks the marble is in the basket** – Baron-Cohen et al., 1985, 1986). I later found that the minority of autistic children who were unimpaired at this level were nevertheless impaired at the next level up, in their ability to make *second-order* belief attributions (of the form **John thinks that Mary thinks the icecream van is in the park** – Baron-Cohen, 1989a). This raised the hypothesis that autism may be a case of *specific developmental delay* in the acquisition of a theory of mind, with different autistic children delayed at different points in this developmental sequence. The more recent research suggests there may be yet *earlier* delays in arriving at the stage of joint-attention behaviours, and we hypothesize that this may be a necessary first step in the normal construction of a theory of mind.

Some predictions follow from this specific developmental delay theory. First, autistic children who fail tests of proto-declarative pointing will also fail tests of first-order belief attribution. Secondly, those autistic children who do pass tests of proto-declarative pointing may succeed on tests of first-order belief attribution, but even these are likely to fail to understand second-order beliefs. This specific developmental delay model is shown in box 16.3.

The general assumption in the specific developmental delay theory is that autistic children's physical–causal knowledge is mental age appropriate and the only delayed aspect of their development that is specific to autism is in their theory of mind. Currently, we could sketch in some age/stages in the theory as follows: in terms of their theory of mind, most autistic children of less than four-years-old (in producing no joint-attention behaviours) may be similar to normal six-month-olds. After this, some autistic children may develop proto-declarative pointing and pretend play, although its late emergence means it remains impoverished. And years later still, some autistic children may progress beyond this level and succeed at understanding beliefs, although they remain very odd socially as a result of such a severe specific delay. We are currently collecting longitudinal data to test these notions further.[8]

Conclusions

In this chapter I have begun to sketch a model of the *emergence* of a theory of mind which attempts to account for the data from both normal and

Box 16.3 Developmental stages in the understanding of beliefs (normal timescale: on left; autistic[a] timescale; on right)

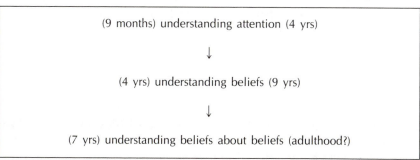

(9 months) understanding attention (4 yrs)

↓

(4 yrs) understanding beliefs (9 yrs)

↓

(7 yrs) understanding beliefs about beliefs (adulthood?)

[a] This suggested autistic timescale may be a generous one: nine years is the earliest age at which we have found autistic children who can make first-order belief attributions, but for many autistic children the delay may be more severe than this. For yet others, there may be no development in their theory of mind at all (Humphries and Baron-Cohen, 1990).

autistic children. This model is in one sense a radical one, in that it places the onset of a capacity for metarepresentation in human development earlier than has hitherto been argued. On the other hand, it is consistent with analyses which do their utmost to avoid unnecessarily rich attributions in infancy (Stern, 1985).

The central distinction in my theory between understanding seeing versus understanding attending hinges on the latter requiring representation of the object of something perceived as 'interesting' (etc.) to the viewer. It is noteworthy that, in Bates et al.'s (1979) view, 'protocommunications' are all about sharing *interest* in objects. In this sense, appreciating that objects may or may not be of interest to others may be the drive behind all communication, and may help to explain why, even in those autistic children whose syntax, lexicon, phonology and even semantics are all intact, spontaneous communication in terms of two-way sharing of interests is seldom seen (Baron-Cohen, 1988).

In closing, we should keep in the mind that caregivers of autistic children are no different from caregivers of other children in the social input they provide (Cox, Rutter, Newman and Bartak, 1975), and yet autistic children are severely delayed in the development of a theory of mind. Such children therefore allow us to begin to answer the question 'Which cognitive structures and processes must be present for an infant to be able to take advantage of the "tutorial environment" (Butterworth and Grover, 1988) that their caregiver provides as part of social experience?' We know that all caregivers, the world across, spend many enjoyable hours during the infant's first year of life playing the 'peekaboo' game (Bruner, 1983). We can surmise that, apart from its possible role in developing turn-taking skills (as Bruner has discussed), this game functions to focus the infant on the seeing–attending distinction. Quite whether children who lack the concept of attentional states, such as our model postulates autistic children do, could enjoy such games, becomes an important question for future research.

ACKNOWLEDGEMENTS

I am grateful to Alan Leslie, Peter Hobson, Vasu Reddy and Sue Leekam for comments on an earlier draft of this chapter. Parts of this work were presented in talks at the MRC Cognitive Development Unit, London (May 1989), at the Oxford Workshop on Children's Theories of Mind (Chair: Paul Harris, June 1989), and in the Symposium on Pointing at the BPS Developmental Psychology Conference, University of Surrey (Chair:

George Butterworth, September 1989). Figure 16.1 was drawn by Cathy Clench, St Bartholomew's Hospital, Medical Illustration Department, London.

NOTES

1 A summary of these two theories can also be found in Baron-Cohen (1988).
2 Fodor obviously didn't know about autistic children when he wrote this. Such children may be the exception to his statement about there being 'no human group that doesn't explain behaviour by imputing beliefs and desires to the behaviour'. Note that it was from anthropology that he expected any challenge to this statement to come, but as it has turned out, the challenge has come from abnormal psychology.
3 Such an experiment is currently being tried by Maggie Minter and Peter Hobson of the Institute of Psychiatry, London (personal communication).
4 Butterworth (chapter 15) cites the aphorism of 'When the finger points at the moon, the fool looks at the finger' to highlight the view that comprehension of proto-declarative pointing is linked to cognitive development. The results from the study reported here (Baron-Cohen, 1989b) can clarify this further: although a minimum MA of ten to 14 months may be necessary in order to understand proto-declarative pointing, low IQ by itself is *not* a cause of failure to comprehend proto-declarative pointing, as the non-autistic developmentally delayed control subjects demonstrate.
5 Leslie's (1987a) theory pinpointed the origins of metarepresentation at about 14 to 18 months of age, with the emergence of pretend play. His amended theory (Leslie and Happé, 1989) suggests that the origins of metarepresentation predate this, in being based in 12-month-olds' ostensive communication. The theory I am developing here suggests that the origins of metarepresentation may predate even this: that in understanding that others have attentional states, infants of seven to nine months reveal their capacity for metarepresentation.
   Naturally, this does not imply that infants understand that other people have *beliefs (that x)*, but understanding attention may imply they understand that other people can *think (of x)*, to use Perner's (in press b) distinction.
6 Trevarthen and Hubley's (1978) notion of primary intersubjectivity is based on reciprocity seen between the infant and his or her caregiver. Stern (1985, p. 135) argues that there is no evidence that this is inter-mental, and moreover, unlike the behaviours comprising Trevarthen and Hubley's notion of secondary intersubjectivity, reciprocity in the neonatal period is not unique to humans but is seen in other social animals.
7 In parallel studies between London and Madrid, Juan-Carlos Gómez, Wendy Phillips and I are currently exploring how autistic children use eye gaze in situations where they desire an object.
8 Ages in this paragraph are relative indications of some predictions this theory makes. Until good longitudinal data is available, these ages will remain as heuristic estimates.

17

Perceptual Origins and Conceptual Evidence for Theory of Mind in Apes and Children

DAVID PREMACK AND VERENA DASSER

'Does the Chimpanzee have a theory of mind?' The question Premack and Woodruff (1978) posed over ten years ago, raised the curtain on what has turned out to be an extremely productive decade. Although most of the work accomplished in this busy time deals not with the ape but with the child, the basic issues are the same in both cases.

1 Does the individual attribute states of mind to another individual, states that he considers to be the cause of the other one's behaviour?
2 What is the nature of these states? For instance, are they exclusively perceptual (e.g., I believe that he *sees* X) or also motivational (e.g., I believe that he *wants* X), or are they both of these and informational as well (e.g., I believe that he *believes* X)? The distinction is important because informational states (e.g., *belief*) appear to be uniquely complex.
3 What is the developmental course of this competence? For instance, do any of the states have perceptual origins?
4 Can these questions be addressed on the basis of non-verbal evidence? Although this requirement is posed most dramatically by the ape, it is not escaped even when working with the child, for then one wants assurance that the child's failures are not owed simply to language difficulties. Fortunately, with the child (though not the animal) one can take into account the convergence of verbal and non-verbal evidence.

Two Levels

Theory of mind, like any other major competence, can be studied on both a perceptual and conceptual level, and we will provide examples of both levels in this paper. On the perceptual level one relies almost exclusively on habituation/dishabituation procedures. The individual is shown stimulus events of one kind or another; when her reactions are appropriate, one makes two kinds of claims: first, the individual perceives certain distinctions; secondly, the perception is the input to a slightly higher-order device that has interpretation as its output.

Consider now the conceptual level on which we also study theory of mind. Here we supplant habituation/dishabituation with higher-order measures involving judgement and choice. We require the individual to indicate which is the positive and which the negative exemplar of a distinction, eliciting this information by explicit questions, in some cases, and by non-verbal procedures, e.g., match-to-sample, in others. We use these higher-order measures because, no longer interested solely in what the individual can perceive or recognize, we want to know whether the individual can make instrumental use of what he perceives.

The distinction between recognition of a distinction, on the one hand, and instrumental use of the distinction, on the other, reflects the growing appreciation of the difference between implicit and explicit processes. Although numerous examples of this distinction can be found in the literature, we present yet another example, one germane to the present discussion since it applies to both 18-month-old-children and chimpanzees.

Habituation/dishabituation studies show that the chimpanzee (not to mention the child) can distinguish not only the sameness/difference of objects but also the sameness/difference of relations. Thus, the duration for which the infant looks at an object A is longer when A is preceded by B than by A. More interesting, however, the infant also responds longer to AA (a pair of identical objects) when it is preceded by EF than by BB and longer to CD when it is preceded by BB than by EF. That is, the homogeneous cases, *same* followed by *same* (and *different* followed by *different*) lead to less responding than do the heterogeneous cases, *same* followed by *different* (and vice versa). Thus, the infant recognizes the sameness/difference not only of objects but also of relations.

Nevertheless, though the infant can *recognize* the sameness/difference of both objects and relations, and in addition readily *match* like objects, the infant cannot match like relations. For instance, it cannot match AA to BB (or CD to EF) – the very same stimuli used in the habituation tests – though it can readily match A to A, B to B, C to C, etc. (Premack, 1988a).

Moreover, though in time the infant's failure to match relations is overcome, the failure is hardly short lived. Most children cannot match relations until at least four-years-old, and apes cannot match them at all unless trained in special ways (Premack, 1983, 1988a). In short, the results of the habituation/dishabituation procedure do not predict those of the higher-order measure, and therefore one must take care to distinguish perception from conception, i.e., to distinguish the evidence that warrants the two levels of processing.

Many studies fail to make this distinction and, for example, speak freely of 'infant's concepts' at a time when the only data available are those of simple habituation/dishabituation. The claim is premature for the evidence available is strictly perceptual. Some would warrant this claim simply on the grounds that the infant generalizes, but this does not justify claiming conception, for generalization is also a property of perception. To show that the perceptual distinction is one the individual can use, and thus that the process is conceptual, one needs evidence beyond that of mere generalization. Here we provide examples of both the perceptual and conceptual levels, starting with the former.

The Infant's Theory of Self-Propelled Objects

We began our work on the perceptual level with this hypothesis: the perception of intention, like that of causality, is a hard-wired perception based not on repeated experience but on appropriate visual stimulation. In the case of causality, thanks largely to Michotte (1963), and more recently Leslie and Keeble (1987), in the case of infants we can specify the stimulation: basically it is temporal and spatial contiguity between appropriate events. What is the analogous stimulation in the case of intention?

Picture the infant as dividing the world into two kinds of objects: those that are and those that are not self-propelled. Self-propelled objects are those objects that can both move and stop moving without assistance from another object; non-self-propelled objects cannot. The non-self-propelled object can have as its initial state either rest or motion, but in either case it will retain this state unless acted upon by another object or force. Elsewhere we take up the psychophysics of how the infant discriminates the two classes of objects (Premack, in preparation); here we simply assume that the discrimination is one the infant can make.

Our first argument is this: just as causality is the infant's principal hard-wired perception for non-self-propelled objects, so intention is its principal hard-wired perception for self-propelled objects. Here is a more complete statement of the argument:

first, the infant perceives certain properties, e.g., one object is moved by the other under conditions of temporal and spatial contiguity, versus the object is self-propelled; second, the infant not only perceives but also interprets, i.e., the infant's perception is the input to a slightly higher-order device that has interpretation as its output. The interpretations in the two cases are causality and intention, respectively. (Premack, 1990).

Now suppose we show the infant not one but two self-propelled objects and, in addition, make a special arrangement between the two objects. We arrange what we call a BDR sequence, where B stands for base, D for deflection from base, and R for recovery or return to base. The movements constituting B, D and R can take innumerable forms and we have only begun to look at their possible composition rules. Consider an example instead. Two balls, one larger than the other, appear on the screen and bounce together for five seconds; that constitutes base. Next one of the balls gets 'stuck' in a virtual hole, i.e. stops moving and remains immobile; that is deflection from base. Finally, the other ball 'frees' the 'stuck' one, i.e., contacts the immobile ball after which it moves; that is return to base.

Our second argument is this: although presentation of a single self-propelled object leads to the perception of intentional movement, adding the BDR relation leads to a further perception. Specifically, the infant perceives one object as having a goal – that of affecting the other object. (Additional perceptions, concerned specifically with reciprocation, may also occur at this point but we shall not discuss them here.)

To demonstrate our second argument, we used habituation/dishabituation in conjunction with a role reversal paradigm (Dasser, Ulbaek and Premack, 1989). Since the subjects in this experiment were not infants but young children, three and a half to five and a half years old, we present this experiment not to make claims about infants, but to illustrate the test paradigm. To demonstrate that BDR leads to the perception of a social goal – that one object intends to affect the other object – we divided the children into two groups, and habituated one of them to a BDR sequence, the other to the reverse sequence RDB. Then we carried out a role reversal in both sequences, i.e., the ball that freed the stuck ball in the first sequence now became stuck itself, and was freed by the other ball. We showed BDR with role reversal to the first group, RDB with role reversal to the other. As we predicted, in the case of BDR, role reversal produced significant dishabituation, whereas in the case of RDB it did not.

Actually, the results were somewhat more complex. With young children, three and a half and younger, the results were exactly as described. However, with older children role reversal produced significant dishabituation in the case of both BDR and RDB. Fortunately, we had obtained similar results some years earlier in a study concerned with the effect of violating the sequence in picture stories (Poulsen, et al., 1979). Whereas presenting the pictures out of order had no effect on older children, it had a profound effect on younger ones. When asked to describe the individual pictures, younger children now said things like 'he's here . . . and he's here' rather than 'he's over here because he's afraid', omitting specifically reference to the intentional component (ibid., 1979). We argued that older children already knew the story schemata; therefore they needed only the elements, being capable of putting them into order themselves. But younger children did not know the schemata, hence they needed not only the elements but also the properly ordered elements. We would now make for the BDR sequence the same argument we made earlier for the picture story.

For some purposes, it is of interest to reformulate our original contrasts, drawing them along somewhat different lines. For instance, we contrasted induced movement (that leads to the interpretation of *causality*) with self-propelled movement (that leads to the interpretation of *intention*). This can be reformulated by treating intentional movement as itself a form of causality, i.e., as movement that is caused *internally* rather than *externally*. Then all movement is caused, some of it externally, some of it internally. Similarily, the contrast between intentional movement in the one-object and two-object cases can be redrawn. One can grant the perception of *goal* in both cases, reserving specifically social goal for the second case. These reformulations alter the focus but not the substance of the infant's theory.

It is essential to recognize that however we formulate the distinctions, the infant's theory of self-propelled objects is a highly restricted one. In proposing that the interpretations of causality, intentional movement and social intention originate as hard-wired perceptions, we by no means argue that all 'fundamental ideas' have similar origins. Indeed, we do not argue that most of the components which, along with intention, make up theory of mind have such origins.

For example, though we claim that when the infant is shown BDR, it perceives one object as having the goal of affecting the other object, we do not claim that it perceives either object as perceiving that the other object has a goal. That is, we do not claim that the infant can perceive second-order intentions. One has only to look closely at the test requirements that such a claim would impose to see that the infant is highly unlikely to be able to meet such requirements.

Similarly we do not claim that the infant perceives informational states of mind, in particular *belief* – an uncommonly strong state of mind – or even *expectancy* – a notably weaker state of mind (see Premack, 1988b, for preliminary treatment of distinction between *belief* and *expectancy*). We base our negative judgement here on the same kind of argument. The test requirements entailed by such claims are likely to exceed the infant's capacities. To be sure, wisdom councils running the tests, but it is not lack of wisdom that councils doubt.

In brief, the theory of self-propelled objects we claim for the infant is a relatively modest one. The interpretations the infant makes on appropriate perceptual inputs are intentional movement and social goal (or the equivalent). For the moment, these are the only components of theory of mind for which we find plausible *perceptual* origins. To bring other states of mind into the child's theory of mind will require arguments beyond those presented here.

The Conceptual Level: Next Versus Relevant

In turning now to the conceptual level, we content ourselves with just one item, improving the diagnostic power of one of our original tests for the claim that chimpanzees have a theory of mind. The test in question is the one in which the chimpanzee Sarah was shown videotapes in which a human actor appeared to have a problem (Premack and Woodruff, 1978). For instance, the videotape showed the actor inside a cage jumping up and down apparently struggling to obtain bananas that were inaccessible in a variety of ways. In one case, they were out of reach overhead, in another case they lay outside the cage, in yet another they were blocked by an intervening box, etc. Many of the problems given the actor were modelled after those Wolfgang Köhler actually gave his apes 60 years earlier (1927).

After showing Sarah the brief videotape depicting the problem, she was given either two or (in some tests) three large photographs, one of which depicted a solution to the problem. For example, the photographs depicting solutions to the problems showed in one case the actor stepping up onto a chair (fruit overhead), in another reaching out with a stick (fruit outside cage), and in yet another displacing a box (fruit impeded by box). The trainer handed Sarah the photographs in a large manila folder and then left the room. Sarah made her choice, after removing the photos and laying them out, placed it in the designated location, and then rang a bell summoning the trainer. The trainer returned either to give differential feedback or to praise all of Sarah's choices, depending on the test. Sarah (now in her early thirties, then a mere teenager) was remarkably successful from the beginning, choosing the right alternative on the first trial in nearly all cases (Premack and Woodruff, 1978).

What can be said of an individual who like Sarah picked the right alternative on the first trial of nearly every problem? Notice what 'right' means: the alternative is a *solution* to the actor's *problem*. Thus, stepping up onto a chair is a solution to the actor's problem, for it enables him to get the bananas. Note that 'solution' presupposes 'problem' – the two are interlocking concepts – and that a 'problem' is not an entity that is physically instantiated by the videotape. The videotape shows no more than a sequence of events, such as, for example, the actor jumping up and down with bananas overhead. This is not a problem, nor does it become one unless it is interpreted in a particular way.

Once the jumping individual is perceived as having the *intention* of getting the bananas, as *wanting* the bananas, as *trying* to get them, the sequence becomes a *problem*, and it then becomes sensible to choose *solutions*. But not until the sequence is interpreted in this general manner does the consistent choice of solutions make any sense.

In fact, not everyone to whom we have given this test consistently chooses solutions. About fifty per cent of children between three and three and a half did not choose solutions (Premack and Woodruff, 1978). Moreover, the failure of young children to choose solutions was not explained by their unfamiliarity with cages and out-of-reach bananas. When the films were reset in a suburban location, e.g., a child actor jumping for chocolate chip cookies on top of a refrigerator, the children did no better. Instead of solutions, these three-year-olds chose alternatives physically matching some evidently salient item in the videotape. For example, they sometimes chose a yellow flower evidently because it matched the yellow of the bananas. Choices of this kind suggest that the child has not interpreted the videotape, not perceived a problem; or that any interpretation he may have made is weak relative to the simple perception of the immediate sensory properties contained in the videotape.

Individuals who consistently choose solutions do so, we argue, because they perceive problems. They interpret the actor's behaviour, where interpretation means: assign states of mind to the actor, e.g. 'wants the bananas', is 'trying to get them', 'has the intention to . . .', etc.

Rebuttals to this argument have taken several forms, some of them wide of the mark, e.g., Sarah was 'taught to' do this (Dennett, 1988). This 'explanation' ignores the fact that since Sarah was correct from the first trial there was no need to teach her. It commits a more serious error: it supposes that one could teach her, i.e., could teach an individual who did not perform correctly from the start. How would you teach such an individual? We have no idea and suggest that proponents of this alternative have no idea either. Consider a more serious rebuttal, one that may be the best of the lot (Bennett 1988b).

This is the proposal that the choice of correct alternatives does not require attributing states of mind at all. It requires only knowledge: an understanding of what the actor must do to solve the problem. For example, to choose correctly in the case of the actor jumping to reach the bananas, one needs only to know what acts will benefit the actor and what will not, e.g., that stepping up onto a chair will be helpful whereas reaching sideways with a stick will not.

Now, there is no doubt that in order to pick the right alternative and thus solve the problem, one must have knowledge of this kind. But is knowledge alone sufficient? Can one pick the right alternative simply by knowing 'what comes next'? Or does the choice of correct alternatives require interpreting the actor's behaviour, assigning states of mind to him, and hence require a theory of mind?

There is as it turns out an admirably direct way to test between these interpretations. However, the outcome of this test always seemed so self-evident to one of us that for years he was perfectly content to let the test stand as a *Gedanken*experiment (cf. Premack and Woodruff, 1978). Unfortunately, however, though *Gedanken*experiments have the advantage of speed, of not requiring that one spend hours in foul-smelling rooms, they tend to persuade only those who are already committed. They do not carry the weight of an actual experiment and attract new adherents (often, too, they do not clarify all the details – 'details' that sometimes turn out to be critical).

We therefore recently turned the *Gedanken*experiment into an actual experiment. Before turning to the real one, however, consider a brief account of the *Gedanken*experiment; it will clarify the idea that stands behind the actual experiment.

Return to the actor who is jumping up and down, struggling to obtain the bananas out of reach overhead. We prepare a special film, one making only a small change in the original. Again, the actor jumps up and down, evidently trying to reach the bananas; now, however, at some point he stops, hitches up his trousers, and then in a moment resumes jumping. We thoroughly familiarize our subjects with this film. Then we present the film, stopping it exactly at the point where the actor's next act is hitching up his trousers.

We offer our subjects three alternatives: 'next' – the actor hitching up his trousers; 'relevant' – the actor stepping up onto a chair, and 'irrelevant' – the actor reaching out with a stick. The subject's task is to pick one of the three alternatives.

'Next' is self-explanatory, being literally the temporally next act in the sequence. 'Relevant', the second alternative, is an act that satisfies the actor's intentions, and therefore presupposes a theory of mind. Whether an act does or does not *satisfy* is defined by the intention the viewer attributes to the actor. For example, if the viewer assigns the actor the intention of getting the bananas, then stepping up onto a chair is relevant; if, however, he is seen as exercising (and the bananas just happen to be overhead) then stepping up onto a chair is not relevant. 'Irrelevant', the third alternative, is simply any act that is neither of a kind that will realize the actor's intentions, nor the temporally next act in the sequence. For more than a decade, this remained a *Gedanken*experiment – we prepared no special films – for it seemed self-evident that any one who passed the standard version of the test would never choose either 'next' or 'irrelevant' alternatives; he would choose only 'relevant' ones.

Experiment: Next versus Relevant

Although the original *Gedanken*experiment was designed for chimpanzees, the chimpanzee laboratory has since been closed, so what began as a *Gedankenexperiment* for apes ended up as a real experiment for children.

Subjects: The subjects were 24 children, all of them students in a village or small-town day school. There were eight three-year-olds (average age 44.1 months, range 39 to 47 months, 4 males, 4 females); eight four-year-olds (average age 54.3 months, range 50 to 59 months, 3 males, 5 females); and eight five-year-olds (average age 62.1 months, range 60 to 66 months, 2 males, 6 females).

Procedure: each child was tested individually on six films, three films per session. The child was familiarized with each film by being shown it twice in a row; on the third presentation, the film was stopped at a particular point and put on hold (so that an image remained on the screen). The child was then given three alternatives, each a large coloured photograph, laid out in a triangular form, with the position of the photographs in each category randomly varied from film to film. The order of the films was randomized over the children, and there was an average of eight days between the two sessions. When shown the alternatives, the child was told: 'Choose what comes next in the movie.' All of the child's choices were praised or approved of.

Fourteen days (on average) after the last experimental session, the children were again shown the three alternatives presented with each film, this time without the film being shown. The child was told: 'Pick the picture you like best.'

The six films are briefly described below:

1 Actor tries to hammer a nail into wall using only his hands. Stops, looks at his wrist watch, and resumes hammering.
2 Actor tries to open a cookie box using only his hands. Stops, pushes one of his sleeves back, resumes handling box.
3 Actor tries to listen to record player, handles and shakes it but there is

no record on it. Picks up tissue from floor, blows nose, resumes handling record player.

4 Actor jumps up and down trying to reach bowl of oranges. Stops, wipes kitchen counter with towel, resumes jumping.
5 Actor is locked in cage, tries to get out. Stops, kicks soccer ball, resumes trying to get out.
6 Actor, locked in cage, tries to reach toy car outside of cage. Stops, pulls hood over head, resumes trying to reach toy car.

The average duration of the films was 39 seconds, plus or minus 8.1, range 30 to 58 seconds. The actor in films 1 and 2 was a nine-year-old boy, in films 3 to 6, a five-year-old boy. The three alternatives given with each film are described in table 17.1.

Results

The main results are summarized in Tables 17.2 and 17.3. The predominant choice in all age groups, as shown by both tables 17.2 and 17.3, was the relevant alternative. Four- and five-year-olds, however, did make some use of the 'next' category, and three-year-olds some use of the 'irrelevant' category. Three-year-olds chose 'irrelevant' alternatives significantly more often than five-year-olds (Mann-Whitney-U test, P 0.05, 2-tail); the only statistically significant difference among the three groups.

The use of irrelevant alternatives by the youngest group recalls the fact, mentioned above, that about half the children in this age group fail the

Table 17.1 Alternative choices following each of six films

Film	Next	Relevant	Irrelevant
1	Looks at watch	Hammers with hammer	Raises hand towards ceiling
2	Pushes sleeve back	Holds scissors against box	Holds cup against box
3	Picks up tissue	Puts record on	Ties shoe
4	Wipes kitchen counter	Steps on chair	Pulls hood over head
5	Kicks ball	Key in hand	Examines glasses
6	Pulls hood over head	Reaches out with stick	Sits on large ball

Table 17.2 Number of choices made by each age group of the three categories of alternatives

	Relevant	Next	Irrelevant
3-years-old	27	7	14
4-years-old	27	14	7
5-years-old	31	14	3

Table 17.3 Number of subjects in each group showing preference for a category of alternative

	Relevant	Next	Irrelevant
3-years-old	6	1	1
4-years-old	6	2	0
5-years-old	7	1	0

standard version of the test (Premack and Woodruff, 1978). Three-year-olds who pass the standard test – choosing solutions (rather than physically matching items) – appear to perform like older children on the present test, choosing relevant rather than either next or irrelevant alternatives.

Even the limited use of 'next' by the older children is of interest. The reader will recall that the instructions given the child were 'Choose what comes next in the movie'. Thus the children were explicitly told to take that which comes next. Some of them apparently did just what they were told to do, and that they did – in the face of an obviously powerful competing disposition – reflects the extraordinary control that language already exerts on children even as young as these.

One can interpret the results in a way that gives emphasis to either of the two dispositions. (1) So strong is the disposition to pick the relevant alternative that it all but overrode the explicit verbal instruction to do otherwise. (2) Language has a determinate impact on the older child; despite the strong 'natural tendency' to choose the relevant alternative, some children followed the instruction and chose that which was next.

A simple way to support this argument would be to repeat the present experiment without the use of verbal instructions. Do the experiment as one would do it with the chimpanzee: present the alternatives, and say nothing. Under these circumstances, the child should have no disposition to use the 'next' category. A comparison of the experiment with and without 'next' instructions would be most instructive. It would show how much the use of 'next' is induced by instruction, as well as how much greater is the use of 'relevant' when it is not interfered with by a competing disposition.

Finally, the control condition – presenting the same alternatives without showing the films, and telling the child to take the picture he liked best – established that the children's choices could not be explained by simple preference. Twenty-one children were re-tested under the control condition (three chose not to be tested again), and of these only three showed a preference for the alternative they chose in the experimental sessions. Eleven of the 21 chose a picture other than the one they chose in the experimental test more often that they chose the same one, and seven chose a different one equally often as the same one they chose in the experimental test.

In summary, the results of the experiment corroborate the conclusions which the Gedankenexperiment recommended as being too obvious to require an experiment. One does not predict the behaviour of the other one simply on the basis of the temporal order of his behavioural sequence. Instead, one attributes intentions to the other one. Why? The principal gain may be a reduction in one's perceptual and mnemonic burden. Having attributed an intention, one need no longer perceive and seek to remember every thing the individual does. Instead, one can ignore irrelevant acts – acts that do not satisfy the intention – and attend only to those that are relevant, i.e., do satisfy the intention. Notice, however, that to do this effectively presupposes that one can discriminate between acts that do and do not satisfy an intention. Clearly, therefore, one needs knowledge to understand the other one. But the knowledge is not that of the temporal sequence of the other one's behaviour. Rather it is knowledge of a kind that enables one, first, to assign the right intention, and second, to discriminate between acts that do and do not satisfy the intention.

Although the Gedankenexperiment was designed for apes, when thought turned into action apes turned into children. Does the performance of children permit us to say anything about how apes would perform if given the same test? Nothing final, of course; how apes would perform can be determined only by testing them. Nevertheless, we can in the meantime venture some educated guesses based on previous child–ape comparisons.

Typically, chimpanzees pass non-verbal cognitive tests that are passed by three-year-old children; they fail if the child must be older, say, four-years-old, before passing the test. In a large series of comparisons (summarized in Premack, 1988a), we have only one exception to this rule of thumb. Sarah violated the rule in successfully conserving liquid and solid quantity (Woodruff, Premack and Kennell, 1980); she should not have passed this test since children are older than four when they pass. Worse still for the rule of thumb, when we taught children Sarah's plastic words for same/different, making it possible to test them exactly as we had her, children still failed where Sarah succeeded (Premack, 1983). We had thought that Sarah's success was owed to a cleaner (less ambiguous) test than children are sometimes given, but this was not the case. Still, this is the only violation of the rule. Otherwise, if three to three and a half year old children passed the test, so did Sarah. Therefore, the success of the younger children on the present test suggests that Sarah and other able chimpanzees may also pass it.

Incidentally, the rule of thumb is designed, of course, for non-verbal cognitive tests, not species-specific abilities. The language that children master even before three-years of age is not duplicated by the ape, nor on the other side of the coin are the chimpanzee's physical feats, tree climbing or a gallop that overtakes most dogs, matched by the child. Comparing apes and children on cognitive tests has produced one interesting outcome. Whereas sensory motor measures (grasping, sitting, walking, etc.) yield the traditional neoteny ordering – monkey, ape, human – cognitive measures do not. From perhaps the child's eleventh month, human exceeds ape (and ape monkey) – with the human advantage increasing thereafter – the reverse of the usual neoteny order (Premack, 1988a).

The Chimpanzee's Theory of Mind: Current Verdict

We close by summarizing what we presently know of the chimpanzee's theory of mind. The chimpanzee has passed tests suggesting that it attributes states of mind to the other one. These states, however, are either motivational (e.g., he *intends* to get the banana – Premack and Woodruff, 1978) or perceptual (e.g., he *sees* which container is baited – Premack, 1988b). Decisive evidence for the attribution of informational states is still lacking.

Tests the chimpanzee has failed largely concern attribution of informational states. Though the indeterminacy of negative evidence is well known, here for whatever it is worth is a partial list of Sarah's failures. (1) She did not distinguish between *know* and *guess*, between an informational condition that would permit an individual to *know* about an outcome versus one that would only permit him to *guess*. (2) She did not distinguish between the different kind of knowledge one would associate with two-year-old and six-year-old children, and hence between the different solutions children of these ages would give when confronted with the same problems.

At the time we gave these tests we did not fully appreciate their difficulty. Only later, after giving the same tests to four-year-old children, and finding about 80 per cent of them fail the first test (*know* versus *guess*) and about 30 per cent the second test, did we properly appreciate their difficulty.

To alleviate this problem, we designed a non-verbal version of the *false belief* paradigm – which however Sarah also failed (Premack, 1988b). But were *we* successful: was this test really less difficult than the previous two? Unfortunately, we cannot say for we have yet to give the test to children. The performance of children is virtually the only measure of difficulty we have at this time.

The continued lack of clear evidence for attribution of informational states by animals is compatible with an early speculation by Premack and Woodruff (1978). They argued that informational states are more complex than motivational ones, and that this difference would be reflected in both the phylogenetic and ontogenetic data. The speculation appears to be confirmed by recent child data; children are reported to attribute motivational states appreciably earlier than informational ones (Wellman chapter 2; Baron-Cohen, chapter 16).

On the other hand, the negative experimental evidence is incompatible with the anecdotal literature. There claims of attribution of *belief* are made not only for apes but even for monkeys. For example, a female baboon, when accepting grooming from a sub-adult male, 'hides' her lower body behind a rock from her mate. She hides, we read, so that her mate will not *believe* she is doing anything wrong (Jolly, 1988). Claims of this kind – which hardly bring credit to the anecdotal approach – suggest that the rules for attributing mental states are not yet sufficiently well formed to be understood by all parties.

We began with the distinction between perceptual and conceptual levels, between the distinction that a species can merely recognize, on the one hand, and those it can use instrumentally, on the other. Unfortunately, we have yet to try either apes or monkeys for their interpretation of self-propelled objects, and thus have no perceptual level evidence in animals. It is highly desirable to obtain such evidence, however, for it is already clear that apes and children differ on the conceptual level. The advanced attributional competences of the older child do not, so far as we know, appear in the ape. What is the source of these differences? Can they be detected on the perceptual level? Or do they appear only on conceptual levels? A species comparison on both perceptual and conceptual levels will help clarify the attributional systems of both humans and animals.

18

The Emergence of Metarepresentation in Human Ontogeny and Primate Phylogeny

Andrew Whiten and Richard W. Byrne

A two-and-a-half year old child engages in a deceptive act: she bites her hand and shows it to the teacher, indicating that another child did this to her (LaFreniere, 1988). In attempting such deception, a child evidences two cognitive abilities which go beyond any primary representation of the world whose function is to represent perceived reality as faithfully as possible: the ability to *pretend* that something has happened which really has not; and an ability to *model the mind of another human*, in this case appreciating that the teacher is likely to give the evidence a false interpretation (that the other child was the culprit), rather than the one the child knows to be the literal truth.

In deception like this, the cognitive operations of pretence and mindreading naturally go together (Jolly, 1985, p. 412). However, a child may mindread without deceiving or otherwise pretending: and conversely, may indulge in pretend play when alone. It is therefore quite another matter to argue, as does Leslie (1987a; chapter 5), that there is a fundamental cognitive substrate underlying both solitary bouts of pretence, and the inherently social phenomenon of a theory of mind. Leslie draws on a range of sources, including logic, philosophy of language, and particularly the developmental psychology of autistic and non-autistic children, in support of his case: yet, all the data derive from humans. We here suggest that a comparative, evolutionary approach to the same phenomena now supports and extends the idea that pretence and mindreading are part of a fundamental cognitive pattern.

Leslie's Model

The theory of mind which lies behind our every-day social behaviour is characterized by the use of mental state terms such as *believe* and *think* (chapter 1). Philosophers of mind have shown that such terms exhibit very special logical properties, and Leslie (1987a) proposes that there is a striking isomorphism between the three major types of logical property and three major diagnostic features of pretend play observed in children (see box 18.1).

We note that the three-part isomorphism is not as neat as Leslie implies.

Box 18.1   Isomorphism of Forms of Pretence and Mental State Logic

---

Type 1

Logical property of mental state term: non-entailment of existence
Assertions involving mental state terms do not logically entail the existence of embedded referrents: 'I *fear that* the monster behind the door will bite me' still makes sense even if no monster exists.

Corresponding form of pretence: imaginary object
E.g. Viki's imaginary pull-toy.

Type 2

Logical property of mental state term: referential opacity
A proposition involving a mental-state term does not have to admit substitution of one description of a referent with an alternative logically correct referent: 'I believe that the chimp behind the bush will bite me' does not entail I believe this about Fifi, even when the chimp truly is Fifi.

Corresponding form of pretence: object substitution
E.g. Austin and Sherman's doll; Koko's trunk.

Type 3

Logical property of mental-state term: non-entailment of truth
A proposition involving a mental-state term does not logically imply the truth/ falsehood of propositions embedded in them: 'The belief that the chimp will bite me may be unfounded.'

Corresponding form of pretence: pretend properties
E.g. Austin and Sherman's doll?

For further explanation see text, and Leslie (1987).

A pretend 'property' (such as imaginary dirt on a doll's face) may be detached to be an object; an imaginary object must have pretend properties; and in all three cases, there is some non-entailment of truth. But the implication of these criticisms is just that in some incidents of pretend play, more than one diagnostic feature may be manifest; even all three: in principle, one might play with an imaginary white stick, pretending it is a blue horse!

Leslie argues convincingly that the isomorphism between the properties of mental state terms and those of pretend play is not coincidental, but signifies a fundamental psychological achievement which can generate both pretence and an ability to represent the mental states of others. What these two share is that they are *representations of representations* – labelled variously as second-order representations (Dennett, 1988) or metarepresentations (Pylyshyn, 1978; Leslie, 1987a, see chapter 1).

In the case of mental state terms, what 'second-order' means is fairly obvious: the child's mind represents a mental state in another's mind, *believing* (for example) that her father *thinks* there is a mouse behind the chair.

In the case of pretence, the implication is less obvious (Leslie, 1987a, 1988). The key point is that in pretence, as strictly defined by Leslie, two simultaneous representations of the world must coexist in a precise relationship. When a child talks into a banana as if it were a telephone, what differentiates pretence from other reasons why the child might act as if the banana were a telephone (e.g. mistaking the banana for a telephone) is that the child has a primary representation of the object as a banana and, simultaneously, a representation of it as a telephone. Although these representations must be tied to the same physical object, it is crucial for the continued coherent functioning of primary, faithful representations (the object as banana) that the pretend representation (the banana as telephone) is coded or marked off in some way as metarepresentational, a process Leslie dubs *decoupling*. Pretence once coded in this way can be elaborated through the application of normal inference procedures, such that a truly empty cup full of pretend water, if tipped, should be expected to produce pretend spillage, perhaps requiring pretend mopping up. Such elaboration by a child can be taken as *diagnostic* of a full-blown mode of pretend representation, and it will be argued further below that such evidence exists also for certain non-human primates. For the present, the important point is that the pretend representation is *derived* from a primary one and is thus *second order*: it is explicitly coded as such and basic rules governing primary representations of the world are suspended (box 18.1).

If both pretence and mindreading do indeed rest upon a shared foundation, then we would expect linkage in their emergence over the course of a child's development. Quantitative assessment of whether such a correlation can be detected is not yet available; furthermore, the links expected are not straightforward in so far as mindreading will require supplementary cognitive abilities, like inference, for expression: representing pretence in others is different from representing their false belief, for example. Nevertheless, Leslie can note in support of his model that early true pretence tends to be manifested towards the end of the second year (e.g. Piaget, 1962; McCune-Nicolich 1981), to be followed closely by use of mental state terms in language (e.g. Shatz, Wellman and Silber, 1983). More compelling is the evidence from studies of autistic children, that the two critical abilities show simultaneous deficits, as would be predicted (chapters 5 and 16). Autistic children have been reported to show little or no pretend play (Wing, Gould, Yeates and Brierly, 1977; Baron-Cohen, 1987 for a review) and also, more recently, to show severe deficits in mindreading, such as the ability to represent another person's false belief (Baron-Cohen, Leslie and Frith, 1985, 1986; Leslie and Frith, 1988; Perner, Frith, Leslie and Leekham, forthcoming). Down's syndrome children examined in these studies showed neither deficit. The striking correlation between the two deficits in the autistic children is therefore unlikely to be the result of general retardation and indeed has been demonstrated for children of average IQ: it thus provides support for Leslie's basic contention with respect to the development of metarepresentational ability in the human child.

We now consider if pretence and mindreading in non-human primates fit this pattern.

Pretence in Other Primates

Recall that the strict criterion for pretend play is that implications are elaborated within the pretend mode, as in the spilled (empty) cup being followed by mopping up. Accepting this severe criterion, several clear reports of spontaneous pretence can be offered for the two species of chimpanzee, our closest primate relatives. Since it is largely in their detail that they convince, some will be quoted quite fully.

Imaginary Objects and Properties

The classic record comes from Viki, the chimpanzee home-reared by the Hayes (Hayes, 1951):

Very slowly and deliberately she was marching around the toilet, trailing the fingertips of one hand on the floor. Now and then she paused, glanced back at the hand and resumed her progress . . . Viki was at the pull-toy stage when a child is forever trailing some toy on a string . . . Dragging wagons, shoes, dolls or purses, her body assumed just this angle . . . She interrupted the sport one day to turn and make a series of tugging motions. That is, they would have been called tugging had there been a rope to tug, which of course there was not. She moved her hands over and around the plumbing knob in a very mysterious fashion; then placing both fists one above the other in line with the knob, she strained backward as in a tug of war. Eventually there was a little jerk and off she went again, trailing what to my mind could only be an imaginary pull toy.

And two weeks later she 'stopped once more at the knob and struggled with the invisible tangled rope. But this time she gave up after exerting very little effort. She sat down abruptly with her hands extended as if holding a taut cord.'

Here Viki, in her tugging and apparent efforts to untangle the non-existent cord, and in her reaction to its becoming freed, shows just the sort of elaboration required by the strict definition explained above. Moreover, an imaginary object, for instance the cord, appears to be invested with pretend properties, such as being tangled around the knob.

For some time, the records from which this extract is taken, although they covered several days of behaviour and several pages of careful description, stood alone. More recently however, Savage-Rumbaugh and McDonald (1988) have reported in more summary fashion on pretend play in several chimpanzees trained to communicate using keyboard symbols (Kanzi is a pygmy chimpanzee, the others are common chimpanzees):

Kanzi frequently pretends to hide invisible objects in piles of blankets or vegetation. Later he will pretend to take them out and pretend to eat them, at times even acting as though he has gotten a bad bite. He then spits out the invisible object and comments 'bad'. All the while there is really nothing there. Kanzi also engages the participation of others in these 'invisible object' games by giving them the invisible object and then watching to see what they do with it.

From the account given, it appears that this behaviour was not demonstrated to the animal by the trainers, and the authors go on to explicitly reject this possibility in the next record:

Sherman and Austin engage in similar pretend eating games. They have also pretended that a fearsome animal was housed in an empty cage by making Waa barks and attacking the empty cage. This behaviour was not demonstrated

for them, but occurred after they watched a tape of King Kong who was
housed in a similar cage.

A further record involving one of these subjects is documented in a videotape
(Savage-Rumbaugh, 1986b, associated with Savage-Rumbaugh, 1986a). The
chimpanzee takes a spoon, dips it in an empty jar, and then acts as if feeding
itself with the non-existent food so obtained.

Evidence from non-play contexts is consistent with these records. Thus,
in describing the tactics used by chimpanzees in reconciliation following a
fight, de Waal (1986; record 86 in Whiten and Byrne, 1986) notes that:

> On several occasions feigned interest in small objects served to break the
> tension and attract the adversary . . . One male suddenly discovered something
> in the grass and hooted loudly, looking in all directions. A number of chimpan-
> zees, including the adversary, rushed to the spot. Each time, the others rapidly
> lost interest, whereas the two males stayed. Still avoiding eye-contact, they
> made all kinds of excited sounds while touching and sniffing the discovery
> (which I have never been able to identify) . . . These reconciliations give the
> appearance of being facilitated by an 'excuse'. The fact that, besides the
> discoverer, his adversary was equally fascinated by an object that induced so
> little interest in others suggests that the adversary also understood the purpose.
> It is tempting to regard this face-saving tactic as a collective lie, i.e. one party
> deceiving, and the other acting as if deceived.

Object Substitution

Evidence for this is by contrast more marginal. From one point of view,
this is surprising: one might expect that pretence elaborated around the use
of a 'prop' would be easier than totally fabricating an object, as in the
previous examples. Perhaps pretence using a prop is more *difficult* because
of interference from perception of the real nature of the prop?

The clearest record comes from the videotape mentioned above (Savage-
Rumbaugh, 1986b). One of the two common chimpanzees, in playing with
a doll, sticks his finger in its mouth and then withdraws it quickly, shaking
it as if bitten. He repeats this twice. Thus, the doll is being treated *as if* it
were a real animate being. Compared to a child using a stick as a horse, or
a banana as a telephone, this of course represents a relatively 'weak' substitution in so far as the doll bears many points of similarity with the literal
counterpart.

This raises a further, more general issue of how pretend play as defined
in the foregoing is to be distinguished from mere generalisation in the
functional object play found in many mammalian species (Fagen, 1981).
Take the example of a kitten playing with a ping-pong ball. It seems clear

that the ball is substituting for prey such as mice which in the natural case the mother brings back live for the kitten to play and practise with (Ewer, 1968). Is the kitten pretending the ball is a mouse? The answer depends, of course, on definitions. According to the strict specification of pretence referred to above, we would require that the kitten holds simultaneous primary (ball) and meta- (mouse) representations. But it seems possible, even plausible, that all that is happening here is that prey-catching play behaviour is being elicited by the presence of the perceptual stimulus array (size, movement and so on) to which it is functionally set to respond. Only one representation would thus exist. This is akin to that of *mistaking* one object for another, one of the explanations for acting *as if*, which Leslie's specification of pretence is designed to exclude: however, it need not imply that the kitten cannot *distinguish* a ball from a mouse – only that with respect to play, they share some stimulus properties, sufficient to elicit the same behaviour pattern.

The chimpanzee playing with the doll appears to go beyond this. He conformed to the operational criterion referred to earlier – that true pretence be manifest in elaborations of play which exhibit the working out of new implications within the pretend mode. Unlike the case of the kitten's ball, it is difficult to see the doll as displaying a 'stimulus property' of biting.

It is difficult to imagine what the kitten could do which would be equivalent, because we are dealing with behaviour all within the natural repertoire of prey-catching play. Thus even if the ball rolls into a mouse-hole and the kitten 'elaborates' on the pretence by sitting down to wait for it to come out, this could be interpreted simply as behaviour released by the natural set of cues. For this reason we must expect some difficulty in deciding one way or the other about whether object play with substitute objects really involves pretence in observations in the wild, including those on primates.

A different basis for inferring pretend-object substitution comes from attempts to teach apes sign language. Although early claims about what aspects of language can be mastered have been disputed (Terrace et al., 1979), Savage-Rumbaugh (1986a) has provided careful evidence that communication can be truly symbolic. In this context consider the following transcription of signing to her teacher, B. Hiller, by the gorilla Koko, during a bout of drinking through a fat rubber tube (Patterson and Linden, 1981).

K: sad elephant
B: what mean?
K: elephant
B: you sad elephant?
K: sad . . . elephant me . . . elephant love thirsty

B: thought you gorilla
K: elephant gorilla thirsty
B: you gorilla or elephant?
K: elephant me me . . . time
B: time for what?
K: time know Coke elephant good me
B: want drink good elephant?
K: drink fruit
B: (showing Koko the rubber tube) what this?
K: that elephant stink
B: that why you elephant?
K: that nose

Although the signs are jumbled and the referents are unclear for 'sad', 'love' and 'time know', a plausible implication is that the tube is being treated as a pretend substitution for an elephant's trunk.

In summary, there is evidence for the existence of pretence in great apes. While some evidence, such as that in the one gorilla record above, is only suggestive, we interpret the data as compelling, particularly in chimpanzees and in the case of imaginary objects, where similar observation comes from different animals and different observers.

Savage-Rumbaugh and McDonald suggest that such behaviour is limited to symbol-using apes; but whether so much can be ascribed to Viki, who only acquired a handful of demand vocalizations, is surely in doubt. What certainly is shared by those apes referred to above is being raised by humans. However, it is hard to imagine that the ability to pretend could emerge simply as the result of this experience, in a species which did not already use the underlying competence in its natural existence. Goodall (1986), summarizing 25 years of detailed recording in the wild, is aware of the problem in identifying pretence. Having referred to the Viki records quoted above, she is able to surmise (p. 591) only as follows:

> Wunda picked a tiny twig, perched herself on a low branch of a sapling in the same attitude as her mother, and poked her little tool down – into an imaginary nest? And when she subsequently withdrew it, how do we know that it was not swarming with a record, though nonexistent, catch?

Perhaps even in what she did, she was 'pretending to fish' – but because this is just part of chimpanzees' repertoire in the wild, we are not convinced any more than in the case of the kitten's play discussed above. If Wanda were capable of pretend play (strictly defined), we could expect her to pretend to bite off the non-existent ants, chew them up, and/or express their taste. Although the same objections of 'natural repertoire' could be advanced even if she did, such elaboration of pretence would surely be more convincing. The fact that it has not been seen lends support to the proposal that human-rearing is important. A possible answer to how such a fundamental ability could, then, emerge out of the blue in human reared apes emerges in the application of the other, mindreading part of Leslie's model to primates, discussed overleaf.

Lack of Evidence in Monkeys

Do chimpanzees (and perhaps other apes, which have up to now been studied less intensively?) provide the only evidence for pretence, and the other anthropoid primates – the monkeys – lack the facility? Given the possible significance of human rearing in its manifestation, we turn first to the literature on *hand-reared* monkeys. Although several reports exist in the literature, some of them offering detailed documentation of a range of behavioural capacities including play, nothing corresponding to the behavioural sequences described above appears to have been documented (Bolwig, chacma baboon, 1959; Hopf, squirrel monkey, 1970; Bertrand, stump-tailed macaque, 1969, 1976).

Turning to wild monkeys, the most obvious cases to consider are those from the large corpus of records of tactical deception in primates, analysed by Whiten and Byrne (1986, 1988a,b; Byrne and Whiten 1987). Consider, for example, records of distracting others by looking into the distance, *as if* there were a predator there. The question is, is the monkey pretending that there is a predator there? Do we see elaborations, working through the implications of a pretend predator? Certainly, alert looking is accompanied in some records by alarm vocalizations: but it is possible that these are just part of the routine of acting as if a predator is there, and not in the same category as Viki's novel generation of untangling her string. The same argument can be applied to other monkey records in the corpus.

In summary, compelling evidence for 'full-blown' pretence is restricted to apes, and then principally to chimpanzees, with whom we last shared an ancestor only four to seven million years ago (Sibly and Ahlquist, 1984; Hasegawa, Kiskino and Yano, 1989). Monkeys, with whom the last common ancestry was 20 to 30 million years ago, have not offered such evidence.

Mindreading in Nonhuman Primates

Although 'imputation of like self-consciousness to others' was posited for chimpanzees by Lloyd-Morgan as early as 1930, and possession of a 'theory of mind' was explored experimentally more recently (Premack and Wood-ruff, 1978), there has been little systematic attempt to examine the evidence for such hypothetical abilities in the natural behaviour of primates (see chapter 1). Byrne and Whiten (1987; chapter 9) and Whiten and Byrne (1988a, b) have thus now reviewed the data available on spontaneous deceptive acts in primates for evidence of mindreading. If there is a funda-mental ability underlying both pretending and theory of mind, then on the basis of the review above, we would expect the best evidence for mindreading in primates to be found for chimpanzees, and perhaps for other apes. This is in fact currently the case. Chimpanzees not only account for a disproportionately high number of records in the corpus, but more importantly, offer the strongest indications that an agent entertains some concept of deception itself, distinguishing between overt behaviour and the deceptive intentions which sometimes underly it (Byrne and Whiten, 1988b, section 5). One type of evidence for this – retribution – emerged when a researcher (F. Plooij), struggling with the too close attentions of a highly habituated young female, used a tactic he had observed in the chimpanzees: he looked attentively into the distance. The female looked in the same direction, then back to the observer, and finally went off to search for the non-existent focus of attention. But failing to find any, she returned, struck the observer and then, in contrast to her earlier pestering, ignored him for the rest of the day, which Plooij interpreted as her classifying his act as deceptive (ibid.). The other type of evidence concerns counterdeception, of which we catalogued seven cases. All concerned chimpanzees. The most striking was of a chimpanzee who, on observing another acting as if no food was available at a feeding hopper (when it actually was, although according to a rota only this second chimpanzee would be allowed access) appeared to depart. In fact he went only a little way and hid behind a tree from where he watched until the first chimpanzee took the food, whereupon he went and snatched it (ibid.). He thus demonstrated an ability to divorce a non-literal interpretation of the world (the true intent of the first chimpanzee) from a primary one (the apparent intent). (See chapter 9 for other discussion of these and related cases.)

There is a strong need for experimentation to complement the corpus of naturalistic observations from which these examples are taken. That which has been undertaken so far offers support for the conclusion that chimpan-zees could represent others' wants or intents (Premack and Woodruff, 1978) but could not represent others' beliefs (Premack, 1988a). However, as Premack comments on the latter, 'Negative outcomes seldom lend them-selves to diagnosis. Sarah could have failed for any of dozens of reasons.' As is often the case, failure on the task may be explicable by something as simple as lack of motivation.

Although neither naturalistic observation nor experimentation can yet provide a watertight conclusion, they are mutually consistent in offering support for mindreading capacities in chimpanzees. By contrast, we do not have equivalent records for monkeys, despite the fact that some taxa of monkeys are well represented in the deception corpus (Whiten and Byrne, 1988a). We thus reach the nub of what this paper proposes: that there is a broad *correspondence* between the occurrence of the two phenomena of mindreading and pretend play within a *phylogenetic perspective*, just as has been claimed in the case of human *developmental* change, reviewed earlier.

There may well be a more fine-grained correspondence, at the level of 'marginal' mindreading capacities. Whiten and Byrne (1988b) showed that by far the greater part of the corpus of tactical deception was concerned with the monitoring and manipulation of the attention (particularly visual attention) of others. There is evidence in the partial hiding achieved by some monkeys (as well as apes, but so far, not the more 'primitive' prosimian primates with whom we shared a common ancestor yet further in the past – about 65 million years ago) that actions are being finely tuned, not to the animal's own perception of the world, but to the view which another individual has of the situation. Representation of another's view, or their visual attention, is not mindreading according to the strict criterion of referential opacity (Quine, 1961; Dennett, 1983), which bars 'seeing' as a mental state, in contrast to such phenomena as 'intending' or 'believing' (see chapter 1). However, for an animal to monitor closely another's view of the world is surely a candidate step along the way to mindreading; and if there *is* a relation between this simple step and the mindreading of chimpanzees, a corresponding correlation in the child development work becomes of interest. This again refers to the capacities of autistic children. Despite the deficits in mindreading and pretend play already outlined, autistic children have been found to perform quite adequately in tasks requiring the representation of what another person can see (Hobson, 1984; see chapter 16). Thus comparisons within both child development and primate taxa suggest a distinction between a capacity for visual perspective-taking, and a more advanced state marked by the co-occurrence of capacities for mindreading and pretence. The simpler ability may plausibly represent a stepping stone to the emergence of the more advanced cognitive complex, whether in ontogeny or evolution.

The tentative pattern which is thus presented by the evidence reviewed so far is shown in table 18.1. That mindreading is manifest in natural contexts, whereas pretend play is only apparent in non-natural environments, suggests that metarepresentation may have evolved initially to support the first of these. If second-order capacities have been selected for in chimpanzees, their natural function appears to be to underwrite these ani-

Table 18.1   Metarepresentations in Primates

	Pretence	Mindreading	Imitation
Chimpanzees	yes	yes	yes
Gorillas	?	?	?
Monkeys	not shown	perspective-taking only	not shown

mals' acknowledged Machiavellian expertise (de Waal, 1982; Byrne and Whiten, 1988a; Whiten and Byrne, 1989). Pretend play may emerge as a product of such abilities only in the rarefied environment of rearing by humans – although it must be acknowledged that methodological difficulties may have prevented pretend play being so clearly recorded in the wild.

Imitation and Second-Order Representation

As table 18.1 indicates, imitative ability is a further respect in which chimpanzees (and perhaps other apes) appear to differ from monkeys, on current evidence. Although it is commonly assumed that monkeys are proficient imitators, recent analyses have expressed scepticism about this. Passingham (1982) emphasized the distinction, within observational learning, between true imitation, in which the form of an act is copied, and stimulus enhancement, where the observer animal's attention is merely drawn to relevant aspects of the task by the behaviour of the observed individual: the façade of imitation then results merely from trial-and-error learning. In this context, Passingham reviewed experimental studies, and could find little basis for accepting the reality of imitation in monkeys. Recent laboratory and field studies have lent further support to this conclusion (Whiten, 1989). The classic textbook imitation example of potato and wheat washing by Japanese macaques has been subjected to searching criticism (Green, 1975a; Galef, forthcoming) and Visalberghi and Fragaszy (forthcoming) have shown that monkeys can readily acquire such behaviours without use of imitation. By contrast, Passingham noted that observational and experimental studies offer overwhelming support for the reality of imitative abilities in the chimpanzee (e.g. Hayes and Hayes, 1952).

Perhaps then a larger pattern exists than Leslie has suggested already. Imitative copying (at least in the visual mode) like pretence and mindreading, may involve second-order representation, in so far as the acts done by (and perhaps the intentions of) the model have to be translated from what is involved in doing them from the model's point of view (perceived *from* the imitator's point of view), *into* a metarepresentation permitting their performance from the imitator's point of view. From the perspective of the potential imitator, the primary representation of an act like termite fishing will be very different according to whether it is done by self or by other, and to derive one from the other appears to be beyond the capacities of most primates. Imitation, then, also fits the pattern proposed in table 18.1, raising the prediction that autists should also have difficulties in imitation.[1]

A Cluster of Metarepresentational Capacities?

A number of other capacities which appear to be special to chimpanzees as opposed to other non-human primates, or apes as compared to monkeys, deserve mention in the context of table 18.1. Given the preliminary nature of some of the evidence already reviewed in the foregoing, these further possibilities will be given only brief treatment.

Indirect Sensorimotor Coordination

When presented with a mirror-image of themselves, monkeys treat it as an image of a strange conspecific. They interpret mirror images of other monkeys correctly: for instance, using the mirror sight of a familiar animal to give advance warning of its arrival (Anderson, 1984; Mitchell, 1989). Most mammals fail to interpret mirror images correctly and soon habituate to them. By contrast, chimpanzees and orang utans have been shown to treat their image as a reflection of themselves, using it to guide their hand to wipe off a spot of paint applied to their foreheads under anaesthetic (Gallup, 1970, 1982; Anderson, 1984). More recently, Menzel, Savage-Rumbaugh and Lawson (1985) showed that chimpanzees but not macaques have a similar capacity to use a video image of their hand accurately to guide arm movements, and they therefore argue against treating the earlier mirror experiments as essentially demonstrating capacities for self-aware-ness.[2] Rather, what all the ape successes do have in common is a facility for going beyond a primary appearance – the face or hand of an apparent conspecific – and instead guiding one's own actions by indirect feedback. What this feedback must involve is a capacity to represent the remote representation of parts of self available in the mirror or video image: second-order representation.

Tool Use

Chimpanzees are pre-eminent amongst non-humans in their capacities to use and make tools, and to do this with forethought, as evidenced, for example, by the collection of relevant materials at remote sites beforehand (Goodall, 1970; McGrew, et al., 1979; Boesch and Boesch, 1984; Beck, 1980 and Passingham, 1982 for surveys). Foresightful tool use, as in the example of the branch trimmed for use as a probe, requires a capacity to generate, simultaneously with the primary perception of the branch as branch, a metarepresentation of it as probe.

Insight

In the classic paradigm used by Kohler, in which an out-of-reach lure is retrieved by chimpanzees through some novel use of boxes stacked to stand on, and/or use of two sticks to fabricate a long pole or rake, the essential nature of the underlying cognitive capacity is one of seeing beyond the primary perception, to new opportunities provided by the materials to hand. Thus, we are really talking about a particular subset of tool use which is marked by clear innovation. There is surely a close similarity between pretence, and the creative insight involved in re-interpretation of an object as a tool: 'I *pretend* this rock is a hammer' . . . 'Aha, I could *use* this rock as a hammer'. Insight and tool use thus fall into the same category as pretense, with respect to the building of metarepresentations from primary ones.

Having thus arrived at insight, we must ask whether the subject matter of this paper is really 'just' intelligence, of which the second-order capacities of pretence and mindreading might be simply specific manifestations? Although the autistic and Down's syndrome child comparison reviewed above offers evidence of a dissociation of mindreading and intelligence as we measure them in children, it may well be that folk perceptions of 'intelligence' in animals are based on somewhat different criteria. Possibly what convinces those who interact intensively with them that chimpanzees are 'intelligent' is a facility in second-order representation. But merely to label certain animals as particularly intelligent advances behavioural science little: we need to take the concept of intelligence apart (Whiten and Byrne, 1988c). To the extent that the subject matter of this paper could be said to be 'intelligence', the value of the analysis must lie in this dissection of component cognitive capacities.

ACKNOWLEDGEMENTS

We are grateful to the following for comments on early drafts of this manuscript: F. de Waal, P. Harris, A. M. Leslie, E. Visalberghi, E. S. Savage-Rumbaugh and R. J. Sternberg.

NOTES

1 Paul Harris has pointed out to us that evidence already exists on impairments of imitation in autism (Curcio, 1978; Jones and Prior, 1985).
2 Since writing this paper our attention has been drawn to a paper by Gallup (1982) in which he used his conclusions about self-awareness, based on mirror self-recognition tests, similarly to predict a chimpanzee superiority in mindreading.

19

The Work of the Imagination

PAUL L. HARRIS

Strive to read a text of the Second Century with the eyes, soul, and feelings of the Second Century; let it steep in that mother solution which the facts of its own time provide; set aside, if possible, all beliefs and sentiments which have accumulated in successive strata between those persons and us.

M. Yourcenar, *Memoirs of Hadrian*

Mental Simulation

Recent work in developmental psychology has shown that young children explain and predict behaviour in terms of every-day mental concepts, notably beliefs and desires (Astington, Harris and Olson, 1988). From this evidence, some have concluded that children adopt a *theory* of mind (Perner and Wimmer, 1989; Wellman, forthcoming, chapter 2). I shall argue instead that children engage in an increasingly sophisticated process of mental simulation that allows them to make quasi-theoretical predictions (Harris, 1989; Johnson, 1988). Mental simulation depends on the capacity to engage in two successive steps: (1) to imagine having a particular desire or belief, and (2) to imagine the actions, thoughts or emotions that would ensue if one were to have those desires or beliefs. The products of such a simulation can then be attributed to other people who do have the simulated desires or beliefs. My analysis incorporates the notion of role-taking (Chandler and Boyes, 1982; Flavell et al., 1968) but seeks to show how such a process might operate in early childhood. It provides a framework for interpreting two reasonably well-established facts: (1) the increasing accuracy with which children can diagnose mental states, and (2) the deficits shown by autistic children in making such diagnoses. I shall first state my position in terms of three bald claims.

1   *The capacity for pretence*. By the age of two to three years, children can imagine having a mental state of belief or desire that they do not have. For example, they can imagine wanting a drink of milk when they are not thirsty.

2   *Reasoning with pretend premises*. Having entertained such premises, children can coordinate them with further premises. These may consist in (1) premises that are known to be true (e.g. 'the cup has no milk inside it' when it is empty), or (2) premises that have no counterpart in reality (e.g. 'the cup has milk inside it' when it is empty). Provided these additional premises make reference in an anaphoric fashion to entities mentioned in the initial premises (e.g. a desire for *milk*) children will be able to arrive at new conclusions that follow either causally or logically by coordinating the two sets of premises. For example, they can imagine the emotional reaction of someone wanting a drink of milk either to a cup that is empty or to a cup that contains (pretend) milk.

3   *Altering default settings*. When they imagine states of belief or desire, children do so against a background of default settings. Unless an imagined premise overrides the default setting, it will remain operative. Within the theory to be developed, default settings correspond to two distinct states: current Intentional states of the self and current states of the world (as known to the self). For example, unless the child imagines a desire that is different from what the self wants, the default setting corresponding to what the self wants will be operative. Similarly, unless the child imagines a state of affairs that does not correspond to the assumed state of the world, the default setting corresponding to that state will be operative. Many errors made by children in predicting actions, thoughts or emotions can be traced to a failure to adjust the default settings.

The simulation of a person's mental state (imagining a state of belief or desire) should not be seen as an all-or-none step. There are degrees of difficulty. Roughly speaking, the greater the number of default settings that require temporary suspension, the more difficult the simulation. It is relatively easy to imagine a different Intentional stance towards current reality or future possibilities; this involves a change in one default setting. It is more difficult to imagine a different Intentional stance toward a situation that runs counter to current reality; this involves a change in two default settings. For example, imagining another person's knowledge can involve imagining a different Intentional stance toward current reality. ('This cup has milk in it. I know that it does. He does not know that it does. I can imagine his ignorance.') It may, however, entail imagining a counterfactual situation and imagining a different stance towards that situation ('This cup has milk in it not tea. I know that it does. He believes that it has tea in it not milk.')

Having presented this short overview, I now backtrack to give evidence for each claim.

1 The Capacity for Pretence

Evidence for the ability to imagine mental states that they do not have is to be found in children's pretend play. Like Leslie (1987a), I believe that the precocity of pretend play tells us something important about human intellectual capacities. I prefer, however, to invoke not a single decoupling mechanism that lies at the heart of all modes of pretence, but rather an increasingly complex set of adjustments. Developmental analysis, stretching back to Piaget's early work *Play, Dreams and Imitation* (Piaget, 1962) shows that pretence undergoes elaboration between about 12 and 48 months. Moreover, the attribution of pretend mental states to dolls, and make-believe characters, undergoes an orderly elaboration from about 18 months onward.

Initially, children treat their dolls as passive recipients of their own ministrations: they feed or clothe an otherwise lifeless character. Later, they begin to manipulate the doll as if it were an active agent (Watson and Fischer, 1977). By 24 months, they endow the doll with a variety of mental states – with sensations, perceptions and desires (Wolf, Rygh and Altshuler, 1984). Still later, between three and four years, the doll may be credited with beliefs that fly in the face of the pretend 'facts' as designated by the child. For example, one character is supposedly unaware of the presence of another character, hiding behind a tree (Wolf et al., 1984, p. 202).[1]

I draw two conclusions from these observations. First, sometime after they can engage in object-oriented pretence, children also exhibit a capacity for imagining states of desire, perceptions and belief. Second, this capacity undergoes an orderly developmental elaboration. Like the increasing accuracy of psychological prediction, this elaboration can be explained by assuming that the child starts off with a variety of default settings specifying the current state of the world and the self, and these can be overriden with increasing flexibility.

2 Reasoning from Pretend Premises

That children can not only entertain make-believe premises, but also combine them with further premises to reach novel conclusions has been shown for both syllogistic and causal reasoning. Dias and Harris (1988) gave children premises that ran counter to their real-world knowledge (e.g. 'All cats bark' or 'All fishes live in trees'). Children were then introduced to a new member of the category (e.g. 'Rex is a cat' or 'Tot is a fish'). Finally, they evaluated a conclusion requiring coordination of the two premises (e.g. 'Does Rex bark?' – correct answer: 'Yes', or 'Does Tot live in the water?' – correct answer: 'No'). Four- and six-year-olds could reason consequentially from these counter-factual premises provided they heard them in a make-believe context. For example, if the experimenter said: 'Let's pretend that I am in another planet . . .' and presented the premises with a dramatic intonation as one might in telling a story, children were quite accurate in answering the final question. If, however, the premises were stated in a normal matter-of-fact intonation, children made many more errors (see figure 19.1).

Children in the 'make-believe' condition were also more likely to offer 'theoretical' justifications – justifications that referred to the make-believe premises that they had been given (e.g. "cos cats bark in this planet'). (See figure 19.2).

Children in the 'matter-of-fact' condition, by contrast, were more likely

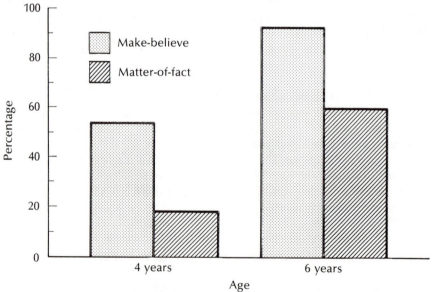

Figure 19.1 *Percentage of correct replies by age and condition.*

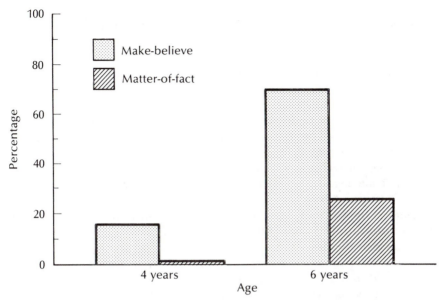

Figure 19.2 *Percentage of theoretical justifications by age and condition.*

to back up their answers by referring to their empirical knowledge (e.g. 'No, Rex doesn't bark because I know that cats miaow') ignoring the initial premises.

These results illustrate how children can reason from counterfactual premises, and also how the default setting (i.e. the assumed state of the world) will be deployed in the reasoning chain, unless there is an explicit prompt to enter the make-believe mode.

In later experiments, we have established three further conclusions. First, a similar pattern of results emerges for *modus tollens* as well as *modus ponens* (e.g. 'All cats bark. Rex does not bark. Is Rex a cat?' – correct answer 'No'). Second, contrary to the standard conclusion from cross-cultural research (e.g. Scribner, 1977) schooling is not a precondition for such consequential reasoning. Unschooled, illiterate children can reason from counterfactual premises showing that it is a universal human faculty rather than a culturally induced form of reasoning. Finally, children's adoption of the make-believe mode can be prompted in a variety of ways (Dias and Harris, forthcoming). For example, (1) a change of intonation, or (2) a reference to a strange planet, or (3) explicit instructions to make a mental image of the counterfactual premises, all boost the number of correct replies (see figure 19.3) and the number of 'theoretical justifications' (see figure 19.4).[2]

Earlier analyses by Piaget (1962) and Isaacs (1930), and more recently by Leslie (1987a; chapter 5) show that children can work out the *causal* consequences of pretend premises. When a cup filled with pretend tea is accidentally knocked over, two-year-olds appreciate that it will need re-filling after the (pretend) spillage. They keep track of the changes in the pretend state of the cup (i.e. from full to empty and back to full) although the cup remains empty throughout (Leslie, 1988a). Isaacs (1930) describes how a three-year-old protested at his companions' failure to take into account the causal consequence of a pretend premise. Having boarded a make-believe ship, he refused to disembark for petrol in 'mid-ocean'; he did so only after steering the ship safely into 'port'. Even chimpanzees seem capable of such consecutive make-believe (Whiten and Byrne, chapter 18); for example, Hayes (1952) describes how Viki pretended to have a toy on a string that she pulled along with one arm trailing behind her; she pretended to disentangle the string and she even responded appropriately to the parallel pretence of her caretaker, staring at the spot on the floor where the invisible rope would have met the imaginary toy.

Children occasionally slip back into the default setting during pretend play. For example, DeLoache and Plaetzer (1985) report the puzzlement of a two-and-a-half year old at his mother's comment when he accidentally

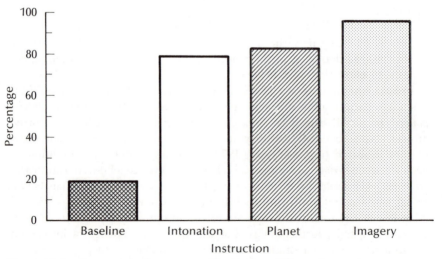

Figure 19.3 *Percentage of correct replies for four different instructions.*

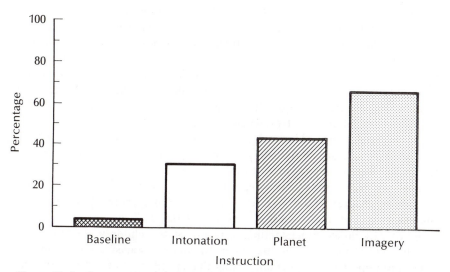

Figure 19.4   *Percentage of theoretical justifications for four different instructions.*

knocked over a cup with pretend tea in it: 'Uh-oh, you spilled your tea. You better wipe it up.' He picked up a sponge, looked at the table-top and asked 'Where?' He appeared to be looking for real tea not pretend tea, and failing to find any, he did not re-enter the make-believe mode and pretend to clean up imaginary tea instead. Here, we have an episode that nicely bridges the results obtained by Dias and Harris (1988) and Leslie (1988a). Without a clear indication (e.g. intonation) that his mother's remark is a continuation of the pretend episode, the child falls back on the default setting (current reality) and taking his mother's remark as a reference to that reality, searches for spilled tea.

Despite such occasional slippage, children's consequential reasoning from pretend premises is precisely what is needed to enable them to draw valid *psychological* conclusions. For example, given the pretend premise that Jack wants Coke, and the further premise that the Coke can is empty, the child can arrive at the conclusion that Jack will be sad. In the next section, we look in more detail at this type of reasoning.

3   Default Settings

Children start to understand other people's mental states by a process of simulation that overrides a background of default settings. I divide these settings into two classes: states of reality, and Intentional states of the self

towards that reality. In daily life, both default settings are normally operative. The child's attention is taken up by some visible or likely target within
current reality and by the current Intentional state of the self toward that
target. For example, the child sees a cup out of reach and points to it
repeatedly, vocalizing at the same time. We describe such an episode quite
naturally by saying that the child wants the cup. Here, an Intentional state
(a desire) is directed toward a likely target (obtaining the cup).

To embark on an act of pretence, the child must adjust at least one of
these default settings. Many of the standard features of pretence (object
substitution; the attribution of pretend properties; and the invention of
imaginary objects; see chapter 18) call for a setting aside of current reality
– 'a decoupling from a primary representation' – to put it in the terms used
by Leslie (chapter 5) and Whiten and Byrne (chapter 18). For example,
the empty cup is treated as if it were full of tea.

To embark on an understanding of mental states, children need to adjust
the default setting that specifies their Intentional stance towards current
reality, as opposed to the default setting that specifies reality itself.[3] Specifically, they need to imagine a different Intentional stance towards reality
from the one that they are adopting.

There are several examples of such understanding. All of them appear to
be available by three years of age. In each case, the child takes the current
state of the world as a given (I include in that world all the hypothetical
but attainable possibilities that it affords (e.g. leaving the table, getting
some toys, going out to play) and conceives of people taking a different
Intentional stance to some portion of that world or its possibilities. Figure
19.5 provides an illustration of what is required. The child (C) must set
aside his or her own mental stance (depicted by continuous and dotted
lines) and imagine having the different stance adopted by another person
(O). This divergence in Intentional stance can occur for both actual targets
(e.g. X – depicted by a continuous circle) or hypothetical targets (e.g. Y –
depicted by a dashed circle). Recent evidence confirms that three-year-olds
are quite adroit at acknowledging such variations in Intentional stance. They
appreciate that people may differ in the targets that they *see, know, expect,
like* and *want.*

Flavell's Level 1 tasks assess whether the child grasps that self may *see*
X whereas another person cannot see X (or the reverse). Three-year-olds
cope well with such tasks (Lempers, Flavell and Flavell, 1977). They can
also cope with questions about knowledge versus ignorance. Thus, although
they *know* the contents of box X, they appreciate that another person may
not *know* its contents (Hogrefe, Wimmer and Perner, 1986; Pratt and
Bryant, forthcoming; Wellman and Bartsch, 1988). Three-year-olds also
understand that people can vary in what they *expect.* They grasp that

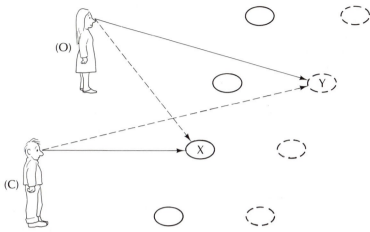

Figure 19.5 *Child (c) and other person (o) adopting divergent mental attitudes to real target (x) and hypothetical target (y).*

although they do not anticipate finding an object in Y, someone else may do so, and search accordingly (Wellman and Bartsch, 1988). They understand that while they may *like* an object X (e.g. they judge that X tastes, smells, or looks good) another person may not like it (Flavell et al., 1989). Finally, they understand that people may not *want* the same outcome. One person may want X but not Y, another may want the reverse. Therefore, a given outcome can cause one person to feel happy and another to feel sad (Hadwin and Perner, 1989; Yuill, 1984).

In all these cases, the child can simulate the reactions of another person by imagining that person's mental stance toward some actual or hypothetical target: seeing or not seeing an object; knowing or not knowing the contents of a box; expecting or not expecting an outcome; liking or not liking an object; wanting or not wanting an outcome. The same analysis allows us to explain how three-year-olds can reconstruct their own past mental states rather than those of another person. We may simply conceptualize (O) not as another person but as a past self with a mental stance that no longer matches that of the current self, which must therefore be simulated. Thus, three-year-olds should grasp that whereas they now expect or see X, earlier they did not. Supportive evidence for this claim comes from Gopnik and Slaughter (1989): most three-year-olds who had formerly wanted X rather than Y could remember that preference, even though they now (having become bored with X) wanted Y rather than X (see chapter 3).

Note that none of these simulations requires that children consider hypothetical targets that are (mistakenly) regarded as part of current known reality. They need only imagine another person – or their past self – aiming, or failing to aim, their mental arrows of seeing, expecting, knowing, liking and wanting at specific targets within the set of actual or possible targets.

A second class of problems does require a simulation of such deviant or mistaken targets. Accurate simulation in such cases requires that the child temporarily overwrite known reality. For example, knowing that a particular target contains X or is a member of category X, the child must keep that knowledge in mind but also imagine a non-existent and conflicting state of affairs (e.g. the object contains Y, or is a member of category Y) temporarily standing in for that portion of reality. Such targets, therefore, are not simply hypothetical or future possibilities (as in figure 19.5); they are non-existent situations that are treated as portions of known reality. In addition, the child must set aside his or her mental stance toward that non-existent state of affairs and imagine a different stance. For example, the child must replace disbelief with belief, non-recognition with recognition, hope with apprehension, and so forth. This type of simulation is illustrated in figure 19.6. It shows the child (C) conjuring up a non-existent reality (Y). This non-existent reality (Y) hovers above that portion of reality that it temporarily countermands (X). A simulation of the other person (O) can only be achieved if the child (C) imagines both this discrepant reality, and the divergent stance that the other person takes toward it.

The evidence for this claim derives from the relative success of four to

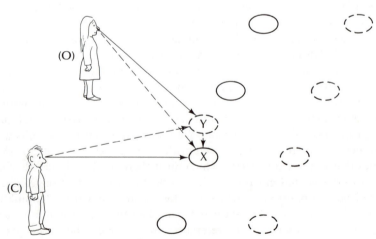

Figure 19.6 Child (c) and other person (o) adopting divergent mental attitudes to target (x) and a hypothetical alternative (y) that might be taken for (x).

five-year-old children (as compared with three-year-olds) in diagnosing what another person *believes, perceives* and *feels*.

Children of four to five years, but not three years, can grasp that while they know that a box contains one thing (e.g. pencils), another person may (falsely) *believe* that it contains smarties (Gopnik and Astington, 1988; Moses and Flavell, 1989). A similar age change occurs for perceptual recognition. Children of four to five years grasp that although they know that the object before them is a sponge, another person denied the possibility of extended perceptual inspection, would *perceive* it as a rock (Gopnik and Astington, 1988). Similarly, they also grasp that although they regard an object as one thing (e.g. as an upright animal) another person in a different position might *perceive* it differently (e.g. as an upside-down animal) (Flavell et al. 1981).

In all these cases, children must conjure up an alternative counterfactual state (Y), temporarily standing in for that reality (X) which they know, or perceive as veridical. Smarties must replace pencils; a rock must replace a sponge; an inverted animal must replace an upright animal. They must also set aside their current sceptical stance toward (Y) and simulate the stance taken by the other person. They must replace disbelief with belief, accurate recognition with illusion, and perception of one orientation with its opposite.[4]

A similar analysis applies to children's reconstruction of their own past mental state rather than another person's current mental state. Children of four to five years but not three to four years appreciate that even though they now believe that an object contains X, or is an X, earlier they thought that it contained Y or took it to be a Y (Flavell, 1986; Gopnik and Astington, 1988; Perner, Leekam and Wimmer, 1987; Wimmer and Hartl, forthcoming).[5]

Finally, we may consider children's understanding of emotion. This is particularly informative because we can devise tasks that require either a simple or a complex shift in the default settings. We have compared these tasks in a recent study (Harris, Johnson, Hutton, Andrews and Cooke, 1989). Children watched while a mischievous monkey played tricks on the other animals. For example, they first learned that Ellie the Elephant has a favourite drink, namely Coke, which is the only drink she likes. They then watched while Ellie went for a walk and Mickey tricked her by replacing the contents of a Coke can with milk, and innocently leaving the Coke can on her table in anticipation of her return. The children judged how Ellie would feel (1) when she first saw the Coke can waiting for her, before she had taken a drink from it and discovered the trick, and (2) after she had taken a drink and discovered the actual contents.

Answers to question (2) require only that children imagine Ellie's state of desire – her preference for Coke – and check that against the actual contents of the can. This case matches the simpler case depicted in figure 19.5.

Answers to question (1) require that children imagine Ellie's state of desire towards Coke as compared with any other drink. In addition, they must imagine her emotional reaction given her mistaken assumption that the can contains Coke. This case, therefore, matches the generic case depicted in figure 19.6.

Accordingly, children should cope much better with question (2) than question (1). This is exactly what we found. Figure 19.7 shows the proportion of correct replies. In answering question 2, all three age groups gave a high proportion of correct replies. For question (1), the proportion is much lower especially among the younger children; they fail to make the necessary adjustments to the default settings, and continue to diagnose the animal's reaction to the actual as opposed to the apparent contents of the container.

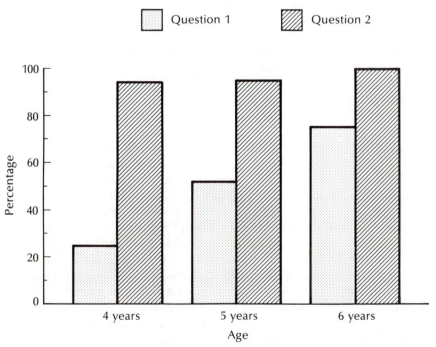

Figure 19.7   *Percentage of correct replies by age and question.*

Children's justifications support this interpretation (figure 19.8). Many younger children said that Ellie would be sad – even before tasting the liquid in the can – 'cos it's milk' or 'because of the trick'. Older children recognized that, as yet, Ellie's hopes would not have been dashed. She would feel happy 'cos she likes it' or 'because she thinks it's Coke'.

Finally, table 19.1 shows that there is a close link between children's judgements about the duped animal's emotion, and their explanations of that emotion. Younger children were mostly wrong on both judgements and explanations; older children were mostly right on both.[6]

Do Autistic Children Lack a Theory of Mind?

Recently, Simon Baron-Cohen, Alan Leslie and Uta Frith have asked whether autistic children lack a theory of mind. They have shown that, as compared with retarded children of the same mental age, autistic children are poor at diagnosing false beliefs (Baron-Cohen, Leslie and Frith, 1985; 1986; Leslie and Frith, 1988; chapters 5 and 16). These tasks require a complex adjustment of the default settings according to my analysis: imagin-

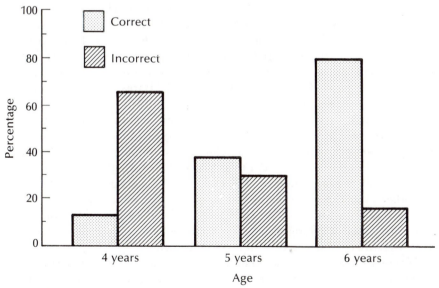

Figure 19.8 *Percentage of correct and incorrect justifications for question 1 by age.*

Table 19.1   Contingency between Predictions and Justifications for each Age Group

Age	Correct predictions	Correct justification	
		3 or more	Less than 3
4-year-olds			
	3 or more	2	1
	Less than 3	0	13
5-year-olds			
	3 or more	5	2
	Less than 3	0	9
6-year-olds			
	3 or more	12	0
	Less than 3	1	3

ing a counterfactual state of affairs, and imagining the other person's stance towards that state of affairs, (as depicted in figure 19.6).

How do autistic children perform if we simplify the task – if we require the type of adjustment depicted in figure 19.5? For example, if we tell them that a story character wants X but not Y (or vice versa) and the character eventually gets either X or Y, can autistic children predict how the story character will feel? This is a very easy task for normal children. Recall that four-year-olds made almost no errors when asked how the tricked animals would react to the actual contents of the container (figure 19.7). Indeed, even three-year-olds do well on such tasks (Hadwin and Perner, 1989; Harris, Johnson, Hutton, Andrews and Cooke, experiment 3, 1989; Yuill, 1984).

In our first study, we compared 20 autistic children and 20 normal children equated for mental age (Harris and Muncer, 1988). We used simple stories about a brother and sister who wanted different things. In each story, their mother announced a treat that matched what one child wanted but not what the other wanted. For example, 'John wants to go to the zoo but Mary wants to go to the swimming-pool; their mother tells them that they are going to the zoo.' We then asked 'How does John feel? And how does Mary feel?' Children listened to three such stories and for each story they were asked about both of the story characters.

Figure 19.9 shows how accurately children judged the story character's feelings. Both groups were likely to say that the characters would be happy even if they did not get what they wanted (mismatch condition) although this error was especially frequent among the autistic children. We interpret

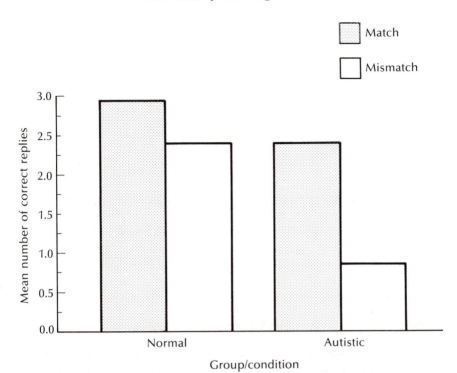

Figure 19.9 *Mean number of correct replies by group and condition.*

it as a failure to adjust the default setting. For example, asked how Mary would feel when their mother said they were going to the zoo, children erred by saying that she would feel happy (a reaction that they themselves would probably have), neglecting to keep in mind Mary's specific desire to go to the swimming pool not the zoo.

As a group, the autistic children performed worse than the normal children. Nevertheless, some autistic children made only a single error or none at all. This is shown in tables 19.2a and 19.2b, in which results for individual children are presented, collapsed over match and mismatch questions. This point emerged even more strongly in a follow-up study when we tested somewhat older, and more able autistic children using the same task. As before, we found that the autistics did worse than the normals as a group, especially on the mismatch condition. Nevertheless, many autistic children (11 out of 20) performed without error.

Baron-Cohen (forthcoming) has pursued these results by contrasting two emotion-judgement tasks. The simpler task, like those just described, called

Table 19.2a   Number of subjects correct on 0–6 desire stories: study 1

	0	1	2	3	4	5	6	N	Mean
Normal[a]	0	0	0	1	3	4	12	20	5.35
Autistic[b]	1	3	4	5	3	0	4	20	3.1

[a] Normals: Mean CA 5 years 4 months; mean MA 4 years 11 months.
[b] Autistics: Mean CA 11 years 6 months; mean MA 5 years 4 months.

Table 19.2b   Number of subjects correct on 0–6 desire stories: study 2

	0	1	2	3	4	5	6	N	Mean
Normal[a]	0	0	0	0	1	1	18	20	5.85
Autistic[b]	0	0	0	5	2	2	11	20	4.95

[a] Normals: Mean CA 6 years 3 months; mean MA 6 years 5 months.
[b] Autistics: Mean CA 12 years 7 months; mean MA 6 years 7 months.

for a single adjustment of the default setting: children simply needed to compare what the story character wanted with the actual outcome. The more difficult task (like the task involving Ellie the Elephant described in the previous section) called for a more complex adjustment of the default setting. The story character was misled concerning the outcome. Hence, children had to set the actual outcome aside, and compare what the character wanted with what the character (mistakenly) expected to get. On the simple task, the autistic children performed worse than normal children, but many autistic children performed without error, corroborating the results depicted in table 19.2a and 19.2b. Indeed, their performance was comparable to that observed in a group of mentally handicapped children of the same mental age. On the more complex task, however, the autistics performed very poorly. Few performed without error, and as a group they did worse than either normal or retarded children of the same mental age.

Drawing these studies together, it is clear that autism does not completely block the normal development of psychological understanding. Rather, it is a deficit that slows development in that domain. In terms of the analysis that I have developed, the autistic child is slow to adjust the default settings. For single adjustments (cf. figure 19.5), autistic children perform worse than normal children of the same mental age. Nevertheless, some perform without error, and their performance as a group may be comparable to that of retarded children. For more complex adjustments (cf. figure 19.6), their lag in performance is much more noticeable: few perform without error, and their performance as a group is inferior to that of both retarded children and normal children matched for ability.

We can arrange 'theory of mind' tasks in terms of the necessity for default adjustment. At the bottom of the ladder are easy tasks – such as the emotion-judgement task that I have described. Higher up the ladder, we find the more complex false-belief tasks used by Baron-Cohen and his colleagues (Baron-Cohen et al., 1985; 1986). Higher up the ladder still, we find the so-called second-order belief-attribution task, that calls for an analysis of what one story character believes about another story character's beliefs. If we examine autistic children of a given mental age, we should find that the emotion judgement task will be solved by the highest proportion and the complex second-order false-belief task by the smallest proportion. The available evidence supports this conclusion. Among autistic children with a receptive verbal mental age of five-and-a-half to six years, about 45 per cent perform either perfectly or make a single error on the emotion-judgement task, 28 per cent solve the simple, first-order false-belief task, and none solves the more complex, second-order false-belief task (combining data from Báron-Cohen, 1989b; Harris and Muncer, 1988; Harris, Coles and Tan, 1989). In summary, the bold claim that autistic children lack a theory of mind is wrong. Some autistic children certainly know something about the way that the mind works although they are much slower to acquire that knowledge than normal children. By analyzing tasks in terms of the default settings that require adjustment, we can predict how poorly autistic children will perform.

Do Normal Children Have a Theory of Mind?

In conclusion, I wish to offer an alternative to the claim that children – whether normal or autistic – are acquiring a 'theory' of mind (Harris, 1989a). I have argued that children make predictions about other people's actions, thoughts and emotions by running a simulation. A simulation calls for a working model of the other person but not a theory. Consider a small-scale working model of an aeroplane. The model aeroplane can be subjected to various forces. For example, a wind tunnel can be created to assess its aerodynamic properties. Observation of the model will produce a stock of generalizations about how it reacts to particular situations. Those generalizations can be used to predict, by analogy, how the real plane will react when faced with the same conditions.

Notice, that without any recourse to theorizing, the model can also be used to make new predictions about how the real plane will behave when facing novel conditions. All that is needed is to mimic those novel conditions with the model, to observe how it reacts, and to make predictions about the real plane, by analogy.

Children are equipped from birth with a working model of the other person. The construction of their own mind is similar in crucial ways to the construction of other people's minds, and it faces the same sorts of conditions. Provided they have some awareness of their own mental states, and of the conditions they face, they can arrive at a set of generalizations about the links between situations, mental states, and action. For example, they can notice the pain that ensues after a fall, or the way in which visual experience changes with direction of gaze. These regularities allow the child to make predictions about other people, by a process of analogy.

These generalizations can be supplemented by the process of simulation described in this chapter. Asked what someone will do, it is important for the child to consider the situation as conceived by the other person. That situation may not correspond to what the child wants or believes, either now or in the past. Effectively, therefore, the child is required to make a prediction about a novel situation. However, so long as the child mimics the conditions that obtain for the other person – imagines the desires and beliefs that other person brings to the situation – the analogy between self and other can be re-established. Simulations of the ensuing action or emotion of the other person will be more or less accurate depending on the degree to which such default adjustments are made. Exactly the same holds for the model plane. If we are to predict the behaviour of a real plane in a hurricane, we cannot simply use any model plane. We must try to construct one that embodies the properties of the actual plane that we are attempting to make predictions about. We must mimic the wing-span of the actual plane and the conditions that it will encounter. Children get better at making predictions to the extent that the working model that they deploy includes such adjustments.

In defence of the claim that children operate with a theory of mind, Wellman (1990) asks how it is that children offer causally relevant explanations of other people's actions. For example, asked whether a story character will feel happy or sad, children focus appropriately on the character's beliefs and desires instead of his or her heartbeat or respiration. He argues that the relevance of children's explanations is easily accounted for if we assume that they have a theory of mind. Faced with an action or emotion, children invoke the theory, and the theory specifies explanatory constructs such as beliefs rather than heartbeats. However, Wellman overstates the appropriateness of children's explanations. Children are sometimes good and sometimes poor at invoking beliefs and desires. They often focus inappropriately on the situation that confronts the story character. For example, asked how a character will feel about a Coke can whose contents have been surreptitiously replaced by milk, young children will often say 'sad – 'cos there's no Coke' even if the character could not possibly know about the replacement (Harris, Johnson, Hutton, Andrews and Cooke, 1989). We need, therefore, to explain children's irrelevant explanations as well as their relevant ones. The simulation model does that quite naturally: the younger child imagines him- or herself confronted by the situation that actually faces the (duped) story character: a Coke can filled with milk. That simulation leads the child to wrongly attribute sadness to the character who wants Coke. Asked to explain that emotion, the child refers to the actual situation. Since nothing has been said about the story character's heartbeat or respiration, it does not enter into either the simulation or the explanation offered by the child.

The older child, by contrast, makes a more extensive adjustment to the default settings – imagines not what it would be like to face the objective situation but what it would be like to face the situation that the character assumes to obtain, namely that the Coke can is full of Coke. This simulation allows an accurate prediction of the character's emotion, and it prompts a different form of explanation: the child mentions not the actual situation but the assumed situation: 'happy, because she thinks it's Coke'.

An emphasis on analogical modelling has two further advantages over the view that children operate with a 'theory' of mind. Wellman insists that children go beyond first-hand experience of beliefs and desires; they elaborate them into theoretical constructs just as scientists invoke theoretical constructs to explain the effects they observe. This raises the awkward question of just how experiences are transformed into theoretical constructs. The present account denies that such a transformation occurs. Children do go beyond first-hand experience but they do not construct a theory. Children have beliefs and desires and they are frequently aware of them. Certainly, by the age of two or three years, they can report their beliefs and desires quite vehemently. That awareness allows the detection of local regularities in experience. The attribution of such regularities to other people is based on an assumed analogy between self and other.[7] Particularly when adjustments are made to the default settings, as described in this chapter, analogical modelling can be highly predictive but it does require the construction of a theory.

Finally, the emphasis on prediction by analogy captures important continuities between child and scientist without obscuring crucial differences. Philosophers of science have stressed that many theories are guided by models or analogies (Hesse, 1966; Kuhn, 1970a; Masterman, 1970). Kuhn

(1970b) acknowledges that a concrete model can play a central role in the establishment of a scientific paradigm. It offers those who subscribe to the paradigm a common way of looking at the various puzzles to be tackled. However, although models and analogies offer guidance, they do not in themselves constitute a theory. The theory takes shape only as the scientific community systematically sorts through those features of the analogy or model that do and do not hold. Scientific progress may therefore undermine the analogy rather than call for its constant re-establishment (as in the case of default adjustment). The ensuing theory will be more focused and certainly more explicit than any analogy or model that gave rise to it. Indeed, especially when formally stated, the resultant theory may be stripped of all signs of the analogy (Hesse, 1966). In short, we can acknowledge that children, like scientists, rely on analogy, while at the same time denying that they proceed to the formulation of a theory of mind. Skilled mindreading – as I hinted at the beginning of this chapter – calls for the imaginative resonance of the biographer rather than the theoretical postulates of the scientist.

NOTES

1 Leslie (1987; chapter 5) notes that two-year-old children readily join in with pretence by other people. He makes the additional claim that this early understanding of pretence-in-others is 'an elementary form of understanding another's mental state'. If he is right, my argument must be wrong. I claim that the understanding of another person's mental state requires a process of simulation or pretence. The implication of Leslie's argument – in combination with my own – would therefore be that the understanding of another's pretence requires that one pretend to pretend. Something is wrong here. Two-year-olds are most unlikely to be capable of anything as sophisticated, yet they do join in with games of pretence initiated by other people. The problem, in my view, is Leslie's assertion that such understanding implies an understanding of another's mental state. I believe that early shared pretence can operate in a much simpler way. An adult acts out a piece of make-believe. To join in, the child needs to recognize what the other person is pretending to do, and also that what they are pretending is not for real. For example, the child needs to recognize that the other person is pretending to pour tea, but that there is no real tea. This may be a lot, but it does not require any insight into the mind of the person pouring the (pretend) tea. In the same way, a theatre-goer need only respond to the play *as if* it were real while acknowledging that it is not; he or she can ignore the mental processes by which the actors produce their performance. They are as irrelevant to an appreciation of the play as the mechanical processes by which the scenery is shifted. Thus, although adults might eventually consider the mental processes

that lie behind a fine piece of acting, they need not do so as they watch the play. Similarly, a child can share another person's pretence without considering that person's mental state.

2 The diversity of these prompts and the convergence of their effects on the child's reasoning lend support to the notion we are dealing not with a local intensification of normal information-processing (e.g. superior attention to, or memory for, words spoken in a dramatic intonation) but rather the triggering of a distinctive 'make-believe' mode of processing.

3 At this point, my position departs sharply from that of Leslie (chapter 5). He subsumes all acts of pretence under a single decoupling mechanism, and predicts that autistic children will be deficient at pretence across the board. By contrast, I distinguish between the adjustment of two different default settings: those specifying current reality and those specifying Intentional states of the self (Harris, 1989a, b). The difficulties displayed by autistic children suggest that they can make the former type of adjustment; they can engage in simple object-directed pretence (Lewis and Boucher, 1988; Boucher and Lewis, forthcoming) even though they have difficulty in imagining other people's mental states.

4 Important differences between my analysis and that of Josef Perner can be made clear by comparing figures 19.5 and 19.6 with the left- and right-hand portions, respectively, of figure 8.1 (Perner, 1988a). According to Perner, a dramatic shift occurs between approximately three and four years. Three-year-olds can conceive of someone being linked with a non-existent situation (e.g. there being chocolate in box Y) by 'thinking of' or 'thinking about' that situation. However, lacking any conception of how someone might represent that situation in their mind and treat it as a guide to reality, three-year-olds do not have any genuine understanding of 'thinking that' or 'expecting that' (Perner, forthcoming a). By contrast, Perner claims, four-year-olds can grasp that the mind is a representational device. As compared with three-year-olds, they do three new things. First, they can engage in metarepresentation: they can conceive of other people constructing a mental representation of a situation. For example, they might conceive of another person entertaining in her mind a representation that depicts chocolate in box Y. Secondly, they grasp that, for the other person, this model can serve as a representation of reality. Thirdly, they grasp that the content of this model (its depiction of chocolate in box Y) may not, in fact, represent the actual situation but a counterfactual situation (because the chocolate is in X not Y).

In comparison with Perner, I attribute more to the younger child and less to the older child. Figure 19.5 credits younger children, including three-year-olds, with the ability to imagine various Intentional states, including beliefs and expectations concerning hypothetical situations, provided those hypothetical situations pertain to as yet unrealized possibilities, rather than to known counterfactuals. Figure 19.6, on the other hand, does not credit older children with metarepresentation, i.e. the capacity to imagine the mental models or representations inside the mind of another person. Like figure 19.5, it credits children with the ability to imagine various Intentional states (including belief), but now these Intentional states may be directed towards a non-existent, counterfactual situation. In particular, figure 19.6 depicts how children can grasp that it is possible to treat a counterfactual situation as a substitute for a portion of reality.

This substitution is depicted in figure 19.6 where (Y) hovers about (X).

Have I introduced Perner's complicated representational machinery in through the back door? When the substitution of Y for X is unpacked, does it not imply that the four-year-old grasps how the mental representation of (Y) is regarded by the other as a representation of the real situation, whereas in fact it misrepresents that real situation which consists in (X)? I do not think so. All the child needs to understand is that anyone who accepts (Y) for (X) would adopt the same stance toward (Y) as they themselves adopt to (X). The situation Y would be accepted as a quite specific part of reality (the part corresponding to X). Nothing more is needed. In much the same way, we might notice that a slot machine will treat a coin that is no longer valid currency as if it were still valid; we can make that assertion – and it will help us to anticipate what the machine will do – without implying that machines have anything like a *representational* device that gives rise to false beliefs (Dretske, 1988). If my analysis is correct, it shows that the claim that children of approximately four years of age grasp the concept of mental representation (Astington and Gopnik, chapter 3; Flavell, 1988; Forguson and Gopnik, 1988; Perner, 1988a; Wellman, forthcoming) is highly questionable.

5 Wimmer and Hartl (1989) and Astington and Gopnik (chapter 3) have suggested that three-year-olds' difficulties in reconstructing their own past false beliefs refute the Cartesian notion that mental states of the self are transparent, and show instead that mental states of the self have to be identified by means of a theory of representation. However, the refutation only follows if it is held (quite implausibly) that all mental states of the self – past and present – are equally transparent. A much more defensible position is that *current* mental states of the self are transparent and reported earlier than those of other people (cf. Harris, 1989a, pp. 56–7). This position is quite compatible with the existence of difficulties in reconstructing *prior* beliefs.

6 Hadwin and Perner (forthcoming) have replicated these results with one important qualification. Some children could accurately diagnose the duped animal's false belief, but still proceeded to misdiagnose the animal's emotion. This lag warrants further research.

7 Wellman (forthcoming) argues that even when children lack crucial first-hand experience, they nevertheless arrive at accurate theoretically based insights into another's experience. For example, Kelli, a blind, pre-school child, realized that her mother could see an object at a distance, provided there were no obstacles between her and the target (Landau and Gleitman, 1985). This argument is flawed, however. Kelli was not completely blind. She could distinguish light from darkness with one eye, and could therefore have learnt first-hand that light can be seen at a distance, provided there is no obstacle.

20

Narrativity: Mindreading and Making Societies

MICHAEL CARRITHERS

In *Actual Minds, Possible Worlds* Jerome Bruner sets out a contrast between what he calls the paradigmatic mode of thought and the narrative mode. The paradigmatic mode is that of mathematics, logic and computing, whereas the narrative mode concerns the human condition. He remarks that the narrative mode is little understood and speculates as follows:

> Perhaps one of the reasons for this is that story must construct two landscapes simultaneously. One is the landscape of action, where the constituents are the arguments of action: agent, intention or goal, situation, instrument, something corresponding to a 'story grammar'. The other landscape is the landscape of consciousness: what those involved in the action know, think, or feel, or do not know, think, or feel. The two landscapes are essential and distinct: it is the difference between Oedipus sharing Jocasta's bed before and after he learns from the messenger that she is his mother. (1986; p. 14)

The notions of a narrative mode, and of a dual landscape, are I think potentially very fruitful. They go to the heart of the human capacity to imagine, to construe and misconstrue, others' mental states. I want to use these ideas to explore an anthropologist's perspective on mindreading.

In *Actual Minds* Bruner was concerned chiefly with the landscape of consciousness and with the narrative mode as exercised by adult competence, especially in literature. Janet Astington has taken the ideas in another direction, towards 'Narrative and the Child's Theory of Mind' (Astington, forthcoming b). She confirms that a crucial change occurs between three and five years of age, when children begin to understand the difference between the two landscapes, the difference between what is true and what someone thinks is true, between 'the weaver *knows* that the loom is empty' and 'the Emperor *thinks* that the loom might have cloth on it'. These issues she approaches from a theory of mind viewpoint, but she hints at something more as well. She notes, for example, that the setting of experimental questions in a story facilitates children's understanding, quite apart from any additional information conveyed. This implies, I think, that the narrative mode might amount to more than the individual theories or competences into which it might be analysed.

In fact in this paper I will propose that we might usefully think of a distinct capacity, *narrativity*, a property of the human species which differentiates it from other species. Mindreading or higher-order intentionality, I argue, is a necessary foundation for narrativity. But that is not the end of the matter, for narrativity provides a yet more powerful form of mindreading. It is narrativity which allows humans to grasp a longer past and a more intricately conceived future, as well as a more variegated social environment. In other words, narrativity supports the more elaborate and mutable sociality which differentiates humans from their cousins, the other social primates. In this perspective the link between the landscape of consciousness and the landscape of action cannot so easily be disjoined for purposes of exposition, as Bruner and Astington did. For in our evolutionary past, as in our later history, the landscapes of action *and* of consciousness have been part of one real and determining flow of deeds and mortal consequences.

My arguments therefore are phylogenetic and sociological rather than ontogenetic and psychological. If they are acceptable, however, they should be able to be translated into a developmental perspective. For example, I think it no accident that the children depicted by Astington above and Astington, Harris, Wellman, and others in this volume – children gradually attaining new and more powerful attributions – can also be depicted in a very different way:

> In every culture, the period of three to five years is one in which children begin to discover wider opportunities for co-operation as well as the harsher aspects of human conflict and aggression. They begin by imitating and comparing, and then gain imagination for real co-operation in a narrative drama where pretended roles complement each other. Emotions of liking and disliking are strongly expressed in play. When play breaks down, fights can become mean and bitter. Friendships and antipathies last, but are open to negotiation and change. Confident and joyful sharing of experiences, and of the motives that give them significance, depends on acceptance of rules and the exercise of communicative skills that facilitate agreement. (Trevarthen and Logotheti, 1989)

This child's world as described by Trevarthen and Logotheti is an altogether more intricate, risky and entangling place. It is in fact more like human social life, and certainly more like the threshold to an adult social life that adult competence must match. To think of people as holding a theory concerning others' ideas and beliefs is perhaps a reasonable first step in trying to understand how we master social complexities. But in order to enter into play, pretend roles, or negotiations over friendship and antipathy, the child – and *a fortiori* the adult – must build a more sophisticated understanding of a social setting than mindreading in a narrow sense can provide.

Research Programmes

I want to begin by stressing that my reasons for thinking so arise from the character of human experience as envisaged by anthropology and not from psychological evidence. I conceive that anthropology has a research programme, as developmental psychology and behavioural biology have theirs, and that these programmes arise in genuine conundrums set by experience. For sociocultural anthropology the conundrum appears in two phenomena, the sheer complexity of human sociality and the wide variation in schemes of sociality.

In box 20.1 I have tried to convey the anthropological programme by contrasting it with others represented in this volume. I envy the elegance of experiment and the rigour of thought demonstrated by many of the papers here, and my attempt to characterize the different paradigms implies no value judgement. Psychologists and behavioural biologists are building a view of humans from the simple to the complex, whereas anthropologists work from the complex to the simple.

I have surely oversimplified, but this series will help me to make three important points.

The first concerns the difference of temporal perspective between the top of the table and the bottom. Humphrey, for example, writes that social primates inhabit a world 'where the evidence on which their calculations are based is ephemeral, ambiguous and liable to change, not least as a consequence of their own actions' (1976: p. 309). The key word is 'ephemeral'. This is not, as I first thought, a world without time, but one whose temporal horizons are very close and which does not, at least so far as the social primates are concerned, suffer the burden of a laboriously planned future or a long remembered past. Similarly the experiments reported in this volume by Leekam, Wellman and Astington and Gopnik are ones which presuppose only a very brief sequence of actions. But in contrast the settings studied under the rubric of (4) in box 20.1, and even more so those under (5) and (6), are ones with broader views on time, bringing into consideration

Box 20.1   Primal Scenes

1   A generic individual (with theories or mind modules) confronts the
    environment.
2   Generic individuals confront each other and environment in a shifting
    social setting with a narrow temporal horizon. (Humphrey's (1976) setting,
    theory of mind experiments.)
3   Individuals typed by age, sex and rank confront each other and environ-
    ment in a face-to-face community over a (relatively short) time period.
    (Achieved or projected longitudinal studies of primate groups – Strum,
    1988.)
4   Role types, based on named individuals but distinguished by achieved
    and/or marked social statuses, relate to each other and environment in a
    face-to-face community with a weighty cultural tradition and complex
    social organization. (Community studies in ethnography.)
5   Named individuals with shifting role types relate to each other and
    environment in a face-to-face community with complex social organiz-
    ation, a long past, an uncertain future, and a rolling cultural heritage.
    (Historically oriented ethnography)
6   Those of five join with others, and against others, in interest groups,
    ethnic groups, and classes to remake their heritage (of role types and
    groups) in the face of shifting global social and social environmental
    forces. (An ideal social anthropology or social history?)

This box gives a simplified comparison of different viewpoints in research on
human sociality.

the lifetime of individuals and the longer continuity – or discontinuity –
over generations or centuries of families and other institutions.

Secondly, the perspectives at the top of the list are socially simple. The
experimental settings reported in this volume have at most three roles:
experimenter, subject and perhaps one other. Even the experimental stories
have only two or three characters. On the other hand humans considered
by anthropologists are socially variegated on many dimensions. Within a
family or small community different kin relations distinguish one person
from another: mothers, mother's brothers, grandparents and great-grand-
parents, daughters, cross and parallel cousins. Beside these relations, and
often involving the same people, other social, political or economic distinctions might be made: woman and (uninitiated) girl, healer and patient,
judge and plaintiff, headman and villager, queen and subject, host and
guest, customer and trader, master and slave.

Finally, the temporal and the social perspectives are intimately involved with each other. For in human societies regarded as such the types or characters are frequently ones arrived at over a large part of a life-cycle: a doctor or healer trains for years, a woman becomes a wife after being initiated and achieving her society's version of the age of reason, a peasant son succeeds to his patrimony as head of household only with age and his father's retirement or death. Moreover, these gradually attained character- istics of persons occur in a mutually construed flow of events extending beyond any one person's life-cycle into the past and the future. The arrival in his hands of his patrimony by the peasant son, for example, is intelligible because of, indeed is constituted by, the previous inheritance by his father and his father's father, and so forth.

Such a flow of events includes performative acts – the vows of marriage, initiation into manhood, conferral of a degree, coronation as a king – the natures of which are constituted by, and are only conceivable within, a wider social and temporal setting: a church, a community, a university. In the larger evolutionary perspective the peculiarity of this human trait is highlighted if we ask how such roles differ from those we might attribute to a social primate of another species. How, for example, might the role 'newly immigrant adult male', a role strongly differentiated in other primate societies, appear among ourselves? And the answer is: in many ways. A new commander is appointed to your unit. A new apprentice joins your company. A lawyer comes to town and hangs out his sign. Such characteristi- cally human movements are only intelligible in the light of, indeed are constituted by, a much larger and more complex social background than those found among our primate cousins.

And finally there are other and larger events which may not be per- formative alone, but which all the same create a new and long-lasting state of affairs and set of characters. A murder takes place, a feud begins, and new identities with new relations of enmity spring into being. Famine strikes and whole regions are rendered refugees and dependents. A colonial power arrives and society is transformed from top to bottom.

Anthropologists, sociologists and social historians have one way of conceiv- ing such events and arrangements, the people involved have another. Differ- ent participants have different understandings of the action. But what I think ineluctably true is that human beings have an effective capacity which enables them to create, to understand and to act within these ramifying complexities, complexities extended through social rather than physical space and unfolding in an event-filled rather than abstract time.

Narrativity

It is this capacity which I want to designate as narrativity, a capacity to cognize not merely immediate relations between oneself and another, but many-sided human interactions carried out over a considerable period. We might say: humans understand *characters*, which embody the understanding of rights, obligations, expectations, propensities and intentions in oneself and many different others; and *plots*, which show the consequences and evaluations of a multifarious flow of actions. Narrativity, that is, consists not merely in telling stories, but of understanding complex nets of deeds and attitudes. Another way to put this would be to say that human beings perceive any current action within a large temporal envelope, and within that envelope they perceive any given action, not as a response to the immediate circumstances, or current mental state of an interlocutor or of oneself, but as part of an unfolding story. (I owe this latter formulation to Paul Harris, personal communication.)

I think it essential that character in narrativity be conceived very broadly, since it must comprehend both individuals as having statuses and roles – that is, as standing in relation to one another – and individuals as having idiosyncratic histories and propensities. On the one hand there must be some room for abstraction, so that people can be understood as acting generally, on a first approximation, with a specific set of obligations and rights: as, for example, a lawyer, or a king, or a mother acts with obligations and rights toward clients, subjects, or sons and daughters. But on the other hand the particularity of one person rather than another, of Hannah rather than Amy, must also be grasped. We must understand not just the type of the grandfather, for example, but also his individual propensities: mellowness or irascibility, friendliness or aloofness, and so forth. Whether or not the Western notion of an individuated personality really grew out of a much earlier sense of people as *personae* or types as Mauss suggested (see Carrithers, Collins and Lukes 1985), narrativity must comprehend both of those possibilities and many others as well.

But characters with their relationships are also set in a flow of events, a plot, with its sense of plans, situations, acts and outcomes. Plots embody what a character or characters did to, or about, or with some other character or characters, for what reasons, and what followed on from that. To comprehend a plot is therefore to have some notion of the temporal dimension of social complexity. This complexity arises from a distinctly human form of causality in which people do things because of what others think and because of how others' places thereby change with respect to their own. By means of stories humans cognize not just thoughts and not just situations, but the metamorphosis of thoughts and situations in a flow of action.

Clearly a very great deal must be involved in the capacity to understand interlinked events in this way. For example, a good deal of the causality woven into a plot consists in characters acting upon their evaluation of others' acts in the light of some standard: I may act, that is, just because I find your action kind or evil, appropriate or silly, and so forth. People also rely upon a folk psychology, some more elaborate and cultivated set of attributions which supplement the basic theories of which Wellman, for example, writes in this volume. But what I want to stress for present purposes is only this: though we can, for purposes of analysis, separate out character and plot, and morality and folk psychology as well, in the flow of action these constituents are all inextricably mingled in a larger and comprehensive understanding of pattern in events. The landscape of consciousness would not be intelligible, would not even exist, were it not meshed with the landscape of action.

Let me use Bruner's example, *Oedipus the King*, to illustrate what I mean. On one hand, Sophocles' play could be no better example of the power and intricacy of immediate and temporally simple human mindreading capacities. From the beginning the drama plays on the difference between the audience's received knowledge of Oedipus' actual condition of incest and parricide and the false state of mind of Oedipus on the stage. To cast the situation in a form which emphasizes the layers of representation and metarepresentation involved we could write:

We *know* that Oedipus *believes* [falsely] that he is innocent, not the cause of the city's pollution.

And even during the early scene with Teiresias, whose prophetic knowledge of the real state of affairs is not accepted by Oedipus, this configuration is wound more tightly until:

We *know* that Oedipus *believes* [falsely] that Teiresias seeks to *deceive* Oedipus and the citizens; but we also *know* that Teiresias *knows* that in fact Oedipus *deceives* himself.

Sophocles drives this interplay of ignorance and knowledge further and further until just before the revelation, when Jocasta implores Oedipus not to pursue his enquiry into his origins: 'I beg you – do not hunt this out – I beg you, / If you have any care for your own life / What I am suffering is enough' (Latimore and Grene, 1954: line 1060).

We *grasp* that Jocasta *fears* that she might *know* what Oedipus *hopes/
fears* the herdsman might *know* about Oedipus' birth.

Looked at in this way, the play is constituted through its use and manipulation of humans' abilities to construe and to track complex states of mind
in oneself and others. The drama is literally made of mindreading. Moreover,
action is set out as taking place in a very narrow time-span, a few hours
perhaps, and only with few characters, so that the dramatic action is a good
deal closer to the experimentalist's chronological and social simplicity than
to the anthropologist's complexity.

But it is misleading to think that the story of Oedipus is circumscribed
by mindreading alone. Narrativity is no less an ingredient of *Oedipus the
King*, and indeed the wider envelope within which the action takes place
covers most of an ordinary human life. It includes the union of Laius,
Oedipus' father, with Jocasta his mother, Oedipus' own birth, his exposure
on the hillside and rescue, Oedipus' murder of Laius, his accession to the
throne and marriage to Jocasta, and the begetting of his children. Without
this framework the short-term play of mindreading would be senseless. And
indeed, since the story of Oedipus looks forward as well to his death and
apotheosis at Colonus and to the fate of Thebes in later episodes, for a
Greek audience the temporal envelope extended into the future as well.

So if *Oedipus the King* is unintelligible without mindreading, it is equally
so without the notions of what a king and a queen are, a husband and wife,
a mother and a son, without the conception of a human life-span and its
proper stations, and without the notion of what constraints and possibilities
govern long-lasting relationships. It would also be unintelligible without
some notion of Oedipus' idiosyncratic character, including the intelligence
and heroism which allowed him to confront the Sphinx and solve its riddle.
Nor could we grasp the action without being able to conceive a change in
such statuses, such as Oedipus' taking of marriage vows or being crowned
king, or Jocasta's giving birth to legitimate children. And finally, I suggest,
it would be incomprehensible were not statuses, changes in status, and the
transformation of relationships, attitudes and beliefs knitted together into a
larger, developing, narrative whole. The fate of Oedipus, to blind himself,
and of Jocasta, to hang herself, would seem poorly motivated had not the
tempo and relation of events, both on stage and in the larger context, led
inexorably to that outcome. It is for this reason that the separation of a
landscape of consciousness from a landscape of action is finally unviable:
for the tale is made indissolubly of Oedipus' relations to others, of the
characters' beliefs, feelings, and intentions in regard to each other, of public
events, and of their unfolding together in a compelling sequence.

Making Society

My proposal is that narrativity, Bruner's narrative mode, constitutes a level of cognitive integration matched to the level of social and interactive integration achieved in human social life. I have elsewhere (1989) suggested that just that capacity for a larger social integration, our distinctly human form of sociality, has been selected for in the process of human evolution. The argument is an elaboration from Humphrey (1976) and Byrne and Whiten (1988b): an increasing capacity to live in groups, to vary the organization of those groups, and to create ever-more complex forms of cooperation within them would, for many reasons, have been to the advantage of members of our species. When Trevarthen and Logotheti wrote of children developing an 'imagination for real cooperation in a narrative drama where pretended roles complement each other', their words had an evolutionary as well as a developmental significance. It is the development and elaboration of cooperation which marks us as a species, and our children begin to be equipped – this is Trevarthen and Logotheti's larger point in their article – to enter into co-operation from the beginning. Moreover I have suggested that we need not conceive the narrativity that was part of that evolution to be a strictly or narrowly linguistic skill, though it is certainly intertwined with linguistic skills in adult humans at present.

It is however misleading to conceive narrativity only after the pattern of an audience understanding *Oedipus*. For that example sets narrativity in a passive mould, as a capacity which enables humans to comprehend successfully a social world already formed, already given and immutable. For purposes of research into mindreading or narrativity it may be easier to take this view, since to consider the social environment as shifting introduces complexities that are very difficult to reckon. But in an evolutionary perspective narrativity must have been important as an active competence as well, one which enabled humans to shape events, and indeed society, through plans or projects. I suggest, in fact, that the human capacity for planning and for having long-term projects is at base no different from narrativity.

As Schmidt and Marsella point out (in chapter 8) a plan may be conceived on a short or a long scale. A plan on a very short scale, such as those envisaged by Humphrey or in some of the experiments reported here, may perhaps be directly grasped as an immediate intention, belief or attitude through mindreading in a narrow sense. Fred's intention as he busies himself with his kettle to offer a cup of tea to his colleague Nigel might be read by a Nigel equipped with higher-order intentionality. But a long-term plan, such as Fred's design to woo Nigel and get him to help Fred displace Angela as head of department, appears only through a grasp of Fred's character and through a casting of events in a long enough perspective. Only then might Fred be understood as a schemer and Fred's actions be revealed as a campaign, not a random series of interactions. More important, Fred could only *be* a schemer if he could project the unfolding of his scheme over a considerable period of time and in the face of shifting vicissitudes. This dimension of human life would appear more clearly if we read *Macbeth* or *Othello* rather than *Oedipus*.

Let me look at the example of Fred more closely. On the one hand there are the larger narrative assumptions which are part of Nigel and Fred's setting, assumptions analogous to those which enable an audience to understand *Oedipus*. Fred and Nigel understand what a chairperson is, what it means for a university to have a relatively democratic structure, and therefore how a chairperson might be chosen or elected. More to the point, they connect these larger assumptions with an actual history, the development of chairpersons' power in their university and Angela's appointment as chair several years ago.

Moreover for Fred there is a yet larger history as well, one which he tells both himself and others. Angela epitomizes an unfortunate and backward influence in (shall we say) the discipline of anthropology. She is steering the department towards biological and evolutionary interests. Fred, as the faithful student of the celebrated Professor Zehetgrueber, represents a more enlightened concern with cultural symbols. This is indeed the department Zehetgrueber founded, the one which should carry forward his project of symbolic anthropology. So apart from personal ambition there is, for Fred at least, a much longer term story, one which transcends his own lifetime and involves in one way or another many others in his discipline.

And there is a finer-grained story too, one which concerns the patterning of events on a day-by-day, even hour-by-hour scale, and the forming of action on that scale. The meeting at which arrangements for electing or re-electing the chairperson is next month. Fred's close friend and ally, Lotte, has agreed with Fred that things have gone too far and that they need to change the direction of the department. They must go to work quickly. They cannot count on everyone agreeing, but there are some who might come around, among them Nigel. Fred agrees to approach Nigel while Lotte approaches others. Indeed – and now we are back with Fred about to offer Nigel a cup of tea – Fred will not mention his conversations with Lotte, for Nigel does not wholly approve of Lotte. Fred will rather address Nigel directly and appeal to his shared concern with symbolic anthropology. And as Fred now hands Nigel that cup of tea, he looks very closely to see Nigel's reaction as the topic of the chair is raised. Fred will be able to narrate to Lotte the course and timing of his conversation with Nigel. From that they will measure Nigel's inclinations and decide how next to move.

The entanglements of this hypothetical sketch are not in their nature, I believe, very different from those of many families or corporations or villages or churches or other social settings. On one hand, Fred could not understand what was going on, let alone act, if he could not put characters together with plots: he could not understand himself as the student of Professor Zehetgrueber, Angela as an abidingly deleterious influence, or Lotte as his ally. On the other hand, the forging and recounting of stories enables him to act. On the larger scale it is the casting of Angela as a villain in the developing story of Zehetgrueber and his apostles that furnishes him with orientation and direction. Fred can understand himself, indeed present himself, as acting for the longer term, not just for whimsy or temporary advantage. And as action develops and circumstances change, he will be able to orient himself according to that narrative . . . or according to some new and further narrative which develops out of it. Fred is not without invention, and he can spin a new tale to match new circumstances.

On a smaller scale Fred's ability to recount Nigel's reactions will form the basis of further policy to be pursued by himself and Lotte. They will understand Nigel partly through the development of his conversation with Fred, and they will remind each other of things that Nigel said or did on other occasions. They will work Nigel into their account of the developing action. And in fact Nigel would be literally incomprehensible to anyone, completely unaccountable, were it not possible for Fred and Lotte so to set him in a narrative frame.

Recapitulation

Let me for the moment leave Fred and Lotte conspiring. I have proposed that narrativity consists in two inseparable traits which I have called 'character' and 'plot', traits which humans attribute to themselves and to the people and actions which surround them. People do not possess characters apart from their place in the developing action any more than plots possess a shape apart from those who participate in them. Neither plot nor character make sense without the other. This inseparability is the central reason why I would wish to see narrativity considered as unitary, rather than as the cumulative effect of separable competences or theories.

Character consists in attributions to persons in action: such attributes can be very varied, ranging from personal attitudes and propensities to the duties and obligations expected of someone acting in a well-understood social role, but in any case the attributes appear only in the course of events,

events which may span a lifetime. Plots in turn consist in series of actions and events which are linked causally through the construal of the propensities and attitudes, the beliefs and understandings, the intentions and interests of those participating in observing them. Fred and Lotte, that is, will act next on the basis of their understanding of Nigel's propensities, beliefs and desires. They will act as they do *because* Nigel inclines towards or thinks or wants this or that, *and because* Nigel's beliefs or desires bear particular consequences in the present flow of action.

If, as I suggest, narrativity is a distinct cognitive power, we need not think of it as being infallible, or as producing a canonical or impersonally correct account. Participants' understandings may be more or less public and agreed, as people agree on who is now chairperson, or they may be more private, hidden or contentious, such as who will be the next chairperson. Nigel no doubt would tell a story different from Fred's, and Angela's would differ again. What all the narrators have in common is the ability to act by virtue of construing a direction in events and a coherence in persons.

In fact there is a certain amount of recursion or embedding involved in such construals: the coherence which Nigel finds will, to the extent that it guides his action, actually render his action coherent and capable of being construed. Consequently Fred may well tell a story which involves the story Nigel tells himself. 'Lotte,' Fred might say, 'Lotte, I think Nigel always thinks of himself as a peacemaker, a true Christian, that's what he did the last time the chair was elected, so if we can go along with that then he might . . . ' The embedding which we find in higher-order intentionality ('I *suspect* that he *thinks* that I *believe* so and so') appears in narrativity, the only difference being that in narrativity temporal and social complexity are encompassed as well.

By connecting narrativity to action I have also tried to suggest that we regard it as more than just a mental capacity for representation. For narrativity is essentially connected to conation and emotion. Stories move us, and move us to action in a way that merely imperative injunctions cannot. It is commonplace of anthropologists that peoples everywhere look to exemplary narratives, myths or legends, for a template of action. In my own fieldwork (1983, 1988) I found that Buddhists in Sri Lanka and Jains in India did indeed often pattern their actions, and indeed whole series of actions, on some narrative precedent enshrined in their scriptures. These narratives are roughly equivalent to Fred's larger story of the heritage of Zehetgrueber and his place in it. What anthropologists find harder to capture is the way in which people – including themselves – find in everyday life the more evanescent narrative structures that allow them to act. Yet if my contention that narrativity is a fundamental and pervasive human trait is true, then it is to the fragmentary and elusive talk of everyday life – what so-and-so did to so-and-so, and what you are going to do about it – that we should look for confirmation. We would expect to find narrative coherence – or better, coherences – even in the absence of clearly marked story-telling. And indeed some anthropologists, notably Schieffelin (1976), have begun to take this tack.

The notion of mindreading is partly an answer to the question: how can humans enter into such complex interactions with each other? What I have tried to suggest is that this question leads on to another, and that is: how can humans form enduring and changing relations with each other, such that they create the intricate and mutable societies in which they live? And I have suggested that narrativity, a capacity to comprehend both long-term experience and elaborate social arrangements, is the answer to this second question. The implications for anthropology of this answer, if it were accepted, might be that we would look less to purely abstracted symbols and the play of symbols as the atoms of human cultural arrangements, and more to plots and characters as embodying a fusion of ideas with action and actors. For my psychological colleagues it might imply that they could look to a level of integration of cognition greater than that embodied in the understanding of immediate intentions and beliefs alone.

21

The Emergence of Mindreading: Steps Towards an Interdisciplinary Enterprise

ANDREW WHITEN

In this final chapter I shall summarize points of contact between the different disciplines represented in the rest of the book,[1] a necessarily personal and selective exercise. I will also indicate the major conceptual and empirical questions which now seem to me to beg further enquiry, for in this book we have focused on 'emergence' not only in the subject matter of mindreading, but in the very field of study itself.

Steps in the Emergence of a Theory of Mind

A number of specific objects of mindreading have been repeatedly treated in the foregoing chapters: *seeing, attending to, wanting, intending,* and *believing* are common examples which can be thought of as delving progressively deeper into the operations of the other's mental apparatus. If we examine briefly the consensus which appears to be arising about the order in which these come to be mastered by the developing child, we can then assess whether a similar hierarchy of competencies is evident in evolutionary constructions based on comparisons between related species. It should be emphasized that this exercise does not imply the discredited expectation that ontogeny should recapitulate phylogeny (Gould, 1978) for any correspondencies which are found to exist between ontogenetic and phylogenetic elaboration may simply reflect general principles in the biological construction of mindreading systems (cf. Parker and Gibson, 1979).

All undated references are to other chapters in this book.

Belief–Desire–Action Psychology

There appears to be general agreement that a child is initiated into the first stage of what we recognize as an 'adult' or mature theory of mind once he or she explains others' actions as the combined result of their desires and beliefs (see accounts by Bennett; Wellman). The belief–desire–action triad is important to our subject both as the bedrock of a mature theory of mind, and also (at first paradoxically) because of the proposal that this achievement is preceded in development (in, say, two-year-olds) by a simpler psychology in which only the desire component is represented (Wellman).

There is more disagreement about when the critical triad is truly mastered. The sternest commentators have argued that a crucial sign is the ability to attribute *false beliefs* to others, for only then does the young mindreader evidence an understanding of the *representational nature* of mental states, so clearly implied when a mental state happens to embody a false or mistaken picture of reality. According to this criterion, a theory of mind is typically the achievement of a four-year-old rather than a three-year-old (Perner, Leekam and Wimmer, 1987). Wellman does not dispute three-year-olds' difficulties with *false* beliefs, but concludes that in all other respects such children do typically show evidence of operating a theory of belief–desire psychological causality. Thus far, then, we have a rough characterization of the achievements of average two-, three- and four-year-olds, as they progressively master attribution of desires, then beliefs and finally, false beliefs.

The two-year-old requires closer scrutiny however. What can it mean to say that he can attribute *desire* and not *belief*, when, according to Bennett 'neither of those can help to explain behaviour except when combined with the other' (p. 97)? Bennett's own answer to this difficulty is that such a young child does use a belief–desire psychology, but only his own beliefs are attributed to the subject. This seems consistent with the performance of two-year-olds studied by Wellman, who correctly predict the behaviour of a character who fails to find what they want at a certain location: perhaps the child successfully predicts further search because the character, like the child himself, should *believe* that searching will satisfy his *want*. But is this necessary? Could not the child attribute to the other a behavioural strategy on the lines of 'if you haven't yet found what you *want*, keep searching'? Belief may be said to be implicit in this formulation, but then that could be true of most behavioural rules and conventions. I think Bennett has thus raised an issue about two-year-olds' mindreading which needs more attention.

Further food for thought is that Wellman, and others including Astington and Gopnik, and Leekam, express the idea that the 'simple psychology' of two-year-olds is fundamentally distinguished by a failure to attribute representations to others: 'simple desires [for, say, an apple] embody no notion of representing an apple in your head, simply *wanting* one' (p. 29). I must confess some difficulty with this. If somebody wants an apple and not a pear, this would seem intrinsically to require some representation of the nature of the want. Moreover, it is difficult to characterize someone *searching for* a wanted object, the task used by Wellman, without some notion of their having an internal representation of that which will constitute a successful outcome. To be sure, two-year-olds' grasp of the representational nature of wants is severely restricted. Indeed as Astington and Gopnik showed, even by three years children typically fail to appreciate certain implications of the representational nature of wants, such as the way they may change over time (even in the case of the child's own wants) and may vary between different people. Nevertheless, Astington and Gopnik's analysis confirms a basic developmental progression from attribution of desires to attribution of belief, in each case attribution of the mental state to others being handled with similar sophistication as attribution to self.

This pattern appears to fit that observed in older autistic children, who can attribute wants even when demonstrating severe difficulties in attributing beliefs (Leslie; Baron-Cohen; Harris). The pattern also appears to be repeated at higher levels of embedding, with attribution of *second-order desires* being easier than attribution of *second-order beliefs* (Leekam). We thus seem to have a very general phenomenon here, and it will be of interest to see if it extends to the phylogenetic picture also. Before attempting that, however, it may help to bring in another key mental state – that of intention (Shultz; Premack and Dasser; Astington and Gopnik). As the latter stress, intentions are allied to desires in their direction of fit with the environment, this direction being the reverse of that for beliefs (see chapter 3, figure 3.1): but *intention* is not the same as *want*; indeed, intention mediates between wants and actions, and handling it is an achievement only of older children, according to Astington and Gopnik's experiments.

How do the comparative data relate to this developmental progression in the reading of others' desires, intentions, knowledge and false beliefs? At present we are far from being able to discuss developmental changes in mindreading in other species, but rather must concentrate on comparisons between taxa. At present, the main phylogenetic comparison feasible is between just one well-studied ape, the chimpanzee (with whom we last shared an ancestor only about 7 million years ago) and various species of monkeys (with whom the split was more like 30 million years ago)(Whiten and Byrne: W&B).

Premack and Dasser (P&D) update the conclusions to be drawn from experiments with chimpanzees. Tests for attribution of what P&D call informational states, such as belief and knowledge, have generally proved negative, as have those with monkeys (Cheney and Seyfarth). Although all these authors naturally regard the negative conclusions derived from these first attempts as tentative, P&D argue by contrast that recent experiments do add further weight to the interpretation that the chimpanzee can attribute *intentions*. Now, in light of the above discussion about children, we need to ask whether the attribution was in fact *intention*, or only *want*. What the chimpanzee chose successfully was a picture of the solution to a problem set to the actor and this could be interpreted as the correct satisfier of the actor's *want*, as much as their likely *intention*. However, Byrne and Whiten (B&W; W&B) have argued that certain counterdeceptions by chimpanzees suggest an ability to distinguish deceptive from true *intent*, and *want* is not so easily substituted here. B&W do not offer evidence of attempts to create (false) beliefs in others. To summarize so far, if, given the uncertainties involved here we collapse wants and intentions into *desires*, the primate studies do then seem to be consistent with the child research in supporting the emergence of attribution of *desire* states before informational states like *beliefs*.

However, this picture is complicated by very recent studies not captured in the earlier chapters. Povinelli, Nelson and Boysen (1989), using experimental designs inspired by those used with children (Wimmer, Hogrefe and Perner, 1988) claim to have found chimpanzees 'capable of visual perspective taking and of using this ability to differentiate between guessing and knowing'. In this study, food was hidden from chimpanzees in such a fashion that a human 'Knower' could, in view of the chimp, observe the hiding, while a 'Guesser' left the room during the hiding. The chimpanzees subsequently showed a preference for the Knower over the now-returned Guesser in using pointing by these individuals as a guide to their own selection of a food location, a preference which was evident from the outset of the tests. This preference extended to a transfer test in which the Guesser covered his head with a bag instead of leaving the room whilst the food was hidden, leading the experimenters to favour 'the hypothesis that chimpanzees, like young children, believe that those who see an object or event have a different understanding of that object or event than a comparable individual who did not see it'. This is consistent with the ambiguous results of a test with parallel design reported by Premack (1988b and chapter 17), in which two of four chimpanzees were successful in discriminating knower and guesser. Interestingly, the one chimpanzee of the four who performed poorly in the experiment by Povinelli et al. was Sarah, the subject of Premack's (1988b) negative result in tests of both knowledge and false-belief attribution. Thus there is now some support claimed for chimpanzees, at least, taking account of informational states in others, which the monkeys in Cheney and Seyfarth's tests failed to do (although in the context of very different experimental designs). Povinelli and his colleagues are now replicating their study directly with monkeys, so we may hope for further clarification of the possible superiority of chimpanzees in mindreading about knowledge states.

To further complicate the picture, the proposition that attribution of belief is an advanced and late-emerging capacity in pre-school children is itself challenged. Dunn (1988 and chapter 4) notes how frequently the young child's spontaneous behaviour in the home gives evidence of specific mindreading capacities which tend to have been demonstrated by rigorous experiments only at later ages. For example, deception, accompanied by explicit reference to the child's own and to others' intentions, was observed in the second year. Chandler, Fritz and Hala (1989) were thus able to caricature two scientific camps: the 'boosters' – workers, typically taking an ethological approach, who see early evidence of theory of mind – and the 'scoffers' – typically strict experimentalists holding up *false-belief* tests as the litmus test confining theory of mind to older preschoolers. Chandler et al. noted the importance attributed to deception in the case of animal research, and aimed to resolve the dispute between the two camps by studying spontaneous deception under controlled, experimental conditions. Children were pitted against an adult in a hide-and-seek game intentionally kept computationally simple. While the adult was out of the room, a doll was made to hide a prize in one of several alternative containers. The doll left inky footprints, and the game offered to the child was to help the doll mislead the adult returning to search for the treasure. In summary, nearly all the two-and-a-half and three-year-olds took active steps to mislead, including wiping out trails and laying false ones. Such results, Chandler et al. firmly conclude, establish beyond reasonable doubt that even two-and-a-half-year-olds already practise a variety of deceptive strategies that necessarily presuppose a working knowledge of false beliefs. Acceptance of such a claim has implications beyond child development: given Premack and Dasser's 'rule of thumb' that 'typically, chimpanzees pass non-verbal tests that are passed by three-year-old children', chimpanzees could be expected also to invent deceptive tactics designed such that they will create false beliefs in others.

And of course we know their design does have this *effect* on the duped opponent (de Waal, 1986; B&W; W&B). This is one reason why I expect that the experiment by Chandler et al. will not immediately resolve the debate. Since a deceptive act must be innovative to give evidence of *intentionally* creating a false belief, boosters will probably find their observations under natural conditions more impressive than the 'set-up' hide-and-seek experiments, in which children were both encouraged to deceive, and given prior experience in the non-verbal techniques they were later able to deploy deceptively. Even an arch-scoffer may say as much, finding in primate data: 'reports of spontaneous deception in novel situations a more convincing indication that apes have a theory of mind (e.g. de Waal, 1986) than deceptive acts that are the results of a history of laborious conditioning (Woodruff and Premack, 1979)(Perner, 1988b, p. 291).

In addition, the scoffers will apply their own trade, and offer interpretations of the childrens' acts not yet ruled out experimentally: perhaps that wiping out tracks effects *ignorance* rather than *false belief*; or that false trails may be laid only to affect behaviour, as in merely leading the adult to a false destination (Sodian, Hains, Taylor and Perner, 1989). Having said all that, we surely need more work which presents the challenge Chandler et al. do. Ethological observers of both children and animals need more often to appreciate the alternative explanations of their observations which it may take an experiment to distinguish (even a one-off experiment – see Dennett's [1983] 'Sherlock Holmes' method'). Equally, many experimentalists need to take more seriously the implications of records of spontaneous, sophisticated mindreading which jar with the more conservative conclusions drawn on the basis of performances under the constraints of the experimentalist's laboratory.

Precursors

What others want   We have already noted the proposition that a possible precursor of belief–desire theory of mind is a simpler desire psychology, and that there is evidence of this in two-year-olds and in chimpanzees. Wellman points out that a simple psychology of this sort is not only a step towards a more sophisticated one, but is immediately useful to the individual in predicting how people will act to fulfil their desires, such as searching in locations where the object of the want is likely to be found. I suggest that it could also provide a basis for social manipulation and deception, employing the rule that a strong want will displace a competing but weaker one in determining someone's action. If I want something that you have got to first, I could try to distract you from it by offering you something else I know you will desire more. Consider an example of *distraction* in baboons (records 62 and 83 in Whiten and Byrne, 1986; expanded upon by Strum at the Mindreading Symposium: Strum, 1989). A male baboon, Dr Bob, had killed a young antelope and would not give any to Peggy. Eventually she took to grooming him, and when he relaxed and lolled back, Peggy took the meat and ran. Later the episode recurred, but now Dr Bob kept a firm hand on the meat while he was groomed. Peggy then moved off, and targeted an attack on another close female associate of Dr Bob. Dr Bob wavered, looking back and forth between his meat and the female who needed his support against Peggy. He finally went to the aid of the female, leaving the meat, which was then snatched by Peggy. *If* (as Strum believes) such actions were novel, then Peggy offers us evidence that her actions were constructed on the basis of what might best be called a motivational analysis, employing the rule about conflicting wants outlined above, just as the young child might employ the rule to get her baby brother away from the toy she wants, offering him another one (and if that fails, choosing *another* motivator). Peggy did not peremptorily groom Dr Bob and make a snatch at the meat, but waited until his motivational state was such that, lolling back for more grooming, he relaxed his grip on the meat. More importantly, when this tactic failed later, Peggy flexibly deployed a different one, engineering an opportunity for Dr Bob to help a friend, which he would want to do more than stay with his meat.

At present, this seems to be the best type of evidence available that monkeys take account of others' desire states. Its weakness lies, firstly, in the difficulty of being assured that Peggy did invent the behaviour rather than discovering it through a prior history of trial and error, for which we have to rely on the judgement of the observer: Strum's baboons *were* observed daily over many years, but even tighter biographies may be required as the key to clearer interpretations of such naturalistic evidence in future (Strum, 1988). Secondly, there is the question of in what sense Peggy's action, even if innovative, utilized a general predictive rule about conflicting *wants*, as opposed to a prediction about specific competing actions (such that if Dr Bob can be made to defend the other female, he is likely to leave the meat). Following Gómez's notion of an 'implicit hypothesis of mind' we must ask whether even such an apparent action-analysis by Peggy relies on an 'implicit hypothesis of motivational conflict' – a plausible foundation for the evolution of deeper mindreading. Were further evidence to reveal a greater repertoire of alternative tactics in cases like Peggy's distraction of Dr Bob, the possible representation of others' wants by such animals begs more serious attention from us for reasons of parsimony – in two senses. It is in such circumstances that the representation of others' wants becomes a parsimonious cognitive faculty for the animal itself, and therefore likely to be favoured by natural selection; simultaneously it becomes parsimonious for the scientist to account for the observed complexity of repertoire by attribution to the animal of this level of mindreading (see Bennett; also Dawkins, 1976; Whiten and Byrne, 1988a). I see this conceptual approach to both the nature of mindreading and its study as analogous to that traditionally treating states like hunger and thirst as 'intervening variables' which parsimoniously account for complex webs of cause and effect in animal behaviour (Hinde, 1970, p. 195).

What others see, notice or attend to From the interdisciplinary point of view, Baron-Cohen's incorporation of *attention* into the modelling of childrens' development of a theory of mind is of great interest. In analysing our first corpus of data on tactical deception, we indeed found little evidence for the representation of knowledge or desire states in monkeys, compared to apes (see above; W&B, 1988a, chapter 18; B&W, chapter 9); what we did find was that the bulk of the episodes in both monkeys and apes concerned the *monitoring and manipulation of others' visual attention* (Whiten and Byrne, 1988b). Perhaps then, this is the basis of further parallels between developmental and evolutionary emergence of mindreading.

As with the attribution of wants, the question of how much mindreading is going on in such cases is a slippery one, but this very slipperiness is likely to be important given our interests in how mindreading gets launched. At one extreme, to attribute to another *attending to* something is only to say they are *looking at* it, which in turn can be exhaustively described in readily observable behavioural and spatial terms. *Seeing*, to the extent it fails the opacity test, also falls short of being in the same mental-state category as *knowing*, for example (see chapter 1). At the other extreme, two individuals acting in the same way, at the same location, may nevertheless *attend to*, *notice*, or even *see* quite different things, distinctions clearly in the realm of mindreading. Perhaps attribution of seeing, attending or noticing at the behavioural extreme precedes, and can provide an evolutionary (and developmental) entry into, attribution of them at the more mentalistic level.

The ability to represent what another sees is dependent on a number of subcomponents whose emergence needs to be traced in both development and evolution. One involves monitoring the orientation of others' head and eye movements, extrapolation from this direction of gaze to the environment permitting the attribution of *looking at x* or *seeing x* or even *attending to x*. Such abilities appear amongst the most widespread and primitive of those we here consider, being shown early in human infancy (Butterworth), in autists with theory of mind impairment (Baron-Cohen), in birds (Ristau) and in monkeys (Menzel and Johnston, 1976; Whiten and Byrne, 1988b). As Butterworth shows, even within this component different stages of expertise are to be discriminated.

A second aspect of such geometric computations is an ability to detect the existence or occlusion of a line of sight to specific locii. Children at least as young as two-and-a-half-years-old appreciate the role of occlusion in hiding games, as demonstrated in experiments by Flavell, Shipstead and

Croft (1978). B&W and Whiten and Byrne (1988a) present records of deceptive concealment in monkeys as evidence of this ability. Particularly important here is manoeuvring by the agent such that part of itself is hidden, although it still keeps an eye on the opponent, ruling out the explanation of moving until one can't oneself see the opponent. Even here chimpanzees seem to be yet more sophisticated, using just hand or leg to conceal rather precisely an erect penis from a particular competitor who would take exception to this signal (de Waal, 1986).

Taken together, computation of gaze direction and clear line of sight should be sufficient to attribute looking at, and usually seeing, a particular thing (excepting rare complications such as blindness, illusions and hallucinations). More complex geometric computations may be necessary to judge *how* the object of sight will look from the other's point of view, such as inversion on viewing two objects from the opposite side (e.g. Flavell, Everett, Croft and Flavell, 1981). But even though such abilities can be expressed as exercises in observation of behaviour (gaze) and three-dimensional geometry, they are surely important in the study of mindreading's origins. First, the result of the computations is *in effect* to put one individual into the shoes of the other, able to 'see the world from their point of view' (hence the alternative expressions applied to the ability – *visual perspective taking* or *perceptual role taking*). Putting this the other way round, even where I consider what you must be seeing as a mental state, the way I must determine what you see is by the same computations as specified above. Secondly, when we think of what a monkey or a young child can *achieve* with a simple attribution of what others can (or cannot) see, Gómez and I are of like mind and I can do no better than again quote part of his eloquent analysis (see also Gómez, forthcoming; Whiten and Byrne, 1990):

> 'prelinguistic one-year-olds and gorillas show that they have at least a rudimentary understanding of the perceptual abilities of people and their relation to the behaviours they can subsequently generate. They seem to understand that an agent's behaviour may depend upon what he is attending to. Thus, they seem *somehow* to take into account the mind of the other . . . They can be said to have something like a latent hypothesis of mind, rather than a theory of mind.'

Presumably such an understanding underlies the deceptive partial-hiding tactics of monkeys and apes mentioned above, which are clearly designed to avoid punitive actions by others which would result if they saw what the agent is hiding. Any infant or animal who attends closely to the seeing–action complex, in which psychological causality is implicit, is surely preadapted for the acquisition of a deeper mindreading in which the causality comes to be further modelled using attributions of wants, beliefs and so on.

The notions of *attention* and *noticing* have the power to take the mindreader deeper into the other's mind, as Gómez and Baron-Cohen point out. Baron-Cohen draws the distinction between a child's behavioural and geometric analysis of another's seeing such as I outlined earlier, which can be handled by *primary representation*, and the analysis of another's attention to foci of interest within the visual field, attention in this sense being itself representational and thus requiring *metarepresentations* on the child's part. Consistent with this, Baron-Cohen finds autistic children passing tests of attribution of seeing, yet showing impairments in production and comprehension of proto-declarative pointing at potential foci of shared interest with another person.

Formal experimental analysis of the attribution of attention in this sense is yet to be done in children or animals. Perhaps the most relevant data in primates come from those classes of deception where the perpetrator inhibits its own attention so as to manipulate that of others. The examples are few but at present they concern only our two closest relatives – gorilla and chimpanzee – and it will of course be of interest if this bias is maintained. In these cases the observer has recorded the agent noticing a choice and somewhat obscured food item, but then inhibiting gazing at it while competitors are present, staying or returning to take it later when the others have left. The agent is thus taking into account the ability of the others to take into account its own attention as a guide to the location of delicacies – a sort of arms race in attentional embedding (insert 'interested in' as 'z' in figure 1.1b above; see also Whiten and Byrne, 1988b). The point most strongly suggesting that this involves attribution of attentional states of the sort discussed by Baron-Cohen is that the apes only bother to do this in the case of small food items which the competitors are unlikely, of their own accord, to *notice*. Are autists able to withhold attention in similar circumstances?

The Nature of Mindreading

Both within and between the camps of the interdisciplinary authorship, getting to grips with the essential nature of mindreading has revealed some shared preoccupations, and some excitingly different theoretical approaches.

One aspect of this is the attempt to understand how the cognitive capacities required in components of mindreading relate to other major cognitive abilities in evidence at corresponding stages. Leslie, W&B and Harris, for example, all consider links between mindreading and *pretend play*, which shares the property of going beyond the individual's current primary representation of reality. For similar reasons both Harris and W&B discuss (not necessarily playful) *imagination*. These three papers find that a range of empirical findings, including stages of development in normal children, impairments in autistic children, and phylogenetic differences, can all be brought to bear on the patterns of cognitive links hypothesized. It is perhaps early days for such ambitious theory building, but these current attempts start to expose both conceptual differences (e.g. see Harris, notes 1 and 3) and the empirical matters which need more attention in order to resolve them, such as differences within the overall category of pretend play.

Harris's paper raises another controversy in his proposal that five-year-old children do not operate with a theory of mind as most authors conclude, but rather engage in mental simulations. In the preface I have already indicated that, despite acquiescence in using the current dominant expression – 'theory of mind' – for the title of this book, I feel a more neutral term should be used to label the basic attribution of mind states to others: 'mindreading' has been promoted here as an appropriate term, but Humphrey's 'natural psychology' (1980) and Morton's 'mentalizing' (1989) are alternatives. This leaves as a separate question *how* mindreading is achieved, with alternatives including theory of mind, simulation, or the direct perception implied by Dasser, Ulbaek and Premack (1989) with respect to recognition of intention (Premack and Dasser).

It would be premature to cast judgement on the theory of mind versus simulation debate: clearly its implications go beyond child development to any mindreading creatures or machines. The essential distinction is not a straightforward one, as suggested by the fact that the terms 'theory' and 'model' are often used interchangeably in psychology and indeed science generally (cf. Harris). We are still only at the start of debates about just what the proposed differences should imply and what predictions can be tested to discriminate them. Thus Harris is clear on how his proposal that the child operates two default cognitive settings (one for world states and another for her intentional states) differs from those of other authors and why the data from both normal and autistic children support his contention: but it is not so clear why the idea of two default settings could not equally be incorporated into a theory of mind. The metaphor of the mental 'model aeroplane' seems at first sight useful in helping us appreciate what is distinctive in the idea of mental simulation – indeed, it is interesting, in the context of the discussion of pretend play above, that Fagen (1976) argued that play itself must be seen as a simulation, and was also led to use the metaphor of a model plane in explanation. However, the aeronautical engineer has a 'real' model plane in her wind tunnel, and the child does not have such a real model plane in his head: is the metaphor therefore likely to mislead us? Perhaps using formalisms like the computational ones of Shultz and

B&W will help to specify more precisely the supposed essential difference between simulation and theory; between, for example, 'representing what another thinks' and Harris's 'imagining having a thought and attributing the products to another'.

Testing that the child uses introspection to further its mindreading capacity is not easy. The fact that children appear to code their own wants and beliefs at the same ages as those of others is circumstantial evidence against it, as Astington and Gopnik emphasise. Gallup (1988) has made an ingenious suggestion for a type of experiment which may help on this question. Gallup's proposal is that the ability to use one's own mental experiences to mindread the better could be tested in the case of a monkey's ability to attribute blockage of *seeing* in other monkeys wearing a blindfold, by first letting the subject itself wear the blindfold.

The Functional Significance of Mindreading

Much of the research effort to date has focused on just what mindreading abilities a particular child or primate possesses, with the emergence more recently of attempts to understand underlying mechanisms and processes of change like those reviewed so far. Attention to the functional significance of all this has by contrast been limited.

Consider again the baboons Peggy and Dr Bob, contending for Dr Bob's meat. Having failed on the second attempt to gain the meat by grooming, Peggy might, if not a mindreader, have been stuck for an alternative tactic. However, if by contrast the grooming was a tactic aimed at *distracting* Dr Bob's *attention*, she might, when this failed, efficiently select from her repertoire of attention-distractors another to achieve this same goal, distracting his attention now by chasing another female associate of his (a somewhat different account to that based on motivational analysis earlier, although equally speculative!). As noted above, this is just the sort of thing an older child might do as it runs through different distractive ploys so as to get a toy away from its younger sibling. Mindreading about such attentional states (here in particular knowing that the other *tends to attend to only one thing at a time*) should make for sophisticated powers of social influence.

The potential significance of such mental economy and efficiency were alluded to by Wellman, Astington and Gopnik, Bennett, and Schmidt and Marsella (see also chapter 1, and Whiten and Byrne, 1988a). Some of the naturalistic ethological approaches, both to animals (e.g. B&W; Gomez; Ristau) and to children (e.g. Dunn; Reddy) start to attend to the functional outcomes of mindreading, but there is still much scope for deepening our understanding by asking just when mindreading helps, what it achieves, and equally, where the subject could get by without it. Carrither's chapter is important in setting out some of the wider social, temporal and cognitive contexts in which the functional significance of mindreading must be pursued. I hope and expect that a 'pragmatics of mindreading' will be an important future step, as in earlier progress in the study of language acquisition.

References

Ackerman, B. P. 1981: Young children's understanding of a speaker's intentional use of a false utterance. *Developmental Psychology*, 17, 472–80.

——1983: Form and function in children's understanding of ironic utterances. *Journal of Experimental Child Psychology*, 35, 487–508.

Altmann, S. A. 1988: Darwin, deceit and metacommunication. *Behavioral and Brain Sciences*, 11 (2), 244–5.

Amarel, S. 1967: An approach to heuristic problem solving and theorem proving in the propositional calculus. In J. F. Hart and S. Takasu (eds), *Systems and Computer Science* (Toronto: University of Toronto Press).

——1983: Problems of representation in heuristic problem solving: Related issues in development of expert systems. In R. Groner, M. Groner and W. F. Bischof (eds), *Methods of Heuristics* (Hillsdale, NJ: Lawrence Erlbaum).

Anderson, James R. 1984: Monkeys with mirrors: some questions for primate psychology. *Journal of Comparative Psychology*, 99, 211–17.

Anderson, John R. 1983: *The Architecture of Cognition* (Cambridge, MA: Harvard University Press).

——1987: Causal analysis and inductive learning. *Proceedings of the Fourth International Machine Learning Workshop* (Palo Alto, CA: Morgan Kaufmann Publishers), 288–99.

Andrews, J., Rosenblatt, E., Malkus, U., Gardner, H. and Winner, E. 1986: Children's abilities to distinguish metaphoric and ironic utterances from mistakes and lies. *Communication and Cognition*, 19, 281–98.

Arduino, P. J. and Gould J. L. 1984: Is tonic immobility adaptive? *Animal Behaviour*, 32, 921–3.

Argyle, M. and Cook, M. 1976: *Gaze and Mutual Gaze* (Cambridge: Cambridge University Press).

Arsenio, W. F. and Ford, M. E. 1985: The role of affective information in social-cognitive development: Children's differentiation of moral and conventional events. *Merrill-Palmer Quarterly*, 31, 1–17.

Astington, J. W. 1989a: Children's understanding of prior intention. Unpublished manuscript, Ontario Institute for Studies in Education.

——1989b: Developing Theories of Mind: What develops and how do we go about explaining it? Paper presented at the symposium 'Theoretical Explanations of Children's Understanding of the Mind' at the Biennial Meeting of the Society for Research in Child Development, Kansas.

——Forthcoming a: Intention in the child's theory of mind. In C. Moore and D. Frye (eds), *Children's Theories of Mind* (Hillsdale, NJ: Erlbaum).

—— Forthcoming b: Narrative and the child's theory of mind. In B. K. Britton and A. D. Pellegrini (eds) *Narrative Thought and Narrative Language* (Hillsdale, NJ: Erlbaum).

Astington, J. W. and Gopnik, A. 1988: Knowing you've changed your mind: Children's understanding of representational change. In J. W. Astington, P. L. Harris and D. R. Olson (eds), *Developing Theories of Mind* (New York: Cambridge University Press).

Astington, J. W., Gopnik, A. and O'Neill, D. 1989: Young children's understanding of unfulfilled desire and false belief. Unpublished manuscript, Ontario Institute for Studies in Education.

Astington, J. W., Harris, P. L. and Olson, D. (eds), 1988: *Developing Theories of Mind* (Cambridge: Cambridge University Press).

Barkow, J. H. 1976: Attention structure and the evolution of human psychological characteristics. In M. R. A. Chance and R. R. Larsen (eds), *The Social Structure of Attention* (New York: Wiley).

Baron-Cohen, S. 1985: Social cognition and pretend play in autism. Unpublished doctoral thesis, University College, University of London.

—— 1987: Autism and symbolic play. *British Journal of Developmental Psychology*, 5, 139–48.

——1988: Social and pragmatic deficits in autism: cognitive or affective? *Journal of Autism and Development Disorders*, 18, 379–402.

——1989a: The autistic child's theory of mind: a case of specific developmental delay. *Journal of Child Psychology and Psychiatry*, 30, 285–97.

——1989b: Perceptual role-taking and proto-declarative pointing in autism. *British Journal of Developmental Psychology*, 7, 113–27.

—— 1989c: Are autistic children behaviourists? An examination of their mental-physical and appearance–reality distinctions. *Journal of Autism and Developmental Disorders*, 19, 579–600.

——1989d: Joint attention deficits in autism: towards a cognitive analysis. *Development and Psychopathology*, 1, 185–9.

——Forthcoming a: Autistic children's understanding of some causes of emotions. *Child Development*.

—— Forthcoming b: The theory of mind in autism: how specific is it? *British Journal of Developmental Psychology*. Special issue on Children's Theories of Mind.

Baron-Cohen, S. and Charman, T. 1990: Testing the metarepresentation theory of autism. Unpublished manuscript, Institute of Psychiatry.

Baron-Cohen, S. and Humphries, S. 1990: Is there any development of a theory of mind in autism? A six-year follow-up study. Unpublished manuscript, Institute of Psychiatry.

Baron-Cohen, S., Leslie, A. M. and Frith, U. 1985: Does the autistic child have a 'theory of mind'? *Cognition*, 21, 37–46.

——1986: Mechanical, behavioural and intentional understanding of picture stories in autistic children. *British Journal of Developmental Psychology*, 4, 113–25.

Bartsch, K. and Wellman, H. M. 1989: Young children's attribution of action to beliefs and desires. *Child Development*, 60, 946–64.

Bates, E. 1976: *Language and Context: The Acquisition of Pragmatics* (New York: Academic Press).

Bates, E., Benigni, L., Bretherton, I., Camaioni, L. and Volterra, V. 1979: Cognition and communication from 9–13 months: correlational findings. In E. Bates (ed.), *The Emergence of Symbols: Cognition and Communication in Infancy* (New York: Academic Press).

Bates, E., Camaioni, L., Volterra, V. 1975: The acquisition of performatives prior to speech. *Merrill-Palmer Quarterly*, 21, 205–26.

Bateson, P. P. G. 1984: Ontogeny. In D. J. McFarland (ed.), *The Oxford Companion to Animal Behaviour* (Oxford: Oxford University Press).

Beck, B. B. 1980: *Animal Tool Behaviour* (New York: Garland Press).

Bennett, J. 1964: *Rationality* (London: Routledge and Kegan Paul). Reissued in 1988: Indianapolis: Hackett.

——1976: *Linguistic Behaviour* (Cambridge: Cambridge University Press). Reissued in 1989: Indianapolis: Hackett.

——1988a: Thoughts about thoughts. *Behavioural and Brain Sciences*, 11, 246.

——1988b: Thoughtful brutes. *American Philosophical Association Proceedings and Addresses*, 62, 197–210.

——1990: How is cognitive ethology possible? In C. Ristau (ed.), *Cognitive Ethology: The Minds of Other Animals* (Hillsdale, NJ: Erlbaum).

Bertrand, M. 1969: *The Behavioural Repertoire of the Stumptail Macaque* (Basel, Karger).

——1976: Acquisition by a pigtail macaque of behaviour patterns beyond the natural repertoire of the species, *Zeitschrift für Tierpsychologie*, 42, 139–69.

Bloom, L., Lightbown, P., Hood, L. 1975: Structure and variation in child language. *Monographs of the Society for Research in Child Development*, 40 (2, serial no. 160).

Boesch, C. and Boesch, H. 1984: Mental map in wild chimpanzees: an analysis of hammer transports for nut cracking. *Primates*, 25, 160–70.

Bolwig, N. 1959: A study of the behaviour of the chacma baboon, *Papio ursinus*, *Behaviour*, 14, 136–63.

Boucher, J. and Lewis, V. 1990: Guessing or creating? A reply to Baron-Cohen. *British Journal of Developmental Psychology*, 8, 205–6.

Bower, G. 1981: Mood and memory. *American Psychologist*, 36, 129–48.

Bowerman, M. 1976: Semantic factors in the acquisition of rules for word use and sentence construction. In D. Morehead and A. Morehead (eds), *Normal and Deficient Child Language* (Baltimore, MD: University Park Press, 99–179).

Boyd, R. and Richerson, P. 1985: *Culture and the Evolutionary Process* (Chicago: University of Chicago Press).

Bratman, M. 1984: Two faces of intention, *Philosophical Review*, 93, 375–405.

Braverman, M., Fein, D., Lucci, D. and Waterhouse, L. 1989: Affect comprehension in children with pervasive developmental disorders. *Journal of Autism and Developmental Disorders*, 19, 301–16.

Brazelton, B. 1982: Joint regulation of neonate-parent behaviour. In E. Z. Tronick (ed.), *Social Interchange in Infancy: Affect, Cognition and Communication* (Baltimore: University Park Press).

Brentano, F. von 1874/1970: *Psychology From an Empirical Standpoint*, ed. O. Kraus trans. L. L. MacAllister (London: Routledge and Kegan Paul).

Bresina, J. L., Marsella, S. C. and Schmidt, C. F. 1987: Predicting subproblem interactions, *Technical Report LCSR-TR-92*, Laboratory for Computer Science Research, Rutgers University.

Bretherton, I. and Bates, E. 1979: The emergence of intentional communication. In I. C. Uzgiris (ed.), *Social Interaction and Communication during Infancy* (San Francisco, CA: Jossey Bass).

Bretherton, I. and Beeghly, M. 1982: Talking about internal states: The acquisition of an explicit theory of mind. *Developmental Psychology*, 18, 906–21.

Bretherton, I., McNew, S. and Beeghly-Smith, M. 1981: Early person knowledge as expressed in gestural and verbal communication: When do infants acquire a 'theory of mind'? In M. E. Lamb and L. R. Sherrod (eds), *Infant Social Cognition* (Hillsdale, NJ: Erlbaum).

Brown, J. 1989: Conversations about feelings, Unpublished Master's thesis. Pennsylvania State University.

Bruner, J. S. 1975: The ontogenesis of speech acts, *Journal of Child Language*, 2, 1–19.

——1976: From communication to language – a psychological perspective. *Cognition*, 3, 255–287.

——1983: *Child's Talk* (Oxford: Oxford University Press).

——1986: *Actual Minds, Possible Worlds* (London: Harvard University Press).

Burghardt, G. M. 1988: Anecdotes and critical anthropomorphism. *Behavioral and Brain Sciences*, 11, 248–9.

——1990: Cognitive ethology and critical anthropomorphism: A snake with two heads and hog-nose snakes that play dead. In C. A. Ristau (ed.), *Cognitive Ethology: The Minds of Other Animals* (Hillside, NJ: Erlbaum).

Butterworth, G. E. 1987: Some benefits of egocentrism. In J. S. Bruner and H. Haste (eds), *Making Sense: The Child's Construction of the World* (London: Methuen).

——1989: Discussant's comments, delivered at the symposium on 'The Emergence of Mindreading', BPS Annual Conference, University of St Andrews, St Andrews.

Butterworth, G. E. and Adamson-Macedo, E. 1987: The origins of pointing – a pilot study. Paper presented at the Annual Conference of the Developmental Psychology Section of the British Psychological Society, York.

Butterworth, G. E. and Cochran, E. 1980: Towards a mechanism of joint visual attention in human infancy. *International Journal of Behavioural Development*, 19, 253–72.

Butterworth, G. E. and Grover, L. 1988: The origins of referential communication in human infancy. In L. Weiskrantz (ed.), *Thought Without Language* (Oxford: Oxford University Press).

Butterworth, G. E. and Grover, L. 1989: Joint visual attention, manual pointing and pre-verbal communication in human infancy. In M. Jeannerod (ed.) *Attention and Performance XIII* (New York: Lawrence Erlbaum).

Butterworth, G. E. and Jarrett, N. 1980: The geometry of pre-verbal communication. Paper presented at the annual conference of the Developmental Psychology Section of the British Psychological Society, Edinburgh.

Byrne, R. W. Forthcoming: Using anecdotes to distinguish psychological mechanisms in primate tactical deception. In R. W. Mitchell (ed.) *Anthropomorphism, Anecdotes, and Theory in the Study of Animal Behavior.*

Byrne, R. W. and Whiten, A. 1985: Tactical deception of familiar individuals in baboons. *Animal Behaviour*, 33, 669–73.

——1987: A thinking primate's guide to deception. *New Scientist*, 116, (1589), 54–57.

——1988a: Towards the next generation in data quality: a new survey of primate tactical deception. *The Behavioral and Brain Sciences*, 11, 267–273.

——(Eds) 1988b: *Machiavellian Intelligence: Social Expertise and the Evolution of Intellect in Monkeys, Apes and Humans* (Oxford: Oxford University Press).

——Forthcoming: Tactical deception in primates: the 1990 database. *Primate Report.*

Campbell, R. N. 1988: Discussant's comments in the symposium 'New evidence on the child's theory of mind', presented at the BPS Developmental Section Annual Conference, Harlech, Wales.

Campos, J. J. and Stenberg, C. R. 1980: Perception, appraisal and emotion. The onset of social referencing. In M. Lamb and L. Sherrod (eds), *Infant Social Cognition* (Hillsdale, NJ: Erlbaum).

Carey, S. 1985: *Conceptual Change in Childhood* (Cambridge, MA: MIT Press).

Carlson, V. 1980: Differences between social and mechanical causality in infancy. Paper presented at the International Conference on Infant Studies, New Haven, CT.

Carrithers, M. 1983: *The Forest Monks of Sri Lanka: An Anthropological and Historical Study* (New Delhi, Oxford University Press).

——1988: Passions of nation and community in the Bahubali Affair. *Modern Asian Studies*, 22, 815–44.

——1989: Sociality, not aggression, is the key human trait. In S. Howell and R. Willis (eds), *Societies at Peace: Anthropological Perspectives* (London: Routledge and Kegan Paul).

Carrithers, M., Collins, S. and Lukes, S. (eds) 1985: *The Category of the Person: Anthropology, Philosophy, History* (Cambridge: Cambridge University Press).

Chance, M. R. A. 1956: Social structure of a colony of *Macaca Mulatta*. *British Journal of Animal Behaviour*, 4, 1–13.

——1967: Attention structure as the basis of primate rank orders. *Man*, 2, 503–18.

Chandler, M. J. 1977: Social cognition: a selective review of current research. In

W. F. Overton and J. M. Gallagher (eds), *Knowledge and Development* (New York: Plenum).

Chandler, M. J. and Boyes, M. 1982: Social-cognitive development. In B. Wolman (ed.), *Handbook of Developmental Psychology* (Englewood Cliffs, NJ: Prentice-Hall).

Chandler, M. J. and Helm, D. 1984: Developmental changes in the contributions of shared experience to social role-taking competence. *International Journal of Behavioral Development*, 7, 145–56.

Chandler, M. J., Fritz, A. S. and Hala, S. 1989: Small-scale deceit: deception as a marker of 2, 3- and 4-year-olds' early theories of mind. *Child Development*, 60, 1263–77.

Chapais, B. 1988: Rank maintenance in female Japanese macaques: experimental evidence for social dependency. *Behaviour*, 104, 41–59.

Chapman, D. 1987: Planning for Conjunctive Goals. *Artificial Intelligence*, 32, 333–77.

Cheney, D. L. and Seyfarth, R. M. 1981: Selective forces affecting the predator alarm calls of vervet monkeys. *Behaviour*, 76, 25–61.

——1985: Vervet monkey alarm calls: manipulation through shared information? *Behaviour*, 94, 150–66.

——1990: *How Monkeys See the World* (Chicago: University of Chicago Press).

Chevalier-Skolnikoff, S. 1986: An exploration of the ontogeny of deception in human beings and non-human primates. In R. W. Mitchell and N. S. Thompson (eds), *Deception: Perspectives on Human and Nonhuman Deceit* (Alba: State University of New York Press).

Chisholm, R. M. and Feehan, D. 1977: The intent to deceive. *Journal of Philosophy*, 74, 3, 143–59.

Chomsky, N. A. 1986: *Knowledge of Language: Its Nature, Origin and Use* (New York: Praeger).

Churchland, P. S. 1984: *Matter and consciousness: A Contemporary Introduction to the Philosophy of Mind* (Cambridge, MA: MIT Press).

Coulter, J. 1979: *The Social Construction of Mind* (London: Macmillan).

Coulter, J. 1979: Transparency of mind: the availability of subjective phenomena. In J. Coulter (ed.), *The Social Construction of Mind* (London: Macmillan).

Cox, A., Rutter, M., Newman, S. and Bartak, L. 1975: A comparative study of infantile autism and specific developmental receptive language disorder: II. Parental characteristics. *British Journal of Psychiatry*, 126, 146–59.

Curcio, F. 1978: Sensorimotor functioning and communication in mute autistic children. *Journal of Autism and Developmental Disorders*, 8, 281–92.

Dale, N. 1983: Early pretend play within the family. Unpublished PhD dissertation, University of Cambridge.

Dasser, V., Ulbaek, I. and Premack, D. 1989: The perception of intention. *Science*, 243, 365–67.

Datta, S. B. 1983: Relative power and the acquisition of rank. In R. A. Hinde, (ed.), *Primate Social Relationships* (Oxford, Blackwell).

Davidson, D. 1980: Psychology as philosophy. In D. Davidson (ed.), *Essays on Actions and Events* (Oxford: Oxford University Press).

Dawkins, R. 1976: Hierarchical organisation: a candidate principle for ethology. In P. P. G. Bateson and R. A. Hinde (eds), *Growing Points in Ethology* (Cambridge: Cambridge University Press).

Dawkins, R. and Krebs, J. R. 1978: Animal signals: information or manipulation? In J. R. Krebs and N. B. Davies *Behavioural Ecology: an Evolutionary Approach* (Oxford: Blackwell).

Dawson, G. and Fernald, M. 1987: Perspective-taking ability and its relationship to the social behaviour of autistic children. *Journal of Autism and Developmental Disorders*, 17, 487–98.

Dawson, G., Hill, D., Spencer, A. and Galpert, L. 1988: Affective exchanges between young and autistic children and their mothers. Paper presented at the International Conference on Infant Studies, Washington DC.

DeLoache, J. S. and Plaetzer, B. 1985: Tea for two: Joint mother–child symbolic play. Paper presented at the meeting of the Society for Research in Child Development, Toronto.

Demorest, A., Meyer, L., Phelps, E., Gardner, H. and Winner, E. 1984: Words speak louder than actions: Understanding deliberately false remarks. *Child Development*, 55, 1527–34.

Demorest, A., Silberstein, L., Gardner, H. and Winner, E. 1983: Telling it as it isn't: Children's understanding of figurative language. *British Journal of Developmental Psychology*, 1, 121–34.

Dennett, D. C. 1978: *Brainstorms* (Montgomery, VT: Bradford Books).

—— 1983: Intentional systems in cognitive ethology: the 'Panglossian paradigm' defended. *Behavioral and Brain Sciences*, 6, 343–90.

—— 1987: *The Intentional Stance* (Cambridge, MA: Bradford Books, MIT Press).

—— 1988: The intentional stance in theory and practice. In R. W. Byrne and A. Whiten (eds), *Machiavellian Intelligence: Social Expertise and the Evolution of Intellect in Monkeys, Apes and Humans* (Oxford: Oxford University Press).

——Forthcoming: Out of the armchair and into the field. *Poetics Today*, Israel.

Dias, M. and Harris, P. L. 1988: The effect of make-believe play on deductive reasoning. *British Journal of Developmental Psychology*, 6, 207–21.

—— Forthcoming: The influence of the imagination on deductive reasoning. *British Journal of Developmental Psychology*.

Dissanayake, C. and Crossley, S. 1989: Behaviour in children with early infantile autism: responsiveness to people. In P. Lovibond and P. Wilson (eds), *Clinical and Abnormal Psychology*. Amsterdam: Elsevier.

Donaldson, M. 1978: *Children's Minds* (New York: W. W. Norton).

Dretske, F. 1969: *Seeing and knowing* (Chicago: University of Chicago Press).

——1988: *Explaining Behavior: Reasons in a World of Causes* (Cambridge, MA: Bradford Books, MIT Press).

Dunbar, R. I. M. 1988: How to break moulds. *Behavioral and Brain Sciences*, 11, 254–5.

Dunn, J. 1984: Emotion and the development of social understanding. Paper presented at the BPS (Developmental Section) Annual Conference, University of Lancaster.

——1988: *The Beginnings of Social Understanding* (Oxford: Blackwell).

Dunn, J., Bretherton, I. and Munn, P. 1987: Conversations about feeling states between mothers and their young children. *Developmental Psychology*, 23, 132–9.

Dunn, J. and Brown, J. 1989: Family talk about feeling states, and children's later understanding of others' emotions. Unpublished manuscript, Pennsylvania State University.

Dunn, J. and Brown, J. Forthcoming: Relationships, talk about feelings, and the development of affect regulation in early childhood. In K. Dodge and J. Garber (eds), *The Development of Affect Regulation* (Cambridge: Cambridge University Press).

Dunn, J. and Dale, N. 1984: I a Daddy: 2-year-olds' collaboration in joint pretend with sibling and with mother. In I. Bretherton (ed.), *Symbolic Play: The Development of Social Understanding* (New York: Academic Press).

Dunn, J. and Munn, P. 1986a: Siblings and the development of prosocial behaviour, *International Journal of Behavioural Development*, 9, (3), 265–84.

Dunn, J. and Munn, P. 1986b: Sibling quarrels and maternal intervention: Individual differences in understanding and aggression. *Journal of Child Psychology and Psychiatry and Allied Disciplines*, 27 (5), 583–95.

El'Konin, D. 1966: Symbolics and its functions in the play of children, *Soviet Education*, 8 (2), 7, 35–41.

Emde, R. N., Klingman, D. H., Reich, J. H. and Wade, J. D. 1978: Emotional expression in Infancy: 1. Initial studies of social signalling and an emergent model. In M. Lewis and L. Rosenblum (eds), *The Development of Affect* (New York: Plenum Press).

Estes, D., Wellman, H. M. and Woolley, J. D. 1989: Children's understanding of mental phenomena. In H. Reese (ed.), *Advances in Child Development and Behavior* (New York: Academic Press).

Ewer, R. F. 1968: *The Ethology of Mammals* (London: Jonathan Cape).

——1969: The instinct to teach. *Nature*, 222, 698.

Fagen, R. 1976: Modelling how and why play works. In J. S. Bruner, A. Jolly and K. Sylva (eds), *Play: Its Role in Development and Evolution* (London: Penguin).

—— 1981: *Animal Play Behaviour* (Oxford: Oxford University Press).

Feffer, M. H. 1959: The cognitive implications of role-taking behaviour. *Journal of Personality*, 27, 152–68.

Fehr, B. J. and Exline, R. B. 1987: Social visual interaction: a conceptual and literature review. In A. W. Siegman and S. Feldstein (eds), *Nonverbal Behaviour and Communication. 2nd Edition* (Hillsdale, NJ: Erlbaum).

Fein, G. G. 1981: Pretend play in childhood: An integrative review. *Child Development*, 52, 1095–118.

Fenson, L. 1984: Developmental trends for action and speech in pretend play. In I. Bretherton (ed.), *Symbolic Play* (New York: Academic Press).

Fikes, R. E., Hart, P. E. and Nilsson, N. J. 1971: STRIPS: A new approach to the application of theorem proving to problem solving. *Artificial Intelligence*, 2, 189–208.

Fischer, M. J. and Immerman, N. 1986: Foundations of knowledge for distributed systems. In J. Y. Halpern (ed.), *Theoretical Aspects of Reasoning about Knowledge*, Proceedings of the 1986 Conference (Los Altos: Morgan Kaufmann).

Flavell, J. H. 1978: The development of knowledge about visual perception. In C. B. Keasey (ed.), *Nebraska Symposium on Motivation*, vol. 25 (Lincoln: University of Nebraska Press).

——1985: *Cognitive Development* (Englewood Cliffs, NJ: Prentice-Hall).

——1986: The development of children's knowledge about the appearance–reality distinction. *American Psychologist*, 41, 418–25.

—— 1988: The development of children's knowledge about the mind: From cognitive connections to mental representations. In J. W. Astington, P. L. Harris and D. R. Olson (eds), *Developing Theories of Mind* (New York: Cambridge University Press).

Flavell, J. H., Botkin, P. T., Fry, C. L., Wright, J. W. and Jarvis, P. E. 1968: *The Development of Role-Taking and Communication Skills in Children* (New York: Wiley).

Flavell, J. H., Everett, B. A., Croft, K. and Flavell, E. R. 1981: Young children's knowledge about visual perception: Further evidence for the Level 1 – Level 2 distinction. *Developmental Psychology*, 17, 99–103.

Flavell, J. H., Flavell, E. R., Green, F. L. and Moses, L. J. 1989: Young children's understanding of fact beliefs versus value beliefs. Unpublished manuscript, Department of Psychology, Stanford University.

Flavell, J., Green, F. L. and Flavell, E. R. 1986: Development of knowledge about the appearance–reality distinction. *Monographs of the Society for Research in Child Development*, 51, 1.

Flavell, J. H., Shipstead, S. G. and Croft, K. 1980: Young children's knowledge about visual perception: Hiding objects from others. *Child Development*, 49, 1208–11.

Fodor, J. A. 1983: *The Modularity of Mind* (Cambridge, MA: MIT Press).

——1985: Fodor's guide to mental representation: The intelligent auntie's *vade mecum*. *Mind*, 94, 76–100.

——1987: *Psychosemantics: The Problem of Meaning in The Philosophy of Mind* (Cambridge, MA: Bradford Books/MIT Press).

Fogel, A. and Hannan, T. E. 1985: Manual actions of nine to fifteen-week-old human infants during face to face interactions with their mothers. *Child Development*, 56, 1271–9.

Fogel, A. and Thelen, E. 1987: Development of early expressive and communicative action: reinterpreting the evidence from a dynamic systems perspective. *Developmental Psychology*, 23 (6), 747–61.

Forguson, L. and Gopnik, A. 1988: The ontogeny of common sense. In J. W. Astington, P. L. Harris and D. R. Olson (eds), *Developing Theories of Mind* (New York: Cambridge University Press).

Forgy, C. L. 1981: OPS5 user's manual. *Technical Report CMU-CS-81-135*, Department of Computer Science, Carnegie-Mellon University.

Franco, F. and Butterworth, G. E. 1988: The social origins of pointing in human infancy. Paper presented at the Annual Conference of the BPS Developmental Psychology Section, Coleg Harlech, Wales.

Frith, U. 1989: *Autism: Explaining the Enigma* (Oxford: Blackwell).

Galef, B. G., Jr Forthcoming: Tradition in animals: field observations and laboratory analyses In M. Bekoff and D. Jamieson (eds), *Interpretation and Explanation in the Study of Behaviour: Comparative Perspectives* (Westview).

Gallup, G. G., Jr 1970: Chimpanzees: self-recognition. *Science*, 167, 86–7.

——1982: Self-awareness and the emergence of mind in primates. *American Journal of Primatology*, 2, 237–48.

——1988: Toward a taxonomy of mind in primates. *Behavioral and Brain Sciences*, 11, 255–6.

Gallup, G. G., Jr, Cummings, W. H. and Nash, R. F. 1972: The experimenter as an independent variable in studies of animal hypnosis in chickens. *Animal Behaviour*, 20, 166–9.

Gelman, R. and Baillargeon, R. 1983: A review of some Piagetian concepts. In J. H. Flavell and E. M. Markhain (eds), *Handbook of Child Psychology, Volume 3, Cognitive Development* (New York: Wiley).

Gentner, D. 1983: Structure mapping: A theoretical framework for analogy. *Cognitive Science*, 7, 155–70.

Gibson, J. J. 1966: *The Senses Considered as Perceptual Systems* (London: George Allen and Unwin).

Golinkoff, R. M. 1983: Infant social cognition: Self, people, and objects. In L. Liben (ed.), *Piaget and the Foundations of Knowledge* (Hillsdale, NJ: Erlbaum).

Golinkoff R. M. and Kerr J. L. 1978: Infants' perception of semantically defined action role changes in field events. *Merrill-Palmer Quarterly*, 24, 53–61.

Gómez, J. C. 1990a: Primate tactical deception and sensorimotor social intelligence. *Behavioral and Brain Sciences*, 13, 414–5.

——1990b: Causal links, contingencies and the comparative psychology of intelligence. *Behavioral and Brain Sciences*, 13, 392.

——Forthcoming a: The emergence of intentional communication as a problem-solving strategy in the gorilla. In S. T. Parker and K. Gibson (eds), *Language and Intelligence in Monkeys and Apes: Developmental Perspectives* (Cambridge: Cambridge University Press).

——Forthcoming b: *El Desarrollo de la Comunicacion Intencional en el Gorila*. PhD dissertation, Universidad Autonoma de Madrid, Madrid.

Goodall, J. 1970: Tool-using in primates and other vertebrates. In D. S. Lehrman, R. A. Hinde and E. Shaw (eds), *Advances in the Study of Behaviour* (New York: Academic Press).

——1986: *The Chimpanzees of Gombe* (London: Harvard University Press; Belknap).

Goodson, J. L. and Schmidt, C. F. 1988: The design of cooperative person–machine problem solving systems: A methodology and an example. In S. Robertson and

W. Zachery (eds), *Cognition, Computing and Interaction* (Norwood, NJ: Ablex).

Gopnik, A. 1990: Developing the idea of intentionality: Children's theories of mind. *Canadian Journal of Philosophy*, 20, 89–113.

Gopnik, A. and Astington, J. W. 1988: Children's understanding of representational change in its relation to the understanding of false belief and the appearance–reality distinction. *Child Development*, 59, 26–37.

Gopnik, A. and Graf, P. 1988: Knowing how you know: Young children's ability to identify and remember the sources of their beliefs. *Child Development*, 59, 1366–71.

Gopnik, A. and Seager, W. 1988: Young children's understanding of desires. Unpublished manuscript, University of California at Berkeley.

Gopnik, A. and Slaughter, V. Forthcoming: Young children's understanding of changes in their mental state. *Child Development*.

Gottman, J. and Parker, J. (eds) 1986: *Conversations Among Friends* (Cambridge: Cambridge University Press).

Gould, J. 1986: The Lowe and Costello Symbolic Play Test in socially impaired children. *Journal of Autism and Developmental Disorders*, 16, 199–213.

Gould, S. J. 1978: *Ontogeny and Phylogeny* (Cambridge, MA: Harvard University Press).

Green, S. 1975a: Dialects in Japanese monkeys: vocal learning and cultural transmission in locale-specific behaviour? *Zeitschrift für Tierpsychologie*, 38, 304–14.

—— 1975b: Communication by a graded vocal system in Japanese monkeys. In L. A. Rosenblum (ed.), *Primate Behavior* Vol. 4 (New York: Academic Press).

Grice, H. P. 1957: Meaning. *Philosophical Review*, 66, 377–88.

Griffin, D. R. 1976: *The Question of Animal Awareness*, 2nd edn 1981 (New York: Rockefeller University Press).

—— 1984: *Animal Thinking* (Cambridge, MA: Harvard University Press).

Grover, L. 1988: Comprehension of the manual pointing gesture in human infants. Unpublished PhD thesis, University of Southampton.

Guillaume, P. 1962: *Imitation in children* (Chicago: Chicago University Press) (first published in French 1926).

Gyger, M., Karakashian, S. J. and Marler, P. 1986: Avian alarm-calling: Is there an audience effect? *Animal Behaviour*, 34, 1570–2.

Hadwin, J. and Perner, J. Forthcoming: Pleased and surprised: children's cognitive theory of emotion. *British Journal of Developmental Psychology*.

Halpern, J. Y. and Moses, Y. 1984: Knowledge and Common Knowledge in a Distributed Environment. In *Third ACM Symposium on Principles of Distributed Computing*, 50–61.

Harding, C. G. and Golinkoff, R. M. 1979: The origins of intentional vocalisations in prelinguistic infants. *Child Development*, 50, 33–40.

Harris, P. L. 1989a: *Children and Emotion: The Development of Psychological Understanding* (Oxford: Blackwell).

—— 1989b: The autistic child's impaired conception of mental states. *Development and Psychopathology*, 1, 191–6.

Harris, P. L., Coles, T., and Tan, J. 1989: Performance of autistic children on simple psychological problems. Unpublished paper, Department of Experimental Psychology, University of Oxford.

Harris, P. L., Johnson, C. N., Hutton, D., Andrews, G. and Cooke, T. 1989: Young children's theory of mind and emotion. *Cognition and Emotion*, 3, 379–400.

Harris, P. L. and Gross, D. 1988: Children's understanding of real and apparent emotion. In J. W. Astington, P. L. Harris and D. R. Olson (eds), *Developing Theories of Mind* (Cambridge: Cambridge University Press).

Harris, P. L. and Muncer, A. 1988: Autistic children's understanding of beliefs and desires. Paper presented at the British Psychological Society Developmental Section Conference, Coleg Harlech, Wales.

Hasegawa, M., Kishino, H. and Yano, T. 1989: Estimation of branching dates among primates by molecular clocks of nuclear DNA which slowed down in Hominoidea. *Journal of Human Evolution*, 18, 461–76.

Hauser, M. D. and Wrangham, R. W. 1987: Manipulation of food calls in captive chimpanzees. *Folia primatologica*, 48, 207–10.

Hayes, C. 1951: *The Ape in Our House* (New York: Harper)

Hayes, K. C. and Hayes, C. 1952: Imitation in a home-raised chimpanzee. *Journal of Comparative Physiological Psychology*, 45, 450–9.

Heider, F. and Simmel, M. 1944: An experimental study of apparent behaviour. *American Journal of Psychology*, 57, 243–59.

Hennig, C. W. 1977: Effects of simulated predation on tonic immobility in *Anolis carolinensis*: The role of eye contact. *Bulletin of the Psychonomic Society*, 9, 239–42.

Heelas, P. 1981: *Indigenous Psychologies* (London: Academic Press).

Hertzig, M. E., Snow, M. E. and Sherman, M. 1989: Affect and cognition in autism. *Journal of the American Academy of Child and Adolescent Psychiatry*, 28, 195–9.

Hesse, M. B. 1966: *Models and Analogies in Science* (Notre Dame, IN: University of Notre Dame Press).

Hilton, C. E. 1986: Hands across the old world: the changing hand morphology of the hominids. Unpublished paper, Department of Anthropology, University of New Mexico.

Hinde, R. A. 1970: *Animal Behaviour: a Synthesis of Ethology and Comparative Psychology*, 2nd edn (London: McGraw Hill).

Hinde, R. A. and Atkinson, S. 1970: Assessing the roles of social partners in maintaining mutual proximity, as exemplified by mother–infant relations in rhesus monkeys. *Animal Behaviour*, 18, 169–76.

Hobson, R. P. 1984: Early childhood autism and the question of egocentrism. *Journal of Autism and Developmental Disorders*, 14, 85–104.

—— 1986a: The autistic child's appraisal of expressions of emotion. *Journal of Child Psychology and Psychiatry*, 27, 321–42.

—— 1986b: The autistic child's appraisal of expressions of emotion: a further study. *Journal of Child Psychology and Psychiatry*, 27, 671–80.

—— 1989a: Beyond cognition: a theory of autism. In G. Dawson (ed.) *Autism: Nature, Diagnosis, and Treatment* (New York: Guildford Press).

—— 1989b: On sharing experiences. *Development and Psychopathology*, 1, 192–204.

—— 1990: On acquiring knowledge about people, and the capacity to pretend: A response to Leslie. *Psychological Review*, 97, 114–21.

Hobson, R. P., Ouston, J. and Lee, A. 1988a: What's in a face? The case for autism. *British Journal of Developmental Psychology*, 79, 441–53.

—— 1988b: Emotion recognition in autism: coordinating faces and voices. *Psychological Medicine*, 18, 911–23.

Hogrefe, G., Wimmer, H. and Perner, J. 1986: Ignorance versus false belief: A developmental lag in attribution of epistemic states. *Child Development*, 57, 567–82.

Holland, J. H., Holyoak, K. J., Nisbett, R. E. and Thagard, P. R. 1986: *Induction: Processes of Inference, Learning and Discovery* (Cambridge, MA: MIT Press).

Hopcroft, J. E. and Ullman, J. D. 1979: *Introduction to Automata Theory, Languages and Computation* (Reading, MA: Addison-Wesley).

Hopf, S. 1970: Report on a hand-reared squirrel monkey (*Saimiri sciureus*). *Zeitschrift für Tierpsychologie*, 27, 610–21.

Howell, S. and Willis, R. 1989: *Societies at Peace: Anthropological Perspectives* (London: Routledge and Kegan Paul).

Humphrey, N. K. 1976: The social function of intellect. In P. P. G. Bateson, and R. A. Hinde (eds), *Growing Points in Ethology* (Cambridge: Cambridge University Press).

——1980: Nature's psychologists. In B. Josephson and V. Ramachandran (eds), *Consciousness and the Physical World* (London: Pergamon Press).

——1982: Consciousness: a just-so story. *New Scientist*, 95, 474–8.

——1983: *Consciousness Regained* (Oxford: Oxford University Press).

——1986: *The Inner Eye* (London: Faber and Faber).

——1988: Lies, damned lies and anecdotal evidence. *Behavioral and Brain Sciences*, 11, 257–8.

Isaacs, S. 1930: *Intellectual Growth in Young Children* (London: Routledge and Kegan Paul).

Johnson, C. N. 1982: Acquisition of mental verbs and the concept of mind. In S. Kuczaj, II (ed.), *Language Development, Vol 1: Syntax and Semantics* (Hillsdale, NJ: Erlbaum).

——1988: Theory of mind and the structure of conscious experience. In J. W. Astington, P. L. Harris and D. R. Olson (eds), *Developing Theories of Mind* (New York: Cambridge University Press).

Johnson, W. L. 1985: Intention-based diagnosis of errors in novice programs. Unpublished PhD thesis, Yale University.

Jolly, A. 1966: Lemur social behaviour and primate intelligence. *Science*, 153, 501–6.

——1985: *The Evolution of Primate Behavior*, 2nd edn (London: Macmillan).

——1988: The evolution of purpose. In R. W. Byrne and A. Whiten (eds), *Machiavellian Intelligence: Social Expertise and the Evolution of Intellect in Monkeys, Apes, and Humans* (Oxford: Oxford University Press).

Jones, V. and Prior, M. 1985: Motor imitation abilities and neurological signs in autistic children. *Journal of Autism and Developmental Disabilities*, 15, 37–46.

Kasari, C., Sigman, M., Yirmiya, N. and Mundy, P. Forthcoming: Affective characteristics of autistic children. In B. M. Prizant and B. Schaechter (eds), *Autism: the Emotional and Social Dimensions* (Boston: The Exceptional Parent Press).

Kawai, M. 1958: On the system of social ranks in a natural group of Japanese monkeys. *Primates*, 1, 11–48.

Keddy Hector, A., Seyfarth, R. M. and Raleigh, M. J. 1989: Male parental care, female choice, and the effect of an audience in vervet monkeys. *Animal Behaviour*, 37, 262–71.

Kendon, A. 1967: Some functions of gaze direction in social interaction. *Acta Psychologica*, 26, 22–63.

Kenny, A. (ed.) 1970: *Descartes: Philosophical Letters* (Oxford: Clarendon Press).

Klahr, D., Langley, P. and Neches, R. (eds), *Production System Models of Learning and Development* (Cambridge, MA: MIT Press).

Klinnert, M. D., Campos, J. J., Sorce, J. F., Emde, R. N. and Svejda, M. 1983: Emotions as behaviour regulators: Social referencing in infancy. In R. Plutchik and H. Kellerman (eds), *Emotion: Theory, Research and Experience*, vol 2 (New York: Academic Press).

Kohler, W. 1917/1927: Intelligenzprufungen an Anthropoiden. *Abhandlungen der Preussische Akademie der Wissenschaften. Physikal – Mathemat. Klasse* (English edn: *The Mentality of Apes*, 1927, Routledge and Kegan Paul).

Krebs, J. R. 1977: The significance of song repertoires: the Beau Geste hypothesis. *Animal Behaviour*, 24, 475–8.

Krebs, J. R. and Dawkins, R. 1984: Animal signals: mindreading and manipulation. In J. R. Krebs and N. B. Davies (eds), *Behavioural Ecology: An Evolutionary Approach* (Oxford: Blackwell).

Kuhn, T. S. 1970a: Reflections on my critics. In I. Lakatos and A. Musgrave (eds), *Criticism and the Growth of Knowledge* (Cambridge: Cambridge University Press).

——1970b: *The Structure of Scientific Revolutions* 2nd edn (Chicago: University of Chicago Press).

Kummer, H. 1982: Social knowledge in free-ranging primates. In D. R. Griffin (ed.), *Animal Mind – Human Mind* (Berlin: Springer-Verlag).

LaFreniere, P. J. 1988: The ontogeny of tactical deception in humans. In R. W. Byrne and A. Whiten (eds), *Machiavellian Intelligence: Social Expertise and the Evolution of Intellect in Monkeys, Apes and Humans* (Oxford: Oxford University Press).

Laird, J. E., Rosenbloom, P. S. and Newell, A. 1987: Chunking in Soar: The anatomy of a general learning mechanism. *Machine Learning*, 1, 11–46.

Landau, B. and Gleitman, L. R. 1985: *Language and Experience: Evidence from the Blind Child* (Cambridge: Harvard University Press).

Landau, B. and Spelke, E. 1988: Geometric complexity and object search in infancy. *Developmental Psychology*, 4, 512–21.

Landry, S. and Loveland, K. 1989: Communication behaviours in autism and developmental language delay. *Journal of Child Psychology and Psychiatry*, 29, 621–34.

Langdell, T. 1981: Face perception: an approach to the study of autism. Unpublished PhD thesis, University College, University of London.

Langley, P. 1987: A general theory of discrimination learning. In D. Klahr, P. Langley and R. Neches (eds), *Production System Models of Learning and Development* (Cambridge, M.A.: M.I.T. Press).

Latimore, O. and Grene, D. (eds) 1954: *Sophocles I* (Chicago: University of Chicago Press).

Leekam, S. R. and Perner, J. 1990: Does the autistic child have a metarepresentation deficit? Paper presented at the Fourth European Conference on Developmental Psychology, University of Stirling.

Lempers, J. D., Flavell, E. R., and Flavell, J. H. 1977: The development in very young children of tacit knowledge concerning visual perception. *Genetic Psychology Monographs*, 95, 3–53.

Leslie, A. M. 1982: The perception of causality in infants. *Perception*, 11, 173–86.

—— 1984: Infant perception of a manual pick-up event. *British Journal of Developmental Psychology*, 2, 19–32.

—— 1986: Getting development off the ground: Modularity and the infant's perception of causality. In P. van Geert (ed.), *Theory Building in Development* (Dordrecht: North Holland).

—— 1987a: Pretence and Representation in infancy: the origins of 'theory of mind'. *Psychological Review*, 94, 84–106.

—— 1987b: A 'language of thought' approach to early pretence. In J. Montangero, A. Tryphon and S. Dionnet (eds), *Symbolisme et Connaissance*, cahir no. 8 (Geneva: Foundation Archives Jean Piaget), 133–44.

—— 1988a: Some implications of pretence for mechanisms underlying the child's theory of mind. In J. W. Astington, P. L. Harris and D. R. Olson (eds), *Developing Theories of Mind* (Cambridge: Cambridge University Press).

—— 1988b: The necessity of illusion: Perception and thought in infancy. In L. Weiskrantz (ed.), *Thought without Language* (Oxford: Oxford University Press).

Leslie, A. M. Pretence. Paper presented at the annual meeting of the British Psychological Society Developmental Section, Coleg Harlech, Wales, September.

—— In preparation: The precocity of pretence: Causal inference, communication, and theory of mind.

Leslie, A. M. and Frith, U. 1987: Metarepresentation and autism: How not to lose one's marbles. *Cognition*, 27, 291–4.

—— 1988: Autistic children's understanding of seeing, knowing and believing. *British Journal of Developmental Psychology*, 6, 315–24.

—— 1990: Prospects for a cognitive neuropsychology of autism: Hobson's choice. *Psychological Review*, 97, 122–31.

Leslie, A. M. and Happé, F. 1989: Autism and ostensive communication: The relevance of metarepresentation. *Development and Psychopathology*, 205–12.

Leslie, A. M. and Keeble, S. 1987: Do six-month-old infants perceive causality? *Cognition*, 25, 265–88.

Leung, E. H. L. and Rheingold, H. 1981: Development of pointing as a social gesture. *Developmental Psychology*, 17, 215–20.

Lewis, C. 1987: Composition of productions. In D. Klahr, P. Langley and R.

Neches (eds), *Production System Models of Learning and Development* (Cambridge, MA: MIT Press).

—— 1988: Why and how to learn why: Analysis-based generalization of procedures. *Cognitive Science*, 12, 211–56.

Lewis, V. and Boucher, V. 1988: Spontaneous, instructed and elicited play in relatively able autistic children. *British Journal of Developmental Psychology*, 6, 325–39.

Lieberman, N. 1977: *Playfulness: Its Relationship to Imagination and Creativity* (New York: Academic Press).

Lloyd-Morgan, C. 1930: *The Animal Mind* (London: Edward Arnold).

Loveland, K. and Landry, S. 1986: Joint attention and language in autism and developmental language delay. *Journal of Autism and Developmental Disorders*, 16, 335–49.

Maccoby, E. M. and Martin, J. A. 1983: Socialization in the context of the family: Parent–child interaction. In P. H. Mussen (ed.), *Handbook of Child Psychology*, vol. 4 (New York: Wiley).

McCune-Nicolich, L. 1981: Toward symbolic functioning: Structure of use of early pretend games and potential parallels with language. *Child Development*, 52, 785–97.

McGhee, S. 1989: Humor and the development of social understanding. Unpublished Master's Thesis, Pennsylvania State University.

McGinn, C. 1982: *The Character of Mind* (Oxford: Oxford University Press).

McGrew, W. C., Tutin, C. E. G. and Baldwin, P. J. 1979: Chimpanzees, tools and termites: cross cultural comparisons of Senegal, Tanzania and Rio Muni. *Man*, 14, 185–214.

MacWhinney, B. and Snow, C. 1985: The child language data exchange system. *Journal of Child Language*, 12, 271–96.

Machiavelli, N. 1532: *The Prince*, translated by G. Bull (1961) (London: Penguin).

Maratos, O. 1973: The origin and development of imitation in the first six months of life. Unpublished doctoral dissertation, University of Geneva.

Markova, I. 1982: *Paradigms, Thought and Language* (London: Wiley).

Marler, P., Karakashian, S. and Gyger, M. 1990: Do animals have the option to withhold signals in inappropriate social circumstances? In C. A. Ristau (ed.), *Cognitive Ethology: The Minds of Other Animals* (Hillside, NJ: Erlbaum).

Marr, D. 1982: *Vision* (San Francisco: W. H. Freeman and Co.).

Massey, C. M. and Gelman, R. 1988: Preschooler's ability to decide whether a photographed unfamiliar object can move itself. *Developmental Psychology*, 24, 307–17.

Masterman, M. 1970: The nature of a paradigm. In I. Lakatos and A. Musgrave (eds), *Criticism and the Growth of Knowledge* (Cambridge: Cambridge University Press).

Meltzoff, A. N., and Moore, M. K. 1977: Imitation of facial and manual gestures by human neonates. *Science*, 198, 75–8.

Menzel, E. 1974: A group of young chimpanzees in a one-acre field. In M. Schrier and F. Stolnitz (eds), *Behaviour of Non-human Primates*, vol. 5 (New York: Academic Press).

Menzel, E. and Halperin, S. 1975: Purposive behaviour as a basis for objective communication between chimpanzees. *Science*, 189, 652–4.

Menzel, E. and Johnson, M. K. 1976: Communication and cognitive organization in humans and other animals. *Annals of the New York Academy of Sciences*, 280, 131–42.

Menzel, E., Savage-Rumbaugh, E. S. and Lawson, J. 1985: Chimpanzee (*Pan troglodytes*) spatial problem solving with the use of mirrors and televised equivalents of mirrors. *Journal of Comparative Psychology*, 99, 211–17.

Menzel, E. 1988: Mindless behaviorism, bodiless cognitivism, or primatology? *Behavioral and Brain Sciences*, 11, 258–9.

Michotte, A. 1963: *The Perception of Causality* (London: Methuen).

Miller, G. A., Galanter, E. and Pribram, K. H. 1960: *Plans and the Structure of Behaviour* (New York: Holt, Rinehart and Winston).

Miller, P. and Garvey, C. 1984: Mother–baby role play: Its origins in social support. In I. Bretherton (ed.), *Symbolic Play: The Development of Social Understanding* (New York: Academic Press).

Mitchell, T. M., Utgoff, P. E., Banerji, R. 1983: Learning by experimentation: Acquiring and refining problem-solving heuristics. In R. S. Michalski, J. G. Carbonell and T. Mitchell (eds), *Machine Learning: An Artificial Intelligence Approach* (Palo Alto, CA: Tioga Publishing Co.).

Mitchell, R. W. 1986: A framework for discussing deception. In R. W. Mitchell and N. S. Thompson (eds), *Deception: Perspectives on Human and Non-human Deceit* (Albany, NY: State University of New York Press).

——1989: Recognizing one's self in a mirror. A view from comparative-developmental psychology. Unpublished manuscript, Department of Psychology, State University of Memphis, Tennessee.

Mitchell, R. W. and Thompson, N. S. 1986: Deception in Play between Dogs and People. In R. W. Mitchell and N. S. Thompson (eds), *Deception: Perspectives on Human and Nonhuman Deceit* (Albany: State University of New York Press).

Mitchell, S. 1989: Exploring the autistic child's theory of mind. Unpublished manuscript, Department of Experimental Psychology, University of Oxford.

Moller, A. P. Forthcoming: False alarm calls in the great tit (*Parus major*) and deceptive acquisition of resources. *Behaviour*.

Moore, C. and Frye, D. (eds), *Children's Theories of Mind* (Hillsdale, NJ: Erlbaum).

Morton, J. 1989: The origins of autism. *New Scientist*, 1694, 44–7.

Moses, L. J. and Flavell, J. H. forthcoming: Inferring false beliefs from actions and reactions. *Child Development*.

Mundy, P. and Sigman, M. 1989: The theoretical implications of joint-attention deficits in autism. *Development and Psychopathology*, 1, 173–84.

Mundy, P., Sigman, M., Ungerer, J. and Sherman, T. 1986: Defining the social deficits in autism: the contribution of nonverbal communication measures. *Journal of Child Psychology and Psychiatry*, 27, 657–69.

Munn, C. A. 1986: The deceptive use of alarm calls by sentinel species in mixed species flocks of neotropical birds. In R. W. Mitchell and N. S. Thompson (eds), *Deception: Perspectives on Human and Nonhuman Deceit* (Albany, New York: State University of New York Press).

Murphy, C. M., and Messer, D. J. 1977: Mothers, infants and pointing: A study of a gesture. In H. R. Schaffer (ed.), *Studies in Mother–Infant Interaction* (London: Academic Press).

Neves, D. 1978: A computer program that learns algebraic procedures by examining examples and working problems in a textbook. In *Proceedings of the Second National Conference of the Canadian Society of Computational Studies of Intelligence*, Toronto.

Newell, A. and Simon, H. A. 1972: *Human Problem Solving*. (New York: Prentice-Hall).

Newell, A. and Simon, H. A. 1976: Computer science as empirical inquiry: symbols and search. *Communications of the ACM*, 19 (3), 113–26.

Olson, D. R. 1988: On the origins of beliefs and other intentional states in children. In J. W. Astington, P. L. Harris and D. R. Olson (eds), *Developing Theories of Mind* (Cambridge: Cambridge University Press).

Ozonoff, S., Pennington, B. and Rogers, 1990: Are there emotion perception deficits in young autistic children? *Journal of Child Psychology and Psychiatry*, 31, 343–63.

Parker, S. T. and Gibson, K. 1979: A developmental model for the evolution of language and intelligence in early hominids. *Behavioral and Brain Sciences*, 2, 367–408.

Passingham, R. E. 1982: *The Human Primate* (New York: W. H. Freeman).

Patterson, F. and Linden, E. 1981: *The Education of Koko* (New York: Holt, Rinehart and Winston).

Pazzani, M. J. 1987: Inducing causal and social theories: A prerequisite for explanation-based learning. *Proceedings of the Fourth International Machine Learning Workshop* (Palo Alto, CA: Morgan Kaufmann Publishers).

Perner, J. 1988a: Developing semantics for theories of mind: From propositional attitudes to mental representation. In J. W. Astington, P. L. Harris and D. R. Olson (eds), *Developing Theories of Mind* (Cambridge: Cambridge University Press).

Perner, J. 1988b: Higher-order beliefs and intentions. In J. W. Astington, P. L. Harris and D. R. Olson (eds), *Developing Theories of Mind* (Cambridge: Cambridge University Press).

——Forthcoming a: *Towards Understanding Representation and Mind* (Cambridge, MA: Bradford Books, MIT Press).

——Forthcoming b: Is 'thinking' belief? Reply to Wellman and Bartsch. *Cognition*.

——Forthcoming c: On representing that: The assymetry in children's understanding of belief and desire. In C. Moore and D. Frye (eds), *Children's Theories of Mind* (Hillsdale, NJ: Erlbaum).

Perner, J., Frith, U., Leslie, A. M. and Leekam, S. R. 1989: Exploration of the autistic child's theory of mind: knowledge, belief and communication. *Child Development*, 60, 689–700.

Perner, J., Leekam, S. R. and Wimmer, H. 1987: Three-year-olds' difficulty with false belief. *British Journal of Developmental Psychology*, 5, 125–37.

Perner, J. and Wimmer, H. 1985: 'John thinks that Mary thinks that . . .' Attribution of second-order beliefs by 5- to 10-year-old children. *Journal of Experimental Child Psychology*, 39, 437–71.

—— 1989: Theory formation and children's understanding of the mind. Paper presented at the Society for Research in Child Development meeting, Kansas.

Piaget, J. 1929: *The Child's Conception of the World* (New York: Harcourt, Brace).

—— 1936: *La Naissance de l'Intelligence chez l'Enfant* (Neuchatel: Delachaux et Niestlee).

—— 1951: Symbolic Play. In J. S. Bruner, A. Jolly and K. Sylva (eds), *Play – Its Role in Development and Evolution* (1976) (London: Penguin).

—— 1952: *The Origins of Intelligence in the Child* (New York: Basic Books).

—— 1962: *Play, Dreams and Imitation in Childhood* (London: Routledge and Kegan Paul).

—— 1965: *The Moral Judgement of the Child* (New York: Free Press) (Originally published, 1932).

Piaget, J. and Inhelder, B. 1948/1956: *The Child's Conception of Space*, trans F. J. Langdon and J. L. Lunzer (London: Routledge and Kegan Paul).

Poulin-Dubois, D. and Schultz, T. R. 1988: The development of the understanding of human behaviour: from agency to intentionality. In J. W. Astington, P. L. Harris and D. R. Olson (eds), *Developing Theories of Mind*, (Cambridge: Cambridge University Press).

Poulin-Dubois, D. and Shultz, T. R. Forthcoming: The infant's concept of agency: The distinction between social and nonsocial objects. *Journal of Genetic Psychology*.

Poulsen, D., Kintsch, E. and Premack, D. 1979: The effect of order on story comprehension in children. *Journal of Experimental Child Psychology*, 28, 379–402.

Povinelli, D. J., Nelson, K. E. and Boysen, S. T. 1989: Inferences about guessing and knowing by chimpanzees (*Pan troglodytes*). Unpublished manuscript, Yale University.

Pratt, C. and Bryant, P. E. Forthcoming: Young children understand that looking leads to knowledge (as long as they are looking into a single barrel). *Child Development*.

Premack, D. 1983: The codes of man and beasts. *Behavioral and Brain Sciences*, 16, 246–70.

——1988a: 'Does the chimpanzee have a theory of mind?' revisited. In R. W. Byrne and A. Whiten (eds), *Machiavellian Intelligence: Social Expertise and the Evolution of Intellect in Monkeys, Apes and Humans* (Oxford: Oxford University Press).

——1988b: Minds with and without language. In L. Weiskrantz (ed.), *Thought Without Language* (Cambridge: Cambridge University Press).

——1990: The infant's theory of self-propelled objects. *Cognition*.

——In preparation: *Social Cognition*.

Premack, D. G. and Woodruff, G. 1978: Does the chimpanzee have a theory of mind? *Behavioral and Brain Sciences*, 1, 515–26.

Preyer, W. 1896: *The Senses and the Will* (New York: Appleton).

Pylyshyn, Z. W. 1978: When is attribution of beliefs justified? *Behavioral and Brain Sciences*, 1, 592–3.

Quine, W. V. 1961: *From a Logical Point of View* (Cambridge: Harvard University Press).

Radke-Yarrow, M., Zahn-Waxler, C. and Chapman, M. 1983: Children's prosocial dispositions and behaviour. In P. H. Mussen (ed.), *Handbook of Child Psychology*, vol. 4 (New York: Wiley).

Reynolds, V. 1988: Tactical deception: a likely kind of primate action. *Behavioral and Brain Sciences*, 11, 262.

Ridgeway, D., Waters, E. and Kuczaj, S. A. 1985: The acquisition of emotion descriptive language: Receptive and productive vocabulary norms for ages 18 months to 6 years. *Developmental Psychology*, 21, 901–8.

Riguet, C. B., Taylor, N. D., Benaroya, S. and Klein, L. S. 1981: Symbolic play in autistic, Down's, and normal children of equivalent mental age. *Journal of Autism and Developmental Disorders*, 11, 439–48.

Ristau, C. A. 1983a: Intentionalist plovers or just dumb birds? Commentary on D. C. Dennett 'Intentional systems in cognitive ethology: "The Panglossian Paradigm" defended'. *Behavioral and Brain Sciences*, 6, 373–5.

——1983b: Language, cognition and awareness in animals? In J. A. Sechzer (ed.), *The Role of Animals in Bio-medical Research. Annals of the New York Academy of Science* (New York: NYAS). 406, 170–86.

——1988: Thinking, communicating, and deceiving: Means to master the social environment. In G. Greenberg and E. Tobach (eds), *Evolution of Social Behavior and Integrative Levels*, T. C. Schneirla Conference Series (Hillsdale, NJ: Erlbaum).

——1990: Aspects of the cognitive ethology of an injury feigning plover. In C. A. Ristau (ed.), *Cognitive Ethology: The Minds of Other Animals* (Hillsdale, NJ: Erlbaum).

Rizzo, T. 1989: *Friendship development among children in school* (Norwood, NJ: Ablex).

Robertson, S. S. and Suci, G. J. 1980: Event perception by children in the early stages of language production. *Child Deveopment*, 51, 89–96.

Rosenschein, S. J. 1985: Formal theories of knowledge in AI and robotics, *Technical Note 362*, SRI International.

Rubin, K. H., Fein, G. G. and Vandenberg, B. 1983: Play, In P. H. Mussen (ed.), *Handbook of Child Psychology*, vol. 4 (New York: Wiley).

Russell, J., Sharpe, A. and Mauthner, N. Forthcoming: Deception in autistic children. *British Journal of Developmental Psychology*.

Russow, L. M. 1986: Deception: A philosophical perspective. In R. W. Mitchell and N. S. Thompson (eds), *Deception: Perspectives on Human and Nonhuman Deceit* (Albany: State University of New York Press).

Rutter, D. R. 1984: *Looking and Seeing* (Chichester: Wiley).

Rutter, M. 1978: Language disorder and infantile autism. In M. Rutter and E. Schopler (eds), *Autism: a Reappraisal of Concepts and Treatment* (New York: Plenum).

Sacerdoti, E. D. 1977: *A Structure for Plans and Behaviour* (New York: Elsevier).

Sarria, E., Riviere, A. and Briose, A. 1988: *Observation of communicative intentions in infants*. Paper presented at the Third European Conference on Developmental Psychology. Budapest, Hungary.

Savage-Rumbaugh, E. S. 1986a: *Ape Language: From Conditioned Response to Symbol* (New York: Columbia University Press).

——1986b: *Ape Language: from Conditioned Response to Symbol*. Videotape adjunct to Savage-Rumbaugh, 1986a.

Savage-Rumbaugh, E. S. and McDonald, K. 1988: Deception and social manipulation in symbol-using apes. In R. W. Byrne and A. Whiten (eds), *Machiavellian Intelligence: Social Expertise and the Evolution of Intellect in Monkeys, Apes and Humans* (Oxford: Oxford University Press).

Savage-Rumbaugh, E. S., Date, J. L., Lawson, J., Smith, S. T. and Rosenbaum, S. 1983: Can a chimpanzee make a statement? *Journal of Experimental Psychology: General*, 112, 457–92.

Scaife, M. and Bruner, J. S. 1975: The capacity for joint visual attention in the human infant. *Nature*, 253, 265.

Schaffer, R. 1984: *The Child's Entry into a Social World* (London: Academic Press).

Schieffelin, F. 1976: *The Sorrow of the Lonely and the Burning of the Dancers* (New York: St Martin's Press).

Schmidt, C. F. 1976: Understanding human action: recognizing the plans and motives of other persons. In J. Carroll and J. Payne (eds), *Cognition and Social Behavior* (Hillsdale, NJ: Erlbaum).

——1985: Partial provisional planning: Some aspects of commonsense planning. In J. R. Hobbs and R. C. Moore (eds), *Formal Theories of the Commonsense World* (Norwood, NJ: Ablex).

Schmidt, C. F., Sridharan, N. S. and Goodson, J. L. 1978: The plan recognition problem: an intersection between psychology and artificial intelligence. *Artificial Intelligence*, 2, 45–83.

Scoville, R. 1984: Development of the intention to communicate: The eye of the beholder. In L. Feagans, C. Garvey and R. Golinkoff (eds), *The Origin and Growth of Communication* (Norwood, NJ: Ablex).

Scribner, S. 1977: Modes of thinking and ways of speaking: Culture and logic reconsidered. In P. N. Johnson-Laird and P. C. Wason (eds), *Thinking* (Cambridge: Cambridge University Press).

Searle, J. R. 1983: *Intentionality: An Essay in the Philosophy of Mind* (Cambridge: Cambridge University Press).

Sexton, M. 1983: The development of the understanding of causality in infancy. *Infant Behavior and Development*, 6, 201–10.

Seyfarth, R. M. 1978: Social relationships among adult male and female baboons, II. Behaviour throughout the female reproductive cycle. *Behaviour*, 64, 227–47.

Seyfarth, R. M. and Cheney, D. L. 1988: Do monkeys understand their relations? In R. W. Byrne and A. Whiten (eds), *Machiavellian Intelligence: Social Expertise and the Evolution of Intellect in Monkeys, Apes and Humans* (Oxford: Oxford University Press).

Shapiro, T., Sherman, M., Calamari, G. and Koch, D. 1987: Attachment in autism and other developmental disorders. *Journal of the American Academy of Child and Adolescent Psychiatry*, 26, 480–4.

Shatz, M., Wellman, H. and Silber, S. 1983: The acquisition of mental verbs: a systematic investigation of the first reference to mental states. *Cognition*, 14, 301–21.

Shaw, P. 1989: Is the deficit in autistic children's theory of mind an artefact? Unpublished manuscript, Department of Experimental Psychology, University of Oxford.

Sherman, P. 1977: Nepotism and the evolution of alarm calls. *Science*, 197, 1246–53.

——1985: Alarm calls of belding's ground squirrels to aerial predators: Nepotism or self-preservation? *Behavioral Ecology and Sociobiology*, 17, 313–23.

Shultz, T. R. 1980: Development of the concept of intention. In W. A. Collins (ed.), *Development of Cognition, Affect and Social Relations. The Minnesota Symposium on Child Psychology*, vol. 13 (Hillsdale, NJ: Erlbaum).

——1987: Learning and Using Causal Knowledge. Paper presented at the Meeting of the SRCD, Baltimore.

—— 1988: Assessing intention: A computational model. In J. W. Astington, P. L. Harris and D. R. Olson (eds), *Developing Theories of Mind* (Cambridge: Cambridge University Press).

—— Forthcoming: Modelling embedded intention. In C. Moore and D. Frye (eds), *Children's Theories of Mind* (Hillsdale, NJ: Erlbaum).

Shultz, T. R. and Kestenbaum, N. R. 1985: Causal reasoning in children. In G. J. Whitehurst (ed.), *Annals of Child Development*, 2, 195–249.

Shultz, T. R. and Shamash, F. 1981: The child's conception of intending act and consequence. *Canadian Journal of Behavioural Science*, 13, 368–72.

Shultz, T. R., Wells, D. and Sarda, M. 1980: Development of the ability to distinguish intended actions from mistakes, reflexes, and passive movements. *British Journal of Social and Clinical Psychology*, 19, 301–10.

Sibley, C. and Ahlquist, J. 1984: The phylogeny of the hominid primates, as indicated by DNA hybridization. *Journal of Molecular Evolution*, 20, 2–15.

Siegler, R. S. 1986: *Children's Thinking* (Englewood Cliffs, NJ: Prentice-Hall)

Sigman, M. and Ungerer, J. 1984: Attachment behaviours in autistic children. *Journal of Autism and Developmental Disorders*, 14, 231–44.

Sigman, M., Mundy, P., Ungerer, J. and Sherman, T. 1986: Social interactions of autistic, mentally retarded, and normal children and their caregivers. *Journal of Child Psychology and Psychiatry*, 27, 647–56.

—— 1987: The development of social attachments in autistic children. Paper presented at the SRCD Conference, Baltimore.

Sleeman, D. H. 1983: Inferring student models for intelligent computer-aided instruction. In R. S. Michalski, J. G. Carbonell and T. M. Mitchell (eds),

Machine Learning: An Artificial Intelligence Approach (Palo Alto: Tioga).

Smith, C., Carey, S. and Wiser, M. 1985: On differentiation: A case study of the development of the concepts of size, weight, and density. *Cognition*, 21, 177–237.

Smith, W. J. 1990: Animal communication and the study of cognition. In C. A. Ristau (ed.), *Cognitive Ethology: The Minds of Other Animals* (Hillsdale, NJ: Erlbaum).

Smuts, B. B. 1985: *Sex and Friendship in Baboons* (Hawthorne, NY: Aldine).

Snow, M. E., Hertzig, M. E. and Shapiro, T. 1987: Expression of emotion in young autistic children. *Journal of the American Academy of Child and Adolescent Psychiatry*, 26, 836–8.

Sodian, B. and Frith, U. 1990: Can autistic children lie? Paper presented at the Fourth European Conference of Developmental Psychology, Stirling.

Sodian, B., Harris, P. L., Taylor, C. and Perner, J. 1989: Early deception and the child's theory of mind: false trails and genuine markers. Unpublished manuscript, Department of Experimental Psychology, University of Oxford.

Sokolov, E. N. 1960: *Perception and the Conditioned Reflex* (New York: Macmillan).

Sperber, D. and Wilson, D. 1986: *Relevance: Communication and Cognition* (Oxford: Blackwell).

Stefik, M. 1981: Planning with Constraints (Molgen: Part 1). *Artificial Intelligence*, 16, 111–40.

——1981: Planning and Meta-Planning (Molgen: Part 2). *Artificial Intelligence*, 16, 141–70.

Stern, D. N. 1985: *The Interpersonal World of the Infant* (New York: Basic Books).

Strum, S. C. 1988: Social strategies and primate psychology. *Behavioral and Brain Sciences*, 11, 264–5.

—— 1989: Monkeying around or mindreading? A baboon's eye view. Paper presented at the symposium 'The Emergence of Mindreading: Evolution, Development and Simulation of Second-order Representations', St Andrews, Scotland.

Sussman, R. L. 1988: Hand of *Paranthropus robustus* from member 1, Swartkrans: fossil evidence for tool behaviour. *Science*, 240, 781–4.

Swettenham, J. 1990: The autistic child's theory of mind: a computer-based investigation. Unpublished PhD Thesis, University of York.

Tager-Flüsberg, H. 1989: An analysis of discourse ability and internal state lexicons in a longitudinal study of autistic children. Paper presented at the SRCD, Kansas City, April 1989.

Terrace, H. S., Petito, R. J., Sanders, R. J. and Bever, T. G. 1979: Can an ape create a sentence? *Science*, 206, 891–902.

Thibadeau, R. 1986: Artificial perception of actions *Cognitive Science*, 10, 117–49.

Thompson, R. A. 1987: Empathy and emotional understanding: the early development of empathy. In N. Eisenberg and J. Strayer (eds), *Empathy and its Development* (Cambridge: Cambridge University Press).

Tizard, B. and Hughes, M. 1984: *Young Children Learning* (London: Fontana).

Trevarthen, C. 1977: Descriptive analyses of infant communicative behaviour. In H. R. Schaffer (ed.), *Studies in Mother–Infant Interaction* (London: Academic Press).

——1980: The foundations of Intersubjectivity: development of interpersonal and cooperative understanding in infants. In D. Olson (ed.), *The Social Foundations of Language and Thought: Essays in Honour of J. S. Bruner* (New York: Norton).

—— 1987a: Sharing makes sense: intersubjectivity and the making of an infant's meaning. In R. Steele and T. Treadgold (eds), *Language Topics: Essays in Honour of Michael Halliday* (Amsterdam: John Benjamins Publishing Co.).

—— 1987b: Universal cooperative motives: How infants begin to know the language and culture of their parents. In G. Jahoda and I. M. Lewis (eds), *Acquiring Culture: Cross-cultural Studies in Child Development* (Kent: Croom Helm).

Trevarthen, C. and Hubley, P. 1978: Secondary intersubjectivity: confidence, confiders, and acts of meaning in the first year. In A. Lock (ed.), *Before Speech: the Beginning of Interpersonal Communication* (New York: Academic Press).

Trevarthen, C. and Logotheti, K. 1987: First symbols and the nature of human knowledge. *Cahiers de la Fondation Archives Piaget* (Geneva).

——1989a: Child and culture: genesis of cooperative knowing. In A. Gellatly, D. Rogers and J. A. Sloboda (eds), *Cognition and Social Worlds* (Oxford: Clarendon Press).

——1989b: Child in society, and society in children: the nature of basic trust. In S. Howell and R. Willis (eds), *Societies at Peace: Anthropological Perspectives* (London: Routledge and Kegan Paul).

Ungerer, J. and Sigman, M. 1981: Symbolic play and language comprehension in autistic children. *Journal of the American Academy of Child Psychiatry*, 20, 318–37.

Vygotsky, L. 1933: Play and its role in the mental development of the child. In J. S. Bruner, A. Jolly and K. Sylva (eds), *Play – Its Role in Evolution and Development* (Harmondsworth, Middx: Penguin, 1976).

——1962: *Thought and Language* (Cambridge: MIT Press) (first published in Russian, 1926).

Visalberghi, E. and Fragaszy, D. Forthcoming: Do monkeys ape? In S. Parker and K. Gibson (eds), *Comparative Developmental Psychology of Language and Intelligence in Primates* (Cambridge: Cambridge University Press).

Watson, M. W. and Fischer, K. W. 1977: A developmental sequence of agent use in late infancy. *Child Development*, 48, 828–36.

Waal, F. de 1982: *Chimpanzee Politics* (New York: Harper and Row).

——1986: Deception in the natural communication of chimpanzees. In R. W. Mitchell and N. S. Thompson (eds), *Deception: Perspectives on Human and Nonhuman Deceit* (Albany: State University of New York State).

——1989: *Peacemaking among Primates* (Cambridge, MA: Harvard University Press).

Wellman, H. M. 1988: First steps in the child's theorizing about the mind. In J. W. Astington, P. L. Harris and D. R. Olson (eds), *Developing Theories of Mind* (New York: Cambridge University Press).

—— 1990: *The Child's Theory of Mind.* (Cambridge, MA: MIT Press/Bradford Books).

Wellman, H. M. and Bartsch, K. 1988: Young children's reasoning about beliefs. *Cognition*, 30, 239–77.

—— 1989: 3-year-olds understand belief: A reply to Perner and more. *Cognition*, 33, 321–6.

Wellman, H. M. and Estes, D. 1986: Early understanding of mental entities: A reexamination of childhood realism. *Child Development*, 57, 910–23.

Wellman, H. M. and Woolley, J. D. 1990: From simple desires to ordinary beliefs: The early development of everyday psychology. *Cognition*, 35, 245–75.

Whiten, A. 1989: Transmission mechanisms in primate cultural evolution. *Trends in Ecology and Evolution*, 4, 61–2.

Whiten, A. and Byrne, R. W. 1986: The St Andrews catalogue of tactical deception in primates. *St Andrews Psychological Reports*, 10, 1–47.

——1988a: Tactical deception in primates. *Behavioral and Brain Sciences*, 11, 233–73.

——1988b: The manipulation of attention in primate tactical deception. In R. W. Byrne and A. Whiten (eds), *Machiavellian Intelligence: Social Expertise and the Evolution of Intellect in Monkeys, Apes and Humans* (Oxford: Oxford University Press).

——1988c: Taking (Machiavellian) intelligence apart. In R. W. Byrne and A. Whiten (eds), *Machiavellian Intelligence: Social Expertise and the Evolution of Intellect in Monkeys, Apes and Humans* (Oxford: Oxford University Press).

——1989: Machiavellian monkeys: cognitive evolution and the social world of primates. In A. R. H. Gellatly, D. R. Rogers and J. A. Sloboda (eds), *Cognition and Social Worlds* (Oxford: Oxford University Press).

——1990: Primates' appreciation of physical and psychological causality. *Behavioral and Brain Sciences*, 13, 415–9.

Whiten, A. and Milner, P. 1984: The educational experiences of Nigerian infants. In H. V. Curran (ed.), *Nigerian Children: Developmental Perspectives* (London: Routledge and Keegan Paul).

Whitten, P. L. 1987: Infants and adult males. In B. Smuts, D. L. Cheney, R. M. Seyfarth, R. W. Wrangham and T. T. Struhsaker (eds), *Primate Societies* (Chicago: University of Chicago Press).

Wimmer, H., Gruber, S. and Perner, J. 1984: Young children's conception of lying: Lexical realism – moral subjectivism. *Journal of Experimental Child Psychology*, 37, 1–30.

——1985: Young children's conception of lying: Moral intuition and the denotation and connotation of 'to lie'. *Developmental Psychology*, 21, 993–5.

Wimmer, H. and Hartl, M. Forthcoming: The child's understanding of own false beliefs. *British Journal of Developmental Psychology*.

Wimmer, H., Hogrefe, J. and Perner, J. 1988: Children's understanding of informational access as source of knowledge. *Child Development*, 59, 386–96.

Wimmer, H., Hogrefe, J. and Sodian, B. 1988: A second stage in children's conception of mental life: Understanding informational accesses as origins of knowledge and belief. In J. W. Astington, P. L. Harris and D. R. Olson (eds),

Developing Theories of Mind (New York: Cambridge University Press).

Wimmer, H. and Perner, J. 1983: Beliefs about beliefs: Representation and constraining function of wrong beliefs in young children's understanding of deception. *Cognition*, 13, 103–28.

Wing, L., Gould, J., Yeats, S. R. and Brierly, L. M. 1977: Symbolic play in severely mentally retarded and in autistic children. *Journal of Child Psychology and Psychiatry*, 18, 167–78.

Winner, E., Windmueller, G., Rosenblatt, E., Bosco, L., Best and Gardner, H. 1987: Making sense of literal and nonverbal falsehood. *Metaphor and Symbolic Activity*, 21, 13–32.

Winston, P. H. 1980: Learning and reasoning by analogy: The details. AIM 520, *Artificial Intelligence Laboratory* MIT.

Wittgenstein, L. 1953: *Philosophical Investigations* (Oxford: Blackwell).

Wolf, D. 1982: Agency and experience: A longitudinal case study of the concept of independent agency. In G. E. Forman (ed.), *Action and Thought* (New York: Academic Press).

Wolf, D. P., Rygh, J. and Altshuler, J. 1984: Agency and experience: Actions and states in play narratives. In I. Bretherton (ed.), *Symbolic Play* (Orlando, FA: Academic Press).

Woodruff, G., Premack, D. and Kennell, K. 1980: Conservation of liquid and solid quantity in chimpanzee. *Science*, 33, 269–71.

Wrangham, R. W. 1975: The behavioural ecology of chimpanzees in the Gombe National Park, Tanzania. PhD dissertation, Cambridge University.

Wrangham, R. W. and Nishida, T. 1983: *Aspilia* spp. leaves; a puzzle in the feeding behaviour of wild chimpanzees. *Primates*, 24, 276–82.

Yirmiya, N., Kasari, C., Sigman, M. and Mundy, P. 1989: Facial expressions of affect in autistic, mentally retarded, and normal children. *Journal of Child Psychology and Psychiatry*, 30, 725–35.

Yuill, N. 1984: Young children's coordination of motive and outcome in judgements of satisfaction and morality. *British Journal of Developmental Psychology*, 2, 73–81.

Yuill, N. and Perner, J. 1987: Exceptions to mutual trust: children's use of second-order beliefs in responsibility attribution. *International Journal of Behavioural Development*, 102, 207–23.

Yourcenar, M. 1954: *Memoirs of Hadrian* (New York: Farrar, Straus and Giroux).

Zaitchik, D. 1990: When representations conflict with reality: the preschooler's problem with false beliefs and 'false' photographs. *Cognition*, 35, 41–68.

Zinober, B. and Martlew, M. 1985: Developmental changes in four types of gesture in relation to acts and vocalizations from 10–21 months. *British Journal of Developmental Psychology*, 3, 293–306.

Index